925

Philosophical essays on Freud

Philosophical essays on Freud

Edited by
Richard Wollheim

GROTE PROFESSOR OF THE PHILOSOPHY OF MIND
AND LOGIC IN THE UNIVERSITY OF LONDON

and

James Hopkins

LECTURER IN PHILOSOPHY, KING'S COLLEGE
LONDON

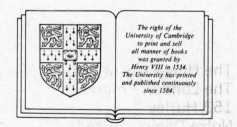

The right of the
University of Cambridge
to print and sell
all manner of books
was granted by
Henry VIII in 1534.
The University has printed
and published continuously
since 1584.

Cambridge University Press

Cambridge
London   New York   New Rochelle
Melbourne   Sydney

Published by the Press Syndicate of the University of Cambridge
The Pitt Building, Trumpington Street, Cambridge CB2 1RP
32 East 57th Street, New York, NY 10022, USA
10 Stamford Road, Oakleigh, Melbourne 3166, Australia

First published 1982
Reprinted 1984

Printed in Great Britain at the Pitman Press, Bath

Library of Congress catalogue card number: 82-1123

The editors and publisher would like to thank the following for their
permission to reprint material in this volume: Basil Blackwell and the
University of California Press for L. Wittgenstein, *Lectures and
Conversations*, ed. C. Barrett, 1966 pp. 42–52; Basil Blackwell for L.
Wittgenstein, *Lectures in Philosophy Cambridge 1932–35*, ed. Alice
Ambrose, 1979 pp. 39–40; Routledge and Kegan Paul and Humani-
ties Press for selection from H. Fingarette, *Self-Deception*, 1969; Eyre
Methuen and Philosophical Library Inc. for J-P Sartre, *Being and
Nothingness*, trans. H. Barnes, 1956, pp. 47–54; the *International
Journal of Psycho-analysis* for S. Hampshire, 'Disposition and Mem-
ory', *IJPA*, 43, 1962, pp. 59–68; *The Journal of the Theory of Social
Behaviour* for B. R. Cosin et al., 'Critical Empricism Criticized: The
Case of Freud', *JTSB*, I no. 2, 1972, pp. 121–51.

British Library Cataloguing in Publication Data

Philosophical essays on Freud.
1. Freud, Sigmund
I. Wollheim, Richard   II. Hopkins, James
150.19'52   BF173.F85

ISBN 0 521 24076 X   hard covers
ISBN 0 521 28425 2   paperback

Contents

CONTENTS

Introduction:
philosophy and psychoanalysis

JAMES HOPKINS

The essays in this volume are about philosophical issues arising from the work of Freud. They differ in approach and opinion, although most are written in the tradition of analytical philosophy. Readers who lack familiarity with psychoanalysis or philosophical discussion of it may find it useful to be given some perspective on the issues involved, and some indication as to how they are connected with one another. This introduction, therefore, consists of two parts. The first describes one of the most widely discussed topics from the encounter between analytical philosophy and psychoanalysis, and considers its bearing upon the exegesis and verification of Freudian theory. The second comments briefly on the essays, relating them to the issues described.[1]

I

Philosophy aims, among other things, at clarity of understanding and the demarcation of knowledge. These aims are linked in the philosophical consideration of theories used in explanation; for a correct understanding of the nature of a theory may be required for judging how far explanations using that theory contribute to knowledge. Clarity of this sort about psychoanalytic theory has, it seems, been difficult to attain. In particular, the relation of Freud's explanations to those in physical or experimental science has long been a matter of dispute. Recently this dispute has taken a particular form.

In a number of remarks dating from his lectures in Cambridge in the nineteen thirties, Ludwig Wittgenstein suggested that a psychoanalytic explanation of what someone did was liable to confuse reasons with

---

[1] The view of psychoanalytic theory indicated in what follows was suggested to me particularly by the second chapter of Hanna Segal's *Introduction to the Work of Melanie Klein* (London, 1973). I am also indebted to work on Freud by Richard Wollheim and to him and Anita Avramedies, Joanna Bosanquet, Jerry Cohen, Greg DesJardins, and Colin McGinn for helpful comments on the first draft of this introduction. I should also like to express my gratitude for the use of disguised material to an analyst who will remain anonymous.

causes, where investigation of the former were based upon what a person said, whilst the latter were associated with laws and could be investigated through experiment. These remarks and others passed into the philosophical literature as enforcing a distinction between the reasons on which an agent acted and the causes of his action, and particularly influenced subsequent work on psychoanalysis. Thus in *The Unconscious* Alisdair MacIntyre wrote, 'Freud calls the unconscious motive "the driving force behind the act". In other words he tries to treat unconscious motives both as purposes and as causes. This is simply a confusion.'[2]

More recently, analysts themselves have been concerned with similar distinctions. Thus in 1966, H. J. Home wrote

In discovering that the symptom had meaning and basing his treatment on this hypothesis, Freud took the psychoanalytic study of neurosis out of the world of science and into the world of the humanities, because meaning is not the product of causes but is the creation of a subject. This is a major difference: for the logic and method of the humanities is radically different from that of science, though no less respectable and rational and of course much longer established.[3]

Similarly, Charles Rycroft has argued that Freud's procedure was 'not the scientific one of elucidating causes but the semantic one of making sense', and that in failing to recognize this analysts lay themselves open to attack from those who see that 'psychoanalysis cannot satisfy the canons of those sciences based upon the experimental method, but who believe that if they can demonstrate its inadequacy as a causal theory, they have proved that it is nonsense'.[4]

In these and a number of related writings we find the psychoanalytic study of the reasons, intentions, or meaning of what someone does contrasted with the scientific investigation of causes. This contrast is used to support two related but distinct claims. First it is argued, as against Freud, that these different kinds of investigation are investigations of different things, i.e. that reasons are not causes. Secondly, it is argued, as against some critics of Freud, that psychoanalytic investigation has a different logic, or requires to be judged by different canons or standards, from those appropriate to physical science.

We can assess these claims by considering the contrast upon which they are based, between the investigation of causes and that of reasons or meanings. This can be brought out by comparing explanations citing causes with those citing reasons.

[2] London, 1968. MacIntyre revised this view in later work. See for example his article on Freud in the *Encyclopaedia of Philosophy*, vol. 3, pp. 249–52 (Macmillan, New York, 1967).

[3] 'The Concept of Mind', *International Journal of Psycho-Analysis*, 1968.

[4] *Psychoanalysis Observed* (Penguin, London, 1968), especially pp. 9–20.

Introduction

To be familiar with the everybody properties of objects – their hardness, fragility, solubility, etc. – is to know something about the way events involving them will cause others, and to apply to them the assumption that, in Hume's terms, like causes will have like effects. (It is plausible that a cognitive orientation towards objects, as well as a readiness to learn such things about them, is part of our evolutionary adaptation.) Thus suppose someone strikes a match and it lights, and we hold, correctly, that the striking caused the lighting. Then we should expect that if a similar match were to be struck in a like way, it too would light. Conversely, if another match were struck and failed to light, we should assume that this was due to some difference in the construction or composition of the match or the circumstances of its striking. To think this way, it seems, is already to connect the idea of a cause with that of a lawlike regularity in nature. For if we could specify how a match and striking would have to be in order to satisfy the maxim that like causes have like effects in relation to a given lighting, then we could use those specifications to state a law. It would be to the effect that whenever an event of kind S (like the striking) befalls an object of kind M (like the match) it causes an event of kind L (like the lighting).

Science enables us to formulate such laws. They cannot generally be stated in everyday terms, but require vocabulary drawn from theory. The way objects behave causally is explicable by reference to how they are constructed, so that an investigation of the way objects are made goes together with an attempt to form precise and specific laws about causal sequences involving them. A match, for example, will be constructed in a particular way of certain materials, known to ignite in ordinary circumstances at a given temperature, to which the friction of a striking can heat it. This kind of information is encoded in generalizations about substances and their behaviour which can be used to specify what matches and strikings must be like if the latter are to cause the former to light. These generalizations, in turn, are explicable by a more fundamental account of the way things are composed and the behaviour of their parts. Thus a given material will be composed of particular kinds of molecules in a characteristic arrangement, heating by friction will be a transfer of kinetic energy to those molecules, ignition a chemical change involving them, and so on, all such changes occurring in accord with laws of nature which are of pervasive application, and linked to their instances by mathematical deduction.

Theories embodying such laws can be used to predict events, and to explain their occurrence by showing them to be instances of general patterns in nature. Thus such theories can be tested relatively simply, by observations and experiments designed to determine whether the kinds of events they predict actually occur. This use of laws for explanation, prediction and test is characteristic of the method associated with the physical sciences, and has seemed to some philosophers and psychologists to provide canons or standards for judging whether a theory is scientific, or has empirical significance. The application of such standards to Freud's work has commonly resulted in a demand that specific and reproducible behavioural consequences – analogous to predictable observations or results of experiment – be derived from Freudian theory.[5]

We also have a natural ability to understand one another as persons. This scheme of understanding seems fundamental to our conception of the mind, and rejecting it seems scarcely intelligible. Within it we represent one another as rational, purposive creatures, fitting our beliefs to the world as we perceive it and seeking to obtain what we desire in light of them. (Again it seems plausible to speculate that a readiness to use this scheme, together with language, is a result of evolution and consequently innate. Certainly we can imagine that it facilitates survival by enabling the individual to adjust his behaviour in all kinds of ways to that of others, and makes articulate co-operation possible.) We do this partly through the ascription of reasons.

So, for example, we spontaneously interpret what a person does by reference to his intentions or purposes in acting.[6] These we understand in terms of the reasons on which he acted, involving beliefs and desires or other motives. Let us assume a case in which someone performs a communicative action by speaking: he says, simply enough, that the ice is thin, which he does by making some sounds, uttering the words 'The ice is thin'. We can take him to have uttered those words with a certain intention or purpose, namely, to say that the ice is thin. This will be because of certain desires and beliefs. He will have wanted to say that the ice is thin, and believed that uttering those words would be a way of doing so. There would also be further reasons for this action, and so further desires and beliefs related to it. Thus the agent might have wanted to warn someone against the possibility of falling through the ice, and thought that saying that the ice is thin would be a way of doing so; and so on.

Regarding a person's action in light of his reasons in this way makes it intelligible to us. We can see his aims in acting and why they were

[5] On this demand see, for example, Karl Popper, *Conjectures and Refutations* (Routledge, London, 1963), p. 38n; also Ernest Nagel, in *Psychoanalysis, Scientific Method, and Philosophy* (University Press, New York, 1959), p. 40; and others in that volume.

[6] Much of this discussion of reasons and causes is based on the papers in Donald Davidson's *Essays on Actions and Events* (Oxford, 1980). These have had wide influence, and should be consulted by anyone in search of further information on these topics.

important to him, and thus recognize that if we had such motives we should have reason to act in the same way. Also, we understand much of what is referred to as meaning by way of knowing reasons. The meaning of an action, for example, is sometimes explicated by some aspect of what the agent thought or felt about it. The meaning of a movement, sign, or symbol used in communication is often understood by reference to the kinds of communicative actions it is used or intended to perform. Thus the meaning of a word or sentence is partly to be understood through its use for the purpose of saying certain things, and hence the reasons for which it is uttered.

Citing a belief and desire as a reason for an action of a certain kind serves to explain the action by explaining the agent's desire to perform an action of that kind. The beliefs and desires cited in the example above thus purport to explain the agent's desire to utter certain words and his desire to say that the ice is thin, but give no explanation of his desire to warn. A belief and desire which can be used to explain another desire in this way are logically related to it in content. We can bring this out by saying that beliefs and desires involve thoughts. Where a belief and desire can explain a further desire, we can say, the thoughts associated with the explaining belief and desire are such as to entail the thought associated with the desire which is to be explained.

Thus suppose that the agent in the example desired to issue a warning and believed that saying that the ice is thin would be a way of doing so, and for this reason desired to say that the ice is thin. Someone who desires to issue a warning believes, or has the thought, that issuing a warning would be desirable in some way. The thought that issuing a warning would be thus desirable and the thought that saying that the ice is thin would be a way of issuing a warning together entail the thought that saying that the ice is thin would be desirable in that way. (We can see that if the former thoughts are true the latter must be.) This latter thought is that involved in the agent's desire to say that the ice is thin.[7]

The same connections hold in a family of cases of reasons for belief. Someone's reason for believing (or coming to believe) that it is summer may be that he believes that swallows have come and that swallows come only in summer; or his reason for ceasing to believe that no one can be trusted may be that he has learned of an honest man. These are instances of the more general idea that we can cite reasons where someone forms or holds a belief because of beliefs that entail it, or ceases to hold or fails to form one because of beliefs that contradict it (entail its negation). This is a parallel of the idea that we can cite reasons where, as above, someone

[7] Parallel considerations apply for motives which involve thinking something necessary or obligatory, so far as these differ from desires.

forms or keeps a desire because of desires or beliefs whose thoughts entail its thought. Also, we can sometimes say that a person lacks or loses a desire or belief where he lacks or loses reasons – that is, desires or beliefs which are connected with it in the relevant way by entailment.[8] All these cases of explanations by reasons, therefore, involve processes or relations of thought which are in accord with logic. So each can be seen as an instance of the idea that persons are rational.

Each of the thoughts involved in the desires and beliefs that we ascribe in giving reasons is connected in content with indefinitely many others. This means that each desire and belief must be accompanied by many others, with which it is connected in content. Suppose, for example, that someone believes that thin ice is dangerous. Then, it seems he must have further beliefs – about what ice is, what it is for ice to be thin, what for something to be dangerous, in what way thin ice is dangerous, and so on. Without these beliefs the initial one would be empty. Further beliefs are required to determine how the initial one represents things, and what role it might play in thought or action. In isolation a belief could have no representation or role, and hence no content. So it seems that any belief must go with other beliefs with which it coheres, in the sense that these others contribute to determining its content.

Ordinarily in assuming that someone believes that thin ice is dangerous we assume (as we say) that he knows what ice is, what it is for ice to be thin, and so on. This means that we attribute further beliefs to him, such as that ice is frozen water, that a person falling through ice will enter almost freezing water, that ice is thin (is rightly called 'thin') when it will not support the weight of a person, and so on. These enable us to understand, so to speak, what he believes in believing that thin ice is dangerous, and so what this means for his thought and action. It seems indeterminate precisely which beliefs must cohere with a given belief in this way, but clearly there must be very many, and they must overlap in content. A similar point applies to the content of desires.

So far we have sketched two kinds of explanation, related to causes and reasons, or to the physical and the mental, respectively. Explanations of each kind use deduction to bring information to bear on what is to be explained. The first enables us to describe events as instances of physical laws, and has one use in giving a deeper account of the causal and

---

[8] Reason requires that beliefs be consistent, but not desires. Contradictory desires cannot of course both be satisfied, but the beliefs or thoughts involved in them may be consistent. When Brutus says 'As he was valiant, I honour him; but as he was ambitious I slew him' he expresses consistent thoughts involved in his presumably inconsistent desires towards Caesar.

dispositional properties of objects. The second enables us to describe beliefs or desires as derived from reasons, by exhibiting the thoughts in the former as following from the thoughts in the latter. We can see something more about how these kinds of explanation are related by further consideration of the components of reasons.

Desires and beliefs involve dispositions to thought and action; for having a reason involves having a disposition to what it is a reason for. Someone who desires to swim, for example, has a disposition to swim, in the sense that if certain conditions were fulfilled he would swim. (We shall consider the conditions later.) Likewise a person who desires to swim and believes that moving his body a certain way would be a way of doing so has a disposition to move his body in that way. And similarly, as we know, a person has a disposition to come to believe consequences of his beliefs, and to disbelieve what is inconsistent with them, even if he is unaware of doing so.

This means that desires and beliefs involve dispositions of a special and complex kind. The reasons for desire and belief we have so far considered are themselves combinations of desires and beliefs; so desires and beliefs act in combination to produce further desires and beliefs. The thoughts involved in the reasons we have so far considered entail, or have as their logical consequences, those involved in the desires and beliefs for which they are reasons. So the way desires and beliefs act in combination to produce others is a logical function of their contents. The possession of desires and beliefs thus implies the possession of dispositions to form further desires and beliefs, through the interaction of the desires and beliefs themselves. Our knowledge of reasons shows that we know something of these dispositions and interactions *a priori,* in accord with our own natural logical understanding.

Dispositions are often characterized in terms of their manifestations and vice-versa. Thus solubility is understood in connection with dissolving, fragility with certain kinds of breaking, and so on. In the case of the dispositions involved in desires, this is particularly clear: the description of a desire for action specifies the kind of action a disposition to which is involved in the possession of the desire. For this reason the citing of dispositions in explanation of their manifestations, or desires to perform certain kinds of actions in explanation of actions of those kinds, would often give little or no information. This redundancy is transcended in contrasting ways in the two kinds of explanation we are considering.

In the physical case we can eliminate reference to a disposition in explanation in favour of theoretical descriptions of the objects which have it. These descriptions and others of the events which trigger the disposition can be integrated with laws of nature to yield descriptions of the events which are its manifestations. This not only provides explanation of the manifestations and a detailed account of how they are produced, but also elucidates the disposition itself. We can see that objects have a particular disposition in virtue of satisfying a particular theoretical description, since this makes prediction of the characteristic manifestations possible. Thus objects are inflammable in virtue of composition related to a certain chemical change, fragile in virtue of molecular structure, and so on.

In the psychological case, rather than state the desire whose disposition is manifest in the action, we cite reasons, desires and beliefs, from which this desire is derived. Since indefinitely many other desires and beliefs could have acted in combination to produce the desire visible in the action, this is informative. And clearly there is much information we can bring to bear in this way. Because we can cite further reasons for the desires and beliefs given in such an explanation, and because each desire and belief involves others in its content, we can understand a single action as issuing from a network of reasons which can be traced through in many ways.

Underlying any disposition are the mechanisms by which the events which are manifestations of it are produced. We know that the mechanisms underlying the dispositions involved in desires and beliefs are those of the human body, and in particular the brain. We regard the body as a natural object, whose physical operations and alterations – including those involved in perception, thought, and action – can be fully explained in physical terms alone. Thus when someone sees something, desires it, and reaches for it, we think there is a network of causally connected events, linking his eyes, brain, the muscular contractions involved in reaching, and so on, for all the events constituting this manifestation of the disposition involved in desire. If we knew enough about the body we could trace through this network, explaining later events by reference to earlier ones and the structure of the body, in the manner described above. This seems to apply to all the events in which dispositions connected with the mind are manifested, so that the only mechanisms involved can be said to be those of the body.

Since desires and beliefs involve dispositions whose underlying mechanisms are causal, they have a causal role, and can in this sense be regarded as causes. Reasons can therefore be regarded as causes of actions, desires and beliefs as causes of desires and beliefs, and so on. This means, moreover, that the logical role of desire and belief, which we can know *a priori* by understanding their contents and how they are related, displays for us their causal role. For example, we thus know that among the causal powers of the belief that all men are mortal is that of producing, together with the belief that Socrates is a man, the belief that Socrates is mortal. Again, among the powers of a desire to signal is that of producing, together with a belief that waving one's hand would be a way of signaling, a desire to wave one's hand. So, finally, we can see that explanation by reasons brings information to bear which is ultimately causal; it does so by the specification of patterns of causes which operate in combination, rather than through the exhibition of causal sequences as instances of laws.

Since this fits with what we know about the body it should not seem counterintuitive. Also, if we assigned reasons no causal role, it seems we could not understand how someone's reaching for an apple could be prompted by desire or guided by the belief that it was in front of him. This does not, however, mean that desires and beliefs could be explicated by reference to physical states (of the brain, for example) in the same way that physical dispositions like fragility can. Each desire and belief can act in combination with indefinitely many others, the result always depending on the combined contents of the interacting attitudes. The dispositions involved in desires and beliefs, therefore, have no fixed physical or behavioural manifestations. So there can be no possibility of elucidating a desire or belief by producing an explanation of any fixed physical or behavioural range of events. Desires and beliefs seem irreducible by this kind of explanation. (Recognition of this may have been one source of the belief that reasons could not be causes.)[9]

Acknowledgment of the causal role of reasons thus does not imply that descriptions in terms of desires and beliefs can figure in the kind of explanation by predictive laws which we associate with physical science. Apparently they cannot. The systematic variation in the manifestations of the dispositions associated with desires and beliefs seems to ensure that these notions can play no role in laws for physical or behavioural prediction. Also, we can see that we cannot form a law connecting desire and action by specifying the conditions in which the disposition to action involved in a desire will be manifested – or, more shortly, the conditions in which an agent with a desire will act. We cannot strengthen or formalize our intuitive capacity to predict in this way, because such statements of conditions will always be circular, in the sense that the

[9] In this connection it is worth noting that in one characteristic use of the notion of a physical state or property we do not take states or properties (but rather the objects which have them) to enter causal relations. There is thus an intuitive dissonance in the attempt to construe desires and beliefs on the model of such states or properties. Desires and beliefs can be thought of as realized by mechanisms of the brain which discharge their causal role. Such mechanisms might cause action in the appropriate circumstances, might interact with one another to produce further mechanisms structurally related to those from which they were derived, etc. The idea that the content of one thought involves that of others, however, suggests that distinguishable mechanisms will not correspond to individual desires and beliefs.

criterion of application of one notion will be stated in terms of other notions which the first was used to explicate. We shall take the simplest possible example, but this still requires going through some complex statements to see.

Suppose we try to specify some conditions for action on a particular desire by saying that someone who has a desire to swim will actually swim if (i) he is able to swim (where this includes being in the right circumstances), (ii) he is aware that he is able to swim and (iii) there is nothing else he would rather do than swim. Now to apply this we should have to be able to specify the conditions in which a person is able to swim. A person who is able to swim, presumably, is one who will actually swim if (i) he is aware that he is able to swim and (ii) he desires to swim and (iii) there is nothing he would rather do than swim. Again, if there is nothing a person would rather do than swim, it seems that if (i) he is able to swim and (ii) he is aware that he is able to swim and (iii) he desires to swim, then he will actually swim. This, it seems, takes us back to where we began.

It seems that such cycles can be enlarged or multiplied but not eliminated. We cannot measure strengths of desires, degrees of belief, preferences for ways of doing things, or the other factors which combine to determine a course of action. So in trying to state when a desire will produce an action we must assign to it a strength or role which ensures that it rather than other desires will be acted on ('nothing else he would rather do' above); then in explicating this strength or role we have to say that a desire which has it, rather than others, will produce action. Similarly, if we tried to state when a person would give up one belief because it contradicted another (as we know frequently happens) we should have to say not only that he was aware of the contradiction but also that he held one belief sufficiently more strongly than the other; and then the same kind of circle would recur.

The circularity is comparable to that involved in saying that an inflammable substance will ignite if made hot enough, while using ignition as the final criterion for sufficiency of heat. The statement is true, and also it is informative in describing cause and effect in a quantitative relation which is verifiable in experience. Beyond this, however, it provides no way of specifying when something will ignite. It is the same, I think, with the conditions of action we have been describing.[10] We can

[10] We do have indications of strength of desire by which we can tell that increase in it renders action more likely, and we often know when a person's desires are strong enough for him to act at once given an opportunity. Desire and action, like heat and ignition, admit of description in this very simple quantitative way without further measure. This, however, does not suffice to impose upon desire even a scale of levels whose place in an order could

see why this should be so. The explanations by reasons we have considered involve the assumption of processes or relations of thought which are in accord with logic. Each such assumption is an instance of our guiding general hypothesis in understanding one another, that persons are rational. Neither this hypothesis nor logic, however, can tell us how a person with certain beliefs and desires will think or act in a given situation.[11] For this, further information would be required than that brought to bear in explanations by reasons.

The preceding considerations tend to show that explanations involving reasons are not to be assimilated to explanations using predictive laws such as are found in physical science. They display causal information, it seems, in a different but certainly no less essential way. This means that our accounts of reasons cannot be tested through the use of laws putatively employed in them, such as those generalizing over beliefs, desires, or actions in the ways described. Nevertheless, it seems clear that we can be regarded as implicitly performing a suitable kind of testing in this field. And it seems that this does involve generalizations, if not at the level of those we have so far rejected.

We can regard ourselves as taking each interpretive explanation as liable to confirmation or disconfirmation through coherence or dissonance with other explanations of the same kind. Each such explanation involves the attribution of desires and beliefs. Each of these, moreover, is associated with many others, which cohere with it and help to fill out its content. Where the desires and beliefs in one explanation cohere and overlap with those of others, the explanations are mutually confirming. (Where they contradict or fail to cohere they are mutually disconfirming.) Since explanations by reasons are thus confirmed (or disconfirmed) by relation to others, giving the best account of an agent's actions requires fitting the pattern of his actions to the pattern of his motives as a whole, so as to achieve the greatest coherence.

Thus a judgment that an agent wants to warn someone about the danger of thin ice will fit with other interpretations of his actions which, for example, represent him as knowing what ice is, knowing thin ice is dangerous, thinking the danger might be avoided by warning, having a kind of concern which would prompt warning, and so on and on. It would not seem to fit (although it might be made to) with the falsity of any of these. Each of these judgments would likewise fit or fail to fit with

be correlated with something, let alone any stronger form of measure such as is used for temperature.

[11] The implication of both the laws of logic and the general assumption of rationality in explanations by reasons may of course engender the impression that laws are involved in a different way.

others which could be made on the basis of the interpretation of action, and so on and on. Finally, the judgment that an agent thinks he can say that the ice is thin by uttering 'The ice is thin' will be supported by other of his actions (particularly those performed by or in response to speech) which also confirm his understanding of English. So, although we interpret actions intuitively one by one, we can be regarded as understanding them in relation to each other more or less overall, constructing patterns of explanation which increase coherence and so give greater understanding of the content of reasons and their role in producing action.

This kind of verification through coherence of reasons can be compared to the statistical testing of hypotheses. If an hypothesis is to be tested in this way it must at least tentatively be interpreted as explaining and implying a range of correlations. If many of these obtain the hypothesis and interpretation are confirmed, whereas if they do not then either the hypothesis or interpretation is disconfirmed. Explanations by reasons can be taken to imply that desires and beliefs involving the thoughts of the reasons will figure in the explanations of other actions, and that those involving thoughts which contradict those in the reasons will not. It seems that we implicitly frame and confirm such hypotheses continually, in the course of understanding one another as rational agents in the sense described above.

The assumption that we can understand one another in this way entails that each of us will so behave that what he does can be interpreted cogently in terms of reasons. In this sense the assumption involves a general prediction about behaviour. It also entails that for practically every action reasons are to be found which cohere with those for many other actions, and this is a strong generalization about reasons and actions. The fact that such generalizations obtain enables us to verify or falsify explanations by reasons in the manner indicated. And our success in explaining actions in this way sustains the generalizations themselves.

The foregoing discussion of explanation and confirmation in everyday psychology may help to show why Home rightly thought it relevant to speak of a different logic and method for the humanities, and why Rycroft felt that psychoanalysis was misjudged if taken on the model of physical science (a point mistakenly put, if the preceding argument is correct, in terms of causality). This brief discussion of interpretation does not of course constitute an account of method. Still it seems appropriate that explanations displaying patterns of derivation among causes operating together should be sustained by a sort of holistic coherence.

Support of this kind might be regarded as increased if the cohering explanations could be assigned some weight in abstraction from their place in the overall pattern of successful explanation. Such weight would be provided by the supposition, mentioned above, that this kind of co-ordinating mutual understanding is part of our adaptation. On this assumption we might expect the exercise of understanding in common-sense psychology to appear merely intuitive and scarcely capable of further elucidation, especially by comparison with the achievements of science. For this is how it would be if the interpretive capacity (like that for the perception of ordinary physical things) was put in a certain natural harmony with its objects by the processes of evolution.

We noted above some connections between reasons and meaning. In his psychoanalytic work Freud characteristically found the meaning of a dream, symptom, or other phenomenon by understanding it as a wish-fulfilment. What is meant by this can be seen in a simple example. Freud observed that frequently when he had eaten anchovies or some other salty food before sleeping he would dream that *he was drinking delicious cool water*. After some repetitions of the dream, he would wake up thirsty and get a drink of water. (This common dream has of course a counterpart concerning urination.)

In dreaming Freud produces an imaginative representation of himself as doing and experiencing something, that is, drinking. Also it seems that while sleeping, Freud desired or wished to drink. He was in a state such that if he had been aware of it and able to describe it he would have recognized it as one of desiring or wishing to drink (as he did on waking).[12] So clearly the content of Freud's desire is related to that of his dream. Since the desire is to drink, and the dream is that he is drinking, the dream represents the gratification of the desire, or represents the desire as fulfilled.

Dreams and other imaginative representations involve something like experience, belief and feeling. In dreaming he is drinking the dreamer has an experience as of drinking, and in some sense believes this. Still, this experience of gratification or satisfaction must be regarded as imaginary or, as Freud says, hallucinatory. For no water was in fact drunk, and the dreamer's genuine thirst remains unsatisfied.

It seems that the content–content relation between desire and dream in this case is strong evidence that it is no accident that the dream

[12] Desires seem more closely related to possibilities of action than wishes, in the sense (for example) that a person is better said to wish than to desire that his past life had been different. Desires clearly go together with related wishes, and both involve unfulfilment or frustration which we may imagine away. So I shall use either notion as required to facilitate discussion.

accompanied the desire. Rather, it seems, we should suppose that the desire caused the dream. This consideration is evidently reinforced by what we have learnt above about the connection between content and causal role. The dream is thus an imaginative representation of the experience of the satisfaction of a desire, caused by that desire. These are, I think, the central features of a (Freudian) wish-fulfilment; the fulfilment in such cases being imaginary or hallucinatory.

Any structure with these features, it seems, will involve a twofold denial or falsification of reality – a falsification, in psychoanalytic terms, of inner and outer reality. In representing an unfulfilled desire or wish as gratified, a wish-fulfilment falsely represents the psychological state of the agent. Thus the dreamer, while thirsty, experiences himself as drinking. Further, in representing the agent as gratifying rather than suffering his unfulfilled desire or wish, a wish-fulfilment falsely represents the activity of the agent. The dreamer, asleep, takes himself to be active, drinking.

Although there are other cases of dreams in which the content of the representation and that of the desire represented as gratified are independently and easily determined, those with which Freud was mainly concerned are less easy. Most dreams can rightly be seen as wish-fulfilments only when their content is compared with desires inferred from the memories, ideas, etc., which the dreamer associates with the content of the dream. These can be considered, moreover, only if the dreamer enters a frame of mind in which they can emerge, and pursues them and submits them to investigation.

So for example one of Freud's patients dreamt that she wanted to give a supper party but was unable to do so, since she had only a little smoked salmon and was unable to get anything else. The dream could be seen as wish-fulfilling only in light of the the recollection that an underweight friend of whom she was jealous (and whose favourite food was smoked salmon) had the day before enquired when she was to be asked to another meal. Not giving a supper party with smoked salmon could thus be seen to fit, among other things, her desire not to feed her rival.[13]

Finally, and especially in cases of conflict, a dream may represent the gratification of a desire symbolically. Thus after a session in the back of a car during which – with some difficulty – she restrained herself, a girl dreamt that she was in the car with her boy friend; he took out his knife and cut an item of her clothing. Again, a man dreamt that a young girl closely related to him offered him a flower, and he took it – this seemed a beautiful dream; later he dreamt (as he put it) he was deflowering her, and awoke in anxiety.

[13] 1900b, IV, 147.

Symptoms occasionally have a fairly obvious representational content. Freud describes an intelligent and unembarrassed-looking girl who came for examination with two buttons of her blouse undone and one of her stockings hanging down, and showed her calf without being asked. Her main complaint was that she had a feeling in her body as if there was something 'stuck into it' which was 'moving backwards and forwards' and was 'shaking' her through and through. Sometimes it made her whole body feel 'stiff'.[14] Generally, however, they can be treated as wish-fulfilling only where associations or other information make it plausible to assign to them both a content and an appropriate relation to a desire.

Consider, for example, the obsessional patient referred to as the table-cloth lady.[15] Many times a day she would run from her room into a neighboring one, stand beside a table, ring for the maid, and send her away again. The compulsion to repeat this apparently meaningless action was perplexing to the patient, and presumably wearing for the maid. Part of the significance of the symptom emerged with two observations. The patient recalled that on her wedding night her husband – from whom she had separated and who was much in her thoughts – had been impotent. Many times he had run from his room into hers to try to have intercourse, and finally, saying that he would feel ashamed before the maid when she came to make the bed, poured some red ink on the sheets – but in the wrong place. To this the patient could add that when she rang she stood in such a way that the maid should see a prominent stain on the tablecloth. So it appeared that the symptom was a representation of events on her wedding night, with the difference that she ensured that the maid should see the stain. It does not seem easy to determine the content of this representation precisely. Freud remarks that the symptom shows wish-fulfilment (the husband is represented as potent), a sort of identification (with the absent husband, whose part the patient plays), and representation by means of a familiar symbolism (table and cloth for bed and sheet.) Also, the activity of the maid – in service, as it were, to the patient's representing imagination – shows a way in which the production of wish-fulfilling representations can involve co-operative or coercive activities among persons. So far as living persons are used in representations which involve symbolism, metaphor, or likeness to what they represent, wish-fulfilment is potentially an important social matter.

Finally, the role of wish-fulfilment as regards memory is exemplified in the following material from a young man who, despite a desire to settle down with a girl he loved, felt compelled to make other girls fall in love

[14] 1900b, V, 618.
[15] 1916, XVI, 263.

with him and to behave in what he considered an unduly seductive and promiscuous way. He began analysis by saying that being outside the consulting room door (while the analyst was with another patient) before his first session had reminded him of being outside the shut door to his parents' bedroom when he was little. Later he remembered something: he was very young, in his parents' bed (he could remember the pyjamas he was wearing, from early childhood) . . . his mother seemed to be rolling back and forth against him, as if excited and yearning, almost in tears . . . he too was excited. It could be ascertained fairly certainly that the memory related to a period when he used to cry at night and was sometimes allowed to come into his parents' bed. It was not his mother, however, but he who had rolled excitedly. The transformation in his memory was apparently wish-fulfilling.[16]

Now it is natural to suppose that the explanation of wish-fulfilment is the same kind as that of action. This seems to have been the assumption

---

[16] On this topic Eysenck and Wilson write that 'Certainly Freud's choice of words is often curiously indecisive, as if he were afraid to say something that could be tested in any rigorous way. Cioffi urges us to "consider the idioms in which Freud's interpretations are typically phrased. Symptoms, errors, etc., are not simply *caused by* but they 'announce', 'proclaim', 'express', 'realize', 'fulfil', 'gratify', 'represent', 'imitate', or 'allude to' this or that repressed impulse, thought, memory, etc." . . . these phrases may have been used to avoid refutation, as Cioffi suggests.' (*The Experimental Study of Freudian Theories*, London, 1973, p. 11. The reference is to F. Cioffi, 'Freud and the Idea of a Pseudo-Science', in R. Borger and F. Cioffi, *Explanation in the Behavioural Sciences* (Cambridge, 1970), p. 496.)

The suggested criticism seems based upon misunderstanding of Freudian theory. Freud uses 'express', 'represent', 'fulfil', 'realize', and 'gratify' as well as 'cause' in connection with wish-fulfilments not to avoid refutation but because he holds that wish-fulfilments express wishes which are not simply caused by wishes but also represent them as fulfilled, realized, or gratified. He uses 'imitate' because representation may involve an element of imitation, as in the table-cloth lady's imitation of her husband's running. Similarly, because of their role and content, wish-fulfilling representations can be said to announce, allude, etc. The girl's dream above alluded to events in the back of the car, as did the lady's symptom to her wedding night. The analysand's first statement on the couch – about being outside the shut door – both alluded to the past and announced (as first communications in analysis often do) a theme which was to dominate his analysis: his inability to tolerate the exclusivity of his parent's relations in their bedroom. And in connection with this his recall of a distorted memory of being in their bed gave a presumably early example of the defensive *motif* already proclaimed in his symptoms, namely that of representing the others as desiring and frustrated rather than himself. (The transposition of this theme on to the analytical situation, also announced in the first communication, continued with his coming to believe that the analyst envied and admired him, perhaps secretly loved and depended on him, preferred him to all other patients, etc.) On the importance of first communications in analysis see Freud's note at the beginning of the case of the Rat Man, discussed below. (1909d, X, 160n, 200). For description of some of Cioffi's misunderstandings see V. L. Jupp, 'Freud and Pseudo-Science' *Philosophy*, October 1977, pp. 441–53. An aspect of the account of Freud given by Eysenck et. al. is discussed in Conway, 'Little Hans: Misrepresentation of the Evidence', *Bulletin of the British Psychological Society* (1978) 31, 385–7, and Cheshire, 'A big hand for Little Hans', the same *Bulletin* (1979) 32, p. 320–3.

of most philosophers (and analysts) who have explicitly addressed the explanation of symptoms, etc. And this assumption seems to have engendered debate, about the rationality or coherence of wish-fulfilment.

Thus Alexander and Mischel[17] have discussed a hypothetical case of wish-fulfilment in which someone's (Oedipal) wish to kill his father is expressed in his lunging at lampposts with his umbrella, this latter being, it seems, a representation of an attack. They disagree as to whether he can be said to have reason, or good reason, for doing this.

Alexander argues that 'if my wish to kill my father were conscious it would be obvious to me that it was not adequately satisfied by lunging at lampposts'. Hence, he says, 'these "reasons" can be reasons for this behaviour only if they are unconscious for they would not look like reasons if they were conscious'. This, he thinks, shows that in an ordinary sense they cannot be regarded as good reasons, or perhaps as reasons at all. Mischel replies that 'if I (unconsciously) want to kill my father and (unconsciously) identify lunging at lampposts with killing him, then, given this irrational starting point, I do have good reason for lunging at lampposts'. This, he thinks, shows that explanation in this case is analogous to explanation of action by a reason.

The argument seems to turn upon Alexander and Mischel's common assumption that the symptomatic action in question should be explained by the agent's desire to kill his father together with some such belief as, that lunging at lampposts would be a way of doing so. Such a belief would, as Mischel says, identify lunging with killing, and so would fulfil the condition, which Alexander mentions, of ensuring that the desire to kill can be taken as satisfied by lunging. On this reading, Alexander's point would be that the belief that lunging at lampposts is a way of killing one's father would not be credible as a conscious belief, and so cannot serve as a constituent of a reason in the ordinary sense; and Mischel's reply would be that still we have here the elements of a reason, a desire and an (irrational) belief, in the dim light of which the action to be explained would appear desirable.

It would be possible, although it does not seem plausible, to interpret each of the examples we have considered in this way. Thus the table-cloth lady's ritual might be explained by some such desire as to have her wedding night over again except with things right, and a belief

---

[17] P. Alexander, 'Rational Behaviour and Psychoanalytic Explanation', *Mind*, July 1962, 326–41 and a reply by T. Mischel, *Mind*, January 1965, 71–8. On this topic see also R. Audi, *The Monist*, 1972, 444–64. An attempt to reformulate psychoanalytic theory in terms relating to action is in Schafer, *A New Language for Psychoanalysis*, (New Haven, Yale, 1976).

that running to the table, etc., was a way of doing so. The dream of drinking could be explained by a desire to drink and some such belief as, that dreaming of drinking was a way of drinking. Perhaps even the analysand's memory could be explained by his desire to avoid recollection of unrequited desire and his belief that remembering wrongly in this way was a way of doing so. In these accounts, however, we encounter two difficulties. The first is that indicated by Alexander. Even if the desire to be linked to a wish-fulfilling representation is clear, and it seems reasonable to suppose that the representation is caused by that desire, still the belief required to explain the representation in accord with the pattern used to explain actions by reasons seems scarcely comprehensible or coherent.[18] The second, related to this, is that in many cases we cannot plausibly link the content of a wish-fulfilment directly with a desire for action. Thus it does not seem quite right to say that the table-cloth lady's ritual shows her desire to repeat her wedding night; rather insofar as we link it to the past it seems we should say that it expresses her wish that things had been different. These considerations both suggest that we should not describe wish-fulfilment on the pattern of rational action, but rather as activity of the imagination.

We imagine by representing things to ourselves. Since wish-fulfilling activities consist in the imaginative representation of the gratification of desires or wishes, it seems we can regard them simply as forms of imagining that things are as (in some way) we wish they were. Such imagining may be caused by a desire to perform a certain kind of action, but it does not seem to be undertaken because of a belief that it is a way of performing that kind of action. It seems natural, for example, that someone hungry should imagine eating; but this carries no suggestion that he supposes that the imagining is a way of eating. No more is this implied if he hallucinates, and so believes that he is eating. Again, his imagining, like his desire to eat, may show his belief that eating is a way of satisfying hunger; but this is a belief about eating, not imagining.

We can imagine things at will, and imagining may involve experiences of gratification. These facts may suggest that the imagining in wish-fulfilment is a kind of intentional action. In many central cases this does not seem to be so. Some cases, however, may involve a certain kind of primitive confusion about actions and events, or an exercise of will of a kind prior to that in intentional action. An adequate discussion of this

---

[18] Reflecting on this same difficulty W. Alston refers to the possibility 'that the unconscious is quite illogical'. ('Psychoanalytic Theories, Logical Status of', *Encyclopaedia of Philosophy*, New York, 1967, vol. 6, pp. 512–16.) This particular illogicality, if I am right, is simply the result of the imposition of an inappropriate pattern of explanation. See also F. Cioffi, 'Wishes, Symptoms, and Actions', *Proceedings of the Aristotelian Society Supplementary Volume*, 1974, 97ff, and the reply of P. Alexander.

would require detailed consideration of the psychoanalytic account of the development of the mind. Some arguments, however, may serve to indicate a line of thought.

Wish-fulfilment may seem most like action where it is effected by bodily or intentional activity, as in the *tableau vivant* of Freud's obsessional patient or the stabbing with an umbrella discussed above. Someone may indeed imagine himself to be performing one kind of action (attacking his father) by actually performing another (lunging with an umbrella); his imagining, that is, may consist partly in his doing something which symbolizes, resembles, or otherwise represents (to him) what he imagines doing. That imagining may govern someone's intentional actions in this way, however, does not show that the imagining itself is intentional. Characteristically, it seems, the actions will be intentional but the imagining not. This is because imaginative activity seems not to be governed by desire and belief in the way intentional action is. It is not typically undertaken, for example, because of a desire to obtain an experience of gratification and a belief that imagining something would be a way of doing so. The variety of our imaginings seems to outrun any beliefs we might have on this score, and what we imagine, with its pleasures or pains, usually arises in us unbidden. Nor is the enaction of a live representation typically undertaken because of a desire to represent something and a belief that performing certain actions may be a way of doing so. Rather it seems that the mark of the imagination – in this or other forms – is the capacity to create representations which are unanticipated and new. Activity like this could not be governed by beliefs about how to represent things.

We can think of imagining as like breathing, which follows a natural course in adjustment to need unless intention or will intervenes. On such a view the natural activity of imagination would encompass the spontaneous production of images of gratified desire, while willed imagining might hold, recapture, or elaborate these or others from perception or memory.[19] From the outside we can think of the aim of such imagining in terms of the production or alteration of images or experiences. A correct description of the intentions with which such imagining is done, however, must depend upon how the person himself regards his activity. He can be said to intend to imagine or represent only if he can think of his activity in that way. So far as he is unable to distinguish imagining from acting or altering the world, his intentions in imagining must likewise be regarded as confused, unformed, or indeterminate.

We may speculate that in the first months of life, before an infant

---

[19] See Freud's abstract and simplified account of this at 1910a, V, 565 and elsewhere.

comes to think of the objective world and his activities in it as distinct from what he imagines, this indeterminacy is radical and pervasive. In particular, it seems that the infant may picture the world in ways systematically distorted by his wishes, and also as partly subject to his will in the way his imaginings are. In Freudian terms, this would be the period of the domination of the pleasure principle[20] and infantile omnipotence of thought, before the establishment of the reality principle. The willed imagining by which the child alters his world during this period can be regarded as a kind of proto-action; and so far as symptoms and dreams involve reversion to this way of thinking, they can be viewed in the same way.

Looking to Freud's theories in the terms we have been trying to clarify, we can see that one of his central claims was that a wide range of human activities involved the wish-fulfilling representation of certain themes in desire. These included not only dreams, symptoms, slips, and transference, but also those of children at play and adults in serious pursuits (perhaps the table-cloth lady's serious symptomatic play with her maid suggests that these are not entirely distinct categories). This claim, as we can see from Freud's interpretive work, was meant to be supported by a systematic correlation and coherence among the results of the interpretation of wish-fulfillment and action.

Abstracting from the content of Freud's theory, we can think of such a correlation as built up as follows. We can interpret almost any action in terms of reasons which cohere with those for other actions. However, some activities which spring from the mind – dreams, symptoms, irrational actions – appear senseless or unmotivated in some respect. So far as these can cogently be interpreted as involving representation and wish-fulfilment, we can form hypotheses which partly explain them by relating them to desires or wishes. These hypotheses, in turn, can be tested through their coherence or dissonance with the results of interpreting both actions and other putative wish-fulfilments. In addition, they may lead to further interpretations of both actions and other wish-fulfillments. These may be tested as before; and so on. Such a process might lead by cogent interpretive steps to a theory which radically transcended commonsense psychology, and yet was strongly supported by interpretive coherence in the same way.

[20] See 1911b, XII, 215ff, 'Formulations on the Two Principles of Mental Functioning'. For more on the role of imagination in psychoanalytic theory see R. Wollheim, 'Identification and Imagination' in *On Art and the Mind* (London, 1973), and 'Wish-fulfilment' in *Rational Action*, ed. R. Harrison (Cambridge, 1979). Wollheim's account of omnipotence of thought is slightly different from that indicated here.

This extended psychology would supplement the assumption of the rationality of action with another concerning the ubiquity and connectedness of wishful imagining. As interpretive success in commonsense psychology sustains the strongly predictive guiding principle of interpretation that for almost any action reasons are to be found which cohere with those for many other actions, so success in the extended psychology might ultimately sustain the strongly predictive principle that for almost any wish-fulfilment desires are to be found which cohere with those for many actions and many other wish-fulfilments. This would mean that interpretations in the extended psychology could be strongly confirmed or disconfirmed, by very many instances of coherence or dissonance with others. So far as the ascription of new and definite patterns of desires was thus strongly and repeatedly confirmed, an extended psychology of determinate content would be strongly supported, and would itself contribute explanation and coherence to the commonsense psychology upon which it was based.

Also, still abstracting from the detail and content of Freud's theory, we can see how the interpretation of a wish-fulfilling structure in such a psychology may provide a condition for a sort of psychic development. An imaginary experience of gratification is precisely suited to preclude awareness of the desire which causes it, as an illusory experience of drinking may prevent awareness of thirst or a vivid phantasy of being desired may prevent awareness of unrequited desire. Now, for a desire or other mental item to be kept from awareness is partly for it to be kept from interacting – logically and causally – with other desires, beliefs, etc., in thought and action. Hence the desire may remain both ungratified and unmodified, like the dreamer's thirst masked by his illusion of drinking.

Interpretation of such a structure may bring awareness of it, and hence the possibility that it should be changed. This, however, involves acknowledging both the internal and external falsification of reality in it – recognizing an unfulfilled desire together with the fact that a range of apparently gratifying experience was illusory. This is partly modelled in the way a dreamer becomes aware of his thirst, and that his recent experiences of drinking have been chimerical, in waking to get a drink; but the hostility of wishful thinking to awareness of real desire is familiar from other areas of life.

The role of awareness here merits further consideration. Wish-fulfilment involves a certain incoherence or irrationality – the persistence of a desire together with an imaginary belief in, or experience of, its gratification. Likewise unconscious motivation characteristically involves contradictory beliefs or desires, of which the agent is unaware. Suppose, for example, that someone is hypnotized and told that after the trance is over he will open an umbrella whenever the hypnotist gives some signal. He wakes up and seems to remember nothing about the trance, but ascertains where the umbrella is and keeps his attention on the hypnotist. Then at the signal he opens the umbrella, confusedly giving some excuse for doing so.

He is best understood as acting on the hypnotist's instructions. This implies that he believes that he was told to open an umbrella and in some sense desires to do as he was told. He may, however, sincerely deny that anyone has told him this, and he may be strongly opposed to any form of unthinking compliance with instructions. In this sense he has contradictory beliefs and desires. We may assume, as often happens, that if he learnt of the suggestion he would try hard to oppose it, and if he remembered being given it he would lose all desire to act accordingly. This means that a kind of memory and awareness would enable him to act more rationally; that is, to choose the course of action (refraining from opening an umbrella for no good reason) in best accord with his desires and beliefs, all things considered.[21]

This indicates how awareness is central to rationality. A person acts rationally when he acts best to satisfy all his own desires, obligations and so forth, as he sees things. To do so he must choose the most preferable – the most desirable, all things considered, or the best in light of his own motives, whatever they are – of the alternative actions he can perform. So far as his desires, beliefs, or other motives are not adequately reflected in his choices, he may fail to act rationally. What a person is fully aware of, it seems, enters most completely into his processes of thought, and plays its proper role in determining his choices. Sometimes, as in the examples mentioned, awareness may lead to resolution of incoherence or contradiction and hence to a simple and rational change in action. Things are more complicated, however, as regards the kind of motives with which psychoanalysis is concerned.

There is no rational satisfaction for the desires Freud thought represented in the incest and parricide of Sophocles' *Oedipus Rex*, awareness

---

[21] Logical consistency figures at two levels – often not grammatically distinguished – in our description of a person. If we take a person as an object which satisfies psychological predicates, then of course the predicates a person satisfies must be consistent. Also, we regard one another as rational, and so generally consistent in belief. This means that the contents of the beliefs we ascribe to one another will generally be consistent. These are, however, distinct matters. We can, as above, give a consistent description of an imperfectly consistent agent.

It may be tempting to think that such a description leads to contradiction. For, one may say, if he believes that it is not the case that the hypnotist told him to open an umbrella, then he doesn't believe that the hypnotist told him. So it seems that it is the case that he believes this, and also that it is not the case that he believes this; which is a contradiction. Such reasoning is, however, invalid; it requires us to assume the agent's consistency at just the point at which we know it to fail.

of which could not be borne. In theory, so far as the boy explicitly represents such desires as gratified he feels unbearable anxiety and despair at the damage he has done his parents and also fear of retaliation from his father. Yet so far as he acknowledges his parents' love for one another he suffers unbearable jealousy. Hence, in one line of thought, he represents his mother as loving him rather than his father, and his father as jealous rather than himself. This, however, results in fear of his father's jealous hostility and also of the consequences of his own wishful retaliation. So this representation is replaced by one in which the relations between father and son are idealized.

The jealous hatred and desire for possession masked by this idealization may, partly because they are so masked, be rendered unmodifiable by experience. This otherwise enables the boy more fully to appreciate and accept his role as a child who is loved by parents who nurture and care for him, help him to grow up, and so forth; and hence to accept that the way they love him is quite different from the way they love each other. So far as the primitive emotions remain unmodified they may continue to be expressed in representations which cause anxiety (or actual damage), may be guarded against by inhibition, and so on.

The reasons for anxiety will include love and concern for the parents. Hence interpretation of these representations will not tend to bring action on the desires shown in them, but rather modification of these desires and their products through awareness and contact with others in thought. Knowledge that hostility and imagined hostility are based on misconception and wish-fulfilment, for example, may bring a lessening of fear and hatred, and awareness that imagined possession and destruction are illusory may bring relief from guilt. Such changes may in turn diminish the role of such motives in the imagination, and hence the intensity of anxiety and idealization consequent on them.

All this may enable the patient to appreciate and accept more fully his place in the family, and to understand what was done for him as a needful child (rather than an imperious little parent). If so, his representations of possession and damage may be replaced by others which express his desires – previously shown mainly in idealization – to make good the relations between and with his parents which were distorted by his own infantile feelings, and to do other things from love, care, gratitude, and so on. Since these like other representations may involve activities which partly replicate or symbolize what they represent, this may mean an indirect but far-reaching change in action.[22]

---

[22] I should make clear that this sketch of theory is extremely incomplete, and is meant for illustration. Also the emphasis on reparation and gratitude in sublimation is taken from Melanie Klein. (See Hanna Segal, *Klein*, London, 1980.)

According to this last part of the theory, the sublimation of primitive sexual and aggressive desires which follows upon awareness of them and their modification in thought leads to the inception of new desires and interests, and so to more deeply satisfying rational action. This part of the pattern of rational action, however, takes its form and capacity to satisfy partly from its role as benign wish-fulfilment. (So gardening might be thought a continuously satisfying activity because of what it represented as well as because of its instrumental function.) Hence on this view of the working of the mind, it might be said, reason is not so much the slave of the passions as the servant of the imagination.

As the remarks above suggest, the psychoanalytic conception of defence is partly to be understood in terms of the kind of representation we have been considering. For example, in using projection as a defence against feelings of frustration or aggression, a person represents and feels another, rather than himself, to be frustrated or aggressive. This can be a simple wish-fulfilling reversal, such as was to be seen in the memories of the analysand above, who represented his mother rather than himself as yearning for erotic contact. Again, transference, which Freud described from his early work as the patient's tendency to make the analyst the object of the thoughts and feelings involved in his symptoms, consists in the patient's unconsciously representing the analyst as a figure from his past. This is a source of one of the interpretive correlations mentioned above, since if the patient's symptoms arise, as Freud claimed, from the Oedipus complex, then he will unconsciously experience and represent the analyst in the Oedipal terms hypothesized in theory.

This can partly be illustrated by reference to Freud's patient called the Rat Man. He was a lawyer, described by Freud as a young man of value and promise, who suffered from a number of incapacitating obsessions and compulsions. Recently he had been particularly tormented by the thought and fear that a certain punishment, in which rats gnawed their way into the anus of the victim, should be applied to his lady and his father, whom he loved. Thoughts of aggression directed towards his lady and his father were a constant source of anxiety and guilt to him, and he employed special formulae and other means to protect the victims.

The idea of the rat punishment being applied in this way had occurred to him when a Captain (his father had been a soldier) had told him about it on manoeuvres. Also, when this Captain told him of a small debt (his father had incurred a debt while in the army which he had apparently failed to repay) he developed a confused obsession with repaying it, supposing that if he failed to do so the punishment would be applied. The Captain advocated corporal punishment, and seemed to him obviously fond of cruelty. As he told Freud the story of the punishment, the patient's face took on a strange, composite expression, which Freud interpreted as one of horror at pleasure of his own of which he was unaware. And while telling Freud of his attempts to pay the debt, the patient became confused, and repeatedly called him 'Captain'.[23]

His father was dead, but much in his thoughts. This had been evidenced not only by his anxiety, but also by his thinking when he heard a joke that he must tell it to his father, by studying to please his father (but not being able to carry his studies through), and by actually imagining, when he heard a knock at the door, that it might be his father. His relationship with his father had been, as he described it, almost ideal. He said he was his father's best friend, and his father his; and in many respects this seemed to be true.[24] There was only one subject of disagreement between them. His father had been the suitor of a poor girl before marrying the patient's wealthy mother. The son's lady was not rich, and his father had thought the connection imprudent. He seemed to remain poised between his dead father's will and his desire for the lady; and before he had broken down his mother and family had encouraged him to marry a wealthy girl. He had suicidal impulses, and was tormented with self-reproach, as if he were a criminal, for not being present at his father's death. Also, when he had visited his father's grave, he had seen a large beast which he took to be a rat gliding over the grave; he assumed it had been gnawing on the corpse.

Despite his love for his father there seemed in his mind to be a lethal opposition between his father and his own sexual or marital gratification. He remembered before his father died thinking that the death might make him rich enough to marry his lady, and he thought later that his marrying might harm his father in the next world. He had not copulated before his father's death, and had masturbated only a little. From after his father's death, however, he remembered occasions of this which seemed significant because of their connection with the idea of a prohibition being defied.

In response to an interpretation about masturbation and thoughts of death or castration by his father, he remembered a period when he was suffering from a desire to masturbate, but was also tormented with the idea of his penis being cut off. And in connection with this he remem-

---

[23] 1909b, X, 155–320. I have made use of Freud's case notes from the time, appended as 'Original Record of the Case', pp. 253ff, and especially pp. 263–4 and 281–5. The patient's inability quite to distinguish his thoughts of punishment from the occurrence of punishment itself, and his connected belief in the power of his own thoughts may exemplify the kind of omnipotence of thought mentioned above. The 'Captain' parapraxis is an early indication of the transference which emerges fairly clearly at 283–5 and is discussed below.

[24] It may be important that the relationship is represented as one in which there is no disproportion between father and son.

bered that on the occasion of his first copulation he had thought 'This is a glorious feeling! One might do anything for this – murder one's father, for instance.' (He also described a scene which he had been told of from his childhood, when he had been enraged with his father for punishing him, and had abused his father roundly. His father had apparently said that he would be either a great man or a criminal.)[25]

His sense of opposition between his father and his own gratification apparently went back into childhood. He could remember thinking at the age of twelve that a little girl with whom he was in love might be more kind to him if he should suffer some misfortune – such as the death of his father. And even from the age of six, as far back as he could remember things completely, he could recall wanting to see girls naked, but feeling that if he had such thoughts his father might die.

His symptoms and thoughts fairly explicitly represented his father as punitively tortured or killed. According to the fragment of psychoanalytic theory sketched above, these symptoms or thoughts would involve the imaginary fulfilment of hostile wishes which had arisen in childhood when he had perceived his father as prohibiting his possession and enjoyment of his mother and which had remained relatively unmodified by his subsequent experience. To represent these wishes as fulfilled would lead to anxiety or guilt, whereas to represent himself as in possession of his mother and hence prohibiting his father in this way would lead to fear of castration or death. To avoid such jealousy and hostility the relationship would have to be imagined as equal and friendly, or as one of admiration, etc.

The hypothesis that such a complex of wishes and feelings was active would bear upon a number of features of the case. It would partly explain why, despite the genuine friendship between the patient and his father, the patient nonetheless also seemed to feel his father to be a barrier to his satisfaction which could be overcome only through harm or death. This was evidenced in his still hesitating in regard to the relationship of which his father had disapproved, and imagining that consummation of it might bring harm to his father in the afterlife; in his having thought that his father's death might enable him to marry the lady, or that one might murder one's father to enjoy the glorious feeling of sexual intercourse; in his having supposed that if his father died his childhood romance might prosper, or that his father might die as a result of his wishes to see girls naked. It would also partly explain his association of castration with masturbation, and his having begun to

[25] Here interpretation of a theme in the patient's associations had apparently enabled further associations to arise, in which the theme was represented more explicitly. See page 263 for the interpretation, 264–5 for the associations it released.

masturbate mainly after his father's death and then in connection with the idea of a prohibition being defied. It would explain his propensity to think of his father's death or torture, and his guilt and anxiety in doing so; his intensified guilt after his father's death; his suicidal impulses; and so on.

He was extremely reluctant to accept that he might harbour hostility towards his father. When Freud interpreted that there was a wish to kill his father in what he said he replied that he could not believe that he had ever entertained such a wish. Then, apparently disconnectedly, he remembered a story. It was about a woman who as she sat by her sister's sick bed felt a wish that her sister might die, so that she might marry her sister's husband. She thereupon committed suicide, thinking she was not fit to live. He said he could understand this, and it would be right if his thoughts were the death of him, for he deserved nothing less. The story repeated the themes which Freud was interpreting, in particular suicidal guilt because of a death wish consequent upon a desire to marry. Also, although the patient denied the wish he yet considered that he deserved to die because of his thoughts, as if they did reflect his desires or intentions. So despite the patient's denial, Freud could regard his response as partly confirming the correctness of his hypothesis.

Although he denied hostility towards his father, he later began showing hostility towards Freud. This intensified after analysis of a protective formula he used in masturbating.[26] In his deliberate actions he treated Freud with the greatest respect, but he attacked him in his thoughts, which as part of the treatment he put into words. He had phantasies of intercourse and fellatio with Freud's daughter; phantasies of Freud's mother naked, swords stuck into her breast and the lower part of her body and especially her genitals eaten up by Freud and his children (cf. the rats of the torture, and the rat seen in the graveyard);[27] of Freud's mother dead; and so on. These depressed him and also made him fearful.

[26] The emergence of hostility seems to begin with the completion of the *Glejisamen* work on p. 281.

[27] Later associations had Freud's son eating excrement, and Freud himself eating his mother's excrement. Those familiar with psychoanalytic theory will recognise the connection with the patient's attitude towards the lady (who was to be tortured by the rats as well) and to his mother, who was condemned because of her money. And it should be pointed out that although the Rat Man was neurotic, the patterns and phantasies in his associations – including those of attacking the mother's breast and eating into her body – are found in the material of normal adults and children as well.

Freud remarked that the Rat Man's recognition of his identification with rats – and so those of the cemetery and the torture – was part of the analytic work which relieved his symptoms. Elsewhere Freud links the themes found here – of killing and eating a prohibiting and castrating father – with the setting up of the super-ego and the acquisition of guilt. He does not, however, relate this in detail to individual development, but rather (and quite implausibly) ascribes it to events which happened in the prehistory of mankind,

While telling Freud of his phantasies he got up off the couch (as he had in first telling of the rat torture) and walked about the room. He said his reason for doing so was delicacy of feeling – he could not lie there comfortably while he was saying these things about Freud; and he kept hitting himself, as in self-punishment, while saying them.[28] But he agreed he was walking about the room not for this reason, but out of fear that Freud might beat him.

He imagined Freud and his wife with a dead child lying between them, and became particularly afraid that Freud would turn him out. He knew the origin of this – when he was a little boy he had been lying in bed between his father and his mother; he had wet the bed; and his father had beaten him and turned him out of bed.

His demeanour during all this was that of a man in desperation and one who was trying to save himself from blows of terrific violence. He buried his heads in his hands, rushed away, covered his face with his arms, etc. He told Freud his father had a passionate temper, and did not know what he was doing. Later he said he had thought Freud might be murderous, and would fall on him like a beast of prey to search out what was evil in him.[29]

of which he supposed we have phylogenetic memories. Thus he cites a child who wanted to eat some 'fricassee of mother' in connection with the eating of the primal father (1912–13, XIII, 131).

Melanie Klein found such oral themes to be very prominent in the play and speech of children in analysis. Thus a patient 'phantasied about a woman in the circus who was sawn in pieces, and then nevertheless comes to life again, and now he asked me if this were possible. He then related . . . that actually every child wants to have a bit of his mother, who is to be cut in four pieces . . . first across the width of the breast, and then of the belly, then lengthwise so that the *pipi* [penis] the face and the head were cut exactly through the middle . . . he constantly bit at his hand and said that he bit his sister too for fun, but certainly not for love . . . every child took the piece of mother that it wanted, and [he] agreed that the cut up mother was then also eaten' (*Love, Guilt, and Reparation*, London 1975, 70). She was able to place this material in a theoretical framework which coheres with Freud's work but supplements it with an account, among other things, of the role of cannibalistic, coprophagous, and other oral phantasies in early development.

[28] Compare the boy in the last footnote biting himself as he describes his phantasy.

[29] Someone he knew to be constantly making things up had told him Freud's brother was a murderer. Also, he later remembered his sister having remarked that one of Freud's brothers would be the right husband for his lady, and took this as a further cause for jealous hostility to Freud's family. What he had been told does not seem to go far in explaining this scene, since he had been aware of it all along, and it only became important in the context of his transference and emerging parallel memory. Jealousy provoked by his sister's remark would fit in with his transference feelings, but would not itself explain them.

Representation of the analyst or father as a biting or devouring beast occurs elsewhere in the material of Freud's patients, as in other psychoanalyses which reach a certain depth. Little Hans' fear was of being bitten by a horse, which animal Freud took to represent his father. (1909b, X, 5ff). Freud's patient called the Wolf Man represented his father and related figures by fearful devouring wolves. He repeatedly dreamt of six or seven wolves staring at him, riveting their attention on him; as a child he awoke screaming in fear that the

Now fairly clearly the patient's experiencing extreme fear that Freud would beat him and turn him out, while remembering his father's having beaten him and turned him out (of bed),[30] instantiates the assumption that he was experiencing Freud as he had his father in the past. This experience was at first unconscious, then became conscious. That he was beaten and turned out as a result of what he did (with his penis) while lying between his parents is related to the Oedipal theme, and also to his symptoms.

He was lying between his parents, and so preventing his father having access to his mother. His father punished and displaced him, and so prohibited and barred his access. In his thoughts the father who had displaced him from the parental bed likewise stood between him and his lady or his gratification, and so might have to die or be murdered for him to marry or have sexual intercourse. (The symptoms would represent both the hatred of his father for this, and also his maintenance of the prohibition within himself, to avoid the terrible consequences of breaking it.) In his symptoms his father was also subjected to punishment, as in return.

Beneath the patient's attitude of respect and delicacy of feeling towards Freud were the unconscious hostility shown in his associations (for which he punished himself, and which depressed him) and the fear expressed at first in his walking about the room. This would cohere with the assumption that beneath his friendliness and respect for his father there was the hostility and consequent self-punishment and depression shown in his symptoms, and also a fear of his father. The ascription of fear would fit with the way his respect and delicacy of feeling gave way to fear of Freud as a murderer or wild beast, especially since he felt this while remembering and describing his father's (as he saw it) fearful violence. (This would be the coming to awareness, through reliving in the transference, of a repressed fear.)

He expressed his hostility towards Freud in part in the form of phantasies of Freud and his family behaving like the rats of his own symptomatic thoughts of the punitive torture of his lady and his father, and expected a reciprocal punitive hostility from Freud as a wild beast.

wolves might eat him. He linked this with the story of 'The Wolf and the Seven Little Goats', of whom six were eaten. In early sessions he would look towards Freud in a very friendly way, as if to propitiate him, then look away to a large grandfather clock opposite. He was able to explain this to Freud when he recalled that the youngest of the little goats had hidden in such a clock while his brothers were eaten by the wolf. Apparently he was representing himself as the youngest little goat, and Freud as the wolf who might eat him. (1918b, XVII, 9ff). The representation of the parent or analyst as such a beast would be a mirror image (projection) of the desires to devour or attack with the mouth and teeth mentioned in the footnote above.

[30] There may be an identification of the scene of the analysis here with the parental bedroom comparable to that in the case mentioned above.

This would cohere with the hypothesis that he had felt such hostilities towards his father in childhood – so that the thoughts of his symptoms were of infantile origin – and that he had expected a comparable hostility in return.

His fear surfaced in an image of a dead baby, lying between Freud and his wife. This would cohere with his thoughts of Freud as a murderer, and also with his memory of lying between his parents and being punished for what he did, as an image of what the terrifying and punitive father whom Freud now represented might do. Such a dreadful image, moreover, might still involve elements of wish-fulfilment. The child was between the parents, and Freud and his father were murderers, not himself. This image might thus represent the projection of the murderous impulses explicit in his symptoms on to Freud as on to his father. It seems to have been with the occurrence of this image that his greatest fear, and also his conscious remembering, began. An assumption of projection would cohere with his excessive fear of Freud, as well as the general tendency in his associations to present Freud (or his children) as possessing desires related in content to his symptoms. This might also be connected with his idea that he deserved death because of his thoughts about his father.[31]

Having illustrated some aspects of the Freudian concepts of transference, defence, and the Oedipus complex, we can approach the more abstract theoretical notions of ego, super-ego, and id.[32]

So far as the patient's present inner conflicts – like those of the Rat Man – reflect previous conflicts in the world between his own erotic and aggressive impulses and the parental authority which prohibits gratification of them, it seems we must regard the original sources of conflict as in some way replicated now within the patient's mind. We can do so by thinking of the mind as containing parts or agencies.

One part would be the locus of the erotic and aggressive impulses involved in such conflicts. These would appear to be present from infancy, and since they correspond, on the one hand, to the sexual and nurturing feelings involved in reproduction, and on the other to intense desires for killing and death, they can be taken as expressions of

[31] Although I think transference and projection are to be seen in this material, these interpretive remarks are not so much meant to convince on particular points as to indicate the presence of a field of imaginative representation related to Oedipal themes. This material could be linked with many other theoretical considerations, for example Freud's hypothesis that a boy's urination may be an expression of sexual excitement, ambition, and aggression, or the idea that mental projection may go together with bodily evacuation.

[32] See 1933a, XXII, 57–80, 'The Dissection of the Psychical Personality'. The discussion which follows is both selective and supplemented by post-Freudian work.

biologically grounded drives or instincts towards life and death respectively. Since the unrestrained and incoherent operation of these drives would be incompatible with individual survival and co-operative life, they require and receive parental and social control. The locus of these drives and impulses would be the id.

Another part of the mind would discharge in the adult those functions of encouragement and prohibition of instinctual impulse which the parent reforms in relation to the child. This part of the mind would be acquired during maturation, and would be modelled on the role of the parents. Among its functions, therefore, would be those of conscience. This part, the super-ego, would be fully established by the time the individual attains independence and maturity, and its proper functioning would be shown in his capacity to love and work co-operatively in family and society.

To a third part of the mind, the ego, is assigned the function of mediating between the external world and the desires of the id, and later between the id and the super-ego as well. Since the drives of the id are not sufficiently coherent to admit of satisfaction in reality, the ego must be assumed to have the capacities of perception, etc., to learn about reality, and also to be capable of learning to act and to form and modify desires so as to obtain satisfaction in it. One way in which the ego may do this is by following the example provided by other persons.

The reality with which a very young child has contact is significantly constituted by his parents. Parental regulation – control of feeding, imposition of toilet training, encouragement to self-restraint, more grown-up ways, etc. – is in early life liable to be felt especially intolerable and frustrating, and so may be represented in the mind as incoherently demanding, prohibitive, and punitive. Hence this kind of representation may be the basis for the development of the super-ego. The child may begin to achieve regulation of his own impulses, that is, by imagining himself as standing in relation to such a figure; and this kind of representation, in this role, may become a permanent feature of the mind.

Failure by the ego to obtain satisfaction for the desires of the id leads to frustration, whereas failure to act in accord with the demands of the super-ego leads to anxiety. Those desires which are felt most violently to conflict with parental regulation (in particular, those comprising the Oedipus complex) are the greatest source of anxiety, and so have to be kept from the attention of the super-ego. Although these cannot be represented or acted on straightforwardly, they may find expression in wish-fulfillment, provided they are suitably disguised or disowned.

The ego employs various mechanisms of defence to mask the representation of forbidden desires, including symbolism and projection. This latter allows desires which are subject to prohibition to be represented quite explicitly and openly, but as desires of another, and so without provoking anxiety from the super-ego. Indeed, projection can lead to a certain ratification of an otherwise forbidden desire: if the object of malevolent aggressive desires, for example, is represented as having these desires, he can then be thought of as a malevolent and aggressive enemy, and so regarded as a legitimate object of hatred and aggression. (In such a case, as it were, the super-ego joins with the id in aggressive hatred of the object.)

The super-ego is part of the ego, and the development and functioning of the one is bound up with that of the other. Their proper establishment in the young man is achieved through his identification with his father – that is, through his taking as his own a regulative image derived from that of his father as a paternal figure whose encouragements and prohibitions he can accept and on whose model he can love and act. This formative change in his ego and super-ego ensures that his desires and ways of satisfying them no longer require external regulation, and so renders him capable of the autonomous and rational pursuit of his own ends. His incorporating his father's prohibition against incest and correlatively following his father's example in choosing non-incestuous sexual love means that while he becomes like his father in type of sexual love he becomes different from his father in the object of it, so that the sources of Oedipal rivalry between father and son are removed. Thus the final development of the ego and super-ego through identification coincides with the dissolution of the Oedipus complex.

The relative functioning of these parts of the mind, however, may go wrong in a number of ways which impede development. For example, a child's intolerance of the frustrations imposed upon his early desires through his relations with his parents might lead to the formation of a severe super-ego. The anxiety generated by this might lead to a correspondingly severe masking and isolation of the aggressive desires of his id. These in turn could obtain representation as gratified, or legitimate gratification, only through projection. The projection of hostility aroused by frustration or prohibition, however, would serve to reinforce the infantile distortion of the parental images involved in his super-ego. Thus both the severity of the super-ego and the aggression of the id would remain in part unmodified by thought, and hence infantile.

For the boy this would mean that the unconscious images of his father related to the Oedipal period would be hostile and punitive in the extreme, and his own Oedipal desires and hatreds liable to correspondingly severe repression and projection. This in turn would continue to reinforce the distortion of the images of his father involved in his early super-ego. In these circumstances he might be unable to form an integral image of his father as a paternal figure whose encouragements and prohibitions he could make his own, and so be unable to accomplish the complete identification with his father required for the dissolution of his Oedipus complex.

In his failure to love on the model of his father he would neither become like his father in choosing non-incestuous love nor become entirely different from him in his object of sexual love, so that together with his childhood super-ego his early Oedipal emotions would remain partly intact. In his failure to act on the model of his father he would remain subject to unintegrated and archaic desires and demands which he could neither assume as his own nor renounce on the basis of an alternative identification. As his super-ego would retain its immature severity, so the unmodified desires of his id would remain unsatisfied, while his weak or incompletely developed ego could have recourse only to projection, wish-fulfilment which would cause anxiety, and so on.

Such theoretical considerations might cast further light on features of the case already discussed. If the Rat Man's impulses were regulated through his representing himself as in relation to a disciplining paternal figure, it would be intelligible that he should feel such a figure to be opposed to his gratification and so forth. Hence we might better be able to understand the correlative role in the Rat Man of unconscious hostility to his father for prohibiting sexual gratification, images from his childhood of his father as particularly frightening and punitive, a severe conscience resulting in anxiety and suicidal guilt, and also a conscious image, which remained quite disparate from the others, of his father as a close friend. These ideas also might bear on explaining why the Rat Man fell ill when confronted with a choice between being unlike his father (and subject to his father's disapproval) in marrying a poor girl, or like his father (of whom he disapproved in this respect) in marrying a rich girl, as his rich mother encouraged him to do; or again why he developed an obsession over paying a debt, as his father had once failed to do. Here illness seems to be bound up with the kind of identification which is supposed to be formative for the ego and super-ego.

These considerations may also serve to explain something of the Rat Man's behaviour in Freud's consulting room, and perhaps something of the earlier disturbing influence of the Captain with whom he first identified Freud. In the terms under discussion we can say that the Rat Man's terror when his repressions began to lift was at confrontation with an image of his own super-ego, which had been turned by projection, as Freud said in another context, into a pure culture of the death instinct. A link with the super-ego is suggested by the way, as the image became externalized, the Rat Man ceased to inflict upon himself punishment motivated from within as by his conscience, and started rather to fear punishment from without. This punishment was to come from something with murderous impulses, which would fall on him like a beast of prey, so as – and here there is another link with conscience – *to search out what was evil in him.*

The Captain who advocated corporal punishment and spoke of the punishment of criminals by other searching animals may also have been significant because he realized a paternal figure of the Rat Man's imagination. On this assumption the Captain's fondness for cruelty would have been significant precisely because it mirrored cruelty of his own of which the Rat Man was unaware. Some such mirroring is suggested by the fact that the Rat Man followed the example of the Captain in expressing cruelty through the thought of the rat punishment, and also took pleasure in thinking of the punishment being applied. In the case of the Rat Man, however, this was a pleasure of which he was unaware, and which horrified him.

In these theoretical terms the changes in desire, belief, imaginative representation etc. pursued in psychoanalysis are described as involving modifications in structural features of the mind. Where internal conflicts can be externalized, understood, and worked through in transference, or where episodes in which the super-ego took shape can be re-experienced and so considered again, the ego and super-ego admit of change. Ideally such development will facilitate belated completion of the identification required for the dissolution of the Oedipus complex. Any change of this kind, however, will mean an increase in satisfaction (or diminution in frustration) for the desires associated with the id.

I do not wish to suggest that this is the best way to describe these matters, but rather to indicate some of the point of doing so. Even if this is not an ultimately satisfactory way of representing things – and it is worth noting that there is no incoherence in supposing that parts of the mind should do some of the things done by the mind, or that functioning within the mind is in some ways comparable to that among persons – it apparently serves to describe important phenomena, and so deserves continued use until a better description is formulated.

When Freud arrived at his theories of dreams and symptoms he wrote his friend Wilhelm Fliess 'Reality–Wish-fulfilment: it is from this contrasting pair that our mental life springs.'[33] The aspects of the contrast discussed so far do not exhaust its role in Freud's work. It is found also, as noted

---

[33] *The Origins of Psycho-Analysis* (Imago, London, 1954), p. 277.

above, in his idea of primary and wish-fulfilling processes of thought, operating in accord with a pleasure principle, as opposed to secondary, rational processes, devoted to taking account of reality; or again in his remarks about the unconscious being contradictory, unchanging, but subject to wish-fulfilment. As the contrast seemed to Freud to fill our mental life, so it seems to pervade his thought.

The examples given above have been meant to illustrate, not to produce theoretical conviction. Even supposing that psychoanalytic theory were true, it would not be possible to demonstrate it in this way. This is not because psychoanalysis is unscientific or incapable of confirmation. We saw above that just as in commonsense psychology interpretation and verification and falsification are guided and sustained by underlying predictions about reasons and their relations, so in psychoanalysis they can be regarded as guided and sustained by underlying predictions about wish-fulfilments, desires, reasons and their relations. This renders judgments in psychoanalysis, and the theoretical framework itself, verifiable or falsifiable in the same way as those of commonsense psychology. Although this seems as much as could be expected in principle, in practice it does not suffice to produce agreement.

Psychoanalytic like physical theory ranges holistically over a vast number of instances and cases. Although a certain amount of theory may be seen to be applicable in a given case, its justification consists in the way it serves to order and explain the whole field. In the case of psychoanalytic theory, the field is particularly difficult to survey.

Accurate assessment of the explanatory scope and power of a theory can be made only by those who know how to use it. Although ability to interpret in commonsense terms comes naturally, a capacity to interpret in psychoanalytic terms (in any serious way) must be acquired through fairly extensive work and thought, and is therefore relatively rare. The material to which the theory has its central applications, moreover, is mainly outside the public domain. The psychoanalytic interpretation of the unconscious content shown in free associations takes place in conditions of privacy, and the more dramatic and unmistakable manifestations of content typically arise only after interpretation of the right themes has eased repression sufficiently for what is beneath to surface and be expressed.[34] (It is true that everyone can read case material, and

---

[34] Hence these may be missed by psychotherapists who do not give such interpretations, or again by other observers who attend only to material in which the unconscious is not particularly manifest. There is no reason to suppose that the Rat Man's transference or memories of 283–4 would ever have emerged clearly had Freud not given him such interpretations as that of 263 and others later.

also try to interpret his own dreams, slips, etc. Since, however, the grounds for interpretive judgments cannot be represented adequately or extensively in print, and self-analysis is difficult to carry far, the bearing of evidence gained in this way is generally relatively limited.) Hence even if we should accept that analysts who regularly observe behaviour which strikingly exemplifies psychoanalytic concepts have good grounds for theoretical conviction, still there would seem to be no generally available and compelling reasons for others to agree with them.

It may also be, as Freud thought, that there is resistance to the theory. Psychoanalysis is partly concerned with the representation in imagination and thought of activities involving biologically significant organs by which we pass things in and out of our bodies and exchange them with those of others. Since we nourish, live and reproduce through cycles of activity involving these organs, it is not implausible *a priori* that the

In trying to assess the cogency of interpretation by reference to case material B. A. Farrell considers an earlier interpretation given the Rat Man (that which led to his remembering the story of the woman who wished her sister would die) and says that although it may have 'produced some movement' this 'could be explained by an Adlerian theory according to which (as we have seen) L. had feelings of inferiority and resentment at the father, not feelings of an Oedipal character.' In this he follows Popper's claim that every conceivable case of human behaviour could as well be explained by Adler's theory as by Freud's, which he cites with some approval (*The Standing of Psychoanalysis*, Oxford, 1981, pp. 62, 72).

Farrell omits to consider the interpretation of 263, to which the Rat Man responded by reporting that the idea of his penis being cut off had troubled him intolerably at a time when he had desired to masturbate, that he remembered thinking that one might murder one's father for sexual intercourse, and that he was reminded of a scene in which he had been punished and had abused his father – which scene was connected in content with, and led to, that discussed above, in which his memory of being taken from between his parents in bed and punished had surfaced together with an image of a dead baby, his feeling Freud to be murderous, and so on. Since the feelings in this material seem to be fairly specifically Oedipal, it is difficult to see how it could be equally well explained by a theory according to which, as Farrell says, the Rat Man did not have feelings of an Oedipal character towards his father. Vague reference to feelings of inferiority and resentment has no specific explanatory purchase here at all.

The Popperian claim that non-Freudian theories can equally well or easily explain the responses above, or the oral and anal material with which they are interwoven, or many other aspects of this case, seems utterly implausible. Theories qualify as non-Freudian partly through their denial of such Freudian factors as oral sadism, castration anxiety, Oedipal sexual rivalry, transference of early childhood conflicts, and so on. They consequently lack resources for explaining material which is plausibly taken as manifesting these factors.

In this connection it should be remembered that Popper simply made up the examples he used to support and illustrate his claim. Even followers of Popper should agree that this is not an adequate substitute for the consideration of such real and testing examples of behaviour as are provided by the Rat Man. Such examples, however, seem to disconfirm Popper's claim. Farrell tries to support similar claims by examining a transcript of some exchanges in analytically oriented psychotherapy. The material to which he devotes his careful scrutiny, however, contains no distinctively Freudian interpretations, nor any directed to what is repressed or unconscious. So consideration of it is irrelevant to the present point, as is Farrell's invention of an Adlerian version of the same material.

mental representation of them should be of great psychological importance. Nevertheless we know that many people find the contemplation of
such things either fascinating or repulsive or both. Also, if psychoanalysis
were, as presented here, a theory of wish-fulfilment, it would be resisted
whatever its content. It would be in the nature of any such theory to
threaten to awaken people to the content of their unfulfilled wishes and
the illusory nature of the gratifications which mask but do not finally
satisfy them. Any such theory would spawn alternatives which again
represented the wishes as gratified and allowed people to sleep on, and so
forth. It is possible that this has happened.

Empiricist psychologists have tried to test psychoanalytic theory
without relying on the extensive use of interpretive explanations by
which it has been built up and is sustained in use. Many results seem to
have been vaguely favourable to Freud, but complete agreement has not
been achieved.[35] One reason for this comes from the nature of indirect
statistical testing itself, and so may be worth noting here.

Suppose a theory postulates that something unobservable or resistant
to a favoured means of observation occurs, so that the theory cannot be
tested directly.[36] Still it can be tested indirectly, if we can formulate some
testing hypothesis to the effect that if the theory is true certain observable
correlations may be expected to obtain, say in how people will answer
questions when shown pictures or in taking standardized tests, or among
customs in a number of societies.

Now clearly the presence or absence of an hypothesized correlation
will bear upon the testing hypothesis as well as upon the theory itself.
The presence of a correlation can confirm only both together, whereas
absence can disconfirm either one or the other, but not both. Hence
assessment of the outcome of tests will depend partly upon prior

---

[35] Thus Kline (*Fact and Fantasy in Freudian Theory*, Edinburgh, 1972) says in his survey
of the literature that so much 'that is distinctively Freudian has been verified' that 'any
blanket rejection of Freudian theory as a whole (e.g. Eysenck, 1952) simply flies in the face
of the evidence' (pp. 346, 350), while Fischer and Greenberg, in a more recent survey,
remark that they were generally impressed with how often the results of tests had borne out
Freudian expectations. (*The Scientific Credibility of Freud's Theories and Therapy*, New
York and Sussex, 1977, p. 393. Eysenck and Wilson, however, in the book cited above,
continued to regard Freudian theory as disconfirmed or entirely unsupported. For
discussion of the outcome of psychotherapy influenced by psychoanalysis see Sloane, et al.,
Psychotherapy versus Behavior Therapy, Harvard, 1975, and for a recent discussion of
the outcome of various kinds of psychotherapy see Shapiro in the *British Journal of Medical
Psychology* (1980) 53, 1–10.

[36] Thus an academic psychologist might consider that events like the Rat Man's rushing
away, covering his face with his hands, and so forth, *in fear of Freud as representing his
father*, were improperly observable, either because they could normally be observed by only
one person, or because they had to be interpreted in terms of theoretical concepts to be seen
as an instance of the theory. This latter objection would apparently hold for any
interpretive judgment whatever.

attitudes to both theory and hypothesis. A psychologist who regards the theory as more plausible than an individual testing hypothesis will tend to view absence of correlation as casting doubt on the putative test, whereas one who thinks the hypothesis superior will count the result against the theory. Clearly there is room for the operation of prejudice here.

Further, a theory and its associated testing hypotheses will differ in character. The testing hypotheses will link parts of the theory either to behaviour which is directly observable or to some other correlations which are, in a way that the theory itself does not. (If the theory did so, it would not require this kind of indirect testing.) So the testing hypotheses will be more operational or behavioural than the theory itself, and consequently may misrepresent the content or meaning of the theory. For this reason no serious assessment of a theory will involve a general preference for testing hypotheses; any such preference risks implicit systematic distortion of the theory under test.

This means that the evaluation of results may be influenced not only by prior attitude towards theory, but also by general psychological outlook. Someone who favoured a theory and found irrelevant correlations might wrongly claim support from them. But also, someone who was prejudiced against a theory, or again was unduly influenced by behaviourism or operationalism, might systematically favour testing hypotheses at the expense of the theory,[37] thus at once distorting it and representing it as refuted or disconfirmed. It appears that objectivity in this area may be difficult to attain.

II

Of the essays which follow, two are directly addressed to these issues of verification. Cosin, Freeman and Freeman examine some of the demands made on Freudian theory by empiricism, and Clark Glymour discusses a testing strategy he finds in Freud's work in the case used for illustration above. Others are concerned with aspects of the relations between the phenomena known in commonsense psychology and psychoanalytic theory. Sachs discusses what might be called the rational logic of Freud's treatment of the emotions. Hampshire relates the unconscious to memory, and O'Shaughnessy the id to thought and will. Morton describes how everyday psychology has been influenced and extended by Freudian theory.

[37] In this context note Eysenck and Wilson's remarks about how unjustly favourable to Freud it might be to concentrate on positive rather than negative results, at p. xii.

Introduction

Freud's belief that human behaviour could be explained in both physical and psychological terms was considered above. Precisely what it means, however, to think of a physical object in mental terms – for example as having consciousness – or vice-versa has long seemed a philosophical problem. Nagel discusses some of Freud's thought relating to this, and links it to other mentalist theories in psychology, such as those of Chomsky. Wollheim finds in Freud a suggestion that a person in a primitive form of mental organization represents his mind in bodily terms; it follows that these representations may be used for psychological explanation which catches action in the perspective in which the agent sees it.

Freud's physicalism went with a willingness not only to be influenced by various sciences – in particular, biology – but also to use analogies from them in psychological theory. (This may have been a source of Wittgenstein's dissatisfaction.) Hart considers the usefulness of one aspect of this, in his discussion of psychic energy and repression. De Sousa describes some biological aspects of Freud's theories in relation to normative considerations and rationality.

We noted above a tendency to at least apparent paradox in psychoanalytic theory, and also described some mechanisms of defense and a division of the personality. Several essays are concerned with these linked questions of mechanism, division and paradox. Sartre argues that repression, described above in terms of wish-fulfillment, cannot be explicated as the activity of a censoring agent or mechanism, but rather must be understood in terms of the (paradoxical) intentions of the agent, and so assimilated to bad faith. Thalberg considers a range of comparable difficulties, and Fingarette and Pears discuss self-deception and other forms of motivated irrationality in relation to Freud. Suppes and Warren attempt a comprehensive formulation of the mechanisms of defence, whose operation is, as noted, assigned to one part of the personality, the ego. Finally, Davidson considers some connected features of Freudian theory which have been found paradoxical – including reference to psychic causes which are not in the ordinary sense reasons, and the partitioning of the mind into person-like structures which interact with one another – and argues that these are essential to a theory which aims, as Freud's does, to explain action which is irrational.

Conversations on Freud; excerpt from 1932–3 lectures

LUDWIG WITTGENSTEIN

Notes by Rush Rhees after a conversation: summer 1942*

When we are studying psychology we may feel there is something unsatisfactory, some difficulty about the whole subject or study – because we are taking physics as our ideal science. We think of formulating laws as in physics. And then we find we cannot use the same sort of 'metric', the same ideas of measurement as in physics. This is especially clear when we try to describe appearances: the least noticeable differences of colours; the least noticeable differences of length, and so on. Here it seems that we cannot say: 'If A = B, and B = C, then A = C', for instance. And this sort of trouble goes all through the subject.

Or suppose you want to speak of causality in the operation of feelings. 'Determinism applies to the mind as truly as to physical things.' This is obscure because when we think of causal laws in physical things we think of *experiments*. We have nothing like this in connexion with feelings and motivation. And yet psychologists want to say: 'There *must* be some law' – although no law has been found. (Freud: 'Do you want to say, gentlemen, that changes in mental phenomena are guided by *chance?*') Whereas to me the fact that there *aren't* actually any such laws seems important.

Freud's theory of dreams. He wants to say that whatever happens in a dream will be found to be connected with some wish which analysis can bring to light. But this procedure of free association and so on is queer, because Freud never shows how we know where to stop – where is the right solution. Sometimes he says that the right solution, or the right analysis, is the one which satisfies the patient. Sometimes he says that the doctor knows what the right solution or analysis of the dream is whereas the patient doesn't: the doctor can say that the patient is wrong.

The reason why he calls one sort of analysis the right one, does not

* Reprinted from Ludwig Wittgenstein, *Wittgenstein: Lectures and Conversations*, ed. Cyril Barrett (Basil Blackwell & Mott, Oxford; and University of California Press, Berkeley, 1966), pp. 42–52, by kind permission of the publishers.

seem to be a matter of evidence. Neither is the proposition that hallucinations, and so dreams, are wish fulfilments. Suppose a starving man has an hallucination of food. Freud wants to say the hallucination of anything requires tremendous energy: it is not something that could normally happen, but the energy is provided in the exceptional circumstances where a man's wish for food is overpowering. This is a *speculation*. It is the sort of explanation we are inclined to accept. It is not put forward as a result of detailed examination of varieties of hallucinations.

Freud in his analysis provides explanations which many people are inclined to accept. He emphasizes that people are *dis*-inclined to accept them. But if the explanation is one which people are dis-inclined to accept, it is highly probable that it is also one which they are *inclined* to accept. And this is what Freud had actually brought out. Take Freud's view that anxiety is always a repetition in some way of the anxiety we felt at birth. He does not establish this by reference to evidence – for he could not do so. But it is an idea which has a marked attraction. It has the attraction which mythological explanations have, explanations which say that this is all a repetition of something that has happened before. And when people do accept or adopt this, then certain things seem much clearer and easier for them. So it is with the notion of the unconscious also. Freud does claim to find evidence in memories brought to light in analysis. But at a certain stage it is not clear how far such memories are due to the analyst. In any case, do they show that the anxiety was necessarily a repetition of the original anxiety?

Symbolizing in dreams. The idea of a dream language. Think of recognizing a painting as a dream. I (L.W.) was once looking at an exhibition of paintings by a young woman artist in Vienna. There was one painting of a bare room, like a cellar. Two men in top hats were sitting on chairs. Nothing else. And the title: 'Besuch' (Visit). When I saw this I said at once, 'This is a dream'. (My sister described the picture to Freud, and he said, 'Oh yes, that is quite a common dream' – connected with virginity.) Note that the title is what clinches it as a dream – by which I do not mean that anything like this was dreamt by the painter while asleep. You would not say of *every* painting, 'This is a dream'. And this does show that there is something like a dream language.

Freud mentions various symbols: top hats are regularly phallic symbols, wooden things like tables are women, etc. His historical explanations of these symbols is absurd. We might say it is not needed anyway: it is the most natural thing in the world that a table should be that sort of symbol.

But dreaming – using this sort of language – although it *may* be used to refer to a woman or to a phallus, may *also* be used not to refer to that at all. If some activity is shown to be carried out often for a certain purpose – striking someone to inflict pain – then a hundred to one it is also carried out under other circumstances *not* for that purpose. He may just want to strike him without thinking of inflicting pain at all. The fact that we are inclined to recognize the hat as a phallic symbol does not mean that the artist was necessarily referring to a phallus in any way when she painted it.

Consider the difficulty that if a symbol in a dream is not understood, it does not seem to be a symbol at all. So why call it one? But suppose I have a dream and accept a certain interpretation of it. *Then* – when I superimpose the interpretation on the dream – I can say, 'Oh yes, the table obviously corresponds to the woman, this to that, etc.'

I might be making scratches on the wall. It seems in a way like writing, but it is not a writing which either I or anyone else would recognize or understand. So we say I'm doodling. Then an analyst begins to ask me questions, trace associations and so on; and we come to an explanation of why I'm doing this. We may then correlate various scratches which I make with various elements in the interpretation. And we may then refer to the doodling as a kind of writing, as using a kind of language, although it was not understood by anyone.

Freud is constantly claiming to be scientific. But what he gives is *speculation* – something prior even to the formation of any hypothesis.

He speaks of overcoming resistance. One 'instance' is deluded by another 'instance'. (In the sense in which we speak of 'a court of higher instance' with authority to overrule the judgment of the lower court. R.R.) The analyst is supposed to be stronger, able to combat and overcome the delusion of the instance. But there is no way of showing that the whole result of analysis may not be 'delusion'. It is something which people are inclined to accept and which makes it easier for them to go certain ways: it makes certain ways of behaving and thinking natural for them. They have given up one way of thinking and adopted another.

Can we say we have laid bare the essential nature of mind? 'Concept formation'. Couldn't the whole thing have been differently treated?

Notes following conversations in 1943; Rush Rhees

Dreams. The interpretation of dreams. Symbolism.

When Freud speaks of certain images – say the image of a hat – as symbols, or when he says the image 'means' so and so, he is speaking of interpretation; and of what the dreamer can be brought to accept as an interpretation.

It is characteristic of dreams that often they seem to the dreamer to call for an interpretation. One is hardly ever inclined to write down a day dream, or recount it to someone else, or to ask, 'What does it mean?' But dreams do seem to have something puzzling and in a special way interesting about them – so that we want an interpretation of them. (They were often regarded as messages.)

There seems to be something in dream images that has a certain resemblance to the signs of a language. As a series of marks on paper or on sand might have. There might be no mark which we recognized as a conventional sign in any alphabet we knew, and yet we might have a strong feeling that they must be a language of some sort: that they mean something. There is a cathedral in Moscow with five spires. On each of these there is a different sort of curving configuration. One gets the strong impression that these different shapes and arrangements must mean something.

When a dream is interpreted we might say that it is fitted into a context in which it ceases to be puzzling. In a sense the dreamer re-dreams his dream in surroundings such that its aspect changes. It is as though we were presented with a bit of canvas on which were painted a hand and a part of a face and certain other shapes, arranged in a puzzling and incongruous manner. Suppose this bit is surrounded by considerable stretches of blank canvas, and that we now paint in forms – say an arm, a trunk, etc. – leading up to and fitting on to the shapes on the original bit; and that the result is that we say: 'Ah, now I see why it is like that, how it all comes to be arranged in that way, and what these various bits are . . .' and so on.

Mixed up with the shapes on the original bit of canvas there might be certain forms of which we should say that they do not join on to further figures in the wider canvas; they are not parts of bodies or trees, etc., but bits of writing. We might say this of a snake, perhaps, or a hat or some such. (These would be like the configurations of the Moscow cathedral.)

What is done in interpreting dreams is not all of one sort. There is a work of interpretation which, so to speak, still belongs to the dream itself. In considering what a dream is, it is important to consider what happens to it, the way its aspect changes when it is brought into relation with other things remembered, for instance. On first awaking a dream may impress one in various ways. One may be terrified and anxious; or when one has written the dream down one may have a certain sort of thrill, feel a very lively interest in it, feel intrigued by it. If one now remembers certain events in the previous day and connects what was dreamed with these, this already makes a difference, changes the aspect

4

of the dream. If reflecting on the dream then leads one to remember certain things in early childhood, this will give it a different aspect still. And so on. (All this is connected with what was said about dreaming the dream over again. It still belongs to the dream, in a way.)

On the other hand, one might form an hypothesis. On reading the report of the dream, one might predict that the dreamer can be brought to recall such and such memories. And this hypothesis might or might not be verified. This might be called a scientific treatment of the dream.

Freier Einfall and wish fulfilments. There are various criteria for the right interpretation: e.g. (1) what the analyst says or predicts, on the basis of his previous experience; (2) what the dreamer is led to by *freier Einfall*. It would be interesting and important if these two generally coincided. But it would be queer to claim (as Freud seems to) that they *must always* coincide.

What goes on in *freier Einfall* is probably conditioned by a whole host of circumstances. There seems to be no reason for saying that it must be conditioned only by the sort of wish in which the analyst is interested and of which he has reason to say that it must have been playing a part. If you want to complete what seems to be a fragment of a picture, you might be advised to give up trying to think hard about what is the most likely way the picture went, and instead simply to stare at the picture and make whatever dash first comes into your mind, without thinking. This might in many cases be very fruitful advice to give. But it would be astonishing if it *always* produced the best results. What dashes you make, is likely to be conditioned by everything that is going on about you and within you. And if I knew one of the factors present, this could not tell me with certainty what dash you were going to make.

To say that dreams are wish fulfilments is very important chiefly because it points to the sort of interpretation that is wanted – the sort of thing that would be an interpretation of a dream. As contrasted with an interpretation which said that dreams were simply memories of what had happened, for instance. (We don't feel that memories call for an interpretation in the same way as we feel this about dreams.) And some dreams obviously are wish fulfilments; such as the sexual dreams of adults, for instance. But it seems muddled to say that *all* dreams are hallucinated wish fulfilments. (Freud very commonly gives what we might call a sexual interpretation. But it is interesting that among all the reports of dreams which he gives, there is not a single example of a straightforward sexual dream. Yet these are common as rain.) Partly because this doesn't seem to fit with dreams that spring from fear rather than from longing. Partly because the majority of dreams Freud considers have to be regarded as *camouflaged* wish fulfilments; and in this case they simply don't fulfil the wish. Ex hypothesi the wish is not allowed to be fulfilled, and something else is hallucinated instead. If the wish is cheated in this way, then the dream can hardly be called a fulfilment of it. Also it becomes impossible to say whether it is the wish or the censor that is cheated. Apparently both are, and the result is that neither is satisfied. So that the dream is not an hallucinated satisfaction of anything.

It is probable that there are many different sorts of dreams, and that there is no single line of explanation for all of them. Just as there are many different sorts of jokes. Or just as there are many different sorts of language.

Freud was influenced by the 19th century idea of dynamics – an idea which has influenced the whole treatment of psychology. He wanted to find some one explanation which would show what dreaming is. He wanted to find the *essence* of dreaming. And he would have rejected any suggestion that he might be partly right but not altogether so. If he was partly wrong, that would have meant for him that he was wrong altogether – that he had not really found the essence of dreaming.

Notes following conversations, 1943; R.R.

Whether a dream is a thought. Whether dreaming is thinking about something.

Suppose you look on a dream as a kind of language. A way of saying something, or a way of symbolizing something. There might be a regular symbolism, not necessarily alphabetical – it might be like Chinese, say. We might then find a way of translating this symbolism into the language of ordinary speech, ordinary thoughts. But then the translation ought to be possible both ways. It ought to be possible by employing the same technique to translate ordinary thoughts into dream languages. As Freud recognizes, this never is done and cannot be done. So we might question whether dreaming is a way of thinking something, whether it is a language at all.

Obviously there are certain similarities with language.

Suppose there were a picture in a comic paper, dated shortly after the last war. It might contain one figure of which you would say it was obviously a caricature of Churchill, another figure marked somehow with a hammer and sickle so that you would say it was obviously supposed to be Russia. Suppose the title of the picture was lacking. Still you might be sure that, in view of the two figures mentioned, the whole picture was obviously trying to make some point about the political situation at that time.

The question is whether you would always be justified in assuming that there is some one joke or some one point which is *the* point which the cartoon is making. Perhaps even the picture as a whole has no 'right interpretation' at all. You might say: 'There are indications – such as the two figures mentioned – which suggest that it has.' And I might answer that perhaps these indications are all that there is. Once you have got an interpretation of these two figures, there may be no ground for saying that there *must* be an interpretation of the whole thing or of every detail of it on similar lines.

The situation may be similar in dreams.

Freud would ask: 'What made you hallucinate that situation at all?' One might answer that there need not have been anything that *made* me hallucinate it.

Freud seems to have certain prejudices about when an interpetation could be regarded as complete – and so about when it still requires completion, when further interpretation is needed. Suppose someone were ignorant of the tradition among sculptors of making busts. If he then came upon the finished bust of some man, he might say that obviously this is a fragment and that there must have been other parts belonging to it, making it a whole body.

Suppose you recognized certain things in the dream which can be interpreted in the Freudian manner. Is there any ground at all for assuming that there must be an interpretation for everything else in the dream as well? that it makes any sense to ask what is the right interpretation of the other things there?

Freud asks, 'Are you asking me to believe that there is anything which happens without a cause?' But this means nothing. If under 'cause' you include things like physiological causes, then we know nothing about these, and in any case they are not relevant to the question of interpretation. Certainly you can't argue from Freud's question to the proposition that everything in the dream must have a cause in the sense of some past event with which it is connected by association in that way.

Suppose we were to regard a dream as a kind of game which the dreamer played. (And by the way, there is no one cause or one reason why children always play. This is where theories of play generally go wrong.) There might be a game in which paper figures were put together to form a story, or at any rate were somehow assembled. The materials might be collected and stored in a scrap-book, full of pictures and anecdotes. The child might then take various bits from the scrap-book to put into the construction; and he might take a considerable picture because it had something in it which he wanted and he might just include the rest because it was there.

Compare the question of why we dream and why we write stories. Not everything in the story is allegorical. What would be meant by trying to explain why he has written just that story in just that way?

There is no one reason why people talk. A small child babbles often just for the pleasure of making noises. This is also one reason why adults talk. And there are countless others.

Freud seems constantly to be influenced by the thought that a hallucination is something requiring a tremendous mental force – *seelische Kraft*. '*Ein Traum findet sich niemals mit Halbheiten ab.*' And he thinks that the only force strong enough to produce the hallucinations of dreams is to be found in the deep wishes of early childhood. One might question this. Supposing it is true that hallucinations in waking state require an extraordinary mental force – why should not dream hallucinations be the perfectly normal thing in sleep, not requiring any extraordinary force at all?

(Compare the question: 'Why do we punish criminals? Is it from a desire for revenge? Is it in order to prevent a repetition of the crime?' And so on. The truth is that there is no one reason. There is the institution of punishing criminals. Different people support this for different reasons, and for different reasons in different cases and at different times. Some people support it out of a desire for revenge, some perhaps out of a desire for justice, some out of a wish to prevent a repetition of the crime, and so on. And so punishments are carried out.)

Notes following conversation, 1946; R.R.

I have been going through Freud's *Interpretation of Dreams* with H. And it has made me feel how much this whole way of thinking wants combating.

If I take any one of the dream reports (reports of his own dreams) which Freud gives, I can by the use of free association arrive at the same results as those he reaches in his analysis – although it was not my dream. And the association will proceed through my own experiences and so on.

The fact is that whenever you are preoccupied with something, with some trouble or with some problem which is a big thing in your life – as sex is, for instance – then no matter what you start from, the association will lead finally and inevitably back to that same theme. Freud remarks on how, after the analysis of it, the dream appears so very logical. And of course it does.

You could start with any of the objects on this table – which certainly are not put there through your dream activity – and you could find that they all could be connected in a pattern like that; and the pattern would be logical in the same way.

One may be able to discover certain things about oneself by this sort of free association, but it does not explain why the dream occurred.

Freud refers to various ancient myths in these connexions, and claims that his researches have now explained how it came about that anybody should think or propound a myth of that sort.

Whereas in fact Freud has done something different. He has not given a scientific explanation of the ancient myth. What he has done is to propound a new myth. The attractiveness of the suggestion, for instance, that all anxiety is a repetition of the anxiety of the birth trauma, is just the attractiveness of a mythology. 'It is all the outcome of something that happened long ago.' Almost like referring to a totem.

Much the same could be said of the notion of an 'Urszene'. This often has the attractiveness of giving a sort of tragic pattern to one's life. It is all the repetition of the same pattern which was settled long ago. Like a tragic figure carrying out the decrees under which the fates had placed him at birth. Many people have, at some period, serious trouble in their lives – so serious as to lead to thoughts of suicide. This is likely to appear to one as something nasty, as a situation which is too foul to be a subject of a tragedy. And it may then be an immense relief it can be shown that one's life has the pattern rather of a tragedy – the tragic working out and repetition of a pattern which was determined by the primal scene.

There is of course the difficulty of determining what scene is the primal scene – whether it is the scene which the patient recognizes as such, or whether it is the one whose recollection effects the cure. In practice these criteria are mingled together.

Analysis is likely to do harm. Because although one may discover in the course of it various things about oneself, one must have a very strong and keen and persistent criticism in order to recognize and see through the mythology that is offered or imposed on one. There is an inducement to say, 'Yes, of course, it must be like that.' A powerful mythology.

Excerpt from 1932–3 lectures*

I wish to remark on a certain sort of connection which Freud cites, between the fetal position and sleep, which looks to be a causal one but which is not, inasmuch as a psychological experiment cannot be made. His explanation does what aesthetics does: puts two factors together.

Another matter which Freud treats psychologically but whose investigation has the character of an aesthetic one is the nature of jokes. The question, 'What is the nature of a joke?', is like the question, 'What is the

* Reprinted from *Ludwig Wittgenstein: Lectures in Philosophy Cambridge 1932–5*, ed. Alice Ambrose (Blackwell, Oxford, 1979).

nature of a lyric poem?' I wish to examine in what way Freud's theory is a hypothesis and in what way not. The hypothetical part of his theory, the subconscious, is the part which is not satisfactory. Freud thinks it is part of the essential mechanism of a joke to conceal something, say, a desire to slander someone, and thereby to make it possible for the subconscious to express itself. He says that people who deny the subconscious really cannot cope with post-hypnotic suggestion, or with waking up at an unusual hour of one's own accord. When we laugh without knowing why, Freud claims that by psychoanalysis we can find out. I see a muddle here between a cause and a reason. Being clear why you laught is not being clear about a *cause*. If it were, then agreement to the analysis given of the joke as explaining why you laugh would not be a means of detecting it. The success of the analysis is supposed to be shown by the person's agreement. There is nothing corresponding to this in physics. Of course we *can* give *causes* for our laughter, but whether those are in fact the causes is not shown by the person's agreeing that they are. A cause is found experimentally. The psychoanalytic way of finding why a person laughs is analogous to an aesthetic investigation. For the correctness of an aesthetic analysis must be agreement of the person to whom the analysis is given. The difference between a reason and a cause is brought out as follows: the investigation of a reason entails as an essential part one's agreement with it, whereas the investigation of a cause is carried out experimentally. ['What the patient agrees to can't be a *hypothesis* as to the *cause* of his laughter, but only that so-and-so was the *reason* why he laughed.'*] Of course the person who agrees to the reason was not conscious at the time of its being his reason. But it is a way of speaking to say the reason was subconscious. It may be expedient to speak in this way, but the subconscious is a hypothetical entity which gets its meaning from the verifications these propositions have. What Freud says about the subconscious sounds like science, but in fact it is just *a means of representation*. New regions of the soul have not been discovered, as his writings suggest. The display of elements of a dream, for example, a hat (which may mean practically anything) is a display of similes. As in aesthetics, things are placed side by side so as to exhibit certain features. These throw light on our way of looking at a dream; they are reasons for the dream. [But his method of analyzing dreams is not analogous to a method for finding the causes of stomach-ache.†] It is a confusion to say that a reason is a cause seen from the inside. A cause is

---

* G. E. Moore, 'Wittgenstein's Lectures in 1930–33' in his *Philosophical Papers*, (George Allen & Unwin, London, 1959), p. 317.
  † G. E. Moore, ibid, p. 316.

not seen from within or from without. It is found by experiment. [In enabling one to discover the reasons for laughter psychoanalysis provides] merely a representation of processes.

2

Freud, Kepler, and the clinical evidence*

CLARK GLYMOUR

I

Whether or not we should think psychoanalysis a reasonable theory, or even a theory at all in the usual sense, depends on what we think to be the evidence for and against it, and that, in turn, depends on how we think theory and evidence go together generally. On one very influential view of scientific testing what is required in order to obtain evidence for or against psychoanalysis, as with any other theory, is that we deduce from it some claim regarding the correlation of two or more properties – which are of a kind that can be identified without using any psychoanalytic hypotheses – and then subject this claim to the rigors of statistical hypothesis testing. This strategy has been used to test psychoanalysis with very mixed and unpromising results.[1] For several reasons, analysts tend to oppose evaluating their theory solely on the basis of such evidence. In the first place, they claim that the experimentalists' bias for easily manipulated and easily controlled factors results in an undue emphasis on testing psychoanalytic hypotheses that are peripheral to the main tenets of the theory; even worse, the hypotheses tested by experimentalists are often no more than surrogates for the genuine article, and inferences from the falsity of such ersatz hypotheses to the falsity of psychoanalysis are not legitimate.[2] Further, the procedures of experimental psychologists are largely framed within a hypothetico-deductive view of theory testing which, when experiment and theory conflict,

---

* This is a reprint of an essay which appeared under the same title in *Freud: A Collection of Critical Essays*, ed. Richard Wollheim (Doubleday, New York, 1974), from which it is reprinted with permission of the author and the publisher. The 'Afterword' has been written specially for this Collection.

[1] See R. Sears, *A Survey of Objective Studies of Psychoanalysis* (Social Science Research Council, New York, 1943).

[2] These problems and others are discussed in, for example, D. Mackinnon and Wm. Dukes, 'Repression' in L. Postman, ed., *Psychology in the Making* (Knopf, New York, 1962).

does not inform us whether the fault is with some readily abandoned thesis or with the most central tenets of the theory. But the most frequent and most controversial complaint is that evaluations of psychoanalysis which consider only experimental results ignore the evidence available from clinical observations. Analysts contend that the observation of neurotics receiving therapy, of children, and particularly the contents of psychoanalytic case studies, provide the principal sources of evidence for psychoanalysis. Their view was put very bluntly by Freud himself. In the early thirties an American psychologist, S. Rosenzweig, carried out a series of experiments which he thought provided experimental support for psychoanalytic claims about repression. Rosenzweig sent a report of his results to Freud, who replied as follows:

My dear Sir
I have examined your experimental studies for the verification of the psychoan-alytic assertions with interest. I cannot put much value on these confirmations because the wealth of reliable observations on which these assertions rest make them independent of experimental verification. Still, it can do no harm.

Sincerely yours
Freud[3]

By contrast, I think the majority of experimental psychologists who have an opinion regard psychoanalysis as nearly bereft of evidence, and that is because they think clinical evidence worthless. That opinion is evidenced by the title of Sears's survey, a book which does not discuss a single psychoanalytic case study. H. J. Eysenck's statement is unusually vivid but not atypical in its conclusions:

What then is the evidence on which psychoanalysis is based? Essentially it is clinical rather than experimental . . . Suffice it to remember that clinical work is often very productive of theories and hypotheses, but weak on proof and verification; that in fact the clinical method by itself cannot produce such proof because investigations are carried out for the avowed purpose of aiding the patient, not of putting searching questions to nature. Even when a special experiment is carefully planned to test the adequacy of a given hypothesis there often arise almost insuperable difficulties in ruling out irrelevant factors and in isolating the desired effect; in clinical work such isolation is all but impossible. The often-heard claim that 'psychoanalytic hypotheses are tested on the couch' (i.e., the couch on which the patient lies during the analytic session) shows a clear misunderstanding of what is meant in science by 'testing' hypotheses. We can no more test Freudian hypotheses 'on the couch' than we can adjudicate between the rival hypotheses of Newton and Einstein by going to sleep under an apple tree.[4]

[3] Quoted from D. Shakow and D. Rapaport, *The Influence of Freud on American Psychology* (World Pub., Cleveland, 1968), p. 129.
[4] H. J. Eysenck, *The Uses and Abuses of Psychology* (Penguin, London, 1959), p. 228–9.

This is not much of an argument, but it is a common enough view. It stems in part, I think, from what are genuine drawbacks to clinical testing; for example, the problem of ensuring that a patient's responses are not *simply* the result of suggestion, or the feeling, not without foundation, that the 'basic data' obtained from clinical sessions – the patient's introspective reports of his own feelings, reports of dreams, memories of childhood and adolescence – are less reliable than we should like. But neither of these considerations seems sufficient to reject the clinical method generally, although they may of course be sufficient to warrant us in rejecting particular clinical results. Clinicians can hopefully be trained so as not to elicit by suggestion the expected responses from their patients; patients' reports can sometimes be checked independently, as in the case of memories, and even when they cannot be so checked there is no good reason to distrust them generally. But I think condemnations like Eysenck's derive from a belief about clinical testing which goes considerably beyond either of these points: the belief that clinical sessions, even cleansed of suggestibility and of doubts about the reliability of patients' reports, can involve no rational strategy for testing theories. The reasons for such an opinion are not difficult to surmise. Most theories, and psychoanalysis is no exception, deal with putative entities and processes which cannot be identified readily, which are not 'observable'. It may well be thought that the view that psychoanalytic hypotheses are tested on the couch involves the claim that such theoretical entities and processes suddenly and mysteriously become discernible within the analytic hour. Further, although Freud wrote a good deal about method, there is still no treatment of clinical testing which compares in clarity, let alone detail, with standard accounts of statistical hypothesis testing and experimental design. Without such a treatment, clinical testing is bound to seem mysterious and arbitrary to those nurtured on statistical methods.

I think that Eysenck's claim is wrong. I think there is a rational strategy for testing important parts of psychoanalysis, a strategy that relies almost exclusively on clinical evidence; moreover, I think this strategy is immanent in at least one of Freud's case studies, that of the Rat Man. Indeed, I want to make a much bolder claim. The strategy involved in the Rat Man case is essentially the same as a strategy very frequently used in testing physical theories. Further, this strategy, while simple enough, is more powerful than the hypothetico-deductive-falsification strategy described for us by so many philosophers of science.

Before trying to make my case, I would enter two cautions. I am not proposing a theory of the confirmation of theories, only of their testing. I do not know how one puts tests together to establish any degree of confirmation, or if one does at all. Further, I am certainly not claiming that there is good clinical evidence for Freud's theory; I am claiming that if one wants to test psychoanalysis, there is a reasonable strategy for doing so which can be, and to some degree has been, effected through clinical sessions.

II

When considering the objection that psychoanalytic procedures do not provide experimental evidence, Freud sometimes compared psycho-analysis with astronomy: there, too, we must rely on observation since we cannot manipulate and control the heavens. Very well, how do astronomers test their theories? Let us consider the theory comprised of Kepler's laws and their consequences. The laws are these:

1. Each planet and comet moves in a fixed plane in which the centre of the sun is situated; the orbit of such a body is a conic section.
2. For any such body, the ratio of the space described about the sun in an interval of time (i.e., the area of the conic section swept out by the position vector with the sun as origin) to that interval of time is a constant particular to the body.
3. For any two such bodies, moving in closed orbits, the ratio of the squares or their orbital periods is equal to the ratio of the cubes of their average distances from the sun.

Certainly it is very implausible to say, as some philosophers seem recently to have said, that astronomers can look through their telescopes and just *see* the orbits of planets, or their periods or their distances from the sun. And even if we are willing to say such a thing, that is not how astronomers report their observations. What astronomers have claimed to observe, at least in contexts where we and they would agree that Kepler's laws might be tested, are right ascensions and declinations – that is, the locations of a planet on the celestial sphere – at various times, as well as the locations of other bodies (such as the sun) at the same or related times. How are these observations to be used to compare the actual orbits and periods with those required by Kepler's laws? On the deductive account of theory testing they are not to be so used at all. Instead, one deduces from Kepler's laws (together with Euclidean geometry, etc.) some 'purely observational' statement; in this case perhaps some statement roughly of the form 'If the planet is located at x,y (on the celestial sphere) at t, then it is located at $f(x,y, t', t)$ at t'', where 'f' is some explicit function. This 'observational consequence' is then compared with observations in order to test the theory. The disadvantages of such a strategy are well known. Chief among them is the fact that it does not enable us to say anything about which of Kepler's laws are tested by a set of observations. For example, observations of the positions of Mars at various times clearly should not of themselves count as a test of Kepler's third law, but on the deductive account there seems no way to make this exclusion. It is of no avail to claim that the third law is not needed for the deduction of the 'observation statement' since we can trivially reformulate the theory so that none of Kepler's laws are required for the deduction.

If we look at the astronomical writings concerned to show how to compare Kepler's theory with astronomical observations we find a rather different strategy employed.[5] From Kepler's laws there are deduced a vast body of relations among geometrical quantities associated with an orbit. It is shown that given the values of six quantities, called the elements of the orbit, by using various of these relations one can compute the complete orbit of a body in three-dimensional space and also its location in the orbit at any time. Further, again by using these derived relations, which we must think of as forming an integral part of Kepler's theory, we can from as few as three suitably chosen observations of a body compute the elements of its orbit. The strategy for testing Kepler's laws which emerges from these considerations is then roughly as follows: There is a set of quantities, in this case the locations of planets on the celestial sphere, which can normally be determined to good approximation without using (or without assuming the truth of) any of the hypotheses which form Kepler's theory.[6] From a set of values of these *non-theoretical* quantities we can by using certain of the relations occurring in Kepler's theory compute values for other, *theoretical*, quantities such as the orbital elements, period, and so on. Of course it will not necessarily be the case that every set of observations permits the calculation of every theoretical quantity. From values of these theoretical quantities we can, again by using the relations of the theory, compute the values required of other observations. Actually it is important to look at this last step in reverse. From one set of observations we can compute the values of various theoretical quantities by using some of the laws of the theory; we can do the same for another, different, set of observations. If the theory is correct, then the results must be the same in both cases. We can think of

[5] My remarks here and subsequently on this topic are based on Karl F. Gauss's *Theory of the Motion of Heavenly Bodies Moving About the Sun in Conic Sections* (Dover, New York, 1963), and on modern treatments of the orbit problem. I have not read Kepler.

[6] I have discussed this distinction in 'On Some Patterns of Reduction' *Philosophy of Science* 37 (September 1970) pp. 340–53. I there refer to it as a distinction between 'primary' and 'secondary' quantities, a terminology which seems to me now to be cumbersome and unrevealing. I think very nearly the same distinction is introduced by J. Sneed, *The Logical Structure of Physical Theories* (Reidel, Dordrecht, Netherlands, 1971), as a distinction between 'theoretical' and 'non-theoretical' quantities. Both his terminology and this discussion of the distinction seem to be superior to mine.

the strategy of testing as a kind of logical pincer movement: for various of the laws asserting the equality of two quantities, observed values of non-theoretical quantities enable us to use some of the laws of the theory to compute values for the two quantities independently. Our results must then either instantiate the law in question or contradict it; in either case the law has been tested. The crucial point is that *which* laws we can perform this pincer movement on is determined by (a) the other laws in the theory and (b) the particular set of observed quantities. For example, if we have, say, half a dozen complete, suitably chosen observations of the position of Mars on the celestial sphere we can use these data to test many of the relations of Kepler's theory via a logical pincer: we use one triple of observations to calculate a quantity on one side of an equality and another triple of observations to calculate a quantity on the other side of the equality. But we cannot so test Kepler's third law using only these observations. Using either of the triples we can calculate Mars's period and average distance from the sun, but we cannot calculate the ratio of Mars's period to that of any other planet.

I do not suppose that all of this is intelligible; perhaps more of it will be if we consider a simple, entirely contrived example. Suppose that *a, b,* and *e* are three quantities which we know how to determine without using the theory below

(1) $c = R(a)$
(2) $d = S(b)$
(3) $e = T(f)$
(4) $f = U(c)$
(5) $d = V(c)$

where *c, d,* and *f* are *theoretical* quantities and *R, S, T, U, V* are explicit functions and, for simplicity, we will assume all of them to have inverses. Suppose now that by performing some physical operations we obtain values *A* and *B* for quantities *a* and *b* respectively. Which of the hypotheses are tested by this pair of measurements? It is easy to see that 1, 2 and 5 are tested but hypotheses 3 and 4 are not. From *A* and *B* using hypothesis 1 we obtain

$C = R(A)$

and using 2 we obtain

$D = S(B)$.

The derived pair of values *C, D,* is either in accord with or else contradicts hypothesis 5, accordingly as $D = V(C)$ or not, and therefore provides a test of that hypothesis. In a similar way, from these same data, we can test hypotheses 1 and 2. By using only measured values of quantities a and b and whatever hypotheses we please we cannot test hypotheses 3 and 4. For given only values of a and b there is only *one* way to compute a value of f, and that is by using hypothesis 4; similarly, there is only *one* way to compute a value of e, and that is by using 3.

If we had measured and obtained values A and E for quantities a and e respectively, then our measurements would provide a test of hypotheses 1, 3, and 4 but not of 2 and 5. Again, if we have B and E as values of b and e, respectively, then we can test every hypothesis except hypothesis 1.

A satisfactory account of this testing strategy must do a number of things. It must provide a general and precise account of when an arbitrary hypothesis within an arbitrary theory is tested by an arbitrary set of data; it must determine whether, and under what conditions, we can regard those hypotheses used in testing a hypothesis as themselves tested indirectly; it must combine with a theory of error to inform us as to what imprecision is introduced into the computed values of theoretical quantities by imprecision in the values of non-theoretical quantities or by the use of approximation procedures in computing the values of theoretical quantities. I cannot yet give such an account but I am convinced that one can be given. For the present I wish merely to point out that there is here a discernible strategy instances of which we should be able to recognize when we come across them, and that the strategy is apparently superior to the deductivist one for several reasons. It is superior because it permits us to test particular laws, or at least particular subsets of the laws, of a theory, and because it sometimes permits us, when theory and experiment conflict, to identify the faulty hypotheses simply by the use of Mill's methods.[7] Even more, the strategy reveals an apparently unnoticed reason for demanding that our theories be tested on a variety of different kinds of instances, and it provides a framework for understanding the role of approximations in testing theories.

I do not think that the use of this strategy is confined to Kepler's laws, or to astronomy, or even to observational sciences. I think it is frequently a central part of the over-all argument for or against a theory, even in the experimental sciences. Its use is particularly apparent whenever an experimenter attempts to test a theory containing quantities which the experimenter does not know how to determine save by measuring other quantities and computing using some of the very hypotheses to be tested.

---

[7] To see how one might use Mill's methods suppose that in the above example we do three sets of measurements: I) of a and b; II) of a and e; III) of b and e. Suppose further that I and II conflict with the theory, but III does not. I tests hypotheses 1, 2, and 5; II tests hypotheses 1, 3 and 4. Agreement says 1 is at fault. III tests 2, 3, 4, and 5 and agrees with them, so Difference says 1 at fault.

More pertinent to our topic, which in case it be forgotten is Freud, I see no reason why essentially the same strategy cannot be carried out in testing theories the hypotheses of which are not quantitative. In such cases the theory will not relate quantities but, let us say, states of affairs.

By a state of affairs I intend at least such states of persons as those of consciously feeling guilt, having a cough, feeling compelled to utter certain ritual phrases, having a repressed wish, having had a sexual conflict with one's father, and so on. The distinction between theoretical and non-theoretical states of affairs seems to me as intelligible, if not perhaps as precise, as the distinction between theoretical and non-theoretical quantities. Some of the states of persons which Freud describes are of a kind that we might reasonably expect to be able to discriminate without making use of any psychoanalytic hypotheses; other states Freud discriminates only through the use of psychoanalytic theory applied to discernible states of the first kind. All unconscious states are of the second kind, that is, theoretical, and most conscious states and overt actions can reasonably be regarded as non-theoretical for psychoanalysis.

A Freudian application of the testing strategy I have described would, then, go roughly as follows: From non-theoretical states of a patient observed in a clinical setting, other states – whether themselves theoretical or non-theoretical – are inferred by using psychoanalytic hypotheses. Hypotheses which claim that these inferred states obtain only if other states obtain are then tested directly by independently determining, either by theoretical or by non-theoretical means, whether the other states do in fact obtain. The hypotheses used in the theoretical determinations involved in such a test are themselves tested indirectly. The hypotheses of psychoanalytic theory will permit us to infer some states of affairs from others, and we can, just as in the quantitative case, effect a pincer strategy to attempt to determine independently whether the states of affairs related by a conditional or biconditional sentence obtain.

However vague this may be, it is not impossibly so. I think the strategy is clear enough so that we know what it would be like to have a precise philosophical explication of it, even if we have in fact none to give. And that clarity is sufficient, I hope, to enable us to recognize the strategy when it appears in Freud's case studies, and to recognize its similarity with quantitative cases. It is true that Freud nowhere explicitly described such a strategy, although in at least one place he did come close,[8] but this

---

[8] In 'Psychoanalysis and the Establishment of the Facts in Legal Proceedings': 'And now, Gentlemen, let us return to the association experiment. In the kind of experiment we have referred to so far, it was the person under examination who explained to us the origin of his reactions, and the experiments, if they are subject to this condition, will be of no interest

is no objection to the thesis that the strategy is implicit in his case studies. Physicists are notoriously bad at describing their methodology and the epistemic features of their theories; there is no reason to expect a greater accuracy from psychologists. It is not even necessary that Freud used this strategy intentionally, either in the case as it actually developed or in his written account. The essential point is that in the published case study – which closely follows the clinical notes – data sufficient to test certain analytic hypotheses are presented, and the inferential steps necessary to test these hypotheses are exactly the steps Freud traces out in his discussion.

III

I think that something like the strategy I have tried to describe can be teased out of Freud's Rat Man case. More than with other case studies, perhaps, the central interpretations which Freud offers in this case are law-governed. That is, they are backed by appeal to generalizations regarding the states of affairs concerned. The generalizations are typically not the more esoteric claims of Freud's metapsychology, but instead are relatively less exciting 'clinical hypotheses', e.g. that obsessive-compulsives are invariably sexually precocious. It is chiefly these clinical hypotheses which I think are tested, by the strategy I have proposed, in Freud's case study. Of course, even here it is not always entirely clear when Freud's inferences from a non-theoretical state of affairs to a theoretical one are warranted by some general lawlike claim in contrast to those cases in which the inference is only warranted by the fact that it makes a plausible story.

The Rat Man, Paul Lorenz, was in his late twenties when he began his treatment with Freud. He was afflicted with superstitions, feelings of guilt, compulsions, and obsessive fears. He was especially obsessed with

from the point of view of judicial procedure. But how would it be if we were to make a change in our planning of the experiment? Might we not proceed as one does in solving an equation which involves several quantities, where one can take any one of them as the starting point – by making *either* the *a* or the *b* into the *x* we are looking for. Up to now in our experiments it has been the *complex* that has been unknown to us. We have used stimulus-words selected at random, and the subject under examination has revealed to us the complex brought to expression by those stimulus-words. But let us now set about it differently. Let us take a complex that is *known* to us and ourselves react to it with stimulus-words deliberately chosen; and let us then transfer the *x* to the person who is reacting. Will it then be possible to decide, from the way in which he reacts, whether the complex we have chosen is also present in him? You can see that this way of planning the experiment corresponds exactly to the method adopted by an examining magistrate who is trying to find out whether something of which he is aware is also known to the accused as an agent' (1906c, IX, 105–6).

the thought that a torture he had learned of during military service would be applied to his father, who was dead at the time the treatment began, and to a young woman with whom the patient had long been infatuated. The torture required that a person be sat upon a cage filled with starving rats, the top of the cage then slid away, and the victim devoured from the bottom up. Lorenz suffered from fears that unless he did or did not do certain things' the rat torture and other unpleasant events would befall the young woman in this world and his father in the next. He developed intricate and compulsive rituals in the belief that they would protect the young woman, his father, and others from such harms.

The history Lorenz recounted began with his sixth year. Before that age he had only very fragmentary memories, but from six years on his memory was complete. As a child of six or seven he had indulged in sexual play with his nurses and had particularly strong desires to see women naked. The occurrences of these wishes were on some occasions accompanied by a fear of his father's death and by the impression that his parents could read his thoughts. Lorenz did not recall masturbating as a child, and did so only for a very brief period as an adolescent, but he did begin the practice after the death of his father. Despite his deep affection for his father, on several occasions associated with sexual desire, Lorenz nonetheless had thoughts of his father's death, always accompanied by a feeling of dread at such an event. For example, at the age of twelve the thought occurred to him that a younger girl, of whom he was fond, would show him affection if something unfortunate were to befall him, in particular if his father should die. Lorenz was able to recall only one instance of severe and overt conflict, reaching to rage, between himself and his father. At about the age of three or four he was beaten by his father – apparently for biting a nurse – and flew into a rage, calling his father, for want of a more elaborate vocabulary, 'You plate, you towel, you lamp . . .' His mother, who was alive at the time of the analysis, confirmed the details of the incident and its singularity. Lorenz felt a great deal of guilt over his father's death; the reason he offered was merely that he had not been present at the moment of demise but instead had fallen into an exhausted sleep in an adjoining room.

The central features of the explanation which Freud offered for his patient's behavior are that his guilt, obsessions, and compulsions were the result of the conflict between his conscious love and unconscious hatred for his father. The unconscious hatred in turn was the consequence of an acute conflict between Lorenz and his father when the former was a small child; specifically, the hatred was first formed when the father punished young Lorenz for masturbation. Lorenz's obsessions were in fact the result of the re-emergence of repressed wishes formed in his early childhood, but permitted into consciousness only in altered, symbolic form. Of course, there is much more intriguing detail in this case study, but rather than develop it I want to examine in detail how Freud warranted the central features of his account of the case. For the most part, Freud was remarkably explicit, and his use of the testing strategy described earlier is almost obvious.

The first three sections of the case study – which correspond to the first few sessions of the analysis – are devoted to the patient's account of his sexual behavior in childhood and of a particularly exaggerated piece of adult obsessive behavior. Very little is done by way of interpreting either, save that characteristically Freud insisted that the cause of the adult behavior lies in the infantile sexual practices. Freud put his view in perfectly general terms:

(1) Such cases [obsessional neuroses], unlike those of hysteria, invariably possess the characteristic of premature sexual activity. Obsessional neuroses make it much more obvious than hysterias that the factors which go to form a psychoneurosis are to be found in the patient's *infantile* sexual life and not in his present one.[9]

In the fourth section of the case study, Lorenz recounted the 'criminal guilt' he felt at his father's death, and Freud used a psychoanalytic generalization to infer an unconscious state:

(2) Hearing this, I took the opportunity of giving him a first glance at the underlying principles of psycho-analytic therapy. When there is a mésalliance, I began, between an affect and its ideational content (in this instance, between the intensity of the self reproach and the occasion for it) . . . the analytic physician says 'No. The affect is justified. The sense of guilt is not in itself open to further criticism. But it belongs to some other content, which is unknown (unconscious), and which requires to be looked for . . .'[10]

The generalization Freud used in this instance had been stated as early as 1894.[11] In the present case, the use is quite clearly to infer the existence of an unconscious thought for which a feeling of guilt would in fact be appropriate. The generalization in question would, on the account proposed earlier, be tested positively if a state of affairs could be found which, together perhaps with other psychoanalytic hypotheses, entailed the existence of an unconscious thought for which guilt would ordinarily be appropriate. In the very next analytic session, Freud proceeded to establish just such a state of affairs; Lorenz recounted his occasional but recurrent fears and Freud interpreted.

[9] 1909d, X, 165.
[10] Ibid., 174–5.
[11] 1894a, III, 45–61.

(3) These thoughts [of benefits to Lorenz from his father's death] surprised him very much, for he was quite certain that his father's death could never have been an object of his desire but only of his fear . . . According to psycho-analytic theory, I told him, every fear corresponded to a former wish which was now repressed; we were therefore obliged to believe the exact contrary of what he had asserted. This would also fit in with another theoretical requirement, namely that the unconscious must be the precise contrary of the conscious.[12]

A desire for the death of one's father is evidently something which would warrant feelings of guilt. Thus Freud has already given us a small example of a qualitative application of the testing strategy described earlier. Freud proceeded to apply his theory to infer the cause of the patient's unconscious hatred for his father. At this point Freud's discussion loses something of the terse, straightforward character of the previous steps and becomes slightly rambling. Nonetheless it is clear that Freud was making an inference under the compulsion of his theoretical principles:

(4) The unconscious, I explained, *was* the infantile; it was that part of the self which had become separated off from it in infancy, which had not shared the later stages of its development, and which had in consequence become *repressed*. It was the derivatives of this repressed unconscious that were responsible for the involuntary thoughts which constituted his illness.[13]

This generalization, together with the hypothesis contained in the first quotation, requires the conclusion that Lorenz's unconscious hatred for his father resulted from the repression of a conscious hatred for his father during infancy or early childhood, and moreover a hatred which in turn resulted from the young Lorenz's sexual behavior. The only possibility allowed by Freudian theory is that Lorenz came to hate his father because the latter had interfered with his sexual activities. That is exactly what Freud concluded:

(5) The source from which his hostility to his father derived its indestructibility was evidently something in the nature of *sensual desires*, and in that connection he must have felt his father as in some way or other an *interference*. A conflict of this kind, I added, between sensuality and childish love was entirely typical.[14]

Moreover, using the non-theoretical fact that Lorenz's infantile amnesia ended with his sixth year, and using as well the psychoanalytic characterization of the unconscious given in the fourth quotation, Freud was able to locate the time of the original conflict.

[12] 1909d, X, 179–80.
[13] Ibid., 177–8.
[14] Ibid., 182.

(6) This wish (to get rid of his father as being an interference) must have originated at a time when circumstances had been very different . . . It must have been in his very early childhood, therefore, before he had reached the age of six, and before the date at which his memory became continuous.[15]

At this point in the case study, Freud used the information he had obtained about Lorenz to provide explanations of the significance of the patient's various symptoms. He proceeded to conjecture as to the nature of the 'precipitating cause' which triggered the illness in adulthood. These discussions involve few general law-like claims, and they appear to be irrelevant to the testing strategy we are considering. In section g the main lines were taken up again. Freud noted several features of his patient's masturbatory behavior, in particular the fact that as an adult he resumed masturbation after his father's death. Freud put his conclusions as follows:

(7) Starting from these indications and from other data of a similar kind, I ventured to put forward a construction to the effect that when he was a child of under six he had been guilty of some sexual misdemeanor connected with masturbation and had been soundly castigated for it by his father. The punishment, according to my hypothesis, had, it was true, put an end to his masturbating, but on the other hand it had left behind it an ineradicable grudge against his father and had established him for all time in his role of an interferer with the patient's sexual enjoyment.[16]

Freud makes it sound as though this construction was but a conjecture peculiar to this case, and not required by psychoanalytic theory. But that is not correct. For by 1905, two years before the treatment of Lorenz was begun and four years before the case study was published, Freud was already committed to the primacy of masturbation as a form of sexual gratification in infancy and early childhood and as an aetiological factor in neurosis.[17] Indeed, he repeats this commitment in the very same section of the case study from which the previous quotation is taken:

(8) Infantile masturbation reaches a kind of climax, as a rule, between the ages of three and four or five; and it is the clearest expression of a child's sexual constitution, in which the aetiology of subsequent neuroses must be sought.[18]

Let us review what has happened. Starting with the patient's reports Freud used various psychoanalytic hypotheses to determine, first, certain unconscious thoughts and the character of at least one event in the

[15] Ibid., 183.
[16] Ibid., 205.
[17] See the concluding summary in *Three Essays on the Theory of Sexuality*, (1905d, VII, 234).
[18] 1909d, X, 202.

patient's early childhood. The first inference, to the existence of an unconscious thought which would warrant guilt, was tested indirectly and so too was the hypothesis used to make that inference. The states of affairs subsequently inferred are, however, unchecked and their laws thus far untested. Freud had nonetheless arrived at an inferred non-theoretical state of affairs, namely the patient's having been punished by his father for masturbation. Checking independently for the presence or absence of this state of affairs would provide a test of the laws used in making the inference: positive if such an event could be located, negative if it could not be after some reasonable effort. For clarity we can put these several inferences into a kind of diagram:

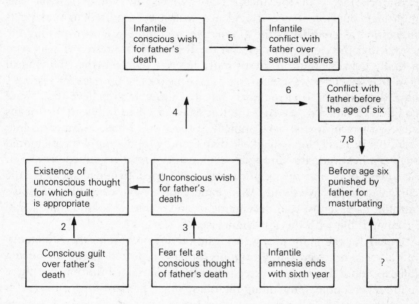

The lower boxes indicate non-theoretical states of affairs which are determined in the case study without the use of psychoanalytic hypotheses; the numbers associated with the arrows are to indicate which quoted passage warrants the inference. The crucial question is whether or not Lorenz was in fact punished by his father for masturbation. Freud reported that immediately after he told Lorenz of his conjecture, the patient recalled the 'You plate, you towel . . .' incident and reported it. Could this be the very event required? Unfortunately, the patient's only memory of the incident was through his mother, who had repeatedly told him of it. But when she was consulted as to the reason for the punishment 'there was no suggestion of his misdeed having been of a sexual character'.[19] Moreover, this was apparently the *only* time the father beat the child.

The chief conclusion I should like to draw from this discussion is that the Rat Man case did provide a test of certain psychoanalytic hypotheses, and in fact a positive test of some hypotheses and a negative test of others. That the inferred castigation for sexual misbehavior was not revealed by the most reliable available means – the memory of an adult observer – is presumptive evidence that something was wrong with Freud's account of the role of psychosexual development in the aetiology of psychoneurosis. The memories of adults are not, of course, infallible; it could have been, as Freud suggested in a footnote, that Lorenz's mother suppressed the sexual character of the incident for which the young Lorenz was punished, but some special evidence would be required to make this suggestion as credible as the alternative, and none was forthcoming.

Whether the clinical evidence of the Rat Man case tested views Freud actually held is bound to be of more interest than whether the clinical evidence tested views Freud could have held. The strategy of testing I have described is so elementary that it is difficult to believe that Freud could have failed to see that the Rat Man case had implications for his views of psychosexual development, if the views I have ascribed to him were his in fact. Nor is it likely that Freud would simply have ignored such implications, for throughout his career Freud remained critical of his own views and seems always to have tried to judge them by the clinical evidence. We should, then, expect some significant shift in Freud's account of psychosexual development, and a shift of a kind that would be compatible with the Rat Man case.

Exactly at the point in the case study that Lorenz's mother's memory of the scene between Lorenz and his father is reported, Freud included a long footnote, running to three pages in the Standard Edition. He there made several points, including the following: The punishment Lorenz in fact received *could have* been either for a sexual misdeed or for some non-sexual misbehavior; interpretation of one of Lorenz's dreams indicated that, unconsciously, he regarded his father as a sexual antagonist; in constructing phantasies about childhood, one sexualizes his memories, 'that is, he brings common-place experiences into relation with his sexual activity and extends his sexual interest to them – though in doing this he is *probably* following upon the traces of a really existing connection',[20] and finally, Freud writes that 'It is entirely characteristic of the nuclear complex of infancy that the child's father should be assigned the part of a sexual opponent and of an interferer with auto-erotic sexual activities;

[19] Ibid., 206.   [20] Ibid., 207 (italics mine).

and real events are *usually* to a large extent responsible for bringing this about.'[21]

The qualifiers 'probably' and 'usually' block any requirement of a *real* conflict between Lorenz and his father, and suggest that, at this period, Freud thought that either real sexual experiences in childhood, or phantasies of them, could serve as aetiological factors in neurosis. If so, then the Rat Man case would not provide a negative test of Freud's hypotheses regarding psychosexual development, but only a negative test of some ersatz theory. I think rather the opposite is the case; I think the qualifications cited above are rather novel in Freud's writings, and are best understood as the very change Freud thought his theory required in view of the negative evidence of the Rat Man case. I shall argue that prior to the Rat Man case, phantasies of childhood sexual experiences were regarded as, at best, screens for memories of real sexual experiences of a different kind. Increasingly after 1909, Freud thought phantasies themselves, even when derived from no real sexual experience, could serve as aetiological factors.

The theory of the psychoneuroses that Freud published in 1896 took the specific cause of hysteria and of obsessional neuroses to be seduction in childhood.[22] In 1897, in a letter to his friend Wilhelm Fliess, Freud renounced the seduction theory, and concluded that many of the seductions reported by his patients were phantasies.[23] But he did not give up the view that the cause specific to psychoneurosis is some kind of sexual experience in childhood. In his first properly psychoanalytic case study, an account published in 1905 of a case undertaken five years before, Freud referred to his view as a 'trauma theory'[24] and took the specific cause of hysteria to be precocious and excessive masturbation subjected to severe repression:

Hysterical symptoms hardly ever appear so long as children are masturbating, but only after a period of abstinence has set in; they form a substitute for masturbatory satisfaction, the desire for which continues to persist in the unconscious until another and more normal kind of satisfaction appears – where that is still possible. For upon whether it is still attainable or not depends the possibility of hysteria being cured by marriage and sexual intercourse. But if the satisfaction afforded in marriage is again removed – as it may be owing to *coitus interruptus*, psychological estrangement, or other causes – then the libido flows

[21] Ibid., 208 (italics mine).
[22] 1896b, III, 162–85.
[23] M. Bonaparte, A. Freud, E. Kris, *The Origins of Psychoanalysis* (Doubleday, New York, 1957), pp. 218f.
[24] 1905e, VII, 27.

back again into its old channel and manifests itself once more in hysterical symptoms.[25]

In the first edition of *Three Essays on Sexuality*, Freud proposed, citing Binet on fetishism, that in both neurosis and perversion the libido is fixated by some precocious sexual experience or other, the outcome being determined by the subjects' constitutionally determined psychological reaction to those experiences.[26] In an essay published a year later, in fact the very essay in which Freud first publicly renounced the seduction hypothesis, Freud claimed that seduction phantasies generally serve as screen memories for real infantile auto-erotic activity,[27] and he reiterated the view that it is a constitutionally determined psychological reaction (excessive repression) to infantile sexual experience which brings about a disposition to neurosis in adulthood.[28]

After the turn of the century and before 1909, Freud's views on the aetiology of neurosis placed decreased emphasis on *traumatic* sexual encounters in childhood, strong emphasis on childhood sexuality, especially masturbation, and regarded the psychological reaction to such experiences as the determining factor in the generation of a neurotic disposition. In this period, and before, there is no statement of the view that sexual phantasies formed in childhood or subsequently, having no real basis in fact, may themselves serve *in place of* sexual experiences as aetiological factors. Then, in 1909 there appeared the footnote discussed above, even while the text of the Rat Man case contains no hint that the events in question may have been phantasized rather than real. Yet after the Rat Man case the view that either infantile sexual experiences *or* phantasies of them may equally serve as aetiological factors became a standard part of Freud's theory. In *Totem and Taboo*, four years after the Rat Man case appeared, Freud emphasized that the guilt that obsessional neurotics feel is guilt over a happening that is psychically real but need not actually have occurred.[29] By 1917 Freud not only listed phantasies themselves as aetiological factors alternative to real childhood sexual experiences, but omitted even the claim that the former are usually or probably based on the latter.[30] Whatever the merits of Freud's revised theory, I think it reasonable to conclude that, to his credit, Freud learned from the experience of the Rat Man case.

[25] Ibid., 79. Two pages later, however, Freud indicates uncertainty as to the universality of masturbation as a cause of hysteria.

[26] 1905d, VII, 154, 190, and 242.

[27] 1906a, VII, 274.

[28] Ibid., 276–7.

[29] 1912–13, XIII.

[30] 1916–17, XVI, 370.

The kind of testing a theory admits depends largely on the strength of that theory itself. Weak theories which embody no putative laws, which concern only causal factors or correlations, may perhaps have to be tested with great regard for statistical methods and experimental controls. But the theory Johannes Kepler proposed long ago was strong enough to be tested in the observatory, and the theory Sigmund Freud developed at the turn of this century was strong enough to be tested on the couch.

Afterword

'Freud, Kepler, and the clinical evidence' was written over a decade ago, and I am not surprised to find that I now have quibbles with some of its claims. The major point of the essay still seems to me quite correct, and I continue to believe that in the Rat Man case Freud brought to bear a strategy for testing hypotheses which is ubiquitous in planetary theory, that he used the strategy to test his views about psycho-sexual development, and that as a result he changed those views in an important way. No doubt the thesis would have been made better and with greater historical veracity if, instead of Kepler, the comparison were with Newton's argument for universal gravitation, or with Eddington's argument for general relativity. And, perhaps, the view of the Rat Man case I presented would have been more credible if the account of testing relations had been more than promissory.[31]

Part of the substance of the essay has been vigorously criticized by Adolf Grünbaum,[32] who objects, first, that the crucial piece of evidence in my reconstruction of the Rat Man case was not clinical at all, but instead obtained outside of the analytic hour, and second, that my treatment of the problem of suggestion in psychoanalysis is overly sanguine and perhaps even naive. I concede both points, although I give them a different weight and interpretation than does Grünbaum.

The testimony Freud obtained from Lorenz's mother is of great importance in my account of the argument of the Rat Man case, and Grünbaum is correct that it is not clinical evidence in the most narrow sense. This does not, however, seem to me of much significance, for it is certainly not *experimental* evidence of the kind H. J. Eysenck seemed to believe requisite for testing the theory, and I expect that in claiming that 'clinical observations' made experimental confirmations, such as those

---

[31] I have attempted to remedy both defects in *Theory and Evidence* (Princeton University Press, Princeton, 1980).

[32] A. Grünbaum, 'Can Psychoanalytic Theory be cogently tested "On the Couch"?', in A. Grünbaum and L. Laudan, eds., *Pittsburgh Series in Philosophy and History of Science*, vol. 8 (University of California Press, Berkeley and Los Angeles, Forthcoming).

attempted by Rosenzweig, supererogatory, Freud meant to include evidence like that obtained from Lorenz's mother.

Suggestion is a more substantial and more complicated topic and several issues must be distinguished. How much Freud's own case studies were vitiated by suggestion, and how sensitive Freud was to the problem, are importantly different issues from those of the general susceptibility of clinical evidence to suggestion. Grünbaum reminds us of the experimental evidence establishing the power of suggestion in clinical settings, and I accept the admonition. Knowing that clinical evidence is subject to suggestion should make us cautious in using that evidence, and it should make us sensitive to indicators that the therapist is determining the responses he receives. I do not see, however, that the experimental knowledge we now have about suggestibility requires us to renounce clinical evidence altogether. Indeed, I can imagine circumstances in which clinical evidence might have considerable force: when, for example, the clinical proceedings show no evident sign of indoctrination, leading the patient, and the like; when the results obtained fall into a regular and apparently law-like pattern obtained independently by many clinicians; and when those results are contrary to the expectation and belief of the clinician. I do not intend these as *criteria* for using clinical evidence, but only as indications of features which, in combination, give weight to such evidence. Two of those features, the first and the last, are present in Freud's Rat Man case.

The knowledge that clinical evidence is liable to suggestion and confounding does not, I think, of itself recommend the policy of dismissing all such evidence, nor does the knowledge that astronomical observations are subject to error recommend the policy of dismissing the evidence of astronomy. In the latter case it is relatively easy to find out something about the limits of error and its dispersion; in the former case it is more difficult. That obliges us, I should think, to use our heads and our good judgment in assaying clinical evidence, and perhaps to seek for finer knowledge of how much error is introduced in clinical proceedings, and in what circumstances. But I think we would not be using our heads if, for example, we took the evidence to be of the same quality in the Little Hans and in the Rat Man cases.

Professor Grünbaum asks whether, if, contrary to fact, Lorenz *had* recalled a conflict with his father during his childhood over sexual conduct, one would thereby have had evidence *for* Freud's views about psycho-sexual development. The trouble with such counterfactual questions is that the answer one is inclined to give depends on what else is assumed, contrary to fact. If the imagined recollection had occurred spontaneously, early on in the analysis and before Freud had told Lorenz of it, the case might have some weight in favour of Freud's hypotheses. Likewise if Lorenz's recollection was corroborated by his mother. How *much* weight is a difficult question which I cannot address; but some. If, by contrast, the imagined recollection had emerged only after Freud's insistence, I would tend to discount it. That is vague enough, I suppose, but it is useless to insist on a precision which the circumstances will not bear.

These questions are, it must be emphasized, largely independent of the historical questions that concern Freud's treatment of evidence in the course of his career, and in defending the structure and value of the core of the Rat Man case, I do not mean to defend Freud's handling of evidence generally. Freud's writings are filled with argument, good and bad, with rhetorical devices masquerading as arguments, with ingenuities of every kind, all in aid of establishing what was to be an empirical science. Most readers of Freud, whether sympathetic or hostile, have fallen well short of separating those circumstances in which Freud uses reason well and forcefully and to good effect from those in which he does something less or worse, and the preceding essay is no more than a contribution to that separation.

The mystery of reason is more vivid and more urgent in Freud than in the works of any other modern writer, and far outstrips the power of our epistemologies to unravel it. That is why Freud still fascinates me.

3

Critical empiricism criticized: the case of Freud

B. R. COSIN, C. F. FREEMAN and N. H. FREEMAN

Within the last decade philosophy of science has developed greatly as a special discipline. Perhaps inevitably, the internal controversies which this expansion has engendered have been difficult to relate to the more general philosophical field. The difficult relationship between philosophy in general and philosophy of science in particular, is an aspect of the difficult relationship between philosophy and scientific theory. The back numbers of reputable journals are littered with articles which either utilize some illusory science as a raw material for practising philosophy on, or which hew so closely to a few minor scientific maxims that their philosophy is deformed. Both these approaches tend towards a sort of eclectic and abstract *legislation* about the nature of science and the conduct of scientific activity.

In the course of this paper we shall have occasion *inter alia* to deal with the following one-sided perspectives. One is the resort to 'common sense' as a court of appeal; often involved with an essentialist view of causation, in particular a reduction to 'constant conjunction'. A second common source of confusion stems from rigid application of criteria based on falsificationist principles. We shall be finding this of particular interest since falsificationism depends upon certain assumptions, a metaphysical theory of truth and a particular view of the relations between facts and theories: assumptions which actually deflect that particular tendency within philosophy of science from dealing with those very methodological problems of scientific discovery and explanation which it formally sets itself.[1]

It is of particular interest to discuss the nature of Freudian theory since it raises *interrelated* problems about the modes of action of scientific theory and about the issues involved in human action—a domain which

[1] In Lecourt's (1970) terms, the question 'A quelles conditions la connaissance que je produis sera-t-elle scientifique?' is replaced by the question 'Quels sont les fondements de la connaissance scientifique?': the latter question is conceived of as epistemologically prior to, and determinant of, science itself, whereas the former question concerns the epistemological advance immanent in scientific development.

is constantly being worked on in contemporary general philosophy. In order to bring out these interrelationships, it is necessary to focus on the theoretical nature of *scientific methodology*. In *Explanation in the Behavioural Sciences* (hereafter referred to as E.B.S.), Cioffi presents a single article concerning the scientific status of some aspects of psycho-analytic theory which exemplifies all of the above points. For expository purposes we shall focus on Cioffi's article, locate it with respect to falsificationism and the British tradition of empiricism, and draw out its methodological implication.

Cioffi's examination of Freud depends on the following linked assumptions:

(a) Basic inconsistencies in Freudian theory, over and above intrinsic unevennesses in its development, can be found by a purely textual examination of Freud's writings (without reference to the practical context of Freud's work);
(b) these inconsistencies reveal the operation of persistent and wilful attempts to avoid confrontation of theory with fact; such that
(c) the resulting theoretical system is essentially unscientific, and, more specifically,
(d) pseudo-scientific in the way in which such systems as 'pyramidology' tend to be.

In what follows we show that Cioffi tries to fit Freudian theory into an inappropriate model of science, and then labels the divergencies as indices of its pseudo-scientific nature.

Conventionalism and refutability

The view of science presented in Cioffi's article is somewhat idiosyncratic. Its points of major impact are clearly related to the early Popperian tradition[2] with specific divergencies. It can be summed up as follows: a scientific theory consists essentially of related hypotheses each of which is empirically refutable, and there is an injunction upon scientists to expose their working hypotheses to (potentially falsifying) severe tests. Analysis of the generation of hypotheses is considered methodologically less important than their refutability.

In *The Logic of Scientific Discovery* (hereafter referred to as *L.Sc.D.*) Popper's abiding concern is to develop criteria for demarcating science from metaphysics. Cioffi is also concerned to distinguish sciences which are genuinely empirical from 'pseudo-sciences'; he emphasizes the prac-

---

[2] It is not necessary here to distinguish the various tendencies within that tradition.

tice of the science rather than the formal characteristics of its theory. He distinguishes between formally defective theses and methodologically defective procedures, and claims (*E.B.S.*, p. 471) that his notion of a pseudo-science is *pragmatic* (procedural) rather than *syntactic* (referring to the logical relations between the theses).[3] This view presents methodology as superadded to theories in use rather than as an integral aspect of the content of, and mutual relationships between, their constituent propositions. In his 'Reply to Farrell' (*E.B.S.*, p. 510) Cioffi says that Popper somewhat 'too baldly' uses the criterion of refutability-in-principle to sum up a whole list of criterial considerations. For it to be scientific a theory must not only be such that a state of affairs which disconfirms it be logically possible, but must also be '*calculated* to discover whether such (disconfirming) states of affairs exists' (*E.B.S.*, p. 472, emphasis added). Thus a crucial element in the criterion for a genuinely empirical science becomes the honesty of the intention of its practitioners. Cioffi's emphasis on the 'pragmatic' notion of a pseudo-science obscures the distinction between a faulty scientific theory and faulty practice by individual scientists. His concentration upon a single man and his published writings makes it easier for Cioffi to conflate the two.

We may note, however, that this error of Cioffi's is fully contained in Popper's work, despite the latter's emphasis on the demarcation between science and metaphysics. For Popper admits that his criterion of demarcation cannot be applied to a theoretical system and thus that this criterion is reducible to 'the norms, by which the scientist is guided when he is engaged in research' (*L.Sc.D.*, p. 50). No sociological or historical analysis of the putative norms is offered, so that the importance of the refutability of hypotheses reduces to moralism (to the demand that this professional duty be central to the scientist's endeavours).

Even where the hypotheses which are part of a scientific theory are logically capable of being refuted the scientist may intervene to forestall the effects of such refutation, by, for instance, modifying the hypothesis so that it is no longer *refuted*. Such devices are particularly used to 'save a theory in time of crisis' (see *L.Sc.D.*, pp. 80 ff.). Manipulation of this kind is termed 'conventionalist', and can, it is implied, seriously retard scientific advance, although the conditions under which it has this effect have been left completely obscure in Popper's writings.[4] The diagnosis of

---

[3] It is interesting to relate this to the tenor of Popper's remark that 'it might indeed be said that the majority of the problems of theoretical philosophy . . . can be re-interpreted . . . as problems of method' (*L.Sc.D.*, p. 56).

[4] For more developed views see Lakatos (1970) and especially Kuhn (1970).

conventionalist stratagems depends crucially on the contrast with the mandatory[5] exposure of hypotheses to severe tests designed to refute them, which is taken as the paradigm of bringing evidence to bear on a theory. We shall argue that this conception of evidence is inadequate, and so the contrast with 'conventionalism' breaks down. 'Conventionalism' as a methodology to be chosen or rejected is a chimaera proceeding from mistaken premises.

Cioffi approvingly quotes Nagel as follows: 'there is surely good ground for the suspicion that Freudian theory can always be manipulated so that it escapes refutation no matter what the established facts may be' (*E.B.S.*, p. 510). And Cioffi asserts more specifically: 'there are a host of peculiarities of psycho-analytic theory and practice . . . which can be understood when they are seen as manifestations of the same impulse: the need to avoid refutation' (*E.B.S.*, p. 473).

There may seem to be something puzzling here. The 'pseudo-sciences' which Cioffi brackets with psycho-analysis, and which include clear cases of non-science such as a conceit of Dante's and a theological aberration of Newton's, are such that 'confrontation with the facts' is not a danger for them (nor even imaginable in many cases). But for psycho-analysis, confrontation with the facts is admitted to be a real danger, which is continually warded off by conventionalist manipulation of theory. In this case, for conventionalist stratagems to be necessary, there must be some facts with which the theory *could* be confronted, which would entail its being empirical at least in some minimal sense. So why does Cioffi present conventionalist manipulation as an argument for the *non*-empirical nature of the theory? Popper, in *Conjectures and Refutations* (hereafter referred to as *C.R.*), provides us with an answer to this question. While conventionalism *is* a guarantee that a theory *had* empirical content, 'such a procedure . . . rescues the theory from refutation only at the price of destroying, or at least lowering, its scientific status' (*C.R.*, p. 37).

Both Cioffi and Popper consistently fail to distinguish between the refutation of a theory and of a constituent hypothesis, and to describe how these are related.[6] This failure raises the question of *how much* conventionalism is criterial for a science being a pseudo-science: is prevarication about one hypothesis a sufficient index? or are we to add up the number of refuted hypotheses and relate them to a threshold for

---

[5] 'what characterises the empirical method is its manner of exposing to falsification, in every conceivable way, the system to be tested' (*L.ScD.* p. 56).

[6] An account of the defects of crude falsificationism in its prescriptive form for research is scattered through Lakatos (1970).

refutation of the entire theory? In this way, even from its own (falsificationist) point of view, this model is involved in difficulties through its failure to deal with theoretical *levels*.

Unless these points are elucidated such a crudely falsificationist view of science can only be understood as demanding that a whole theory be jettisoned if any of its constituent hypotheses, at whatever stage of formalization, meet with a disconfirming instance – for if any part of a theory which fails to account for its subject matter be modified or articulated it can be categorized as the product of manipulation. It is impossible to imagine how such a view of science could account for, or even admit as legitimate, the stage of construction during which a scientific theory is in dynamic relationship with putative data (and in so far as a science is practised rather than merely taught, it remains in this stage).[7] Thus Popper tends to describe theories as '*guesses* about the structure of the world' (*C.R.*, p. 245), and answers the question 'How do we jump from an observation statement to a *good* theory?' – 'by jumping first to *any* theory and testing it, to find whether it is good or not' (*C.R.*, p. 55).

Such difficulties arise for any falsificationist model if it tends to suggest that the implications of refutation of one hypothesis must always be the same for the theory as a whole. It lacks a conception of theoretical structure (with the possible exception of a conception of varying degrees of universality). However, not all propositions in a theory are likely to be of the same logical status or to relate in the same way to its empirical subject matter. Appearances may be deceptive, as in the case of the proposition 'Light travels in a straight line' which, far from being a low level empirical generalization, assigns Euclidean geometry its place in the theory. Another example is Freud's eminently theoretical remark to which Cioffi takes exception, that in certain circumstances where there is no remembering in the usual sense 'dreaming is another kind of remembering', whose subject matter is the theoretical relationship between these concepts.

The meaning of propositions and concepts in a theory depends, of

---

[7] Popper is definite on this point: "The initial stage, the act of conceiving or inventing a theory, seems to me neither to call for logical analysis nor to be susceptible of it' (*L.Sc.D.*, p. 31). (His inappropriate terminology makes theory construction a matter for psychology, not a problem in the logic of knowledge, which 'consists solely in investigating the methods employed in the systematic tests to which every new idea [*sic*] must be subjected if it is to be seriously entertained,' *ibid*.) Popper correctly describes himself as an empiricist (*C.R.*, p. 154). His indictment of inductivism in no way vitiates this, since the central feature of empiricism is not inductivism but the attitude to theory which assigns methodological priority to hypothesis-testing.

course, on their relation to other propositions and concepts in that theory, including the various ways in which the disconfirmation or modification of one proposition or concept may affect the meaning of others. Argument for or against theoretical propositions such as those cited above will refer to their impact on other parts of the theory, and how the meaning-shifts involved in their adoption or exclusion affect the theory's power to describe and explain its data. Some propositions will be more crucial to the theory than others. For instance, while Freud's phylogenetic assumptions are readily detachable from the theory without far-reaching effects on other concepts, the modifications Kleinean psycho-analysts have made in Freud's concept of the Oedipus complex would not have been possible without extensive modifications in his theory of development.

Theories which claim to be scientific must, certainly, contain criteria for telling when a phenomenon has been correctly classified and when incorrectly; when a certain relationship holds and when it does not: it does not follow that to be scientific a theory has to contain criteria for its own total refutation. Recent work in the philosophy of science has suggested that in the physical sciences, which falsificationist models have traditionally been supposed to fit, theories are not discarded in this way but because they are no longer able to generate research problems or because an alternative theory can account for the same subject matter more successfully. To suggest that the claim of psycho-analysis to be empirical must depend upon its ability to specify conditions in which it would be totally wrong,[8] rather than on its criteria for rejecting constituent propositions, is misconceived.

In is relevant to compare, as Cioffi implicitly does, Freudian theory with such 'pseudo-sciences' as numerology and pyramidology. We find that the relationship between their 'findings' and their 'theory' is very different from the analogous relationship in Freudian theory. Properly speaking, numerology and pyramidology are not theories. Theoretical presuppositions *underlie* their activities, and only an examination of these (such as, in some cases, the existence of God as an efficient cause) could make sense of the idea that they are explaining something. But these presuppositions are all borrowed from other fields or from 'common sense'. Nor can the 'findings' of numerology and pyramidology be described as 'facts'. Although they assert that links exist between phenomena previously supposed to be unconnected, these 'findings' of numerology and pyramidology are discrete in the following sense: the

---

[8] 'what kind of clinical responses would refute to the satisfaction of the analyst not merely a particular analytic diagnosis but psycho-analysis itself?' (Popper, *C.R.*, p. 38 n.).

discovery of new 'links' does not alter the meaning of the old, while the old give us no guidance for the discovery of the new. These 'findings' accumulate purely quantitatively, rather than qualitatively as Freudian theory does. There is no reason to believe that a comparison between psycho-analysis and numerology would do otherwise than highlight the differences between them.

Facts and Theory

We have discussed some effects of making the falsification of hypotheses the paradigm of scientific activity. The failure to give methodological priority to the analysis of the structure of theories and the process involved in the generation of hypotheses at various stages of formalization has a further effect: it becomes easy to overlook the theoretical and interpretative nature of description. We argue that facts, which are characterizations of the phenomena which theories are concerned to explain, must necessarily involve theoretical components since they classify and delimit phenomena.[9] Phenomena are *candidates* for status as scientific facts, and theoretical work on them may be viewed as probative: either promoting them to full factual status or relegating them to irrelevance or error. Scientific facts are necessarily an index of the theoretical work involved in their production. The idea that facts are essentially neutral with respect to scientific theory derives partly from the existence of commonsense prescientific concepts[10] (whose theoretical content is not structured in the way in which scientific theories are), and partly from the British empiricist tradition, itself often justified with reference to 'sound common sense'.

The account of falsification we are offered can be seen as a corollary of this view of facts as neutral with respect to theory, which we shall argue is implicit in Cioffi's article. Popper has his own version of the relation between theory and facts, which we shall do well to consider first.

Popper's main criterion for the *scientific* nature of a theory is its *independent testability*.

---

[9] Cf. G. Canguilhem (1968), pp. 16–17: 'La nature n'est pas d'elleême decoupée et repartie en objets et en phenomènes scientifiques. C'est la science qui constitue son object à partir du moment où elle a inventé une methode pour former, par des propositions capables d'êtres composées integralement, une theorie controlée par le souci de la prendre en faute'. Cf. also Feyerabend (1968), p. 27, and of course Parsons (1968), p. 41 n.

[10] We cannot agree with Popper that scientific knowledge is at all like *common-sense knowledge writ large* (*L.Sc.D.*, p. 22; emphasis original). In any case, scientific knowledge cannot be 'writ small', that is, reduced to common sense.

That is to say, apart from explaining all the *explicanda* which the new theory was designed to explain, it must have new and testable consequences (preferably consequences of a *new kind*); it must lead to the prediction of phenomena which have not so far been observed (*C.R.*, p. 241).

The practice of psycho-analysis, he argues, can never supply such tests,[11] while the day-to-day practice of an experimental science may do so.[12] Tests consist in the attempt to confront a hypothesis derived from a theory – one which forbids the occurrence of certain states of affairs – with a true observation statement reporting a state of affairs precluded by the hypothesis. The possibility of such refutations is an important factor in Popper's version of the correspondence theory of truth. For Popper argues against the inductivists that no finite number of confirming instances can *entail* a universal statement, so that while our theories (which include such statements) may *be* true we can never *know* this – no amount of evidence can amount to proof. We know, Popper says, that a true theory would have certain characteristics, such as giving rise to true predictions; he calls this knowledge 'meta-scientific' (*C.R.*, p. 217) and it allows us to conclude that a new theory which makes more and new refutable predictions would constitute an advance over an old one *if it were true*. It cannot, however, tell us whether the theory *is* true, and so the criterion of progress towards the truth (*C.R.*, p. 216) depends upon the theory actually passing severe tests designed to refute it. We cannot know that our theories 'correspond to the facts' – but we can increase the probability of this being the case by exposing them to severe tests. 'If we test our conjecture, and succeed in falsifying it, we see very clearly that there was a reality, something with which it could clash' (*C.R.*, p. 116).

'The status of truth in the objective sense, as correspondence to the facts, . . . may be compared to that of a mountain peak usually wrapped in clouds. A climber may . . . not know when he gets there, because he may be unable to distinguish, in the clouds, between the main summit and a subsidiary peak . . . it will often be easy for him to realise that he has not reached it (or not yet reached it); for example, when he is turned back by an overhanging wall' (*C.R.*, p. 226).

The analogy is an illuminating one, but can falsification, based on the

---

[11] Cf. Popper in *C.R.*, p. 38 n. 'Clinical observations, like all other observations, are *interpretations in the light of theory*; and for this reason alone they are apt to seem to support those theories in the light of which they were interpreted. But real support can be obtained only from observations undertaken as tests (by "attempted refutations") and for this purpose *criteria of refutation* have to be laid down beforehand: it must be agreed which observable situations, if actually observed, mean that the theory is refuted.'

[12] Cf. *L.Sc.D.*, p. 107. Note that Popper represents the daily work of scientists as a process of *testing* theories.

sort of tests Popper describes, be as conclusive as an overhanging wall? Popper does not claim that tests are independent of *all* theory. The observation statements with which the exposed hypotheses are compared must themselves rely on background knowledge, which 'is open to criticism, even though only in a piecemeal way' (*C.R.*, p. 238), but which 'we accept (tentatively) as unproblematic while we are testing the theory' (*C.R.*, p. 390). There can be no doubt that in Popper's theory such observation statements ('basic statements' *L.Sc.D.*, p. 87) *stand in* for the (unattainable) facts. Although he admits that falsification is not conclusive, Popper argues that scientists should behave as if it were (e.g. *L.Sc.D.*, pp. 42, 50, 280). Admittedly they should require that the results of tests be reproducible (*L.Sc.D.*, p. 86), but in the last analysis they agree to carry the critical method no further, at that time. The infinite regress in which his position involves him is recognized by Popper (*L.Sc.D.*, p. 105) and is described as 'innocuous since in our theory there is no question of trying to prove any statements by means of it'. Far from being innocuous, the necessarily inconclusive character of falsification involves Popper in a metaphysical theory of truth as essentially unknowable. Popper claims to have solved the problem of induction by pointing out that 'the acceptance by science of a law or of a theory is tentative only', but falsification seems itself to be no more firmly based. 'Experiences can *motivate a decision*' (to accept basic statements) 'but a basic statement cannot be justified by them – no more than by thumping a table' (*L.Sc.D.*, p. 105, italics in original). Popper adds that should the need arise, the basic statements can themselves be tested further (*loc. cit.*). By this time, however, the theory in whose refutation these statements were used has been decisively rejected, for 'a corroborative appraisal made at a later date . . . can replace a positive degree of corroboration with a negative one, but not vice versa' (*L.Sc.D.*, p. 268).

For Popper truth is synonymous with correspondence with the facts, and as we have seen, 'basic statements' (which are consensual singular existential statements) are treated in his theory as if they were theory-neutral facts. *The method of confrontation between theory and fact Popper regards as unproblematic.*[13] In reality much scientific work consists in the theoretical working out of notions of evidence, of what could count as testing, and notions of how their various propositions

[13] Popper is enabled to present testing as unproblematic because he assimilates scientific explanation to prediction (cf. *L.Sc.D.*, p. 33). But even if this were accepted, whether a hypothesis has or has not been refuted may be in dispute. As Lakatos (1970, p. 102), points out: 'one can easily argue that *ceteris paribus* clauses are not exceptions, but the rule in science'. Even this is a minor question beside the problem of whether a *theory* or *model* has been falsified.

may be rendered dubious or supported (i.e. notions of evidence) are an integral part of scientific theories and the meaning of their constituent propositions. Cioffi also regards such notions as unproblematic, and as ascertainable with no reference to the theory:

The question of the bearing of empirical observation of children on reconstructions based on the use of psychoanalytic method cannot be postponed until the validity of that method is resolved, since the only way of resolving the validity of that method is by determining whether, and to what extent, it accords with empirical observation of children (*E.B.S.*, p. 479).

Apparently the theoretical question of how empirical observation is to be related to a theory is here to be solved by relating empirical observation to the theory.[14]

The notion of facts as neutral with respect to theory lends support to the requirement of theory-free observation for unbiased tests. As we have seen, Popper denies the possibility of theory-neutral facts and of theory-free observation, but his model of falsification depends upon 'tentatively accepted' substitutes which serve the same function. Cioffi does not articulate his own view, but his position on the possibility of direct (pure) observation seems to be cruder and more consistent than Popper's. Thus in the context of an argument about indirect and direct evidence, we find it taken for granted, in the following way.

Here, as elsewhere, Cioffi accuses Freud of deliberately failing to assess his reconstructions of infantile life by direct observation (of children); and of preferring indirect observation based on the analyses of adults. He goes on as follows:

The expression 'direct observation' alternates with 'direct analytic observation' as if they were synonymous, so that it only becomes clear after several re-readings that when Freud speaks of 'the direct observation of children' he is referring to the psychoanalytic interpretation of infantile behaviour (*E.B.S.*, p. 479).

In other words, even where Freud uses 'direct observation' in the sense of looking at the children rather than the adults, this is not the real thing. From the way Cioffi dismisses the idea that observation by child analysts (because they are biased) could be relevant to the assessment of Freud's descriptions of infantile sexuality, it becomes clear that 'direct observation' is, for Cioffi, something a committed psycho-analyst has less chance than anyone of doing. Either Cioffi must specify the kind of training and level of skill required in an observer (and training can hardly be theory-neutral), or he has taken a step from talking as if facts were outside theory to giving them public, commonsense status – as if true

[14] We deal with the substance of Cioffi's point at the end of this section.

facts could not be opaque but must be available to the inspection of any untrained, unbiased observer. Such a step would be disastrous for the physical sciences. Propositions in physics, for example, to which observation is relevant, cannot be assessed by the untrained observer. And in psycho-analysis, while such easily observable behaviour as gestures and speech is relevant to the truth or falsity of statements about unconscious phenomena, the way in which it is relevant is part of the theory.

A further argument about direct versus indirect evidence shows that for Cioffi no psycho-analytic evidence *could* be direct. When Freud remarks that, while observation of small children bears out his interpretation (of deathwishes against the same-sexed parent), the analysis of adult neurotics carried greater conviction, Cioffi comments:

This is as if Holmes, having concluded from the indentation marks on his visitor's walking stick that he was the owner of a dog smaller than a mastiff and larger than a terrier, instead of glancing with interest in the direction from which the animal was approaching, were to turn once again to a more minute inspection of the stick (*E.B.S.*, p. 480).

The analogy cannot hold, for no dog could approach. It rests on the misconception of psycho-analytic evidence as inherently indirect; whereas since it makes no sense to talk of direct access to unconscious phenomena, it makes no sense to talk of indirect access either. Cioffi thinks that to observe children is to obtain direct evidence of the nature of their phantasies, while to *analyse* adult neurotics is to obtain *indirect* evidence of this. We could with more justification describe *psychoanalysis* of children as the best evidence of their phantasies (although many sorts of behaviour might be evidence, and different sorts of evidence might be relevant), and Freud could be criticized for underestimating the possibility of analysing children.

Certainly observation of children, as well as child analysis, yields evidence relevant to psychoanalytic theories of infantile experience and development. But there is no such thing as straightforward, noninterpretative observation. Popper writes: ' "experience" consists largely of expectations and theories and partly also of observational knowledge – although I happen to believe that there does not exist anything like *pure* observational knowledge, untainted by expectations and theories' (*C.R.*, p. 155). We take the stronger position that such concepts as 'tainted' are totally inappropriate here – as is any regret for elusive 'pure observation'. Knowledge involves conceptualizing, and to this extent cannot be divorced from expectations and theories – indeed, it owes its existence to them. In speaking as if tests should be made by carrying out unbiased observation, Cioffi is asking psycho-analysts to test propositions in psycho-analysis in the context of other people's theories, including the attenuated and unrigorous versions of these prevalent in the culture as 'commonsense', or, to use Cioffi's own term, as 'intuition'.[15]

How the trick was done: Popperian precursors of Cioffi's attack

In *Conjectures and Refutations* Popper explains the roots of his system:

My problem perhaps first took the simple form, 'what is wrong with Marxism, psycho-analysis, and individual psychology?' ... I felt that these three theories, though posing as sciences, had in fact more in common with primitive myths than with science ... these theories appeared to be able to explain practically everything that happened within the field to which they referred (*C.R.*, p. 34).

Thus these three 'pseudo-sciences' seemed to him to be characterized by what we may term omnivorousness; every occurrence which was within the range of jurisdiction of the theories was allotted a post-hoc 'explanation' and 'it is a typical soothsayer's trick to predict things so vaguely that the predictions can hardly fail: that they become irrefutable' (*C.R.*, p. 37). Thus the theories cannot benefit from direct experience, since every conceivable case simply becomes absorbed into the theory and counts as an 'additional confirmation'.

It is instructive to look at the method used by Popper in selecting cases to exemplify this (we shall not be concerned with the 'plausibility' of the examples nor of the theoretical components involved, but solely with Popper's technique). He continues: 'I may illustrate this by two very different examples of human behaviour: that of a man who pushes a child into the water with the intention of drowning it; and that of a man who sacrifices his life in an attempt to save the child'. Adler, he says would interpret both as an act of self-assertion, so that he wins on both the swings and the roundabout. On the other hand: 'according to Freud the first man suffered from repression (say, of some component of his Oedipus complex), while the second man had achieved sublimation' (*C.R.*, p. 35).

In the words of Popper's student Agassi, this is intended to convince us that each 'is no explanation ... all these explanations are *ad hoc*. The feeling is conveyed that many cases have been strikingly explained by one single hypothesis', but 'these instances are clandestine instances' (Agassi, 1964, p. 203).

---

[15] Cf. *E.B.S.*, p. 489.

But let us take a closer look at Popper's technique. The insinuation against Adler works in the following way:

(a) Two actions are described as expressing dispositions defined as opposed and incompatible (e.g. criminal and altruistic intentions).
(b) A single theoretical construct is taken from a theorist's work and represented as claiming fully to explain each action.
(c) This opinion is attributed to the theorist concerned.[16]
(d) His theory is forthwith declared pseudo-scientific.

Popper's slur on Freud similarly works by extracting complex theoretical constructs from their contexts and presenting them as empty jargon: the implication being that anyone who used such language to describe something so straightforward must be wrong.

A more convincing example is provided by Agassi who continues the quotation in the following way (no textual reference is given by Agassi).

An example ... which has greatly impressed me is Freud's story of a married woman who unthinkingly signed her maiden name. Freud interpreted this as an unconscious expression of suppressed discontent with her husband and, indeed, he triumphantly added, a few months after her pen slipped in that ominous fashion the poor lady was divorced. This is pseudo-science at its worst: it is a glaring case of a clandestine instance thinly masked as explained instance. Since some married women divorce their husbands without having accidentally used their maiden names, and since other married women use their maiden name by mistake without ever asking for a divorce, clearly in this special case Freud erroneously claimed that the error and the divorce were explained by his theory of slips of the pen.

Agassi's technique here closely follows Popper's. The two actions (see (a) above) are the parapraxis and the divorce, which, however, are presented as different rather than opposed. Freud cites the divorce as evidence for his interpretation of the parapraxis. Agassi assures us that this is 'pseudo-science at its worst' since the two actions do not occur statistically in constant conjunction. Since Freud was not claiming that one action causes the other, such an argument is irrelevant to his point.[17] Agassi follows up his crude *non-sequitur* by stating that Freud believed his 'theory of slips of the pen' explained the divorce. Freud would have claimed no more than that his theory of the unconscious furnished him with a method for explaining slips of the pen. (For this particular

---

[16] The fact that Adler's work is scientifically worthless could never be shown by means of such distortions.

[17] Hempel (1968), pp. 62–4, offers an alternative characterization of the kind of explanation Freud is engaged in here.

parapraxis we have no more than a suggestion. Contrast the detailed explanations to be found in *The Psychopathology of Everyday Life*.) Agassi, whose formalistic position predisposes him to conflate prediction and explanation, tries to represent Freud as making a mediocre *prediction* about the lady's subsequent action. He was not. He was making a diagnosis. Far from entailing a divorce the parapraxis indicated a realm of theory in which expressions of discontent with the marriage take their place.

We may now add to these examples, one taken from Cioffi's article, to which the above considerations apply. On *E.B.S.*, p. 484, Cioffi juxtaposes two quotations from Freud: 'If the father was hard, violent and cruel the super-ego takes over these attributes from him' and 'the unduly lenient and indulgent father fosters the development of an overstrict ego'. Then Cioffi, omitting all cases of *ordinary* leniency or strictness, amalgamates them to form 'If a child develops a sadistic super-ego, either he had a harsh and punitive father or he had an unduly lenient and indulgent one' then reduces them to 'if a child develops a sadistic super-ego, either he had a harsh and punitive father or he had not' and comments that 'this is just what we might expect to find if there were no relation between his father's character and the harshness of his super-ego'. Thus Freud's explanation is concluded to be worthless. Let us see what such treatment would make of *any* explanation of similar form. We select a rigorous case as follows: If a child falls over we could claim to account for this by finding out that he had been pushed violently or that he had been pulled strongly = if a child falls over either he was pushed violently or he was not, and this is just what we would expect to find if there were no relation between the force applied and the speed of the child's descent (or even whether he fell or not). The most consistent explanation would be reduced to rubbish by such a use of the law of excluded middle.

Anamnesis and symptom dissolution

Cioffi offers what seems a truly damning indictment: Freud is presented as claiming that anamnesis of infantile material is causally related to the remission of neurotic symptoms, yet four cases of the relationship between these are shown to be in manifest contradiction with each other. We shall find, however, that Freud is not arguing as Cioffi suggests, but is outlining some problems arising from the action of resistance mechanisms.

Cases of the following four outcomes are described in Freud's work, Cioffi claims (*E.B.S.*, p. 482):

[i] as well as patients who do not recall their infantile sexual impulses and

retain their symptoms, and [ii] patients who do recall their infantile sexual impulses and relinquish their symptoms, we have [iii] patients who do not recall their infantile sexual impulses but nevertheless relinquish their symptoms, and [iv] patients who do recall their infantile sexual impulses and nevertheless retain them. (Numbering inserted.)

It appears that Cioffi has found references to four types of case in Freud, which may be faithfully represented as follows:

(i) $\bar{R}-\bar{D}$

(ii) $R-D$

(iii) $\bar{R}-D$

(iv) $R-\bar{D}$

where R = recall and D = dissolution of symptoms, and $\bar{R}$ and $\bar{D}$ their negations. Freud suggests that there is a *direct* relationship between the two components; so cases (i) and (ii) support Freud. Cioffi suggests that there is *no* relationship between the two components, so cases (iii) and (iv) support Cioffi, if and only if cases (i) and (ii) are found as well.

These bold formulations concerning the cure of neurotic symptoms will strike most readers who are at all conversant with Freud as downright queer, for the force of Cioffi's contrasts depend upon Freud's viewing the recall of the infantile material as both a necessary *and* a sufficient condition for symptom dissolution. The force of case (iii) $\bar{R}-D$ is to show that recall is not necessary, and that of (iv) $R-\bar{D}$ to show that it is not sufficient. Let us examine the evidence.

Cioffi draws his evidence from four sources spanning papers presented in 1909, 1920, 1925, and 1937. Only one of them is a specific case; the other quotations are drawn from expository pieces. The general conjunction between symptom dissolution and recall of infantile sexuality on which Cioffi's contrasts depend, is introduced by the following quotation from a popular lecture at Clark University: 'Starting out from the mechanism of cure, it now became possible to construct quite definite ideas of the origin of the illness' (1910a [1909] xi, 23). However, 'the origin of the illness' does not refer solely to the content of the infantile material, as Cioffi would suggest, for, when this quotation is replaced in its context, we find that 'the mechanism of cure' does not refer to anamnesis of infantile material, but to the breaking down of 'resistance on the part of the patient. It was on this idea of resistance, then, that I based my views of the course of psychical events in hysteria. In order to effect a recovery, it had proved necessary to remove these resistances. Starting out from the mechanism of cure . . .'. Nowhere does Cioffi even allude to the concept of resistance. We shall see how this inexplicable omission invalidates his arguments.

The next quotation from the same source (two lectures later) is presented basically as evidence for (ii) $R–D$ and also for (i) $\bar{R}–\bar{D}$: 'it is only experiences in childhood that explain susceptibility to later traumas [since] it is only by uncovering these almost invariably forgotten memory traces and by making them conscious that we acquire the power to get rid of the symptom' (op. cit., 41). The form in which this quotation is supplied to us may be faithfully rendered as an argument that because there is a necessary connection between R and D, the experiences recalled in R are a sufficient condition for the occurrence of the symptoms dissolved in D. However, if we turn to the original source we see that this is not at all the tenor of Freud's argument, for Cioffi has replaced Freud's 'and' which joins the two propositions he quotes, with his own 'since'. There is absolutely no justification for Cioffi's restructuring of Freud's account, since it does not render the original more coherent or concise. What Freud is actually saying may be gathered by reading on in the original. There we see: 'And here we reach the same conclusions as in our investigations of dreams: the imperishable, repressed, wishful impulses of childhood may without exception be described as sexual'. Freud goes on to continue the main point of the lectures, which is to use his theses on infantile sexuality to illuminate the concept of repression. That is the centre of gravity of the particular paragraph whence Cioffi selects his quotation. Here Freud is *not* concerned to predict cure, and we should *not* be misled into mistaking a sentence in a popular account of sexuality for a scientific statement of his therapeutic theory and practice. In short the conjunction $R–D$ is never discussed, only the conjunction (i) $\bar{R}–\bar{D}$ utilized for expository purposes with regard to repression.

Cioffi's evidence for the conjunction (iv) $R–\bar{D}$ is taken from the 1920 paper 'The Psychogenesis of a Case of Homosexuality in a Woman'. The quotation which we are offered is 'marked progress in analytic under- standing can be unaccompanied by even the slightest change in the patient's compulsions and inhibitions' (1920a, xviii, 163).

However, if we turn to the original source, we shall discover that this is not a therapeutic analysis at all. The young woman was brought to the consulting room by her irate father who 'was determined to combat [his daughter's homosexuality] with all the means in his power . . . if this way failed he still had in reserve his strongest counter-measure; a speedy marriage was to awaken the natural instincts of the girl and stifle her unnatural tendencies', (op. cit., 149). Furthermore it is important to note that 'the girl was not in any way ill – she did not suffer from anything in herself, nor did she complain of her condition . . . and . . . the task to be carried out did not consist in resolving a neurotic conflict' (op. cit., 150). Bearing this in mind we may take a closer look at the quotation which Cioffi has adduced. The context immediately preceding the quotation relates the girl's calm, intellectual comprehension of a point of Freudian theory explained to her by Freud. *En passant* Freud briefly mentions some characteristics of hypnotic treatments and obsessional neuroses and compares them with her marked detachment. The point of comparison is once again, as one might expect, the *resistance*: until the resistance is engaged, any agreement with the analyst is likely to be a mere verbal assent. Freud is drawing to our notice how much of the intellectual faculty may thus by employed in a detached manner, either in the service of the resistance or, as in this girl's case, because of the lack of positive neurotic transference. The question of a 'cure' only arises when the resistance is successfully dealt with. In *no* way is Freud's presentation of this girl's case relevant to Cioffi's (iv) $R-\bar{D}$ and especially not to 'infantile sexual material'.

Cioffi presents as more evidence for (iv) $R-\bar{D}$, that Freud often 'succeeded in . . . establishing a complete intellectual acceptance of what is repressed – but the repression itself is still unremoved'. The original paper is on a technical point: 'the manner in which our patients bring forward their associations . . .' on the role of negation. In the paragraph whence the quotation is torn, the argument runs as follows. The subject matter of a repressed image can become conscious upon condition that it be denied. This taking account of what is repressed is not an acceptance of the content – the intellectual function is, by this subterfuge, distinct from the affective process. 'With the help of negation only one consequence of the process of repression is undone – the fact, namely, of the ideational content of what is repressed not reaching consciousness' (1925h, xix, 236). This quotation makes it quite clear on which theoretical level Freud is arguing. There is no mention of infantile sexuality, nor of symptom formation or dissolution. Whatever one thinks of the complexity of Freud's note, it could hardly be clearer that it is totally irrelevant to the proposition that 'we have patients who do recall their infantile sexual impulses and nevertheless retain [their symptoms]'. The last piece of evidence which Cioffi produces, for the proposition (iii) $R-D$, is exceedingly interesting. This is a quotation taken from Freud's ante-penultimate paper 'Constructions in Analysis', written in 1937, in which he treats of the problem of verifying interpretations. The relevant quotation is as follows: 'Quite often we do not succeed in bringing the patient to recollect what has been repressed. Instead of that, if the analysis is carried out correctly, we produce in him an assured conviction of the truth of the construction which achieves the same therapeutic result as a recaptured memory' (1937d, xxiii, 265–6). Freud goes on to say: 'The problem of what the circumstances are in which this occurs and of how it is possible that what appears to be an incomplete substitute should nevertheless produce a complete result – all of this is material for a later enquiry'. Unfortunately Freud died shortly after these words were written, so this promise remained unfulfilled.[18] The important thing here is, however, Freud's emphasis on the *specifiability in principle* of the circumstances in which symptom dissolution is not preceded by recall of repressed material. The general problem seems to be one of engaging the resistance, rather than merely the content, of the repressed material, by means of a correct construction of the *structure* of the resistance.

We may illustrate the differences between Cioffi's account of psycho-analysis and Freud's own account by considering two quotations:

(a) Psychoanalysis may be described as an attempt to determine the historicity and/or pathogenicity of episodes in a person's infantile past and the character of his unconscious affective life and its influence over behaviour, by the manner in which he responds to assertions or speculations concerning these – not, however, just *any* attempt, but a particular, historically identifiable one which issued in a body of aetiological and dynamic theses, the abiding core of which is the claim that 'only sexual wishful impulses from infancy are able to furnish the motive force for the formation of psycho-neurotic symptoms' (*E.B.S.*, p. 471).
(b) The theory of repression is the foundation stone upon which the 'edifice of psycho-analysis rests, the most essential part of it ... It may thus be said that the theory of psycho-analysis is an attempt to account for two observed facts ... the facts of transference and of resistance', (1914d, xiv, 16).

At no stage does Cioffi deal with such phenomena as transference and resistance, for his abiding concern with infantile sexuality leads him to misunderstand its status in the practical context of psycho-analysis.

Cioffi's tendency, exemplified in this section, to tear quotations from their contexts and misleadingly to paraphrase Freud's argument, is repeated elsewhere in his article.[19] This may perhaps be attributed to his preoccupation with the language of events and with falsification: the concentration upon putative *products* of the work rather than on the

[18] Freud's concept of screen memories (1899a, III) may perhaps be relevant reading on the concept of 'incomplete substitutes'; and also his analysis of dreaming.

[19] For example the account of infantile sexuality on p. 477; the misleading account of Freud and the Hans Herbert case on p. 485; and the quotations from the *History of an Infantile Neurosis* on p. 480.

actual *process* of production. We argue that the latter takes methodological priority, and can only be grasped by focusing upon the structure of theory, and how it constitutes its most basic facts in describing and explaining novel and familiar phenomena.

Aetiology—an exploratory note

Wittgenstein argued that Freud's refusal to attribute changes in mental phenomena to 'chance' must commit him to the search for causal laws.[20] Such a conclusion, however, takes explanation in terms of causal law to be the paradigmatic form of scientific explanation. Thus the Popperian view of science in the light of which Cioffi's criticisms of Freud must be understood sees predictions as the very stuff of science because, by 'forbidding' certain states of affairs, they specify the conditions for their own refutation. Popper writes: 'in order to deduce predictions one needs laws and initial conditions; if no suitable laws are available or if the initial conditions cannot be ascertained, the scientific way of prediction breaks down' (*L.Sc.D.*, p. 205). (That these are *causal* laws is made clear in *L.Sc.D.*, Section 12.) Such assumptions underlie Cioffi's complaints (*E.B.S.*, pp. 478–80) that Freud suggests that certain infantile experiences are pathogenic but, by failing to specify under what conditions the relationship holds, and whether some identifiable groups are less prone than others, leaves the status of the putative relationship in doubt. For Cioffi, either castration threats (for example) are pathogenic or they are not. If they are, then illness will result, and if it does not always result (or if we cannot identify the class of individuals thus prone), then they are not pathogenic. We have met such formulations before (see our discussion of Agassi above, and the Section preceding this one).

The Humean concept of causation on which such an account is based depends on the identifiability of cause and effect as discrete events. But predictions deduced from a causal law are only supposed to hold if certain (often unspecified) conditions are present – and often scientists take an apparently refuted prediction to mean that a supposed causal mechanism has been *impeded*. Popper only partly eschews event language by preferring to speak of 'initial conditions' rather than 'causes', for this version of causality can still be described as the reduction of a process to its supposed elements: the succession of certain events by other events.[21] Popper argues (*L.Sc.D.*, p. 249) that we should not be dissuaded

---

[20] Reported in Barrett (1966). See p. 1 above.
[21] This form of reductionism is exemplified by Cioffi's account of the relationship between anamnesis and symptom dissolution.

from the search for 'pure' cases of a causal relationship. However, the very possibility of 'pure' cases rests on an assumption about the discrete nature of the elements whose relationship is in question. An experiment which attempts to isolate a relationship by holding constant other factors conceived to be relevant is investigating a *different* relationship from one which holds when other factors are present: there is no *prima facie* justification for assuming the first to be a 'pure' form of the second. For example, within the field of animal behaviour, attempts to isolate constituents of behaviour in the laboratory, however well established, are extremely difficult to relate to the animal's life activity in its usual habitat. Some psychologists have concluded that 'interaction' should constitute the subject of their study rather than be treated simply as a barrier to explanation. The impressive advances in developmental psycholinguistics of late have to a great extent involved going beyond the traditional 'event-language' of causality. For many workers in this field, for instance, a conception of structures of development has become theoretically crucial.

Causal explanation is explanatory not because it deduces predictions from causal laws, but when it is part of a theory which outlines the structural relationship between its facts. This relationship may be presented in a schematic form by a model, whether causal or otherwise. Theoretical constructs, by unifying and structuring the facts in a theory, contribute to the determination of their meaning and evidential status. Any philosophy of science which talks in terms of metaphysical and scientific elements and their demarcation *within* a scientific theory,[22] risks misrepresenting this relationship. This is the kind of mistake made by MacIntyre,[23] who argues that the descriptive and unobservable concepts of the unconscious and repression are logically independent of Freud's account of the formation of neurotic symptoms, which may, he thinks, be tested without accepting these theoretical constructs. He fails to realize that by specifying the place of neurotic symptoms and their formation in a model of psychic conflict Freud identifies them: this *involves* relating them to other diverse phenomena, such as parapraxes. Freud's method offers ways of investigating these further relationships. By fragmenting Freud's theory MacIntyre alters the meaning and diminishes the consequences of the abstracted relationships.

The unconscious and the associated concept of repression are the central unifying concepts of Freud's theory, and the model within which they are related to the facts of the theory centres around the dynamic

---

[22] As does Lakatos (1970).
[23] MacIntyre (1958), pp. 67–70.

conception of psychic conflict. The discovery of the resistance, an aspect of repression, was only made possible when Freud abandoned the hypnotic method, and this discovery permitted Freud to understand cures by catharsis *through* the light it cast on the limitations on their scope and permanence. Thus Freud's model of psychic conflict was based on, and constructed out of, continual observation and clinical practice. (Its successful application to dreams, for instance, *followed* its use in the treatment of neurotic patients.)

Freud's theory can be seen as extending the notion of action, by offering explanation in terms of motives and reasons in cases, such as dreams, where such accounts had been considered inappropriate. His explanation of the *genesis* of certain behaviour situates it in its experiential and intentional context and emphasizes the relevance of its social meaning and effect. In terms of the traditional philosophical distinction between causes and reasons such explanation, although it may be genetic (in its stress on the relevance of earlier experience) comes closer to what we may call a reason account than to a causal account. However, the cause–reason dichotomy must not be mechanically applied here, for methodological assumptions underlie it which must themselves be questioned.

Explanation in terms of reasons is often conceived of as rather like the Humean model of causal explanation. The agent's reason for acting in such and such a way, as expressed by him or imputed to him, *precedes* the action and can be described as *making* the agent behave as he does – this sort of formulation is guilty of lending spurious reality to the problem of whether and how reasons could be causes. In fact the reason–cause dichotomy is absurdly narrow. Its application is presumably not supposed to be limited to cases in which the agent has a definite experience of choosing, but to be relevant also to cases where behaviour was 'unthinking' and no reasons were formulated beforehand. In cases like these not every reason account of an action (whether offered by the agent or imputed to him) would be accepted as explanatory: it would be so only if it identified the relationship between the action and the agent's experiences and purposes. Identifying this relationship does not necessitate its expression in terms of a reason account: the reason is merely its subjective form. Thus Freud could use this sort of explanation even where the agent himself could offer no reasons for his action; or where other evidence of how the action related to his experiences and purposes was in conflict with the agent's expressed reasons. (This might be because he is unable to acknowledge his unconscious aims, and not all the experiential context of his action is available to his reflective awareness.) Discovering under which conditions evidence other than the agent's avowals should take precedence is part of the work of Freud's theory.

The main obstacle to the subsumption of reasons under causes (and support of the cause–reason dichotomy) is the notion of freedom. While such and such was a reason for *this* person, then, it might not have been to someone else, or to him on some other occasion – there is something *ad hoc*, it seems, about explanation in terms of reasons, which guarantees that we have a genuine ('free') action. MacIntyre writes:

To describe something, a belief or a piece of behaviour, as an example of wish-fulfilment is to discern a purpose in [it] . . . it is only when we state antecedent conditions given which the agent *could not but* seek gratification in *some such way* as this that we turn wish-fulfilment into a causal concept. So that Freud's ordinary concept of unconscious motive is both of cause behind and purpose in the neurotic conditions (MacIntyre, 1958, pp. 61–2, our emphasis).

MacIntyre is arguing that because of the element of compulsion, what seemed like a reason account in terms of intentions is at the same time a causal account, for the two have become conflated. Instead of critically examining the cause–reason distinction, which he accepts as a given, MacIntyre takes this as a criticism of Freud's theory. But, if it holds, this argument must also apply to everyday explanations of a similar form, which also seek to make actions intelligible by positing certain things about psychology (the *way* in which the agent structures his experience) and by situating his action in the context of his particular experiences. It may be that this context, *in conjunction with* the agent's purposes, limits what we now see as possible courses of action for him. This does not mean that our explanation has retrospectively negated the actor's 'free will', or that it must be couched in terms of a causal law. The action has been rendered intelligible, and this means simply that the explanation is *prima facie* adequate.

The cause–reason dichotomy counterposes 'freedom' of action to the 'compulsion' of causality, as we have seen in the above quotation. In so far as a causal law describes regularities, there is nothing compelling about it, as Hume himself argued. The idea of necessity derives rather from the place of causal laws in theories (the theoretical repercussions of a recognized counter-instance), and from the way in which causal relationships enter into our criteria for identifying objects. In any case, MacIntyre's inference – that if someone *cannot help* doing something, any explanation we offer of this must be causal, is an odd one, and one he fails to defend. 'He cannot help doing it' may have many meanings, and the constraints on the agent may be imposed on him in various ways, often with his agreement and participation. Freud is not saying that behaviour the actor cannot consciously control or understand is the same as behaviour which he can, or that unconscious motives are essentially like preconscious ones. He is, rather, saying something about the relation between them. That a symptom has a certain cultural meaning for the agent and for others, is relevant to its genesis; that someone is deliberately behaving in certain ways must enter into the explanation of why he compulsively behaves in other ways.

Individual differences had been an obstacle to the discovery of *causes* of such syndromes as hysteria. Freud's account, on the contrary, *focused* on the complex mutual interaction between individual and environment, structured in terms of a general model of mental processes. Once hysterical phenomena had been unified through the concept of repression, and a method informed by this concept had had some success, the very diversity of the sources of evidence for repression became a potential strength. On the one hand Freud's explanation of the neuroses was limited to the individual. He came to believe that the neuroses had no specific determinants, and in estimating the pathogenicity of an event for a particular person, Freud was concerned with its meaning *for that person*. (Someone else might experience an apparently similar event in a completely different way.) *But* Freud's explanation was also general, for 'among the tasks with which mental life has to deal, there are a few on which it can especially easily come to grief' (1940b [1938], xxiii, 184). Thus factors (such as habitual coitus interruptus) which make breakdown more likely by increasing the difficulty of the task the ego faces, tend to be pathogenic.

Another kind of generalization is possible to the extent that people share a common language and ways of life. Many of Freud's phylogenetic explanations are enabled to play the role they do in his theory by reference to symbols and stereotypes which are susceptible to cultural or sociological investigation. Freud often tended to underestimate social factors, although he suggests (op. cit., 190n) that the castration complex would not exist in the form he describes 'among peoples and in civilizations which do not suppress masturbation in children'. Someone might ask why the castration complex should exist in our society in cases where no castration threat has been made, and we would look for the explanation in, for example, the social structure of the family and the symbolic relationship between a man's sexual virility and his *social* masculine role. In this kind of way sociology could, to quote Cioffi, help us 'deal with the fact that it is regularly the father from whom castration is dreaded, although [it] is mostly the mother who utters the threat' (*E.B.S.*, p. 481).

Interpretations

The advance of Freudian theory has been to make available to systematic study a new area of inter-related phenomena. In this way Freud can be said to have discovered new facts. Many of the relevant phenomena, and even some of the relationships between them, had long been known in a way. Freud's achievement was to show the basic constitutive principles structuring this material, much of which had been written off as inexplicable or unimportant by contemporary scientists. He did this by a shift of attention, a new approach. For example, what had previously been thought of as gaps in memory (forgetting), Freud suggested was as significant as what was remembered, and could be explained in terms of the content of what was forgotten and its meaning for the person in question. What had previously been thought of as paradigmatically nonsensical and by definition unrelated to waking life (dreams), Freud made sense of by the use of a richer and extended concept of thought. While the extent of individual differences has been seen as the great stumbling block in the way of explaining neurotic symptoms, Freud showed that the content of those symptoms was related to the whole life experience of the persons having them.

The central advance of Freudian theory is to see previously inexplicable behaviour, symptoms, phantasies and dreams of the individual person as explicable *action*, attempts to communicate thoughts, and so on. The central concept which allows this theoretical advance is the concept of the unconscious.

The shift of attention necessary for this theoretical advance is (unsurprisingly) one of the elements of Freudian theory to which Cioffi objects most strongly. How, he asks, could the status of these phenomena as action be demonstrated?

Dora, Paul, etc., could no more *act* as if they had entertained the unconscious thoughts which figure in Freud's reconstructions and to which he attributes their symptoms, than Freud could have acted as if he had dreamt the dream of the Botanical Monograph. Such phenomena are intrinsically linguistic (*E.B.S.*, pp. 494–5).[24]

But, Cioffi goes on to ask, whether 'a belated avowal could transform a happening, like falling, say, into an action. Or a physiological event like menstruation into a performance?'

Action is more relevant here than avowals. While Dora, etc., could say

---

[24] Freud may be to blame here, for he does tend to give the impression that a correct interpretation is not a kind of place-holder for an unconscious thought, but a representation of its linguistic form: this further assumption is not required by the theory.

either that they had, or had not had, such and such unconscious thoughts, this does not help us assess the interpretation. As Freud (op. cit.) is careful to point out their 'yes' is just as irrelevant as their 'no'. What is relevant is (a) how strongly they react; (b) whether the interpretation soon results in fresh memories and other sorts of material relevant to this part of the analysis being brought by the patient; (c) its effects on the symptoms of the patient. An interpretation is not a translation which can be corrected with recourse to a dictionary and grammar book. It inserts itself into an active relationship, and appeals to the need for expression which produced the behaviour. It offers itself, in a way, as a replacement for the symptom or dream and has the inducement of carrying with it the analyst's promised support against possible anxiety consequent upon its recognition. According to Freudian theory, if it be a correct interpretation it will be resisted on the one hand and welcomed on the other.

If the analytic situation is such that the patient and analyst have some kind of transference relationship, an interpretation that is correct enough to express at least some part of the meaning of a piece of behaviour will evoke some response. Freud cites cases in his own case histories where an interpretation had to be discarded because the patient did not respond to it at all – neutrality on the part of the patient and no subsequent connections is, then, a criterion which must lead the analyst to reject an interpretation. If the behaviour is a symptom, it may change in nature or intensity, or vanish altogether, in response to a certain interpretation, or some other part of the patient's behaviour may alter in a way which can be shown to be connected. Freud's description of the Wolf Man case exemplifies this: although progress had been made in the analysis the patient's polite scepticism proved difficult to overcome, until Freud promised to cure his chronic constipation. At this the patient's scepticism became less polite and the conflict between resistance and the desire to get well intensified and 'his bowels started joining in the conversation' – the first sign of his recovery from this symptom. This happened after some years of analysis, during which the patient's intestinal condition had undergone no improvement.

The therapeutic practice of psychoanalysis is of central significance in the question of distinguishing between correct and incorrect interpretations, yet Cioffi refers to this practice only in asides, preferring to concentrate on such works as 'Leonardo', in which the preconditions for judging the correctness or otherwise of the interpretations offered are absent. Works such as these depend on the central body of psychoanalytic practice, and in the absence of analytic material in the true sense we can only say that they offer a possible account.

His tendency to concentrate on those of Freud's works which apply psycho-analytic theory rather than provide evidence for it leads Cioffi to emphasize one criterion for judging interpretations at the expense of others. This criterion is the requirement that an interpretation account for and link together as much as possible of what we know of the person's actions and experience. According to Cioffi this criterion reduces to a simple test by plausibility. This coherence method of judging interpretations is considered by Cioffi to be inferior to real hypothesis-testing, and, indeed, furnishes one of his reasons for distinguishing interpretations from genuinely empirical hypotheses. Cioffi's objections to this criterion cannot be very weighty, since he himself uses a plausibility criterion throughout to *attack* Freudian theory. Thus in one proffered schema of Freud's model of interpretation assessment (*E.B.S.*, p. 494) Cioffi articulates his *own* plausibility criterion: he suggests that perhaps for Freud 'arguments from independent probability and related considerations have no relevance', and clearly believes that they should have. The phrase 'independent probability' has a spuriously quantitative ring. But what can it mean here? Cioffi seems to want to reject the whole concept of the unconscious, claiming that our feeling that there is anything in it (note his own reliance on subjective factors) derives from an imperfect analogy with deliberate lying or omission. But if the unconscious is nonsense, how can such and such an unconscious process be more or less probable, or even more or less plausible? While Freudians can coherently talk about the plausibility of an interpretation *within the context of their theory*, the probability of the unconscious being inconsistent, for instance, which seems to worry Cioffi, can only be estimated in any quasi-quantitative sense within a theory which has a meaning for the concept of the unconscious. '*Independent* probability' is a figment of Cioffi's methodological imagination. It is no more than plausibility, and the claim that Freudian theory is implausible means only that Cioffi himself is unconvinced.

We have outlined some of the criteria by which psycho-analysis distinguishes between correct and incorrect interpretations within the analytic context. Besides the formal requirement that an interpretation account for and link together some of the material brought by the patient, it is also required to affect the further material which he brings. We must note that this kind of evidence is an index not so much of the correctness of the interpretation as of its therapeutic effectiveness *at that stage* in the analysis. For the interpretation to be effective it must be at least partly correct, but the reverse relation need not hold. Cioffi describes such a procedure (*E.B.S.*, p. 494) as using the changes within the analytic situation as symptoms of, rather than criteria for, the correctness of the interpretation. They are in fact both; that is to say, they are *evidence for* its correctness—a possibility which one who draws on Wittgenstein should admit.

Within the confines of this paper, we cannot discuss the nature of psycho-analytic therapy or the development of Freudian and post-Freudian theory. But the ways in which post-Freudian psycho-analysts have built on the advance involved in Freud's theory without accepting it as a whole demonstrate the possibility of disagreement about the evidence for such and such a mechanism or process, without its being necessary to break with Freud's methodology. Freud's views on the psychology of women, for example, have indeed been thought by many psycho-analysts, *from their experience* with children as well as adults to be inadequate to the extent of being wrong, and *within psycho-analysis* alternatives have been developed – something Cioffi completely ignores. Yet these analysts did not have to lay aside Freudian methodology to effect their revision, nor as a result of it were they committed to doing so.

Concluding statement

Current controversy in the philosophy of science has focused on the construction of scientific theories. Views of the nature of evidence for or against scientific theories and their components which reduce it to the occurrence of confirming or falsifying events, and see this single type of evidence as invariant for all scientific theories, have recently been subjected to radical critiques.[25] At their worst such views assimilate all explanation to prediction; such, we have argued, is Cioffi's position. This over-simplification of the ways in which components of scientific theories can be evaluated results from an over-simplified idea of their structure, according to which the function of theories is the production of hypotheses, and explanation consists in such production. In this article we have taken the position that such views preclude an understanding of Freudian theory. We have argued that facts are not automatically related to a theory or its components in a single unambiguous way. The implications of certain facts for a theory or parts of it have to be worked out. This process is an aspect of the discovery of the facts, since it establishes *what* is discovered. In this way the evaluation of components of scientific theories is one of the activities of the theories in question, and

[25] See Harré (1970), especially ch. 1.

may take many related forms, of which the falsificationist view is an essentialist travesty.[26]

References

Agassi, J. (1964). In *The Critical Approach to Science and Philosophy*, ed. M. Bunge, London: Free Press of Glencoe.

Barrett, C., ed. (1966). *Wittgenstein – Lectures and Conversations*, Oxford: Blackwell.

Canguilhem, G. (1968). *Etudes d'Histoire et de Philosophie des Sciences*, Paris: Librairie Philosophique J. Vrin.

Cioffi, F. (1970). In *Explanation in the Behavioural Sciences*, eds R. Berger and F. Cioffi, C.U.P.

Harré, R. (1970). *The Principles of Scientific Thinking*, London: Macmillan.

Hempel, C. G. (1968). In *The Philosophy of Science*, ed. P. H. Nidditch, O.U.P.

Kuhn, T. S. (1970). 'The Structure of Scientific Revolutions', *International Encyclopaedia of Unified Science*, Vol. 2, University of Chicago Pr.

Lecourt, G. (1970). *L'Epistemologie historique de Gaston Bachelard*. Paris: Vrin.

Lakatos, I. (1970). In *Criticism and the Growth of Knowledge*, eds I. Lakatos, and A. Musgrave, C.U.P.

MacIntyre, A. C. (1958). *The Unconscious*, London: Routledge.

Parsons, T. (1968). *The Structure of Social Action*, New York: Free Press of Glencoe.

Popper, K. R. (1960). *The Logic of Scientific Discovery* (revised edn.), London: Hutchinson.

Popper, K. R. (1969). *Conjectures and Refutations* (3rd edn.), London: Routledge & Kegan Paul.

[26] This paper results from a Symposium on Scientific Methodology held in Durham in the summer of 1970. The preparation of the manuscript was supported by the A. J. Wheeler Research Fellowship held by N.H.F. in the University of Durham.

We are particularly grateful to the following people for their useful criticism: Peter Barham, Ben Brewster, Athar Hussain, Branka Magas, Sean Sayers, Michael Stant, Gareth Stedman-Jones, Irving Velody.

4

Freudian commonsense

ADAM MORTON

Diffused Freudianism Many of us take the fact that we have read, talked about, and reflected on Freud's writings to be a fairly important thing about us. We who have this as our only contact with psychoanalysis are often abashed in the face of real initiated analysed and analysing Freudians by the idea that our allegiance is just playful, just the half-hearted (head-hearted) manipulation of the terminology for the sake of intellectual fashion, without an appreciation of the depth of the responses that the *use* of the theory can produce, which give it its real meaning and significance. We are abashed in part by the justice of the accusation. There is a whole direction to Freudianism that we do not see, perhaps do not care to see.

There is also a side to things that we are *better* placed to see. For good or for bad, a diluted influence of Freud has now permeated our age's conception of mind, of motive, action, and morality, as no psychological theory ever before has. It influences our attitudes to ourselves and others in ways that can be separated from our believing any particular theoretical assertions about causes of behaviour or psychological structure. It shapes the styles of explanation and attribution that we are prepared to understand. In this essay I want to do some work towards understanding how this can be, and describe some of the problems it produces, by concentrating on one part of our vernacular psychology, our ideas of character and personality.

Case histories Freud's case histories present one with an array of personalities, which one thinks of as one does of well-drawn figures from literature, or historical figures, or absent friends. (A little like all of these, and a little different.) One knows some aspect of what sort of a person Anna O, Dora, Hans, and so on, are. My impression is that other psychoanalytic writers rarely accomplish this; their cases are just cases. How does Freud do it?

I shall look particularly at the *Dora* and *Little Hans* cases.[1] Between

[1] Among Freud's works I shall refer only to (Dora) 'Fragment of an Analysis of a

60

1905 and 1910, between his discovery of the core of psychoanalysis and his later interest in psychological structures, Freud's writings are particularly relevant to the questions which I shall be concerned with. In the cases of *Dora* (1905) and *Hans* (1909) Freud works out in particular form ideas about personality which are treated in full generality in the 1905 *Three Essays on the Theory of Sexuality*. But in the case studies Freud also seems clearly aware of a problem quite distinct from the theoretical one of explaining the variety of human personalities, namely that of expressing this variety in terms that make them intelligible as personalities

Freud makes or encourages many perfectly commonsensical descriptions of his subjects. Dora is intelligent, choleric, inquisitive, sometimes coy, fairly conventional and also in a way sly and proud. She is not particularly 'neurotic' in manner, in the current sense of the word, in spite of her hysterical symptoms (which Freud tells us rather little about). We learn these things from the episodes in her life that Freud tells us, and from the manner rather than the content of the analytic sessions described for us. Much of what Freud wants to say in description of his subjects cannot be put so idiomatically. Dora is in the grip of layers of erotic feeling: a repressed but relatively recognizable attachment to Herr K, a more primitive fixation on her father, and at a level somewhere between these two a much more opaque attachment to Frau K. She brings to all of these an infantile sense of delight in evasion and a certain orality. The evidence for none of these more characteristically psychoanalytic attributions is incontrovertible, but they all rest on patterns of argument that are familiar from Freud's other work. Dora is also, to introduce a third category of ascription, somewhat afraid of learned men such as Freud, but fairly confident that quick wits and a gently confident assertion of her social prerogatives will see her through.

The case of little Hans could be described in very similar terms. I will not say anything about it until later on where I shall contrast it in some respects with that of Dora. In the Dora case we are given the first category of attributions, the intelligence and inquisitiveness and so on, just anecdotally, as I observed. The second category, the hidden structure of her acknowledged desires, is certainly not given us in anything like the same way. Nor have we anything like the same certainty that Dora *is*

Case of Hysteria' (1905e [1901], VII) (Hans) 'Analysis of a Phobia in a Five-Year-Old Boy', (1909b, X) and *Three Essays on the Theory of Sexuality*, (1905d, VII). I shall presuppose some knowledge of the contents of these. Since the *Dora* case was written largely in 1901, in what I consider Freud's earlier period, the interests I take him to be developing between 1905 and 1910 must be present earlier too. They are however less successfully dealt with in *Dora* than in *Hans*.

fixed upon Herr K, Frau K, and her father in precisely the way described. Freud may be wrong. But there are two different questions here. There is the conventional methodological question of whether on the evidence he presents he is entitled to make these claims. And there is the rather different question that interests me here. It is how Freud succeeds in giving us an impression of Dora's personality-in-depth, an intuitively graspable idea of how her desires are organized, which, justified or not, allows us to think we know about what sort of a person she is. Even if the descriptions and diagnoses Freud gives in his case studies are thoroughly mistaken, the fact that we understand the characterizations he offers (if we do understand them in anything like the way I think we do) shows something remarkable about us, and marks a crucial advance in our culture's resources for thinking of personality.

One typically Freudian device for connecting theoretical, diagnostic judgments and intuitive ones, which Freud makes remarkably little use of in his case studies, is the analysis of verbal slips and practical mistakes. For they are at the same time indices of the kind of state of mind that Freud postulates and actions whose significance is acknowledged by commonsense. Although the relevance of mistakes is ignored by pre-Freudian psychology and philosophy, it has always been a commonplace of everyday life that, e.g. to forget someone's name or their birthday can indicate some less than positive attitude to them, and that one's tongue may express desires one did not know one had. Every novelist knows and uses such evidence and Freud appeals to such literary precedents in several places in order to show that the significance of slips is something we have known all along, even if we have not often admitted the knowledge. And yet nothing important, I think, in any of Freud's famous cases depends on the significance of a mistake.[2] The reason for this is that Freud has other, further-reaching devices, which I cannot describe until I have said more about what I take to be Freud's way of conveying impressions of personality. And before I do that I shall have to say something, however inadequate, about how I take impressions of personality to work in everyday life. To do this I must leave Freud for a while.

γ-concepts I assume that there is something systematic about everyday discussion of mind and action, that behind it there is a vernacular psychology of some power and great flexibility. And although I am far from happy with the idea, I shall go along with the orthodox view that

---

[2] One exception is Dora's forgetting Herr K's birthday. Nothing in the analysis *depends* on this, but it is used in evidence.

the essential core of this commonsense psychology lies in the concepts of belief and desire, and their standard use in explaining while rationalizing an action, as something which the agent believes will lead to a desired end. These are propositions which it is far safer to assume than to defend. All I shall really need from them is some form of the vague idea that we have as part of our culture and condition a systematic approach to problems of explaining and describing each other, and some admission of the possibility that this framework may change in points of detail, perhaps in some structural respects, over time, and that its rightness is in the last analysis a matter of objective fact.

Patterns of explanation in terms of belief and desire need a lot of assistance to engage the particularities of the cases they are supposed to elucidate. Given a list of things believed and things desired – an extensive comprehensive list – what can we say about what the person may do? Almost nothing, since different people will do quite different things to achieve the same ends, and the same desires in different people will lead to different intentions, different goals for action being singled out as the ones to which others are subordinated. What can we say about the reasons why the person may have performed some action? Not much more, since any explanation is quite lacking in force until we have said something to make it reasonable that those were the desires that were acted on, and that those were the means adopted to achieve them. The most we can do is to rule out certain explanations as inapplicable, because the motivation or information they require is not present. Given a statement of a person's character, though, or mood or personality or emotion, belief and desire can be connected with action. If someone is unusually kind, to give a trivial example, it makes sense that they should act on their desire to telephone to warn a friend that there is a bore waiting outside his room, even at the expense of not getting to the pub before closing time.

One way of giving more information about someone, then, in terms of which one can see whether or not a particular explanation in terms of beliefs and desires applies, is through the use of a large category of everyday psychological terms which includes terms of character, personality, emotion, mood, and others less easily classified. I call the whole category that of γ-terms, for reasons outside this essay.[3] The range and character of the γ-terms available in a style of psychological explanation, a particular vernacular psychology, tells a lot about its underlying

---

[3] Because in my *Frames of Mind* (Clarendon Press, Oxford, 1980), vernacular psychology is taken to be centred on terms referring to actions (α), beliefs (β), desires (δ), and personality (γ).

assumptions about human nature and about the kinds of value it can conceive.

Character concepts are probably the most straightforward of all, and illustrate the general point. Courage, kindness, fortitude, meanness, duplicity, describe styles of action and of motivation. They are terms of vernacular psychology. They are also moral terms, in that one could not explain what they mean without at least alluding to a set of values and norms which in various ways they presuppose. Not long ago, the majority of terms which were available for describing the ways in which one person's propensities differ from another's were quasi-moral in the way terms of character typically are. Until recently one would get nowhere trying to register the differences between people that are essential to explaining their actions without the use of a system of terms which presupposes a complex and ultimately tendentious set of ideals (carrying unexamined ideas about class, gender, age, and no end of other things). It is not at all clear to me to what extent one could dissociate oneself from the ideas and still retain the explanatory resources that the system of concepts provided.

Character concepts are no longer central to our psychology. Several tremors in our way of thinking have upset their centrality, one of them due to the diffusion of psychoanalytical ideas into commonsense. One result is that we have now to a large extent replaced the traditional concepts of character with a class of more neutral concepts, which I shall call concepts of personality, for lack of a better term. We speak of people's intelligence, of their sociability, of their compulsiveness, without anything like a direct allusion to the right and the worthy. And even when our concepts are not as neutral as these, when we speak of shyness or aggressiveness or stubbornness, the normative element has retreated a long way, back from the content of the concept to that of various standard moral beliefs. (One could easily and intelligibly use the concept without having the beliefs.)

The contrast between terms of character and of personality, while it may serve to get the general idea across, is too crude either to throw much light on the shift in our repertoire of commonsense γ-concepts for which Freud's writings are in part responsible, or even to help explain the significance of the differences between different types of γ-concepts. In order to move the argument nearer to Freudian issues let me try to say what I take this shift to consist in, by means of an account of the contrasts that structure the γ-concepts.

Three contrasts will do for our purposes. First there is the extent to which the attribution of a term restricts either the motives that one can attribute to an agent or, contrastingly, the kind of motivational process that an agent's motives, whatever they may be, may initiate. The contrast between character and personality makes most sense in these terms. Terms of character pick out typical patterns of belief and, particularly, desire, and say: the agent acts as if his motives were restricted to those satisfying this pattern (satisfying these characteristics). The terms I have been calling terms of personality, though, tend to operate in a rather different way. They instead describe typical processes by which the whole extensive, usually inconsistent, body of an agent's motives resolves itself towards action. For example, compulsiveness amounts to a tendency for a chosen course of action to become autonomous, separated from its original motivation and carried out for its own sake, with all the attention and perseverance that the original reason for choosing it deserved, but eventually in complete independence of that original reason. Characterizations of personality say: this person works out his motives this way, whatever those motives may be. (One can thus see how it is that terms of personality are less suited than terms of character to carry presuppositions about what motives are unseemly.) Let me call states which are like states of character in this respect *restrictive*, and states which are like states of personality in this respect *non-restrictive*.

Another, independent, contrast between γ-terms lies in their permanence. Moods, for example, are transient, or at any rate it is perfectly intelligible for a mood to be ascribable for just a few minutes, and the typical period is a few hours. But states of character must hold for a few hours at the *very* minimum (though one could for example *act* with uncharacteristic honesty for just a few minutes) and the typical period is a matter of years.

The third contrast is in the extent to which an ascription of a γ-term requires the specification of an object for the state. Moods do not have to have objects, and neither do states of character, but emotions do, as to a lesser extent do passions. Or, more accurately, there is a contrast between particular terms of all these kinds over their need for objects, and emotions usually require objects while character concepts usually do not. (Sadness is a mood and requires no object, while hatred is an emotion and does require one. If one hates there is someone or something one hates, if one is sad one need not be sad about anything.[4]) Clearly the attachment of a state to its object is not a simple thing, and clearly the way in which an object is implicated affects the kind of qualification of one's motivation that can be adduced. But I can avoid these complica-

---

[4] I can't begin to refer to the literature on this. The importance of the contrast for my concerns was pointed out to me by Andrew Harrison, and I have benefited from reading a manuscript by Frances Berenson on the subject.

tions for my purposes here. Call a state *referential* if it needs an object, otherwise *non-referential*.

Now I can state what I take to be the heart of the transformation Freud has helped produce in vernacular psychology. Any system of γ-concepts will allow some combinations of these contrasts and disallow others. We once had a system which allowed terms for referential, non-restrictive, short-term states, for example many emotions. And among non-referential states it allowed terms for those which are restrictive and short-term, for example many moods, for those which are restrictive and long-term, for example attributes of character such as courage and kindness, and those which are non-restrictive and long-term, for example attributes of personality such as intelligence or sociability. But it did *not* allow terms for referential, non-restrictive, and long-term. In fact, it was at home with only a few of the possible combinations of contrasts. (Well, with four of the eight possible on my scheme. There are surely in reality far more basic contrasts, though.)

This restriction was not arbitrary. There is no point in having a γ-term unless there is some way of using it to qualify explanations. And this means having principles, general patterns of explanation, rules of thumb, platitudes, which connect the attribution of the term to beliefs, desires, and actions. The traditional vernacular psychology makes the connections in two standard ways. The attribution can state what kind of a person the agent is, understood as what kind of beliefs and desires they are likely to have. One says 'she's too kind (or, too taken with you) to want that' (and therefore there must be some other reason for her action.) Or the attribution can state what kinds of process or experience the agent is undergoing, in which case the agent's motives are not restricted but their mode of thought or motivation is further described. One says, 'He's too unhappy to think it through properly, so he'll probably do what she asks.' The first of these standard connections will involve restrictive terms, typically long-term restrictive terms, such as those of character or attitude. And the second of them will involve short-term non-restrictive terms.

Once one has connections of these two kinds as part of a vernacular psychology, one can get along fairly well without any long-term referential terms, as long as one supposes that whenever a referential state, for example, love, is clearly relevant to the manner in which motivation proceeds, there must be characteristic feelings, for example, the feelings of love, which perturb one's reasoning in the required ways. And there is no need for short-term non-referential, restrictive terms, as long as one supposes that any merely passing constraint on one's motives must be a reaction to some particular feature of one's situation. These suppositions can clearly coexist comfortably with 'Cartesian' views of self-knowledge and 'empiricist' views of the content of the mind, both of which seem not long ago to have had a commonsensical quality that is now hard to recapture.

The resulting scheme is simple and efficient. At the heart of it is an easy pattern which captures all the obvious phenomenological facts and provides a battery of terms to qualify explanations-by-motive, without requiring its users to keep in mind all the possible combinations of contrasts. It looks like this

attitudes: referential, restrictive, long-term	character: non-referential, restrictive, long-term
emotions: referential, restrictive, short-term	feelings: (moods, 'states') non-referential, non-restrictive, short-term

In learning a vocabulary of γ-concepts that fits into such a scheme one has come very close to accepting a metaphysics of mind.[5] For one is implicitly dividing the qualifications of the mind (apart from beliefs and desires) into deep but passing feelings – factors which affect one's mental workings but neither persist nor bear intentional relations to the environment – and more permanent or referential factors which achieve their affects more shallowly, simply by restricting one's motives. No doubt sophisticated explainers have never allowed themselves to be tied too fixedly to any such simple scheme. Improved descriptions of any particular case must often have appealed to the full range of contrasts underlying this simple core. And a number of particular states, includ-

---

[5] There could be even simpler schemes. No doubt the psychology presented in sagas and myths seems simpler, if one sees only the structure that corresponds to parts of ours. And it is evident that even our system of γ-concepts does not really fit either this pattern or the more capacious one I describe below. They are both approximations to a system which is itself more a fixed point to improvise around than a definite limit to our thinking. A better approximation would surely not treat the restrictive–non-restrictive contrast as basic. For there are no doubt essentially different ways in which non-restrictive states can qualify reasoning and motivational processes. I would expect a better classification to take into account (a) the ways in which terms in one category ascribe dispositions to exhibit states described by terms in another category, and (b) the ways in which terms in different categories entail different conceptual clothings for the contents of beliefs and desires. Contrast, for example, perseverance and compulsiveness. Perseverance, against all I say in this paper, is a thoroughly traditional concept which yet fits in my 'personality' pigeonhole. A newcomer like compulsiveness contrasts with it in describing ways in which a desire generates quite unrelated other desires, and in describing characteristic ways in which the agent conceives of (conceptualizes, symbolizes) things.

ing quite unproblematic ones such as impulsiveness and eternally upsetting ones like love and hate, must have always threatened to challenge the limitation of non-restrictive states to the short-term and non-referential. I don't think we find a real category of concepts of personality, of long-term non-restrictive terms, until very recently, though. Freud contributed to this change in two ways. He introduced a category of terms, for example the personality-types associated with the stages of psychosexual development, which qualify people's ways of thinking fairly permanently without restricting their motives, and which are not associated in any direct way with characteristic feelings. The category of (non-referential) long-term non-restrictive terms thus becomes independent of any connection with the category of feeling. Freud also introduced a way of attributing long-term relational states, typically erotically charged attitudes towards particular people, whose influence on an agent's motivation does not depend on their restriction of his motives (or on their production of short-term states). As a result, we get a nice symmetrical arrangement like this.

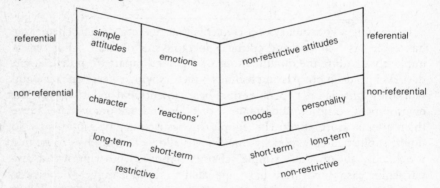

The categories of feeling and character cease to have any particular importance. Much of the category of feeling becomes redundant.[6] Some of the reasons why Freud is able to reorganize the γ-concepts in this way are clear enough. The contrasts on which the new arrangement depends are implicitly present in the older vernacular. I have yet to make it plausible that he does give us an idea of a vernacular, as opposed to a theory, that contrasts its concepts in this way, though I have argued that Freud does in some way give us new intuitive resources for imagining people's personalities. And the theory in which Freud embeds the new concepts, the 1905 theory of psycho-sexual development, does require

[6] Because long-term states no longer need a short-term tie to motivation. Note that one can misunderstand what's happening and interpret the states we can now refer to as new kinds of feeling. That makes psychobabble.

that they have the right properties to take their places in this quasi-vernacular arrangement. Using a term in the context of a scientific theory is evidently a very different thing from using it in everyday contexts of description and imagination, but it is also evident that the terms of that theory have found their way into our ordinary talk. And although most of those who describe their orderly parents as compulsive (I've heard a sitting room described, quite innocently, as 'anal') or who discuss sexual preference in terms of object choice have no sense of Freud's real theory, their use of these terms is often perfectly accurate. It is prompted by the right kinds of behaviour and traceable to the right sort of cause as lying behind them.

Hans and Dora Freud can give senses to long-term referential personality terms because he introduces them in the context of a theory, which brings a new flexibility into the relation between mental states and their objects. Freud introduced the idea of a state with a movable object. A state, he supposes, speaking explicitly of desire but clearly by implication of other states too, can have as its *aim* a fixed function in a person's mental economy and as its *object* whatever at the moment serves when taken *as* object to satisfy that function. I need not spell this out in detail because he does it perfectly clearly himself, and I have elsewhere tried to put the idea into what seems to me the right philosophical context.[7] The importance of the innovation for the attribution of personality terms is twofold. On the one hand, aims that can stay constant through variations in a person's situation and attitudes and can yet be indexed, kept track of, by reference to actual objective objects in the person's surroundings, will clearly provide a way of describing profound and individual characteristics of people in terms of much more accessible things, their behaviour and the objects it is directed at. One can refer to the oral fixation revealed in *this* person by *this* behaviour to *this* object (and *not* to 'orality' as a single explanatory property). And on the other hand, once one sees in this way that states of mind can be permanent, non-restrictive and object-directed, one begins to treat other attributes, particularly states such as love and hate which obviously reveal the characteristic working of a person's motivation, as having some of the features of the technically psycho-analytic attributes.

We don't have a duality of aim and object in commonsense, though, and yet we do now have γ-concepts which are long-term, non-restrictive and referential. Or rather, we struggle to express opinions that seem to require terms for such concepts and sometimes we succeed. Freud's success is mixed, I think. It seems to me that Freud tells the Hans case in

[7] In chapter 5 of *Frames of Mind*.

such a way that a good impression of Hans, and even some of the content of the Freudian aetiology of his phobia, is independent of much understanding of psychoanalytic theory. And I think that the Dora case is in these terms much less successful.

Consider again what we learn about little Hans. Besides the evident commonsense attributes (liveliness, curiosity, irrepressibility), and the characteristically psychoanalytic ones (the classical oedipal desires, the anal sexuality), we are shown a remarkable middle level of attribution. A straightforward example is Hans' infantile fickleness; a series of different people (sometimes adult, sometimes children) succeed one another as objects of his love. There is nothing striking about just this, but then Freud persuades us that it is the same affection that each of these people is the object of. He does so by bringing out constancies in the words and images and actions that express the fastening of Hans' affection on these successive objects. They are thought of as possessed by him in the way that things one has created or imagined could be; they are loved partly in appreciation of their simply being alive, as symbolized by the sometimes mistaken bestowing of a penis. This idea of a passion with a shifting argument place is completely at home in neither ordinary turn-of-the-century vernacular psychology nor technical psychoanalytic theory. It is delicately in between, functioning like a technical term and intelligible in the manner of a vernacular one.

Consider what we learn about Hans' attachment to his father. Working quite commonsensically, simply from his actions, we can see that he is often annoyed with him, usually playfully affectionate, and throughout deeply admiring of and attached to him. The theory that Freud brings to bear on the case does indeed go some way to explaining how this admiration and attachment work and how they are consistent with the episodes of annoyance and with a continued tone of slightly testy resentment. More to the point, though, the way in which Freud applies the theory gives us some idea of how to expand commonsense so as to obtain an intuitive description of Hans' ambivalence. Ambivalence, in fact, has become a term of psychological commonsense, without being too drastically debased from its theoretical meaning. Ambivalence is not intelligible, though, except in terms of persisting non-restrictive attitudes. For the *feelings* of love and hate only appear one at a time, though each attitude persists even while the other is being manifested.[8] In fact, it is essential to ambivalence that the short-term manifestations on which

[8] Patricia S. Greenspan, in 'A Case of Mixed Feelings: Ambivalence and the Logic of Emotion' in *Explaining Emotions*, ed. A. O. Rorty (University of California Press, Berkeley, 1980) points out that in earlier writers like Spinoza ambivalence is only understood as fluctuation of feeling.

introspective self-knowledge is based are not sufficient for its attribution (at least by the person exhibiting it). Or, to put the point differently, in introducing the idea of ambivalence into our vernacular we are deepening our concepts of love and hate. They become more intensional; one loves a person under one description and hates that same person under another. Once we allow ourselves this we can say more, in an untheoretical way, about the character of a particular person's ambivalence.

Hans' ambivalence seems to me intelligible as follows. He is an irrepressible, quick-witted child (Freud: a 'self-assured', 'funny little fellow'), confident, at first at any rate, in his ability to work his way out of situations. He takes the very immediate facts of his five-year-old world without much complaint, assuming that they do not threaten or constrain him in any too vital a way, and assuming that his imagination of unobvious realities is as good as anyone's. His father is a partner in all this, senior and exemplary in strength and knowledge but no threat in social manoeuvring, if confrontation is avoided. See the ease and confidence with which (later in the story, but retaining the earlier manner) Hans catches the contradictions in his father's stories of how God and the stork co-operate to deliver babies, and the finesse with which he cites 'the Professor's' authority to undercut his father's clumsy moralizing, and the wonderfully subtle way he expresses his contempt for his father's reluctance to tell him all he knows about human birth, by alluding back to the images of an earlier conversation when his father was being similarly pointlessly reluctant. The simple part of the ambivalence, then, has little more than a constant amiable and awe-filled respect for father, which can generate anger when the father is being uncooperative and can generate affection when he is being agreeable. This becomes more complicated, though, when, beginning with the birth of his sister, he begins to understand that his parents have knowledge of mysteries about which he can only phantasize, and that some of this knowledge is vital, concerning birth and growth and threatening pain. His accommodation with his parents is upset by this. Perhaps his father is not just a powerful comrade in ignorance; perhaps he knows or intends things dangerous to the future of Hans. (Perhaps he even has the knowledge and power of Herr Reisenbickler, the landlord.) Various graphic dangers have to be disarmed in his dreams. From the earlier stable ambivalence he moves to an unstable one. Now the constant attitude to his father is one of wary respect, which can turn into real love (though his father, having misread Freud, won't believe it) when his father is protecting him or initiating him into mysteries that will some day be at his disposal too, and which can turn into enmity when his father is the agent of forces that can upset his infantile contentment, in particular, his closeness to his mother.

If this is the character of his anxiety, then the very general character of his symptoms falls into place. He wants to stay near the safe and familiar, and avoid anything that might lead him to treacherous mysteries. To say this is of course not to characterize his symptoms in any detail, or to say anything at all about their particular causes, or anything at all about what might alleviate them. Freud's ideas about these must come from his theory, not from the evocativeness of his descriptions.

This is how I read Freud's depiction of little Hans. It does not matter much that other readings are plausible, or that it may be just false of the actual child. The important point is the possibility of a vernacular description of a person's attitudes and motives that captures some of the sense of a psychoanalytic treatment of the behaviour that prompts their assumption. The untheoretical description has many and obvious limitations, but it can sometimes be seen to be true or false just by looking, and it can sometimes allow everyday imagination to tell one what it might be like to satisfy the description.

The case of Dora is harder to handle along these lines. Her attitude to Herr K is indeed ambivalent; it's downright fickle. (Though he seems a charmingly untrustworthy character to whom fickleness is possibly the best response.) And her attitudes to other people, to her father and to Frau K, have the same inconstancy to them. Yet when we look for the constancies underlying these shifting attitudes, we can only find things we need the theory to express, and they are somehow hard to handle in any but a completely theoretical way. The connections between the theoretical and the intuitive seem rather thin here, and one is left with a very incomplete idea of what it is like to be Dora.

She can be fierce, but the connections between this obvious trait and the character of her infantile sadism are just not drawn. Freud tells us that in the second dream 'cruel and sadistic' tendencies find satisfaction, but this judgment depends delicately on the dream's associations and on Freud's intuitions and, more to my point, it reveals no links between the material associated with the dream and the content of the incidents revealing her fierceness (or her pride, her reticence – any of the traits one might expect a connection with). Her fixation on Herr K is long-standing and takes different forms, from sentimental affection to protestations of hostility, and just here one would expect some grasp of the constant themes underlying the varying postures. And one would expect that these themes would trace her attachment to Herr K to her attachments to earlier objects of love, such as her parents, to make sense of the continuing disturbance he caused in her. But we are disappointed. Definite themes of her sexual life emerge, and their connections with infantile oral pleasures begin to become clear, yet this is somehow no help in telling us how her attitude to Herr K is constituted, or even how all this primal material translates into tendencies and styles of liking and disliking.

This is not to say that the case is a failure. Freud's aim in both these cases was first of all simply to produce the material he had elicited and to argue for its relevance to the clinical situation. Secondary to that was the exact aetiology. And even further from his aim was the drawing of intuitive pictures or the expansion of the resources of commonsense. And even in this last respect, he does not do nothing. He gives us glimpses of the infantile desires and attachments that colour her conscious attitudes, and he depicts in conventional terms the manner of the woman, the impression she makes on him, and the atmosphere of the analytic sessions. The failing is that he cannot bring these two, the infantile associations and the adult character, convincingly together. And this is hardly surprising. In the first place, the analysis was broken off just as basic connections were promising to emerge. And in the second place, drawing connections between the theoretical and the intuitive would in this case involve finding expression for very primitive fixations concerned with the establishment of gender and choice of object. Finding a graspable description of what it is to become a man or a woman is something that the whole culture flounders after. The mind that wants description in the Dora case is *younger* than that described in the case of little Hans.

How theory diffuses   How can psychological theory affect the attributions and explanations we make in everyday life? I have described three ways in which psychoanalytic theory affects the vernacular view of mind. First, it affects the range and arrangement of concepts that we can allow into common descriptions. I tried to describe one such effect with respect to what I called γ-terms, the licensing of long-term referential and motivational states. This effect of theory on practice can be quite invisible, since it need not require any injection of typically theoretical vocabulary into common talk. Rather, the relations between terms we already have, and the senses they may bear, is re-thought. This may open up room for entirely new terms, but they do not have to be drawn from the theory whose examples set off the changes. The second effect of psychoanalysis on commonsense is to encourage us to improvise non-exotic analogies of the duality between aim and object. And the third is to lead us to try to capture with the details of our descriptions the symbolic content of the unity that can underlie a person's changing attitudes to an object. These are clearly not the only systematic effects of Freudian theory on vernacular psychology, but they all stem from the same stage in the development of Freud's ideas, and they all reveal as much about commonsense as they do about psychoanalysis.

Psychoanalysis is unusually sensitive to questions of its relation to vernacular ideas, since its hypotheses concern in part the constructions people put on their own and others' actions and its practical import concerns in part the kind of reconstruction people should be led to about their motives and those of others. It should matter, then, what psychological constructions people are actually capable of manipulating in any but the most abstract way. If we want to understand what the possibilities and limits are here, what construals of our motivation we can and cannot see ourselves through, we soon come to a point beyond which philosophical argument is too weak a tool. Only a real empirical social psychology can uncover the structure of everyday thought about mind, and the limits of our ability to imagine personalities. Lacking the science, one is forced to proceed as I have done, simply by looking at cases in which a description of motivation is offered, and presenting one's judgment, as a reflective user of ordinary modes of explanation and imagination, about the extent to which the description succeeds.[9]

[9] Peter Alexander and Andrew Harrison helped me with an ancestor of this paper, Naomi Scheman pointed out several flaws in the penultimate draft, and Flint Schier prompted some last-minute back-pedalling.

5

Disposition and memory[*]

STUART HAMPSHIRE

Preface (1973)

This lecture can be attached to a specific text within Freud's works. *Inhibitions, Symptoms and Anxiety* and *New Introductory Lectures* were two works to which I had been paying special attention while I was writing the Ernest Jones lecture. The lecture purposely avoids any mention of repression; the word nowhere occurs in it. Yet Freud's theory of repression was its starting point. The account that I at that time planned to give of mental dispositions, quite independently of Freud, required a theory of inhibition and of repression. At the same time I found an uncertainty, an apparent hesitation between two distinct views, in Freud's theory of repression. On one view repression of libidinal energies is the universal condition of learning and of conscious, rational planning, and even of the power of normal human thought. On another view repression is represented as the necessary cost of that renunciation of instinctual drives which our civilization demands; the implication is that much of the cost in neurosis may be controllable, and that repression need not be so severe and harmful as it has been. Also, there seemed to be in Freud more than one theory of the relation of anxiety to repression. In *Inhibitions, Symptoms and Anxiety* Freud wrote: 'It was anxiety which produced repression and not, as I formerly believed, repression which produced anxiety.'[1] I was puzzled by these changes, which have consequences for the philosophy of mind.

I now think that the lecture gives too simple an account of the development of secondary dispositions, and of character traits, and of the inhibition of impulses in the process of growing up. I assume here that the unconscious mind develops only from the inhibition of behaviour and that it has no independent nature. I now think, quite independently of

[*] This essay is a revised version of the paper originally given as the Ernest Jones lecture, delivered before the British Psycho-analytical Association on June 15, 1960. The original version was printed in the *International Journal of Psycho-Analysis* 43, pt. 1 (1962), 59–68. Printed by kind permission of the author and the editor of the journal.
[1] 1926d, XX, 108–9.

Freud's theories, that our beliefs and propositional attitudes generally can only be explained by reference to a great variety of unconscious thoughts which constitute the background of our conscious reasoning. The development of secondary dispositions, from childhood onwards, has to be interpreted also as the establishment of memories and fantasies which govern conduct directly, even though the thought may be pre-logical and comparatively unstructured and not easily expressed in words. The anxiety that attaches to threatening and painful thoughts, the repression of them, and the defences against them that are elaborated in conscious attitudes and beliefs, have to be acknowledged as psychical realities, which may or may not have a full and detailed expression in behaviour. I would therefore now qualify the argument of the following pages. Certainly there is a range of dispositions formed as residues of inhibited behaviour, and their expressions are legible for this reason. But these dispositions are further differentiated by thoughts and fantasies which do not have an immediate expression in some corresponding pattern of behaviour.

That much of our thought is not conscious thought, and that be-haviour by itself cannot reveal the specific detail of the thought from which it issues and which it expresses, are conclusions that are scarcely acceptable within an empiricist theory of knowledge. It now seems to me certain that the theory of knowledge has to accommodate the discovery, and the bringing to consciousness, of thoughts which the subject has not known to be his, and which another person usually can only precariously infer from the most indirect evidence.

It is natural to begin with the assumption that infants, like the higher animals, exhibit for our inspection definitely discriminable patterns of behaviour and that at the very beginning they exhibit no powers that are distinctively mental for our easy discrimination, beyond and behind these patterns of behaviour. As young children learn to communicate, and learn routines of demand and response, and as they finally learn to communicate freely in a language, the notion of the mental states that lie *behind* their behaviour and expression, as something distinguishable from them, becomes more and more definitely applicable to them. Part of the process of becoming more and more adult, and of mental develop-ment itself, is the process of learning to inhibit and to control inclina-tions. There is a primary sense of disposition, disposition in the sense of inclination, typically applied to persons rather than to physical objects: the sense in which I may report that I was at a certain moment disposed or inclined to laugh or to cry. A disposition in this sense is something that may occur at a particular moment, may be felt, may be disclosed, and may be inhibited or indulged. When children learn in relations with others to control their own behaviour at will, they will sometimes be in the position of being inclined to do something and yet will refrain from doing it. Concurrently, or a little later, they are also learning to express their inclinations in words, and are learning to identify things and persons and actions as having certain names, or as satisfying certain descriptions. They thereby arrive at the position of often knowing what it is they want, or are inclined, to do, in the sense of being able to say and to think what it is that they want or are inclined to do. They are able to identify their wants and inclinations as directed towards this or that object, or kind of object. The power to identify and declare one's wants and inclinations necessarily brings with it an extension of the range of these wants. Not only is the subject able to discriminate specifically the objects of his inclinations, but also his inclinations can be directed towards objects that are not immediately present to him, and that are not even causally connected with anything present to him. Finally, he acquires, together with the power to name and to describe, the power to place the objects of his inclinations in a clearly identified future, and of his wishes also in a clearly identified past. To learn the use of concepts is, among other things, to be able to give a definite ordering to one's experiences in time. A creature who uses language is no longer confined to an undiscriminated present in the direction of his inclinations and in the objects of his desires.

All this happens to a child in a social context, in primitive dealings with other people. From the beginning he is responding to the meaningful gestures of others. He very soon finds himself in a social world: that is to say, he finds himself learning to observe conventions and rules that conflict with his instinctual needs, and to observe the rules *as* rules. He gradually learns, largely by imitation, routines of behaviour, and he learns also the names and proper descriptions of these routines. Thereafter his inhibition of his inclinations is to be distinguished from the inhibition of a trained animal: of a dog trained to restrain its natural inclination to bite something. Because the child may know what it is he is inclined to do, the question of whether he will do it comes up as a question for him to decide. He may *decide* to restrain his inclination to do something, in a sense of 'decide' that is not applicable to an animal, which is not a potential language-user. Whether we say that the deliberate and self-conscious inhibition of an inclination by a human being is an inhibition in a different sense, a sense not applicable to animals, is a philosophical issue that need not detain us here. Must we recognize a difference of sense when there is a difference in the method of verification attached to a context transferred from its original context? I

77

think not. But whatever answer philosophers may give to this question, it is obvious that we can give a clear sense to the inclinations that lie *behind* a creature's behaviour, when that creature can report that it is, or was, inclined to do something and that it restrained its inclination. An animal which cannot use a language may be trained not to do that which it would naturally do. But that it was on a particular occasion inclined to bark or to bite, although owing to its training it did not in fact do so, must be shown in its behaviour, if it is to have sense at all. One must see it behaving in a constrained way, just as when it is frightened one must see it behaving in a frightened way. (I over-simplify, but broadly this is so.) The inclinations that lie behind the behaviour, the extra dimension that is gradually added to a human being as he grows up to be a language-user, depend for the possibility of their existence on his ability to recognize them as being what they are. This is not only because his disclosures are in the last resort necessary to the confirmation of the existence of the inclination; but also because the action of inhibiting, as an action of his, requires that he recognize his inclination as an inclination of a certain kind.

It will be evident that I am representing a human being's learning of a language as at the same time the acquisition of inclinations which he may on any occasion choose to realize or to inhibit. His full inner life begins with this power of intentional inhibition. To describe the development of conscious emotion in a very simplified form: a creature attacked becomes frightened or angry in the sense that it perceptibly behaves in the way that we would specify if we were asked for the natural response to attack – that is, by flight or counter-attack. At the next stage of mental development away from the primitive reaction, the behaviour typical of anger – i.e. aggression – may be inhibited, and only the physiognomy, or expression, that normally accompanies the behaviour may remain. The important point is that we know that his expression is an expression of anger because we recognize it as the abstracted residue of aggressive behaviour; it is this aggressive behaviour at its vanishing point. At the third stage of inhibition, even this remaining natural expression of anger may be intentionally controlled; perhaps because it is recognized to be a sign of anger that others can interpret as such. When this stage of interiorization is reached, the natural expression of anger may be used intentionally as a sign in letting others know that one is angry. If there is the power deliberately to inhibit the expression, there is also the power to assume the expression, as a gesture, as a means of communication, and in deceit, mimicry and play; or at least the idea of assuming the expression must be present to a man's mind as a possibility, if the habit of concealing has once been acquired.

Part of that which remains as a residue, when both the behaviour and the physiognomy primitively associated with anger are controlled, is the mere feeling as a state of consciousness, the inner perturbation, the affect by itself. It is 'inner' in the sense that nothing of the anger remains to be perceived by an observer. If an observer is ever to know that the subject is angry, he must primarily rely on the subject's avowal of those inclinations, or upon some inference from the situation and from its correlation with these commonly disclosed inclinations. Plainly there will still be many occasions when the inhibition of the natural expression of the anger is incomplete and only partially successful, and when sufficient signs remain as the basis for an inference, or as confirmation of the sincerity of an avowal. On the border line of these two stages of inhibition there will be many impure cases – of angry behaviour half controlled, or of the physiognomy of anger just showing through, in spite of an effort to suppress it. The pure case of mere inclination, as a state of consciousness, with every natural expression of it suppressed, certainly exists; and it is the interesting case, as being part of the pattern of inner, unseen mental states, and of the difficulty, or, as some philosophers have thought, impossibility, of inter-subjective descriptions of them.

A man who feels angry, while concealing every overt sign of his inner perturbation, may not need to exercise his will in the act of concealment. The restraint may already be a habit, natural to him as a civilized man. But the habit of intentional inhibition has been acquired during his lifetime, and acquired gradually as part of the observation of social convention. If he is perturbed in the presence of an attacker, he knows, in a simple case, whether he has the disposition to counter-attack or to escape or both. Therefore he knows, in very simple cases and at a superficial level, whether his excitement is anger or fear, or a mixture of both. He does not have to learn to distinguish anger from fear, as a mere quality of feeling, in the way that he distinguishes one colour from another. He is aware of his own controlled inclination in the situation that confronts him. He feels at once the inclination to flight or to counter-attack and he makes the counter-movement of restraint. If his feelings are complex, in the sense that he is, in the normal sense of these words, both frightened and angry at the same time, he has opposing inclinations towards flight and counter-attack; and these inclinations may again not be translated into spasmodic and interrupted actions, but rather remain as mere inclinations.

I am not of course denying that a man may experience confused and conflicting inclinations, which he may be unable clearly to distinguish and to describe. Nor am I denying that by some methods of analysis, anger and fear may perhaps be shown to be similar and related strategies in the defence of an organism against danger, the one a variant of the other. But it is enough that simple cases of identification of states of consciousness do occur: for it is on these that the whole psychological vocabulary is ultimately founded. We make a mistake if, as philosophers, we think of the emotions and sentiments as primarily something hidden in a man's consciousness and as linked by a contingent and causal relation to their outcome in behaviour: and this has been at least one prevailing picture in contemporary philosophy. The expression of a sentiment or emotion is not something that is extrinsic to the sentiment or emotion itself, as something that may or may not be added to it. On the contrary, that which we call the natural expression is originally constitutive of the sentiment or emotion itself, and may or may not be subtracted from it. This subtraction is the work of a convention-observing creature who already has an intentional control of his behaviour, and who can recognize his own inclinations while refusing to follow them. So much for the simple concept of primary dispositions, or inclinations in the conscious mind, as these are identified at the most superficial level.

You will perhaps at this stage want to ask for the justification of this, or for any other, simplified philosophical theory of the emotions in their relation to behaviour: is this *a priori* psychology, and, if not, what is its scientific basis? What is a philosopher's authority for distinguishing phases of human development beginning with primitive behavioural reactions and ending with inner concealed emotion? What is the purpose, and the criterion of success, in such an inquiry as this? It may seem that any such theory must be tested by the observation of children and by careful experiment; and yet this is not the work of philosophers. The answer is that these considerations about the emotions, which I have been putting before you, very dogmatically and in a very simplified form, are part of a more general, and of course disputable, theory of knowledge, a theory of how concepts must be originally acquired and applied in their normal contexts. I am, or I take myself to be, specifying the implications, and the method of confirmation, attached to uncriticized, ordinary statements about human emotions of the most rudimentary kind. This must be the starting point in prescribing the use of the vastly complex and derivative concepts of psycho-analysis. They also have been developed through many stages of complication and theory, from a rudimentary base in commonplace usage. We have to retrace the path back to this base if we are to understand how they are made up. We have first to see the rudimentary base clearly before us in some simple form, and then we can make the corrections to the commonplace conceptual scheme which the discoveries of psycho-analysis require.

This is the simplified picture of the concept of disposition, in the sense of inclination, which is, I think, the fundamental mental concept. For the conscious mind has to be conceived – at least in the present state of our knowledge – as, at least in part, a vastly complicated set of dispositions of different orders of complexity. I am speaking only of those dispositions that are simple feelings or affects, interpreted as inclinations to behave in certain more or less determinate ways in certain determinate circumstances. But now doubts arise, doubts that infect the whole study of the philosophy of mind at this time. Let it be admitted that it is characteristic of mental, as opposed to physical, concepts that the conditions of their application can only be understood if they are analysed genetically: that is, we need to trace the order in which their use is learnt in the history of any individual, beginning with the primitive concepts of sensation, desire and behaviour, concepts that are applicable also to creatures who are not potential language-users, and showing the use of the more distinctively mental concepts as developing from them in successive stages of interiorization. The use of concepts in communication is learnt in parallel with the development of corresponding powers of mind – the power to feel without acting and the power to think without saying. But 'in parallel' is an inadequate phrase here; for the one conditions, and makes possible, the other in a complex interaction. A child can have desires and intentions, fears and hopes, directed towards future events, only because he has the means of describing and identifying the remote objects that he desires, fears, or hopes. And the more finely discriminated states of consciousness – embarrassment rather than fear, shame rather than guilt, remorse rather than regret – can be attributed to him, only because his thought about himself in relation to external objects is of a degree of elaboration that allows him to decide which of these words accurately represents his state. The refined vocabulary of intentional states requires disclosures, not only of the inclinations, but also of the beliefs that enter into the definition of these states. A man whose state of mind is remorse must, of logical necessity, believe that he has done wrong, and this belief of his must be in principle, expressible.

One could summarize this double development – learning the use of mental concepts and simultaneously acquiring the corresponding powers of mind – as the development of intentional states. An intentional state, like an intentional action, is directed towards an object that is identified as the object of the state by the subject's conception of it as having a certain name, or as satisfying a certain description. Neither intentional states, in this sense of the phrase, nor intention in action, can significantly be attributed to creatures that are not language-users or potential

81

language-users. Such creatures may want and fear, pursue and avoid, certain objects, and we may inquire into, and see, the purposes of their behaviour. We may experimentally distinguish the objects of their desires and fears, their rages and their repugnances; and we may also by experiment distinguish those features of the objects that make them objects of desire and fear, of rage and repugnance. But the intentional object is identifiable, apart from the evidence of variations of behaviour, through the subject's expression of his thought of the object as having a certain name or as satisfying a certain description. With imputations and acknowledgments of beliefs and intentions, which are not simple inclinations to behave in certain ways, we therefore enter another phase of the mind's development.

The first difficulty can now be stated. Infants are born into a social world, and they sooner or later learn to inhibit their inclinations in accordance with social conventions. They learn also conventions of communication in responding to, and imitating, the meaningful gestures of adults. They gradually acquire an inner life of unexpressed feeling, which becomes more and more distinct from their overt behaviour; and they acquire intentions that point forward in time, remote from the observed present, and that may be left unrealized. But their earliest behaviour, and particularly their play, already foreshadows the added depth of concealed disposition, and inner emotion, that will come with their own later recognition of this depth. The signs are legible in their play, and in their ordinary behaviour, of that which is beyond and behind them – namely, dispositions and inclinations that are repressed, contained within the child's mind as affects or inner feelings. But the signs of inner feeling can never at this stage be intentional signs, and they still have to be read by someone other than the subjects themselves.

Neither philosophy nor psycho-analysis can be satisfied at this point. How much is included in the child's response to, and imitation of, the meaningful gestures of adults? Is the play of a child revealing of inhibited dispositions, and therefore of a depth of feeling, unrecognizable by the child itself, in a full sense of disposition and of 'feeling'? The answer to this last question is 'Yes'. But how can this be?

One possibility suggests itself. When a man looks back in memory, later intentional expressions of feeling may sometimes be associated with the memories of the earlier play. He finds a continuity from the earlier to the later, the continuity of a familiar pattern repeating itself. The inner inclination, which, as he is now persuaded, was originally expressed in his play, may later, preserved in unconscious memory, be expressed in intentional conduct; or it may at least be recognized as an inclination to behave in a certain way.

Disposition and memory

The essential problem of the unconscious mind is one of time and of memory. The child's responses to meaningful gestures, and his imitation of them, are the earliest phases of a continuous history, which ends with the use of language, and with those intentions directed towards the future, and those memories of past events, which depend on the use of concepts. The continuity of this history lies in the subject's memory. But the power of memory itself develops from a primitive and pre-conceptual form to an adult's fully articulated dating of his experience in a definite time-order. We may relapse, in dream and fantasy, into the pre-conceptual, childish world, in which past and present are not discriminated by the recognition of memories as memories. But still the power of conscious memory develops alongside these regressions. The word 'development', when we speak of the development of a mind or person, implies an order that is held together by manifold links of conscious, half-conscious and unconscious, memory. Looking back in conscious memory, a person can trace a continuity between that which he may with difficulty remember of his early fantasies and play, and his later self-conscious intentional states; and his earliest surviving conscious memories are still memories of a person already carrying a burden of memories, which are no longer available to him. Then, by analogy, it seems that the actions and experiences that he does still remember were originally desirable or repugnant to him partly at least because of memories of earlier experiences now beyond recall. In investigating the development of a man's body, we take it for granted that its earlier states, taken in conjunction with external factors, determine its later states, and its causal properties, in accordance with a great variety of exact and confirmable natural laws. In investigating the development of a man's inclinations, his emotional development, we cannot always, or even generally, in practice apply such a simple scheme of past states determining future dispositions, although the theoretical possibility is always open. It is a fact that the stored, and potentially available, but still unconscious, memories of the past are influencing present inclinations at any time. But what is contained in the word 'influencing' here? Is this a familiar causal relationship? I am inclined to think not.

Memory of one's own past may take several very different forms. In the most simple case, we may be aware of our memories as memories, and a memory of something that happened may be the fully conscious ground or reason for a present feeling, or for the behaviour that is the natural expression of this feeling. I am inclined to behave harshly towards him because I remember him harassing me. The word 'because' here introduces the reason for, and not only the cause of, my being inclined to behave in this way. But the memory of this same event in the past may have previously existed below the level of consciousness, ready to be evoked as a conscious memory, when the right questions are asked in the right conditions; but the memory is still unrecognized. As soon as the memory is called into consciousness as a memory, the question arises for me – Am I only behaving in this way, and do I only have this inclination, *because of* my memory of this past experience? This might perhaps begin as a causal question, as a matter of objective curiosity about psychology. But it immediately becomes an inquiry into the grounds of my behaviour: are they sufficient grounds or not? I had not realized the fact that I had unconsciously remembered this past experience. This fact – the fact that I had preserved this memory below the level of consciousness – becomes something that I must now take into account in considering my present inclinations. Is it reasonable that this past experience should influence my inclinations and actions in my present situation? Is there a relevant similarity, relevant, that is, to consciously recognized ends, which I can rationally acknowledge, between the past situation and my present situation? Once the question is raised, I may, or may not, consider the past experience relevant to my present situation. This is something that I must now decide for myself.

But at this point any true empiricist will ask – what is the sense of speaking of a memory of a past situation, a memory that exists below the level of consciousness, as a reason for present feeling and behaviour, potentially to be acknowledged as a reason? Is it not clearer, and more economical, in such cases to speak of the past event as the cause of the later feeling or behaviour without the interposition of memory at all? Is it not clearer to speak of memory only as a form of knowledge? And therefore always as conscious memory? I think that the evidence compels us to give the answer 'No' to each of these questions. The bringing to the surface of consciousness of an unconscious memory cannot be assimilated to the discovery of a causal connexion. These are discoveries of quite different kinds, and they require quite different methods of inquiry.

The whole issue of dispositions of the mind, contrasted with the causal properties of physical things, turns on this problem of how far the concept of memory is to be extended. Suppose we allow ourselves to speak of early satisfactions and frustrations of instinctual needs as stored in unconscious memory, and as constituting the reasons, or the motives, for varieties of conduct on many later occasions; then we have already begun to substitute a memory-relationship between past and present, peculiar to mental processes, in the place of the normal causal scheme of the natural scientist. This is exactly what Freud did, from the beginning, in his early studies of hysteria. Had he not taken a leap forward in his discoveries of clinical method, he might simply, as a good empiricist, have correlated early alleged sexual experiences, and then, later, the fantasies of such experiences, with subsequent hysterical disorders as causes to effects. He might have adhered to the normal scheme of natural law, without any doctrine of memory traces, interposed as a middle term. He would thereby have precluded himself from relating his method of treatment to his method of diagnosis within a single theory, each confirming the other. That which is elicited from the unconscious memory is the underlying motive of, or reason for, conduct and inclination; and a motive or reason, unlike a cause, is liable to be immediately acknowledged or repudiated as the real motive, and then judged and criticized by the subject as reasonable or unreasonable. The connexion between the now recalled, unconsciously remembered situation and the later behaviour symptom must be such as to make the behaviour intelligible to him. It is intelligible if it is a variant of behaviour that is normally adapted to the satisfaction of desires, and if this variation is explained as the superimposition of the unconsciously remembered situation on the present situation, then he understands the motive.

There are specifiable differences between the discovery of a correlation between two classes of events in a person's history, the occurrence of one determining, under statable conditions, the occurrence of the other, and the discovery that a memory of something in the past has been continuously the reason for inclination and conduct, unknown to the subject and without his having been aware of the memory as a memory. In the second case the influence of the past is something that may be recognized by the subject as the explanation of his inclination and conduct when he becomes aware of the memory as a memory; and to say that he recognizes the unconscious memory as the *explanation* of his inclination and conduct is not to attribute to him the discovery of a correlation between two classes of events. He finds that the now consciously remembered experience explains his inclination in the same sense that an observed feature of his present situation might explain his inclination; it is the reason of his being inclined to behave in a certain way. But the reason is not to be identified as an objectively observed feature of a present situation, but rather as a feature of a past situation always superimposed upon the realities of the present. When the repressed memory is revived, there is an instant recognition of the continuity and unbrokenness of the memory discernible in a consistent misreading of situations confronting him. When the memory is recognized as a memory, he recognizes also the consistent superimposition of the past upon the present. Then he finds that the now consciously remembered experience explains his inclination in the same way that an observed feature of his present situation might explain his inclination.

The only difference is that, unknown to himself, he has been trying to alter the past instead of acting on the present. It might be shown that there was no universal correlation between the unconsciously remembered event and the later behaviour; and still the subject might be sure that this unconscious memory contains the reason that explains why he, in this particular case, felt and acted as he did. And one of his reasons for being so sure might be that, with his now fully conscious memory of the past event, the inclination to behave and act in the same way returns to him with the same force, even though now, recognizing the past as past and unalterable, he restrains himself. Feeling himself inclined to respond to the fully conscious memory in the same way, he is aware, again by memory, that there is an old cycle repeating itself. Having the memory present to him as a memory, isolated from present realities, he recalls that, at every stage of the repeating cycle, this remembered situation was superimposed upon the present realities, however different, as he now realizes, they were.

The conclusion that, over almost the whole domain of conduct, there are unconscious motives of behaviour to be discovered follows from the hypothesis that there are countless memories below the level of consciousness waiting to be elicited. Where explanations in terms of instinctual needs and rational calculation are inadequate, we can look into the past for explanations of any individual's conduct and inclinations, without recourse to general propositions of natural law, which, in default of experiment, are not generally available. But motives, which explain behaviour and inclination, are one thing and intention is another. 'Intention' is the one concept that ought to be preserved free from any taint of the less-than-conscious. Its function, across the whole range of its applications, is to mark that kind of knowledge of what one is doing, and of what one is inclined to do, that is fully conscious and explicit. I have motives for doing things, or for feeling inclined to do things, and I may have purpose in doing things, without recognizing, and without being aware, that these are my motives and my purposes. When I come to recognize what my motives are, or were, or what my purposes are or were, I may certainly be surprised that these were in fact my motives. I may make a discovery. My motives are typically matters for investigation. But I do not investigate, and then discover, my intentions. I may indeed carry out an investigation to see whether my intentions have been consistently related, as they should be, to my actual conduct, externally regarded; and I may then discover, disagreeably, that in fact they have not. And then I need to look for underlying motives and memories, in order to explain this deviation.

If it is once accepted that there are countless unconscious memories of our past satisfactions and frustrations, we see many of our actions and inclinations as, at least in part, directed towards situations in the past, but superimposed on, and confused with, a present situation. When the memory is brought into consciousness, and we retrace the recurring cycle of motive and conduct back to this starting point, our action may appear as motivated by a desire to alter the past, even though the conscious intention was normally directed to the future. If I am convinced that I would not have formed the intention, had I not had the unconscious memory, I may for some purposes re-describe the conduct by reference to its motive rather than to the conscious intention. Then my conduct can be represented as an attempt to change the past, in defiance of the reality principle. For recognition of reality, as it affects behaviour, is recognition of the *present* situation as present, as opposed to the projection into the present situation of the objects of memory and fantasy. Its opposite, loss of the sense of the present, is a partial regression to the childish, pre-conceptual world in which the objects of conduct and feeling are disconnected from an objectively recognized and definite time-order. The ideally rational man would be constantly aware of all his memories as memories, in so far as they influenced his present conduct and inclinations. Correspondingly, his wishes would be attached to definite possibilities in a definite future, and would not be freely floating fantasies, without attachments to possible occasions. He would always distinguish his present situation from unconscious memories of the past projected upon, and obliterating, the present, and would find his motives for action, in satisfying his instinctual needs, within the objectively observed features of the situation, as he sees it now.

But this is an ideal of rationality that can never be attained – which is perhaps fortunate, since it would leave us without art, without dream or imagination, without likes and dislikes unconnected with instinctual needs, and indeed without any character at all as individuals. It can never be attained, because our secondary dispositions to behave in certain ways in certain situations, assimilated to unconsciously remembered primitive situations, are being formed, and superimposed upon each other, from the beginning of our life. I speak of 'secondary dispositions' here to distinguish dispositions, in the sense of character traits, from dispositions in the sense already mentioned – namely, inclinations to behave in a certain way on a specific occasion. The original formation of secondary dispositions can be traced back to unconscious memories of primitive satisfactions and frustrations of instinctual needs, modified by complicated and continuing processes of repression, projection, displacement, transference, and so on. Ideal rationality, defined as motivation by the recognized features of the present situation alone, together with instinctual drives, would impossibly require that no such dispositions should exist. Every memory of past satisfactions and frustrations would be present to my mind as a conscious memory, and therefore the relevance, for the satisfaction of my instinctual needs, of the past experience to the present situation would be objectively assessed. In fact I necessarily approach situations with already formed dispositions to respond in my conduct principally to those features of them which are easily associated with unconsciously remembered primitive situations. These dispositions, resting on the weight of my earliest memories, constitute my character as an individual. This may be strong or pliable, making me more or less impervious to changing external realities in my feeling and conduct.

It is now possible to see why the genetical method of explanation must lead to apparent paradoxes. In any individual mind, past frustrations and satisfactions, particularly in the earliest phases of the mind's continuous history, foreshadow the direction of later behaviour and inclinations. This foreshadowing is the other face of the fact that experiences that have once aroused strong inclinations are, in one way or another, remembered, if not consciously, then unconsciously. If they are repressed and unconsciously remembered, they remain as unrecognized motives, which explain a recurring inclination to behave in a characteristic way, in comparative independence of the unchanging external realities. A paradox arises when the arrow of historical explanation of a man's secondary dispositions is thought of as causal determination. If the determination were causal, it should allow prediction. But the determination claimed is only the fact that unconsciously remembered situations in the past supply unconscious motives for present conduct and inclination. This confusion has sometimes led interpreters of Freud to speak of retrospective causal explanation, which is a logical absurdity. Of motives it can indeed be said that they explain retrospectively, and that they do not provide a corresponding basis for prediction of future behaviour. In my stating that it was so-and-so that moved me to laugh or protest, I have not so far committed myself to any general proposition which justifies a prediction of my behaviour on future occasions; and least of all is there a basis for prediction when the transition may be made from an unconscious motive to the conscious recognition of it. Once the imposition of the unconsciously remembered past on the present is fully recognized, and the realities of the present situation are no longer consistently misperceived, the foundations of the secondary disposition have been loosened, and therefore the former character trait may be controllable. This character trait was after all something that I found myself to possess, and not something that I had chosen for myself. And now I may be for the first time in a position to choose, within the limits of the other secondary dispositions that constitute my character.

Something is always being added to the weight of motivating memories, both conscious and unconscious, and it is in practice, although not in theory, impossible to isolate the initial conditions on which scientific predictions could be based. It seems that, because of his vastly extended concept of memory, Freud is committed to the reverse of determinism in explaining any individual's emotional development, if determinism is associated with predictability. If we accept the hypothesis of total memory of past satisfactions and frustrations, it certainly follows that we could only approach complete explanations of inclination and behaviour in any individual case through an interminable analysis. The formation of secondary dispositions is a perpetual process, in which recurrent patterns of inclination and behaviour, originally motivated by memories of some primitive situation, are being at all times complicated by displacements and identifications, and by the stress of further frustrations of the dispositions themselves by external realities. And one of the effects and signs of stress, at primitive stages and later, is to make conscious recall more difficult. In any individual case we may be able, by successfully reviving memories, to travel backwards towards the first member of a series, along a series that recalls the recurring motive of inclination and behaviour at every stage. But we cannot infer from this history, or from any finite set of such histories, exactly how the series will be prolonged into the future, if it is prolonged. The vast and continuing accretions of repressed memory provide too many independent variables for any general law of cause and effect to be formulated and tested. We are left only with the recurring pattern itself as a mere tendency; that is, we are left with the old notion of character, of dispositions in the second sense. In extreme cases of illness, a man's character and secondary disposition, which represent attachment, through repressed memory, to the past, will be so strong that patterns of inclination and behaviour will be almost unvarying in changing situations. Selected features of these situations will be read always as changing symbols of emotionally charged features of his primitive past. Then indeed confident prediction may be possible. The cycle of inclination and overt behaviour will simply repeat itself. But when the second dispositions are only of normal (in the sense of 'average') strength, and motives for inclination and action can still be found in changing situations, the interaction between present and past, between fate and character, in forming feeling and behaviour becomes, on this hypothesis, too complicated for scientific prediction.

The second difficulty that we confronted was this: that we should not only attribute motives and purposes that have not been previously recognized by the subject himelf, but also that we should attribute them to children at a stage of development when they would have been incapable of formulating them, or of recognizing their existence in any way. Searching under guidance through repressed memories, and meeting resistance to their recall, an individual will find one of these recurring patterns of motive, of inclination and of behaviour in his history. The recurrence is itself at every stage an instance of unconscious remembering. If the hypothesis of total memory is correct, the earliest memories of the earliest instinctual needs, and of primitive frustrations of instinctual need, must be the terminus of explanation. This is the hard foundation to which we always return in explaining any individual's secondary dispositions. In order to assert the constancy of the motivation from its starting point in the individual's history, and simultaneously to show the motives for the repression of the relevant memory, the early formation of character traits is assimilated to the problem solving of an adult man. It is characteristic of properly causal explanations of mental processes that highly developed and rational processes are assimilated to the more primitive responses to stimulus; for specifically described behaviour has to be regularly correlated with specifically prescribed initial conditions. It is characteristic of an individual psychology based on the memory relationship that the least developed mental processes are assimilated to the rational or problem-solving kind. We look backwards, from the later to the earlier, in order to understand the present as a lightly or heavily disguised re-enacting of the problems of the past. And in extreme cases of neurotic behaviour, the lapse of time, and the development of rational powers of mind, may be virtually left out of the explanation as an irrelevant superstructure.

For centuries the workings of the mind, in forming inclinations and attachments to objects, have been construed by empiricists on a mechanical model, which the causal scheme of explanation seemed to require: the association of ideas. The laws governing the association of ideas were taken to be strictly analogous to the laws governing the movement of bodies. The separate inclinations formed themselves according to universal causal laws. There was no reason to consider the whole set of a man's secondary dispositions, taken as a whole, as ultimately traceable back to a problem presented to him by some primitive situation or situations. For the simple machinery of the association of ideas, Freud substitutes complex activities of projection, introjection and identification in the solution of conflicts. The importance of this substitution, from the philosophical point of view, is just that these activities are represented as activities; and because they are so represented, the underlying motives of them can be investigated. Within this scheme, the question of 'Why?' –

the demand for an explanation in any particular case – does not call for a universally valid psychological law and a statement of initial conditions. Since these processes are represented as activities of mind, the question 'Why?' asks for a description of the situation or situations, and therefore of the given problem, to which these continuing activities were the solution adopted.

The effect of the substitution of the active for the passive mood is that the subject is required to search in his memory for the past situation, as it survives in his mind, and to acknowledge or to disclaim its superimposition on the present. The appeal to his supposed total memory of his unconscious policies in satisfying his instinctual needs, or the needs derived from their frustration, is an appeal to him to understand his own behaviour as a whole, historically: and this form of understanding, the historical and autobiographical form, is taken to be the fundamental form in the explanation of patterns of inclination and conduct. He may resist the appeal and his active exercise of memory may be ineffective. But this failure also will require an explanation in terms of a motive for refusal to remember, and will not be counted as evidence against the hypothesis of total memory itself. If a recurring pattern of feeling and behaviour stands out in an individual's history, and if its first, and only its first, occurrence is explicable by the operation of the instincts against the given resistance of reality, the later instances of the pattern can be traced back, through many complicating stages, to unconscious memories of this primitive occasion.

The whole weight of explaining, and of understanding, human behaviour is placed on the individual subject, as potentially an active, remembering being. Because of this, he can, to some extent, become rather more free and self-determining, through making an active use of memory in disinterring his own unconscious motives, and in acquiring a clearer view of present reality.

6

On Freud's doctrine of emotions*

DAVID SACHS

Talk of a summary kind about Freud has for its byword the claim that unconscious items and processes dominate psychic life. Such talk is of course likely to go farther: due to the unconscious we are creatures curiously heedless of time, creatures fixed in our early if not earliest ways. The unconscious, to put it dramatically, first maddens us and then keeps us mad. Among its achievements are these: we try to gratify wishes that are opposed to each other, indeed wishes whose descriptions may be paradoxical; we mistake as meaningless what is intelligible, and as trivial the important and even portentous; we confuse the scope and character of our acts and intentions; our denials can often be better understood as affirmations, and often too, the converse obtains; again more or less unbeknownst to us, our lives are largely spent in the quest and avoidance of persons and experiences past, in pursuit of and flight from an array of surrogates *for* those persons and experiences, including even antithetical surrogates. Then, too, prominent if not paramount in any résumé of Freud's thought will be statements about his extensions of commonplace notions of sexuality; that among unconscious entities those which enjoy pride of place and power are dispositions to affects or emotions that derive from early erotic experiences and fantasies. Any adequate abstract of Freud's work will also observe that, according to him, everyone is either neurotic or troubled by neurotic tendencies for some appreciable phase or phases of his life.

No doubt any tolerable summary, however quick or breathless, will seize on other salient points in Freud's thought. Mention will be made of his speculations on the origin and development of mankind, on religion, the occult, and the arts; notice taken of his abiding but flexible differences from the rival schools that arose out of his own, particularly the earlier ones, Adler's individual psychology and the analytical

---

* This is a revised version of an essay which appeared under the same title in *Freud: A Collection of Critical Essays*, ed. Richard Wollheim (Doubleday, New York, 1974), from which it is reprinted with permission of the author and the publishers.

psychology of Jung; emphasis will be placed on Freud's changes of view concerning therapeutic practice and, above all, upon the evolution of his metapsychology. In this last connection, although doubtless in others too, there are likely to be certain omissions, in particular omissions that concern Freud's doctrine of emotions or affects.

One important omission, I shall contend, pertains to the five decades of Freud's psychological investigations: to his persistent adherence, in one form or another, to the idea that, between any person's emotions or affects and the causes or objects thereof, there always obtains an actual proportionality or real appropriateness, no matter how discrepant or incongruous those relations may appear to be, and regardless of the person's mental condition, that is, irrespective of whether Freud would deem him psychotic, neurotic, or normal. This claim needs clarification; in what follows I try to clarify it and to show that the attribution to Freud is warranted. At the end I make two observations, the first a suggestion by way of estimating the idea, the second an indication of how, if Freud did hold it, one can thereby be enabled to attain a somewhat novel outlook upon his thought.

I

Among the operative yet unclear expressions that occur in my formulation of the idea I am ascribing to Freud are the phrases 'emotions or affects', 'causes or objects' and 'actual proportionality or real appropriateness'. First, what is the phrase 'emotions or affects' intended to include? Next, what do I mean by 'causes or objects'? Also, can the relation or relations of proportionality or appropriateness be spelled out? For the moment I leave aside the question about the range of emotions or affects, beginning instead with a set of remarks that I hope will indirectly cast some light on the phrase 'causes or objects'. The words 'cause' and 'object' have become jargon in the philosophy of mind; nevertheless, they have played important terminological roles in a controversy which it may be helpful to examine.

Some philosophers hold that, for any instance of a person having an emotion, there is some item which is the emotion's object. Assertions to this effect are regularly accompanied by a warning. The warning alerts us that the item, especially in cases of so-called 'objectless depression', 'free-floating anxiety', and euphoria, is an indefinite collection of more or less randomly hit targets – the objects – of the emotional mood or state. A similar claim is made about certain quite fugitive episodes of emotion or affect: for instance, as when upon waking one just feels – so it is said – good; the claim is that there is no 'just' about it, there is still an item, however diffuse or dim, that serves as the object or objects. It is held that if these putatively 'objectless' states and episodes did not possess at least such tenuous objects, they would not be correctly called instances of emotions or feelings; they are dependent for their conceptual lives upon their frail object constitutions. Other philosophers, while agreeing that in most if not all putatively 'objectless' emotional states and episodes there are the beggarly items to be found hanging about, warn us against regarding them as true or fit objects of emotion. After this divergence, however, there is a joining of forces. Both parties agree that, in Anthony Kenny's words, 'the connection between emotions and their objects is not a contingent one'.[1] Their special concern is to deny that emotions and their objects may be causally connected.

Variations occur upon this theme, variations due to its several possible philosophical motives. The motives are appealed to after making certain assumptions, ones that often hold.[2] Crudely, the assumptions are: when or shortly after a person experiences an emotion, he will be able to say so; he will also be able rightly, even if very roughly, to name or otherwise specify the emotion. At this point one or more of the philosophical motives enters into play. It may be said that, when a person has an emotion and there is some item that is the emotion's object, the person cannot be mistaken as regards at least one identification of it; that is, at least one identification of what is delighting him or making him miserable, what he is feeling hopeful of or fearing, what he is feeling remorseful about or triumphant over, and so on. Or – separately or conjointly – it will be said that the person's identification of the object of his emotion is not a consequence of observation or of any inductive procedure; it is not, as it were, *gathered*, gathered either introspectively or in some other way; it is unmediated. Most commonly the following is said: for a man's identification of the object of his emotion to be an identification of a cause or causal factor of the emotion, he must be able to identify his emotion in a way conceptually independent of – in a manner only contingently connected with – his identification of its object; and this demand, it is said, cannot be met.

There are three claims, then: a person identifies the object of his emotion without any real possibility of mistake; he identifies it without mediation; and a conceptual link holds between his identification of the

---

[1] Anthony Kenny, *Action, Emotion and Will* (Routledge, London, 1963), p. 62.

[2] Here and in much of this section, I am indebted to David Pears' article 'Causes and Objects of Some Feelings and Psychological Reactions', *Ratio* 4, no. 2 (1962), 91–111, reprinted in *Philosophy of Mind*, ed. Stuart Hampshire (Harper, New York, 1966) and in his *Questions in the Philosophy of Mind* (Duckworth, London, 1975); and to J. R. S. Wilson, *Emotion and Object* (Cambridge Univ. Press, Cambridge, 1972).

emotion and his identification or identifications of its object. Philosophers who hold these views often assert that singly or together they are sufficient to show that a man's identifications of his emotions and their objects are not contingently related; or, in any case, that they are not related as identifications of items that could possibly be effects of causes. Following Wittgenstein, they make an additional claim: occasionally emotions, although never merely the effects of their objects, manage to enjoy that humble relationship too. Oddly enough, what appears to be a blatant inconsistency, given the additional claim, seems to have been generally overlooked. The position, again, is that alone or together the alleged incorrigibility, immediacy, and conceptual connection *suffice* to make it impossible for an object of an emotion to be its cause; but it is further acknowledged that, in certain instances, the emotions' objects *are* their causes.[3]

It is my belief that repetition has muffled the clang of the counter-intuitive denial that objects of emotions are often causally related to those emotions. I believe this notwithstanding the lack of clarity of the term, 'object', and the obscurity of the nature of causal relations. A number of refutations of the position have appeared, refutations which have made inroads upon the claim of incorrigibility and which have persuasively argued that the feature of immediacy, insofar as it obtains, is irrelevant to whether the relation often may be causal or not; the refutations have also called into question the view that there has to be a conceptual bond between identifications of emotions and of their particular objects.[4] The refutations have not – though this is a rhetorical complaint – re-evoked the loudness of the denial's counter-intuitive clang. It seems one cannot insist enough upon the notable occurrence of ordinary causal locutions in the examples employed by protagonists of both sides of the controversy, indeed in the very examples used to convey some sense of the role or roles of the term 'object'; nor, apparently, is it quite appreciated how easily, when those locutions are absent from the statement of the examples, the examples can be legitimately construed so as to incorporate those locutions. To turn to a few illustrations, I will quote and comment upon a passage from Miss Anscombe's book *Intention*.

She writes:

in considering feelings, such as fear or anger, it is important to distinguish

---

[3] For one example of the apparent inconsistency see Kenny, *Action, Emotion and Will*, pp. 73 and 75.

[4] See the works by Pears and Wilson cited above; Wilson usefully refers to a number of other relevant writings.

between mental causes and objects of feeling. To see this, consider the following cases:

A child saw a bit of red stuff on a turn in a stairway and asked what it was. He thought his nurse told him it was a bit of Satan and felt dreadful fear of it. (No doubt she said it was a bit of satin.) What he was frightened of was the bit of stuff; the cause of his fright was his nurse's remark. The object of fear may be the cause of fear, but, as Wittgenstein remarks, is not *as such* the cause of fear. (A hideous face appearing at the window would of course be both cause and object, and hence the two are easily confused.) Or again, you may be angry *at* someone's action, when what *makes* you angry is some reminder of it, or someone's telling you of it.[5]

The account Miss Anscombe gives of the child seeing the bit of red stuff can, I believe, be usefully glossed. We may assume the child would not have been frightened had the nurse not spoken as she did; once she has, however, it seems undeniable that the bit of red stuff becomes a causal factor in his fear. For if, after the nurse's words, it were asked, what is making him so afraid, or, indeed, what is causing his fear, a, if not the, natural answer would be: the piece of red stuff. This of course is not to deny that the cause of his being made afraid by it, the cause of its coming to cause him fear, was the nurse's utterance. It may also be useful to take up Miss Anscombe's example of being 'angry *at* someone's action, when what *makes* you angry is some reminder of it, or someone's telling you of it'. The everyday home for the form of words 'what *makes* you angry is some reminder of it, or someone's telling you of it' is where what has caused you to be angry *is* what you are angry about, *is* precisely the reminder or someone's telling you it; but the context shows that Miss Anscombe meant the words to be lodged elsewhere. Plainly, she meant them this way: the cause of your anger is the reminder, whereas your anger's object is the action the reminder reminds you of. But to what extent does this example help us? Granted, the action does not again cause my anger; but surely it could have been both the cause and object of my anger originally – when, say, I witnessed its occurrence.

The passage in Wittgenstein's *Philosophical Investigations* to which Miss Anscombe refers is the *locus classicus* of the controversy: Part I, 476:

The object of fear should be distinguished from the cause of fear. Thus the face that inspires fear or delight in us (the object of fear, of delight) is not thereby its cause but – one could say – its focus[6]

This passage and the pertinent passages in the *Zettel* – 488, 489, and

---

[5] G. E. M. Anscombe, *Intention*, 2nd ed. (Cornell Univ. Press, Ithaca, 1963), p. 16.
[6] I have tinkered with Miss Anscombe's translation.

492 – are plainly consistent with the claim that objects of emotions are also often importantly distinguishable causal factors of them: causal factors to which the emotions *also look*, the emotions' foci, or, to put it literally, what the emotions are felt about or are about.

In the preceding remarks I have wanted to further the clearing away of an obstacle, an obstruction in the path of regarding objects of emotions as often causally related to them. For of course Freud thus conceived them. In whatever way Freud would interpret a putative object of an emotion or affect – whether as a more or less straight-forward causal factor or as largely symbolic of one or more – he understood himself to be investigating largely causal relations. (I would guess that, had Freud come across the philosophical claim that objects of emotions are not often – whether symbolically mediated or not – causes of them, he rightly or wrongly would have reacted with bemusement and scorn, an attitude exemplified by the passage in *An Autobiographical Study* where he says that his avoidance of philosophy was 'greatly facilitated by constitutional incapacity'.[7])

II

Several points should be made concerning what Freud included under the heading 'emotions or affects'. First, a cautionary remark: by '*Affekt*' Freud often did not mean merely or only an emotion or feeling. Often, however, he did, and in speaking of Freud on affects I will depend on this latter understanding of '*Affekt*'. Secondly, he placed among affects certain instances of lack of affect, that is, affectlessness, and I shall follow him in this. Next, for Freud the range of affects includes anything we would unhesitatingly call emotions, emotional states and moods, whether ostensibly objectless or not, and also emotional aspects of desires and impulses; also boredom, malaise, and amusement; also what Descartes called the false emotions experienced by spectators and readers of fictional works, and of course emotions or feelings experienced in dreams. Then, too, Freud includes the affective aspects of many thoughts and impressions, and of course such familiar feelings as ordinary objectless nervousness as well as such infrequent feelings as those of strangeness, familiarity, and déjà vu. Next, although at least as early as the mid-nineties Freud spoke of unconscious feelings of guilt and of repressed self-reproach and found it convenient even four decades later to refer repeatedly to an unconscious sense of guilt and to unconscious

[7] 1925d, XX, 59.

sexual feelings, he had concluded by 1915 that, strictly speaking, there are no unconscious emotions, no unconscious affects or unconscious affect-laden impulses. Needless to say, he continued to maintain that there are more or less structured unconscious dispositions or 'pronenesses' to have feelings; nor did he ever moderate his views on the existence and efficacy of unconscious ideas, motives, intentions, and indeed acts. Yet, for several reasons stated in the third part of his essay 'The Unconscious' (1915e, XIV), reasons often controverted in later psychoanalytic literature,[8] he was always inclined therafter to surround phrases translatable as 'repressed affects', 'unconscious anxiety, guilt, anger', etc. with scare quotes; or, when they were not thus surrounded, to regard them as fairly harmless, even sometimes useful, but nonetheless *loose* phraseology, loose to a degree incompatible with conscientious or scrupulous psychological formulations. This change was no mere terminological shift; it became integral to Freud's metapsychology that emotions and affects should be thought of as 'discharges of excitation' of which the subject had to be to some extent aware. Moreover, the change appears to have been effected quite rapidly: two years earlier, in *Totem and Taboo* (1912–13, XIII, 61), Freud had written, and without apparent qualms, about hostility that could be wholly unconscious but distressingly felt; merely a year earlier, in 'On the History of the Psycho-Analytic Movement' (1914d, XIV), he wrote of affective internal resistances, unconscious resistances affective in origin. A final point here: though Freud was certainly cognizant of attributions of the vocabulary for emotions and feelings in the absence of any 'lively' experience of them, he tended to stress, as it were, felt feelings. Felt, of course, insofar as they involved sensations, sensations however undiscriminated and non-specific, of the cardiovascular and motoric changes that are so often expressive of emotions and affects. These sensations include both those of facial and bodily manifestations of emotions, and also sensations of the actions – or inhibition thereof – that we perform to effect the tendentious aims we typically have when subject to certain feelings.

I shall now elaborate – in an impressionistic but schematic way – what I mean by proportionate or appropriate relations between emotions or affects and their causes or objects. Suppose, e.g. we learn that something has occurred to an individual, something such that understandably enough we expect it will be followed by a certain kind of emotional response on his part; suppose besides that our expectation is not based on any particular psychological information about the individual. What

8 For two discussions and references to others, see the pieces by A. H. Modell and S. E. Pulver in *International Journal of Psycho-Analysis* 52 (1971), 337–46 and 347–54.

we more or less expect in such a case may well not transpire; relative to our uninformed expectation, the affective response might seem to us quite anomalous. In fact, however, there is a plain enough sense in which it could prove anomalous no matter how predictable it would have been had we possessed and utilized considerable relevant psychological information about the individual; could prove anomalous if we also had made allowances required by cultural or subcultural aspects of his environment or environments; could prove anomalous even if we took into account the stage or phase or special circumstances of his life at the time, and further allowed for constitutional or organic peculiarities, permanent or temporary, of the individual. The anomalous response might be any one or more of the following sorts, sorts by no means sharply differentiable: affectlessness, disproportionately slight affect or, contrariwise, disproportionately great affect, and affect without an object. It may well seem that the response could be placed under one or more of these headings, even if we also had discounted the individual's particular temperament, whether it be phlegmatic, excitable, or what have you.

An amplified restatement of the foregoing, one that proceeds in the opposite direction, will be helpful. Suppose that, after any requisite allowances of the kinds mentioned have been made, a person nevertheless could be said to manifest one or another anomaly of affect. My claim is that the anomalies can always be placed under one or more of the following six headings. First, one may experience certain feelings of the type termed 'objectless'. Thus one may feel and show a quite unfocused chronic or intermittent nervousness; or, one may endure noticeable depression and yet sincerely insist that nothing either in general or in particular is depressing one – *mirabile dictu*, one is content excepting only for one's state of mind; or one may feel and vent a dreadful cheerfulness, dreadful for its invulnerability to whatever befalls one. These types of example are 'ideal'; emotional responses, anomalous or not, are usually at least somewhat mixed.

Next, consider anomalies of affect of one or another kind that I shall call 'attenuated object feelings'. To sketch one extreme example and suggest some others: instead of being purely nervous one may be oddly apprehensive; one can experience a sense of threat or menace but have no notion of what, if anything, is under threat or what threatens it or with what it is threatened. Similarly, feelings of hopefulness may be found loosened from their moorings and, somewhat similarly, feelings of guilt, inferiority, etc.

Next, there are – whether disproportionate or proportionate – affective responses that at the very least are doubtfully appropriate. Indeed, feelings that are both disproportionate and inappropriate are so commonplace that examples are unnecessary. Among roughly proportionate but questionably appropriate affects are the feelings of 'counterphobes' – the fears and exultations that tiger-tamers, aerialists and diverse other daredevils experience distinctively, if not solely, in the pursuit of their vocations and hobbies. Also, while one would want to include among excesses of affect the *horror hominis* and *horror feminae* of some female and male homosexual inverts, more moderate aversive homosexual responses, although doubtfully appropriate, could hardly be termed disproportionate.

Excesses of affect include numerous anomalies of feelings. Perhaps most notable among them are certain feelings of fear and many feelings of sexual excitation; they are alike specified by their objects. Conspicuous among such fears, often amounting to terror, are the feelings attached to the large variety of phobias. Other familiar excesses of affect are sexual feelings attendant upon what Freud termed perversions of the sexual aim: narcissistic autoerotism; the couples, sadism and masochism, exhibitionism and voyeurism; and the diverse fetishisms. Then, too, there are many sexual affects connected with what Freud termed inversions of the sexual object: bestiality, paedophilia, and homosexuality. Accompanying these specialities of sexual aim and object are other excessive affects or lack of affect, e.g. overwhelming disgust or utter lack of response upon proximity to or contact with other persons' persons.

The direction in which I have been proceeding is, I trust, clear: from objectless affects to attenuated object feelings to inappropriate affective responses to excessive feelings about objects; and to these headings there needs to be added disproportionately slight responses to objects, and then, past hebetude, affectlessness. This completes the reversal of the direction I followed all too briefly earlier. Once more, my purpose has been to sketch a schema of anomalies of feeling and emotion, a schema, to use Eugen Bleuler's apt figure of speech, of incongruities of affect. The termini of the path I have traversed back and forth are, again, objectlessness and affectlessness.

For Freud, incongruities of affect were symptomatic. Thus variations of trends toward lack of affect and objectlessness enabled, on his view, differential diagnoses of psychotic tendencies and of the psychoses themselves, psychoses constituting the most marked instances of the loss of or flight from reality, including of course within reality nonanomalous affective responses. (To be sure, there are affects that are part and parcel of total or systematic hallucinatory or delusional confusions; their analogues in the lives of psychologically more or less normal persons are the affects experienced in dreams, dreams that we sometimes explicitly and colloquially call 'crazy.'[9]) In some advanced forms of melancholia, that is, of psychotic depression, both affectlessness and withdrawal from objects are to be found together. In such cases, so to say, the two termini coincide.

Doubtless my schema of anomalies of feelings could be improved in a number of ways; the improvements would require complicating it. Before turning to a few of the complications, I want to take up a likely but misguided objection to the schema. The objection, as I conceive it, will take this form: the schema, whatever other failings it may have, cannot pretend to being an analysis of anomalies of affect. This is patently clear in connection with the third of its six headings: inappropriate – whether proportionate or disproportionate – affects. This heading employs the very notion that, presumably, the schema is meant to analyse, namely, the notion of an affect being anomalous or inappropriate. In answer to this objection it should be enough to observe that the schema is not intended as an analysis – however desirable one might be – of the notion of an affect being anomalous. The schema is intended only to serve as *a* specification – one spelling-out – of the varieties of anomalous emotions and feelings; but it does pretend, and not just trivially, to provide a place or places for every instance of affective incongruity.

One important complication of the schema would be an indication of how persons whose lives are troubled by emotional disorder tend to suffer now from one sort of anomaly of affect and then from another or, indeed, are often subject simultaneously to different sorts. Another important addition would provide for certain feelings people suffer due to the incongruities of affect to which they are liable – that is, to sometimes further anomalous feelings whose objects are antecedent anomalous ones. Whatever complications might usefully be incorporated in the schema, my claim again is that it specifies, in however general and unrefined a way, all incongruities of affect; and that, consequently, any emotions or feelings which could not arguably be fitted into it would thereby be appropriately related to their objects or causes, that is, would be nonanomalous affects.

The notion of an affect arguably or not arguably fitting into the schema may well seem problematic; surely, however, it is implausible to suppose that it is devoid of sense. Consider, for instance, some of the examples I placed under the heading of excessive affects: the gamut of feelings of sexual excitation that, according to Freud, are perverted or

---

[9] The comparison is often made in Freud's writings; for a very late statement of it, see *An Outline of Psychoanalysis* (1940a, XXIII, 160–1).

inverted. Of some of those feelings it would certainly be reasonable to claim that they are arguably anomalous; and if one concedes this, one concedes that the notion in question does not lack sense. The same gamut of examples is useful in another connection too, indeed in relation to the central concern of this paper: for Freud's discussions of the affective origins and persistence of the inversions and perversions are among the most prominent applications he made of the idea I am ascribing to him: the idea, once again, that between any person's emotions or affects and their objects or causes there obtains a real appropriateness or actual proportionality no matter how discrepant or incongruous those relations may seem and regardless of the person's mental condition.

To show convincingly that Freud adhered to this idea in one form or other throughout the five decades of his psychological work would require an appeal to all of his pertinent writings, an appeal, that is to say, to at least a majority of his psychological writings. By way of substitute, I will refer at some length to what I take to be a strategic example of the idea's presence in his work, and then briefly touch upon a number of other examples.

When stating and restating the idea, I have used the disjunctive phrase 'causes or objects'. Indubitably whenever someone experiences an emotion that has an object, there are, whether or not the object is among them, causal factors involved. I had, however, a special reason for adverting to causes as well as objects.[10] I repeatedly singled out causes for mention because of the important role Freud allotted for many years – from at least 1893 until the *New Introductory Lectures* of 1933 – to what he called 'sexual noxae' in the causality of the emotional aspect of hysterias and in the effecting of the feelings of debility and anxiety characteristic of neurasthenia, anxiety neurosis, and hypochondria – the disorders he termed 'actual neuroses', as opposed to psychoneuroses. Only at the end of those forty years did Freud completely abandon the view that lack of sexual fulfilment, whether due to abstinence, masturbation, coitus interruptus, or coitus reservatus, effected 'sexual noxae' which in turn effected the marked excitability of many hysterics and the syndromes of feelings which helped enable the differentiation of the actual neuroses both from each other and from the psychoneuroses. He

[10] Perhaps this is a suitable place to emphasize that, in speaking of objects of feelings, I am throughout keeping in mind *intentionality*, i.e. that a person's identification of an object of his feelings may contain terms that lack reference; and that, whether or not this is so, he may be able to make few if any substitutions for those terms that would preserve the truth of his identification, assuming it true to begin with; and that, consequently, existential generalization of his identification would be out of order. (See, for a useful account of the matter, J. R. S. Wilson, *Emotion and Object*, chap. 14.)

conceived of those noxae as similar to known toxic conditions, and of the feelings they generated as comparable to ones that can be induced by certain drugs or glandular deficiencies. Moreover, he thought the sexual noxae – allowing for constitutional differences – proportionate to the affects they caused. Proportionate, that is, however disproportionate or incongruous those affects appeared to be when viewed against the background of the life circumstances – other than the sexual ones, of course – of the individuals who suffered from those disorders.

When Freud completed the assimilation of the actual neuroses to the psychoneuroses – he had always thought some patients were afflicted with both – he interpreted the relevant incongruities of affect in terms of anxiety responses to repressed tendencies, i.e. to unconscious objects, objects in view of which the affects could again be viewed as proportionate.

What then of other anomalous affects? As a matter of theory in regard to the psychoses, and clinically in regard both to psychotic trends and the neuroses, Freud's psychoanalytic interpretations of incongruities of affect *always* try to show that the incongruities are only ostensible. They try, that is, to disclose an actual congruity, a real appropriateness, behind what is taken to be the facade of every apparently discrepant feeling. Thus, on psychoanalytic investigation, the empty spaces of objectless affects are populated: for example, the dejection of depressives is interpreted as self-hatred, and the mania that often alternates with the dejection as relief from the self-hatred. The haze of attenuated object feelings lifts and objects are perceived clearly and forcibly: for example, vague but apprehensive delusions of being observed and watched come to be construed as the workings of a particularly vigilant conscience. Some ostensibly excessive affects, e.g. the ones so noteworthy in compulsive-obsessional neuroses, emerge as fears of ever-tempting transgressions appropriate to those unrelenting feelings. Others, for instance, the *Angst* attached to unrealistic phobic objects, are taken to be symbolic of genuinely terrifying perils; still others, for example, the erotic responses to fetishes, lose their impoverishing extravagance when interpreted as compensatory and reassuring. The counter-phobic objects are viewed as furnishing occasion for an enjoyed mastery at least as representative as direct. Feelings of aversion and distaste give way to forbidden longings, to forbidden possibilities of relishing the distasteful. Inadequate affects are supplemented by recourse to understandably – because, for instance, often traumatically – repressed pronenesses to feeling. The apathy of the melancholiac is traced to mourning over one or another unconscious loss of love. And so on for every anomaly of affect.

III

As far as I have been able to discover, the idea I am ascribing to Freud is nowhere stated in his writings; no doubt if he had stated it he would not have expressed it in the cumbersome way I have found unavoidable. Yet neither in ransacking the corpus of his psychological works nor in searching through commentaries and digests have I been able to find any equivalent to it. On the other hand, in the course of that same search I have not encountered any exceptions to it – instead, only confirmations. If I have not lost my way in this, the ironic upshot is that over the half-century of Freud's psychological investigations he was, unbeknownst to himself, steadily faithful to the idea I have attributed to him. What is more, I am inclined to conjecture that it functioned for him as *one* of the criteria for the correctness of psychoanalytic interpretations of affective disorders.

Persons critical of, or antagonistic to, Freudian doctrines will surely find the foregoing congenial. For if I am right, Freud, although unaware of it, depended – and in a suspiciously *a priori* way – on a crucial and unqualifiedly general view of anomalies of emotion and affect. In fairness, however, it ought to be remarked that if that is the position, it is not without parallel in the origins of other disciplines. In any case, the question of the truth or falsity of the idea is unaffected by Freud's having failed to formulate it. This is of course obvious and would not be worth mention but for the unspeakable quality of the great majority of criticisms of Freud. The value of the idea can only be determined in the ways in which the value of many other Freudian doctrines can be ascertained; and the qualifications required to undertake that task are diverse and rarely found.

To conclude: it is a truism about Freud that he thought that normalcy shades off imperceptibly into neurosis. A prejudice attaches to the way this truism is understood and used. The prejudice shows itself in the contrast between the frequency of claims about the existence of neurotic tendencies in otherwise normal persons and the relative rarity of claims about trends towards normalcy in neurotics and psychotics. That laymen should find this prejudice inviting is, of course, understandable; what is likely to go unnoticed is the deformation of Freud's thought implicit in it. In my belief, the prejudice and consequent deformation tend to be pervasive. For example, people who read Freud know that he regarded dreams as neurotic symptoms, symptoms that occur in all healthy persons. They know too that he argued that dreams, including anxiety and 'punishment' dreams, are surrogates for the fulfilment of wishes. Is there an equal awareness of how comprehensible and useful Freud judged those surrogate fulfilments to be? Again, it is widely known that Freud held that all or nearly all parapraxes are symptomatic, and that he construed them as intentional and meaningful. Is it sufficiently appreciated that in taking them to be meaningful he saw them as clues to needs that their perpetrators possessed but of which they were more or less unaware? Another example: readers of Freud are familiar with his attempt to show that even the most innocent and non-tendentious jokes are instances of reverting to archaic kinds of pleasure. Do those readers have an adequate sense of Freud's understanding not only of the persistence but also of the importance of those kinds of pleasure? Another example: Freud's emphasis on the secondary gain of every neurotic symptom is unmistakable; although such gains cannot compensate for the losses entailed by the disabling character of the symptoms, is Freud's stress on their utility amply recognized?

I have not meant these questions merely rhetorically. Although I am confident that the answers to them are sometimes affirmative, I very much doubt that it is at all common to assemble these questions – to assemble them and related reminders – and thereby enable oneself to grasp the various ways in which Freud's vision was a vision of the normalcy and health that, however obstructed or baffled, lie behind neurosis and psychosis. I have said that on Freud's view the unconscious maddens us and keeps us mad; but he also held that if we could come to terms with it, it would prove the agent and preserver of sanity. That he did thus see it is, I believe, unquestionable. And if, as I have urged, he treated all anomalies of emotion and feeling as only ostensible, taking it as it were for granted that beneath each of those incongruities there is an unconscious but real congruity, it is the more unquestionable.[11]

[11] I am grateful for help and encouragement given me by Philippa Foot, Roger Albritton and George Wilson.

7

The id and the thinking process*

BRIAN O'SHAUGHNESSY

A. Introduction

The concept of the id was formulated by Freud in 1923, in a work entitled *The Ego and the Id*, and it marked the culmination of almost thirty years of empirical investigation and meta-psychological thought concerning the unconscious part of the mind. It is remarkably similar to concepts found in the nineteenth-century German philosophical movement, most especially to Shopenhauerian Will and the Dionysiac of the early Nietzsche; indeed, we must in some sense accept that those two great explorers of the mind had stumbled upon the truth of the id. But I think we can, in addition, discern significant likenesses between the Freudian id and concepts ranging as far afield as the Lockean material substratum and the Kantian noumenon.

It is important to notice the sharp distinction which Freud drew – though not perhaps in so many words – between *a part of* and *a system within* the mind. The id, in Freudian theory, is the mental system that is the repository of the two ultimate instincts, the life and death instincts, Eros and Thanatos. Then while these instinctual contents of the id are in themselves invariably unconscious, so that an entry on their part into consciousness would be possible only in symbolic form, the Freudian concept of the unconscious is not the concept of a particular mental system like the id. Rather, greater or lesser sectors of discrete mental systems jointly constitute the unconscious part of the mind, and do so simply through being something of which people are unconscious. Thus the province of the unconscious encompasses the unconscious part of the ego, which is responsible for mentally self-protective measures like repression; the unconscious part of the super-ego, which is responsible, for example, for the unconscious sense of guilt which may drive an habitual criminal to commit the crimes that repeatedly land him in jail;

---

* This is a reprint of an essay which appeared under the same title in *Freud: A Collection of Critical Essays*, ed. Richard Wollheim (Doubleday, New York, 1974), from which it is reprinted with permission of the author and the publisher.

and, most important of all, it includes the id in its entirety. These unconscious parts of discrete systems form, not one system that is the unconscious, not one system that is the unconscious part of the mind, but the unconscious part of the one system of systems that is – the mind.

In this essay I shall venture to take for granted two basic facts about the mind: the first is its totalized or holistic character, the second is the impossibility of what might be called 'mental physics'. The holism of mental phenomena implies the absence of an *absolute autonomy* on the part of mental events; for the identity of these undeniably real and unquestionably individual events stands essentially behoven to the mental setting in which they occur: that is, they would be other than themselves were the setting to depart from what it is in various specifiable ways. And by 'the impossibility of "mental physics" ', I mean no more than the inapplicability within the mind of a mental scientific explanatory system structured analogously to physics.

My intention is to examine certain phenomena in mental life that make plausible such a theory as that of the id. I shall be concerned with the various forms taken by the central phenomenal process in the mind, the thinking process, and my account will be conditioned by a double preoccupation. One of these preoccupations is *the will*, for I hope to form a clear estimate of the will-status of such thinking processes as creative thinking, the day-dream and the dream. The other is the Freudian account of *mental structure*, for I shall try to characterize these processes in terms of the mental systems, the ego and the id. Indeed, I will try to unite these enterprises, and make evident the close relation that holds between will-status and the locus of the determining centre of the mind; for these are essentially linked. Thus, all acting or willing proceeds exclusively from the ego, never from the id. Action springs from the 'I' in one, never from the 'It'.

Now, the impossibility of 'mental physics' is a direct consequence of the holistic character of the mind (though I do not propose to attempt a demonstration of this thesis here). In fact, it may seem astonishing that causal relations can hold within holistic totalities of the kind of the mind. But they can, and between individual events, despite these apparent counter indications. For mental explanations of mental phenomena, of the utmost certainty, do and must exist; and in depth too, if one thinks of the insights of a non-scientific and gifted observer like Dostoevsky. Paradoxically, however, the region of the mind that offers the greatest resistance to the explanatory enterprise, is the most developed and most characteristically mental of mental phenomena: the thinking process! But what has impressed me, is that a continuity links the *most* self-determined of these, attending, and the *least* self-determined, dreaming;

and that as one moves along this spectrum, *pari passu* the will fades from the scene. But the will is itself a form of mental cause. Therefore as we move across in the direction of the dream, one mental agency is deleted from the causal picture. Moreover, it is the causally central mental agency. Indeed, it is in man the very organ or instrument of reason, being the psychic thrust through which rational self-determination objectifies itself either in the mind or in physical nature.

What, then, is left as sleep descends and the will departs? Or are we to suppose that, with the arrival of sleep, non-mental causes are *all* that operate? But this is highly implausible, for the dream is a describable, even an intelligible, process unity; and this makes it all but impossible to suppose that the early stages of a dream could be of *no* causal relevance to the later stages. It seems that there must be non-rational non-self-determining mental causal forces at work in the generation of the dream. These must at least partially explain, in holistic rather than lawlike manner, why the dream takes the course that it does. Not lying in consciousness, they lie in unconsciousness; and being neither rational nor entirely intellectual, they require as origin something in unconsciousness at least akin to the id. This is the general line of the succeeding argument.

Like the continuity or spectrum mentioned above, this paper also travels in the direction: from self-determination (of the mind's processes) to id-determination (of its processes). The former is the concern of section B, the latter of section C. But in depicting self-determination in B, I want to lay open for inspection the role open to the id in a mind that determines its own movement. It is for this reason that I have seen fit to discuss the problem of *mental creativity*, for the mentally creative situation is *par excellence* a situation in which the id is subordinated to the ego. This is my concern in B; and in C I will consider the dream, where the situation is reversed, and *par excellence* the ego is subordinated to the id.

B. Mental creativity: the internalization by the ego of id forces

The id most reveals itself when the self least determines itself

We will be concerned with those mental phenomena that, as we shall argue, most require explanation in terms of the id. I take these phenomena to be marked by the following features. They are those mental phenomena, of which we are conscious, in which ego-function is at its lowest ebb (which is certainly not to say entirely absent). The most noteworthy example is dreaming. But of course there are others. Thus, while Freud described dreams as 'the royal road to the unconscious', he thought that alongside dreams one could range neurotic and psychotic symptoms, parapraxes and free-associative trains of thought, as the places where the id pre-eminently revealed its existence. Then this is to say that the course of processes like the dream or free-associative trains could be rendered intelligible only through the invocation of some occurrent mental process factor other than the processes occurring in the conscious and unconscious parts of the ego. This factor consists in the so-called primary processes, the processes native to the id. So the theory goes.

Why did Freud think that these phenomena were the sites in which the presence of the id most clearly 'showed through'? If, as is my intention, we confine the question to the central thinking processes of the mind, then the answer is not hard to find. It is because in these processes the *will*, or *choice* or *say*, is least operative. For it is evident that I have less say in what happens in my dreams than in what words will appear in this paper, and there can be no doubt that this is why the dream *must be* the 'royal road' to the unconscious and *probably will be* the 'royal road' to the id. Now, it is true that I have no direct say in determining what will be my visual impression when a certain image impinges on my retina, and it is also true that the formation of that visual impression out of that visual data is the work of unconscious parts of the ego. Therefore an absence of self-determination, taken in the sense of choice or will, is no certain mark of the active presence of the id; and this looks to run counter to the above formula. But the difficulty is resolved if we confine ourselves to the thinking process, for there it seems certain, as a matter of empirical fact, that the less say I have over what happens the more in general the id has say. This is because reason, understanding, intellect, play a less central determining role in such cases. And so I suggest that we proceed with the following simple formula: that the id most reveals itself when self-determination of the mind's thinking processes, taken in the sense of will or say, is at its lowest ebb.

A simple physical image of this mental force situation

Let me illustrate this claim by means of a simple image. Thus it is somewhat as if we were to notice perturbations in the orbits of the more outlying members of a planetary system, and were to argue from the position and character of these deviations to the presence of a hidden disturbing magnetic source lying beyond the outer confines of that system. Thereafter as a result of this discovery we would seek to explain and compute the paths of *all* planets in that system in terms of two variables: an outwardly directed magnetic force; an inwardly directed gravitational force. And the existence, and magnetic character, of the hidden disturbing force will be more nakedly evident the farther the planet under scrutiny lies from the sun. Then in our image the sun is the Apollonian ego, and the dark magnetic sources the Dionysiac id.

Thus being in the neighbourhood of that magnetic source is in many ways analogous to being relatively much determined by processes in the id. And being close to the sun resembles being relatively much determined by ego-processes: either the conscious ego-processes of self-determination or choice, or unconscious ego-processes of an intellectual character. The process of intentionally attending to an item, which I think we must rate as a completely pure example of self-determination, lies, so to say, as near to the sun as possible; an authentic free-associative flow in a psychoanalytic session is situated somewhere in the middle; and hallucinatory processes and dreams, and most especially the dreams of young children and perhaps of great artists, lie as near to that magnetic source as is consistent with remaining within the sway of the sun. We might as well labour the image a little and make this latter requirement, of continuing to describe computable orbits around the sun, stand for the inevitable 'secondary elaboration' that the existence of consciousness strictly demands. (It might even be conjectured, falsely, as I would suppose, that the extremest possible katatonia is the analogue of collapsing into that source!)

Certainly this planetary image is seriously misleading. Yet it helps us appreciate that the id 'shows through' in just those places where the ego is least efficacious. Indeed, adapting one romantic usage, we might say that id most shows through where will is most asleep; for the will, in the romantic sense of *mental force*, is *the* manifestation of an ego that is both large *and* strong; for such an ego is an instrument that is essentially gifted in the sustained art of applying mental force. Then as that magnetic source will be most studied through observation of the paths of outer planets, so it is that from the dream especially we argue both to *the existence* and *the characteristic ways of working* of the primary process. Thus it was from interpreting dreams, as well as symptoms, that Freud was able to say that the primary process was above all noteworthy for two properties that bespeak a tendency towards Dionysian undifferentiation: condensation and displacement.

Mental creativity: the shadow of Dionysus

A process like attending to a sensation, however deep its origins, must if intentional be a pure self-determining. For here a process occurs in my mind simply because I choose that it shall, and the line of its development is determined by nothing but will. Thus far we are concerned entirely with ego-processes. But we take a first step in the direction of the id, and therefore towards a form of *psychic dualism*, when we approach the problem of *mental creativity*.

At once we encounter facts which point towards the presence of more than one ruling deity in the mind. For a deep problem is posed by the fact that much mental activity, and certainly always the most creative, harbours within itself an element that departs from the above simple model of self-determination. I refer to the fact that creative mental activities involve the occurrence of phenomena for which one is responsible *only via the mediation of the activity itself*. I have in mind: those mental events that constitute the advance of the creative activity; for these occur only because that activity brings them into being. For example, thoughts in the course of thinking. In consequence, it may truly be said of the thinking process that it interposes itself between the thinker and his thoughts. Indeed, in general the creative activity must incorporate as an element of itself that which stands at just such a remove of one from the self-determiner creator. The very concept of inspiration demands this. Thus the perpetuation of the creative process depends on the creator's granting a controlled measure of freedom to mental processes upon which he depends. And it involves the unchosen occurrence of ideas which occur only through the mediation of the activity – which is by contrast most assuredly chosen. In the light of this, such a self-determining may be said to gather up into itself the unself-determined. That is, it integrates it into itself.

The power to create exists only because a requisite liberty reigns in part of a mind that is *strong enough* to retain its purposes in the face of such liberty. Indeed, the more exploratory the process, and thus the more of value, the more it occurs only because of this accommodated liberty. But, it might be objected, does not one simply switch on these subordinate mental processes at will? Certainly one does, for it is an activity. Then is it not absolutely analogous to switching on the requisite muscle processes in one's body when one chooses to raise an arm? The answer to this important objection has already been given above. Namely, these two situations differ in the crucial respect that, while one intends the perpetuation of the mental process, one does not intend the mental events its progress involves; and there is simply no analogue of this in the physical situation. Expressing the matter in vague-ish but still revealing language, we might say that this means that those subordinate mental processes have *a life of their own*, and while they move only because we set them in motion they are not the mere instruments of our purposes. They do *our* bidding, but go *their own* way; and this living relationship involves an harmonious division of labour within the psyche. A properly human form of authority is established in such a mind. But so also is duality.

Even the purest ratiocination, if creative, leaves room for the id

We have drawn attention to a quasi-antinomy in the concept of mentally creative self-determination. This led to the realization that some self-determination integrates into itself the unself-determined. But what has that to do with the id? Supposing this is true of an exemplary example of ratiocination, do we not explain each thought in that process when we exhaustively delineate the rational links that tie it to the problem itself, and to the preceding phase of the ratiocinative process? But the truth is, that while we thereby explain *the thought* that we thought, we give thereby no more than a partial explanation of our *thinking that thought*. For having explained a thought by relating it to a problem, we have yet to answer these questions. Why not another thought of equal relevance? Why not nothing of any relevance at all?

It is precisely because the process is creative, as opposed to being something like a mere listing of names, in which case the succeeding phases of the activity would be preordained, that these questions remain unanswered long after we have explained the thought. Of course we can attempt to answer them, invoking relevant factors like the intelligence and talent, the era and training of the thinker. Inevitably, much remains unexplained.

But to this it might be protested: must not these imponderables be intellectual processes, if the thought advances a ratiocinative process? And must they not therefore be unconscious ego-processes, and therefore not id-processes? Now, there can be no doubt that no unconscious intellectual processes are id-processes. But why cannot non-intellectual factors play a causal role in exemplary examples of ratiocination? For example, mental energy. And why should not mental energy be evoked by non-rational forces? Think of the type of mental soil out of which grew certain Newtonian ideas or some of the poems of Yeats. And concerning philosophy, as Nietzsche observed: 'anyone who hears only a "will to truth" in the background surely does not enjoy the keenest hearing'.[1] Then could not non-rational causal factors determine which of a number of equally fruitful lines of inquiry is followed? I conclude that the quasi-antinomy in ratiocination at least allows a gap within which the id might conceivably play a determining role.

While what we have asserted concerning creative activities, holds

---

[1] Friedrich Nietzsche, *Beyond Good and Evil*, par. 10, trans. Marianne Cowan (Henry Ragnery Company, Chicago, 1965).

equally of intellectual and artistic creation; and while in all creative activities the ego is the ringmaster in a psyche wherein unconscious mental processes play a determining role; it would be a mistake to suppose that intellectual and artistic creations emerge out of the same kind of mental processes. I know too little about the mental-structural differences between scientist, philosopher and artist, to be able to speak definitively here, but significant differences in the nature of their creative processes seem more or less to be guaranteed. Thus it seems certain that the id is a more powerful determining force in art than in either philosophy or science. This should hardly surprise us if we bear in mind the kinship between artistic creation and dreaming. It is supported by the fact that, just as the emotions are never rational (which is not to suggest that they are irrational), so it is in the case of the ideas which occur in the creation of a work of art. After all, predominant purposes in art are the *moving* and even the *entertaining* of the spectator. Thus pre-eminently in the case of art we find that the near antinomy in all mental creative processes owes its existence at least in part to the working of the id. Whereas all that we know in the case of intellectual processes is that it is due to the necessary presence of unconscious phenomena. But, as already suggested, no contradiction results from supposing these also to be id-processes.

The parts of the self, bound by Eros, form diverse structures in mental creativity and dream

Our interest in creative mental processes derives primarily from the fact that here, as opposed to pure self-determinings like attendings, there exists a strange explanatory gap, an *hiatus*, within which the id might perhaps function. But what is most interesting is the way it vividly displays the element of *structural hierarchy* in the mind. Thus, while the id doubtless plays a role in creative activity, that role is always enacted *under the auspices of the ego*, which is the focal point of the self that actively creates; for this is a necessary condition of free activity. By contrast, while the ego plays a determining role in dreaming, that role is always enacted *under the auspices of the id*, which is the focal point of the self when consciousness of the world is in abeyance; and this ensures that the dream is not free activity. And so we see the focal point of the self shifting as the state of consciousness alters. I would now like to make a little clearer these twin notions: focal point of the self; structural hierarchy in the mind.

We suppose that id-processes partially determine the course both of the dream and the creative psychical process. Yet a highly significant mental structural alteration occurs as we switch from dream to creative activity. I shall endeavour to shed light on this structural situation by comparing it to an *inter-personal relation*; and, because Freud believed that Eros held the parts of the self together, which may therefore be thought of in personalized terms, I will make that personal relation one of love. Thus it is somewhat as if a lover were selflessly to declaim to his beloved the altruistic message that 'your purposes are mine', only to receive the similarly selfless declamation that 'it is not *mine* that are yours, it is rather that yours are mine'. This possibly archaic situation is to be likened to the above structural switch; and, trite as the comparison may seem, we shall see that it has much to recommend it.

The value of this comparison resides in its capacity to illustrate for us an important property of love. Namely, the capacity of love to create unities in which *the kind of the love* and *the kind of the linked lovers* mutually condition one another, leading to mutual freedom and a predestined division of labour. And so it is in the mind, where Eros holds together parts of the self which perform predestined tasks. We shall find that this holds of creativity and dreaming, but in fact it holds throughout any mind not totally wrecked by illness. Thus the free ego, working harmoniously with a super-ego from which it is barely distinct, is free only because the latter is benign or loving; while by contrast the ego of the melancholic labours, as Freud remarked in *The Ego and the Id*, under a super-ego that has become 'a pure culture of the death instinct'.[2] Similarly, the communication between ego and id that Freud talked of in 'The Unconscious' as a prerequisite of mental health,[3] is possible only where the id is not overloaded with the forces of evil and death. Thus, according to Freudian structural theory, the healthy mind harbours within itself various channels of communication, together with divisions of labour that are thereby made possible. And, ultimately, both are made possible only through the synthesizing influence of the benign forces of love or life, the instinct Eros, originating in the id.

The id as the psychic matter or psychic fuel of mental creation

Let us return to the structural hierarchical differences between dream and creative mental process. We compared the unified parts of the mind to united lovers, the divergent character of those parts of the self corresponding to the diverse natures of the lovers. This is because we supposed there to be two possible mental focal points. These will now be displayed in structural accounts of free creative action, and dreaming, taken in that order.

(1) Concerning free creative action we might say this: 'The creative

[2] 1923b, XIX, 53   [3] 1915e, XVI, 194.

processes in the mind have their own purposes, and these are those of the *self*.' And what we mean is that the mind of the creator spontaneously travels along the inspired paths it follows, only because that creative person has chosen to engage in the creative enterprise. Whereas (2) concerning the dream, the following rather seems apposite: 'While the self that dreams has goals that are its own, these are those of the *dream*.' And we mean that the self that is sleeping has the goals that it has only because the dream determines that it shall. That is, it merely dreams them.

This switch corresponds to a significant structural difference. In the former case, (1), the id is subordinated to the ego, which exploits the id's creative forces in the generation of the active creative process; so that while the ego goes where it wishes, it depends upon the id that it uses. In the latter case, (2), it is the ego that is subordinated to the id, which makes use of the ego's powers of secondary elaboration, and thereby ensures for itself a place in the consciousness of the sleeper and thus an avenue to expression; so that while the id goes where it wishes, it depends for its expression upon the ego that it uses. In those two great phases of the life of the mind, wakefulness and sleep, a different structural relation and division of labour is in each case established, and ego and id perform divergent tasks. More, in either case the focal point or pre-eminent determining centre in the mind correspondingly shifts its locus. For the wakeful it lies in the ego, for the sleeping it is centred in the id.

We assume the id plays a determining role, not merely in the least rational mental processes, such as dreams and hallucinatory psychoses, but in the deepest and most creative human occupations. Then because this generic source of creative impulse finds its naturally appointed (or healthy) role in consciousness in being organized by the active ego, its place in conscious mental life may be likened to that of the raw material stuff in the construction of the artefact. For while the id is not entirely without structure, there is much about it that would recommend this construing of it, or else of the life instinct it harbours, as the sheer formless matter or fuel of the mind.

I think we may justly suppose, following our characterization of creative and therefore relatively integrated activity, that a rich id is ideally subordinated to an ego that possesses the strength, and in consequence the required communicative links with the id, to marshal and put to its uses the untapped riches resident in these mental resources. Rather like a nineteenth-century industrialist harnessing the forces of nature, or like a rider on a horse (as Freud observed),[4] the power of a

---

[4] 1923b, XIX, 25.

powerful ego consists in its capacity to summon up at will, and simultaneously to control and structure, powerful sources lying deep in the id; and in this sense to internalize these psychic forces, thereby assimilating them into the self. For it is in many respects a nineteenth-century image, and I am reminded most vividly of Ibsen's tragic character John Gabriel Borkman, towards the end of the play of that name, addressing by night the minerals buried deep in the nearby mountains: 'I can see the veins of metal stretch out their winding, branching, luring arms to me . . . You begged to be liberated and I tried to free you. But my strength failed me, and the treasure sank back into the deep again. (With outstretched hands.) But I will whisper it to you here in the stillness of the night: I love you, as you lie there spellbound in the deeps and the darkness! I love you, unborn treasures, yearning for the light! I love you with all your shining train of power and glory.'[5] The loss of those now quite inaccessible yet still loved materials, a loss that is explicitly interpreted as symbolic of Borkman's mental tragedy, is the 'objective correlative' of the failure of his ego to establish constructive communicative links with his id, which is in effect that in which his mental tragedy consisted. Those minerals are his own unrealized-forever mental deeps or resources. Indeed, the situation could even be said to represent an ego addressing with love an id which it has proved too weak to harness to its purposes. As Freud observed, in speaking of mental development: 'Where id was, there ego shall be';[6] and what he was referring to was the internalizing, as it were, the mapping and harnessing and civilizing, of the natural and primaeval regions in the psyche.

C. Dreaming: the subordination of ego to id

We shall now pass on from the consideration of controlled pure self-determinings like attending, or controlled impure self-determinings like the creative mental processes of pure thought or art. Instead, we shall turn our attention onto those central thinking processes which are marked by an increasing absence of self-control. That is, day-dream, deep pre-sleep phantasy and dream. Here, as we have already remarked, the id is increasingly visible to eyes that can see. It becomes the focal or determining point in the structural hierarchy in the mind.

We shall, however, begin by examining one important element of the dream. Namely, the unconscious shaping by the ego, the Apollonian

[5] Henrik Ibsen, *John Gabriel Borkman*, trans. William Archer (Heinemann, London, 1910), act 4.
[6] 1933a, XXII, 80.

dream-work,[7] as a result of which the deep instinctual phenomena buried in the id enter in symbolic form into the consciousness of the sleeper. This is none other than the famous 'secondary elaboration' of Freudian theory.

'Secondary elaboration': like a bridge between the atomic and the visible realm

We have spoken of the theory of the 'secondary elaboration' of the primary process. While to many this may seem a somewhat creaking piece of theoretical machinery, conjuring up the image of a perpetually active stage manager scurrying around in the psychic wings, Freud's acceptance of the principle that all thinking processes require perspicuous mental explanation more or less forced him to postulate this theory. I say so for two reasons. First, because the above principle compelled him to postulate id-processes in order to explain the dream (etc.); and secondly, as we shall soon see, because once one accepts the existence of id-processes one cannot but endorse the theory of secondary elaboration.

There is a close analogue between the explanatory role of the id, and that of fundamental particles in present-day physical theory. These last make possible a deep complete explanation of the properties of material stuffs only through contriving to inhabit a categorical limbo lying between matter and energy, for the electron is at once the quantum of negative electricity *and* endowed with mass. Because the most minute speck of sulphur (say), visible only under a microscope as a yellow dot, possesses all the chemical properties of a chunk of sulphur, of sulphur in short, we are compelled to hypothesize explanatory factors lying in the properties of the sulphur to be explained. The realm of the electron cannot be a duplication *in minutiae* of the macroscopic or microscopic realm it explains, if it is to function as a totally comprehensive explanation.

So, I suggest, it is, in the case of the primary processes in the id. If these were a sort of subterranean second conscious mind, wherein reason, self-determination and values held sway, they would fail to perform the deep explanatory task assigned them by Freud. *A priori*, from the very

[7] Compare: Nietzsche, still under the influence of Schopenhauer but already wonderfully original, speaking of the lyric poet: 'As Dionysian artist he is in the first place become altogether one with the Primordial Unity, its pain and contradiction, and he produces the copy of this Primordial Unity as music, granting that music has been correctly termed a repetition and a recast of the world; but now, under the Apollonian dream-inspiration, this music again becomes visible to him as in a *symbolic dream picture*' (Friedrich Nietzsche, *The Birth of Tragedy* [Foulis, London, 1910], p. 45).

structure of these two theories, it is no more possible to introspect or recall id-processes than it is to see the electron or the sulphur atom. As one must lie outside the range of the perceptible, so the other must forever defy the powers of introspectible consciousness. The invisibility of the atom may be likened to the inaccessibility of the id. Both doctrines run counter to common sense, and they are at one in rejecting a philosophy of nature that would be content to regard established surface regularities as final explanatory ultimates. They look for the source of those regularities in something whose ontological status is novel, and whose instances lie outside experience. They continue the pursuit of ultimate truth, knowing they will never arrive at their goal but opting regardless for the search.

Processes in the id could never conceivably fill consciousness

Let me now say why *a priori* id-processes must defy the powers of introspectible or recollective consciousness. Because the consciousness of rational creatures constitutively requires the existence of at least some measure of rational sensitivity to the world,[8] whereas the id is assigned the task of explaining those mental phenomena for which neither intellect nor self-determining choice can be held responsible, it follows that if a mind could be filled with nothing but the primary process, then not even a psychotic consciousness could inhabit the mind at the time. Now, to this it might be objected that people who are completely unconscious sometimes experience dreams, and from this it could be argued that a mind filled with primary process might conceivably be dreaming.

To see why this is impossible, is to see why the secondary elaboration of id-processes is a necessity in the generation of any conscious process that is partly id-determined; and if the dream matches this specification, this must hold of the dream as well. The point turns on the crucially important distinction between consciousness-of-an-item and consciousness-of-the-world, the latter being the condition of wakefulness.[9] Thus a man who dreams is at once unconscious of the world, and conscious of the contents of his dream, even though he is doubtless unaware that those dream contents *are* dream contents. More, because the dream contents are objects of consciousness, there must exist the possibility of recollecting that dream, which is to say, of recollecting a process that he must be

[8] See Brian O'Shaughnessy, 'Mental Structure and Self-Consciousness', *Inquiry* 15 (1972), 43.
[9] Ibid., pp. 41–2.

capable of describing in intelligible narrative. Then that narrative narrates what seemed at the time to him to be true, and this means that in rational creatures the dream takes place under the heading, the true. The conjunction of these two features of human, but not animal, conscious life, is no accident: namely, occurring under the aspect of the true, occurring under the concepts made available to him by the language that he knows. But this is already to locate those dream experiences within the orbit of the ego. It follows that no dream can *consist in* id-processes.

Thus it must be true of any id-determined process of which we are aware, whether contemporaneously or retrospectively, whether when conscious or in a state of unconsciousness, that it owes its place in awareness entirely to the labours of the unconscious portion of the ego. And this is to say that processes of secondary elaboration have occurred. However close certain processes may seem to the id itself, phenomena like hallucinatory episodes or peculiarly raw dreams, it would be impossible for us *ever* to become aware of them unless *at the time* of their occurrence their id-content had already undergone processes of secondary elaboration. Clearly this holds of present phenomena; and it must hold of the past, since it is through memory that those past phenomena enter awareness, and what we now remember must at the time have been an object of our consciousness.

Therefore, were it the case that the mind of the extremest possible katatonic was filled with pure destructive id-processes – which is, I daresay, far from true – it would be logically impossible that he should ever be aware of them. Actually, I suspect that there exist decisive theoretical considerations, most readily expressible in the powerful conceptual framework constructed by Melanie Klein, why this must be a false account of the extremes of schizophrenia. For one thing, it seems to be a case of mental death, for if the forces of death entirely possess something, then that something is dead. But the schizophrenic can part with his schizophrenia only through cure of it. Nevertheless, it would be a mistake to conclude from this that the id lies outside time (like its grandfather concept, Schopenhauerian Will). The id must be temporally diverse, for it must at least in part have its origin in the impact of somatic phenomena on the brain, and it makes its presence felt in the temporally ordered phenomena of consciousness. Thus Freud speaks of primary *processes*, as he was compelled to do, and while id-processes lack the rational structure of ego-processes, in being processes they must be temporally diverse. Therefore, however close it may get to it, the concept of the id is not the concept of a kind of *psychic matter*. It is, as it were, the mere filling of a psychic form that is entirely the work of the ego. It, too, has structure.

Dreaming is thinking when consciousness is unaware of the world

We pass from a consideration of the unconscious ego-processes, the Apollonian dream-work of 'secondary elaboration', as a result of which id-processes in symbolic form enter the consciousness of the sleeper who dreams. And we shall now attempt to characterize, first, the dream, then the day-dream, finally, the deep pre-sleep phantasy. In particular, we shall be concerned to assess *the will-status* of these three phenomena.

The dream is the form that thinking cannot but take, always supposing it continues, as one's state of consciousness switches from wakefulness to sleep. For the dream is a natural continuation of the thinking processes occurring just prior to the onset of sleep. I say so in part because of resemblance between these processes, in part because in either case the state of consciousness is consistent with no other form of thinking. Thus it is surely no contingency, as we reach that rapt state in which we are already well embarked on the road downwards into sleep, that the thinking processes which were unfolding as we first closed our eyes should by then have acquired that peculiar amalgam of drift, intensity and symbolism, all in the absence of words, that marks the transition to sleep and dream. That our thought processes should be of this kind, and the state of consciousness wherein they occur should be as it is, are not distinct states of affairs, since neither could occur without the other. Now, the situation is both similar and strikingly different with the dream: for we can dream when stunned, and fail to dream when asleep; and this shows that dreaming and sleeping must be distinct processes with distinct causes. This is a significant difference between dream and pre-sleep phantasy. Where they are alike is in the fact that sleep is consistent with no other thinking process than dreaming, for one whose thinking processes are as one who is awake must himself be awake! (*Let us not forget that the criteria of consciousness must be internal.*) Therefore I feel entitled to say that dreaming is the form that thinking cannot but take, always supposing it continues, as one's state of consciousness switches from wakefulness to sleep.

So long as we are awake, the onward rush of thought cannot conceivably stop, and therefore *a fortiori* cannot be stopped at will. That is, one awake has no choice but to be thinking (taking 'think' in a sufficiently wide sense). More, if we are awake, then necessarily we have *the power*, call it P, actively to govern the direction of flow of the inevitable stream of ideas. Yet phenomena like day-dreaming suggest that it may be possible to *decline* to put P to use. Even if this is so, there is something else, namely responsibility for our mental processes, which we cannot evade. Thus, because of the special setting in which power P occurs, for it is a power of which we cannot be unaware, it follows that if we are awake then necessarily we must be exercising what might be described as our *say*, call it *S*, over what thinking processes shall occupy our mind. I use this watered-down term, 'say', to indicate our continuing responsibility for our mind's processes, for it seems to me that because of the self-conscious power *P* we must *either* choose *or* permit the mind's processes to be what they are. Thus, at the very least, we exercise this say *S* through *knowingly declining* to put the power *P* to use, which means through permitting a process to occur; while we standardly exercise *S* through *using P* in choosing which processes shall occur.

Therefore the state of wakefulness, over which we have no immediate control, is essentially conjoined with our being not-free not to exercise say over what thinking processes shall occur in our mind. Indeed, the only respect in which we are free in this domain is in our continuing possession of power *P:* namely, the power actively to govern the direction of flow of the inevitable stream of ideas. This power we always have, and are condemned to have, so long as we are awake; and there is no third alternative to either using it or declining to use it. For the state of wakefulness, over which we have no immediate say, is a state marked by the self-conscious possession of that power. In sum: when awake we can choose neither to stop thinking, nor to cease arbiting or exercising responsible say over the processes in the mind. We can merely choose that one or another mental process shall occur.

The day-dream passively and permissively self-determines the day-dream

I introduce the concept of 'say', *S*, the concept of immediate responsibility, as a supplement to that of power to choose, *P*, in order to do justice to the day-dream. For it seems to me that the day-dream is the limiting, and perhaps even the degenerative, case of the self-determination of the thinking process. Now, it is not clear to me whether the day-dreamer exercises his power *P* to determine by choice the thinking process; and this I must emphasize. But what is certain is that the day-dreamer is responsible for the contents of his day-dream, and thus that he is exercising his say *S* over the thinking process in day-dreaming. For if a religious edict were to say, 'One must not permit one's thoughts to stray onto sacred topic *T*', would not one who day-dreams about *T* have disobeyed? Further, in failing to believe in the contents of his day-dream images, the day-dreamer reveals thereby that he knows he is day-dreaming; and this is confirmed by the fact that one who is roused from a day-dream does not at that moment *discover* that he has just been day-dreaming. Now, if we conjoin with this the fact of the continuing presence of the self-conscious power P to determine what mental processes shall obtain at any moment, then I think it becomes evident that, in a quite strict sense, the day-dreamer has responsibility for the contents of his day-dream.

At this point I shall hazard a brief, tentative and highly fallible account of the nature of day-dreaming. It seems to me that the day-dreamer, moved by familiarity (association) and agreeableness (inclination), passively self-determines the day-dream in the mode of permissiveness. That is, the day-dreamer self-consciously permits his thoughts to stray the way that familiarity and agreeableness take them. It is an active consenting to what is at once agreeable, familiar, unchosen; and the best comparison I can offer is that of feminine sexual consent. Its course is desired and permitted, and while it is not initiated it would not have eventuated were it not for that free consent. The conscious day-dreaming self passively conspires with its own easy inclinations. This is the nearest one can get to opting out of the necessity, imposed by sheer wakeful consciousness, of exercising say over the course of one's thinking processes. Indeed, it may even be that the self is active in day-dreaming, but if it is it may be active only in that reduced sense in which the free passive recipient accomplice in an activity engages in that activity.

By contrast, the pre-sleep phantasy pursues its course in a mind not in a self-conscious state. The person on the verge of sleep has not the responsibility or say encountered in the day-dreamer, and this is because he does not know he is merely phantasizing. The proof of this lies in the fact that when one suddenly starts out of such a state, 'coming awake again', one *does* then make the discovery that one was merely phantasizing and, indeed, almost asleep. Therefore in not knowing as he phantasizes that it is mere phantasy, he fails to be in possession of an item of knowledge, 'this process is one that I could control'; and so, peculiarly, it fails to be that which he could control, which is to say that he lacks the power P. Like the dream, it genuinely assumes *the mantle of reality*; whereas the day-dream is seen as *an immediate representation*, now of the past and actual, now of the past and might-have-been, now of the impossible and future, etc. It follows that the pre-sleeper, who is by his state of consciousness compulsorily reduced to the modalities of the here and now and actual, like the dreamer, has not given his consent to what happens in this seeming reality that is a product of his mind. *Mental freedom, and modal sophistication or modal self-consciousness, go together.* For without this, there would be nothing in the mind, as there must be, that relates to the actual processes as does the architect's blueprint to the realized edifice. Therefore the pre-sleeper's conscious values play no overt or chosen role in the genesis of the phantasy. In thus phantasizing, he can be said neither to have abided by, not to have flouted, his conscious values.

A summary of the issues arising from this discussion

At the beginning of section B, we stated that we would be concerned with those mental phenomena most requiring explanation in terms of the id. We took these to be those thinking processes in which ego-function or self-determining will was at its lowest ebb. We saw that in the purest examples of self-determination, such as listening, we were in possession of a total mental explanation of a simple mental state of affairs. For example, it is because I chose to listen to the sound that my attention and the sound are in conjunction. Therefore while my choice may be determined by id-phenomena, it is choice and not id that immediately and completely determines that sound and attention shall conjoin. Therefore the explanation of this conjunction lies entirely in the will of the listener, even if the explanation both of the choice and of the capacity to listen is obscure. Thus the explanatory gap is entirely closed in the case of listening. In consequence, there is little reason to mention the id. And while the id is, in mental creation, a significant factor, the ego and its will determine as organizing forces the terms of reference under which those id-phenomena take place.

How different it is with dreams! Nothing there is predetermined in advance by the choice of the subject. And so the normal causal explanatory factor, present to a greater or lesser degree in our daily waking mental life, is in the dream largely and probably completely absent. I mean: that mental cause – the will of the subject. We suggested that it was this absence that, to Freud, constituted powerful evidence that pre-eminently in the dream the primary processes in the id 'showed through'. Because the normal causal explanation of the course of self-composed thinking processes in waking life is unavailable in the case of the dream, Freud felt that if the dream was to be mentally explained he had to turn to an entirely different processive explanation, one in terms of the primary process. Something whose existence did not depend on that mental cause: the will. Theoretically, it would be open to him to see the dream as nothing but the product of unconscious processes in the ego. But the openly instinctual character of many dreams, in fact of much in human and animal life in general, the close kinship between the work of art and the dream, the similarity of dream contents to neurotic symptoms, jointly constitute a powerful argument for supposing that the missing determining process must be of a different order altogether from the reasoning and organizational phenomena present in the ego.

8

The bodily ego

RICHARD WOLLHEIM

1. 'The ego' Freud writes in *The ego and the id* 'is first and foremost a bodily ego' (1923b, XIX, 26). 'The Bodily Ego', a striking phrase, does not recur in Freud's writings. Nevertheless I believe there to be a thesis of the bodily ego which plays an important part, certainly in Freud's later, but probably also in his earlier, thinking. In this essay I want to consider the nature of this thesis, and to say something about its place within Freudian theory.

2. The thesis of the bodily ego contributes to the question how mind and body are related, or the mind–body problem. Currently, it is true, the problem is interpreted very narrowly, only one relation – that of identity – is taken into account, and only the question whether mind is identical with body is raised. To this question the thesis of the bodily ego has nothing to say, and the contribution that the thesis makes to the mind–body problem becomes apparent only when the full range of theoretically interesting relations between mind and body is taken account of. Let us see how those relations are reached.

To the question whether mind is identical with body or whether for every mental particular – a thought, a feeling, an access of desire – there is some physical particular with which it is identical, the answer may be yes or no. Those who answer yes subscribe to the identity thesis and are, on ordinary metaphysical assumptions, materialists. Those who answer no are generally dualists or epiphenomenalists, unless their no is so hesitant and guarded as to reflect a doubt whether mental and physical particulars are sufficiently well-regimented for identity either to be asserted or to be denied between them.[1] Freud answered yes to this question, he was a materialist, but there are shades and shades of materialism.

[1] See Thomas Nagel, 'What is it like to be a Bat?' *Philosophical Review* 83 (October, 1974), 435–50, reprinted in his *Mortal Questions* (Cambridge University Press, Cambridge, 1979): and Jennifer Hornsby, 'Which Physical Events are Mental Events?' *Proceedings of the Aristotelian Society* 81 (1980–81), 73–92.

Someone who subscribes to the identity thesis might do so for one or other of two different reasons. He might believe that the identities in question are analytic, so that for every mental description of a particular there is some physical description with which it is synonymous. Such a person would accept the identity thesis because he accepts some meta-linguistic thesis which at once entails and trivializes it. But he might not believe in any such synonymy, and for him the identities obtain solely because of what mental particulars are. They are metaphysically rather than analytically true. All who hold the identity thesis for the first of these reasons, and some of those who hold it for the second, are not only materialists but also reductionists: they believe that the mental language is at least in principle eliminable. When the identity thesis is held for metalinguistic reasons reductionism is an obvious consequence, but the connection is less clear in the case of someone who holds it for metaphysical reasons: probably what is at stake is whether mental properties are or are not identical with physical properties. Freud's materialism was not based on linguistic considerations and he rejected reductionism. His theory requires the mental language.

Anyone who is not a reductionist about the mind must ask himself the question, what is so special about mental descriptions? If he rejects the identity thesis, this question asks nothing less than, what is special about mental particulars? If however he accepts the identity thesis, his question may be reformulated as, what is special about a certain subset of bodily particulars?, or what special aspect or aspects of this subset of bodily particulars is it to which we attempt to do justice when we apply mental descriptions to them? It would be in this way that the question presented itself to Freud, and there are two familiar answers, each of which may be thought of as providing a condition for the mental. Each aims at necessity, their disjunction at sufficiency, and in most cases if either is met so is the other. The two conditions constitute a common ground between the dualist, the epiphenomenalist, and the non-reductive materialist.

According to one answer, when we apply mental descriptions to bodily particulars, we do so because the particulars are associated with a phenomenology. The point has been put recently by saying that there is something that it *is like for* the subject that houses the particular to be in the state corresponding to the existence of the particular. According to the other answer, the application of mental descriptions to bodily particulars records the fact that such particulars are associated with an internal representation: in other words, the existence of the particular corresponds to a state of the subject which allows him to be related cognitively, conatively, or affectively to things in the external world (where this includes things in the internal worlds of others) and also to things in his own internal world. (I prefer to say of the particulars to which we apply mental descriptions that they are 'associated' with a phenomenology or with an internal representation rather than that they have a phenomenology or include an internal representation because these latter ways of putting it involve mental predications and it seems right to make such predications of a bodily particular only when it has been picked out by a description in the mental language.)

If either of these answers is correct, or both, the next question to ask is whether they give rise to a further relation between mind and body. If mental particulars, which either are or aren't bodily particulars, have a phenomenology or include an internal representation, does either of these facts relate the mind to the body in a way over and above identity or diversity? Spinoza and William James addressed themselves to just this question. So does the thesis of the bodily ego.

3. Primarily the thesis of the bodily ego says something about the way in which mental states are related to the body through their representational aspect: however this link, as we shall see, is sometimes reinforced by another link which passes through the phenomenology of mental states.

Let us introduce the thesis of the bodily ego through a theory of Spinoza's which also claims that mind and body are related representationally. The theory is very bold, and its claim is that every mental state is representational of a bodily state and specifically of that bodily state with which it is identical. Freud's theory diverges from Spinoza's at three crucial points. First, Freud's theory is not a theory about every mental state. It ranges over primitive states of mind, or states of mind that have fallen under some fairly primitive form of mental functioning. Secondly, Freud's theory concentrates not upon the outward-looking representations that mental states include – that is, those which permit the subject to relate to the world – but upon the inward-looking representations or those by means of which a mental state represents itself to itself. And thirdly – and now we come to the central claim of Freud's theory – it is asserted that those mental states over which the theory ranges represent themselves to themselves as, at least in part, bodily states, though by no means those bodily states with which they are identical. Just which bodily states occur in these self-representations is certainly no arbitrary matter. It has, as we shall see, two determinants. First there is the overall psychic organization of the subject, and secondly there is the precise role or function that the mental state discharges for any subject who has it.

But, first, what is this talk of self-representation of mental states? Why should we be expected to believe in such things? More specifically, if mental states are internally represented, isn't it enough to think that one mental state might be represented by another mental state? – why should we have to believe the surely more cumbrous thesis that (at any rate some) mental states are self-representing?

I suggest that whether a certain mental state is self-representing or not is just the issue whether its efficacy requires that it should be represented in the mind. Once its essential function within the psychology of the person is found to involve a representation of itself, the conclusion seems inescapable that this representation is part of it, i.e. is a self-representation. Of course what such an argument requires is that we should be able to assign to mental states something that may be regarded as their function, but, that this is so is a thesis about the mind which must remain an assumption for the length of this paper. Some difficulties with the thesis may be removed when it is recognized that the function may be, and often will be, a matter of bringing about further mental states. Above, in summarizing the thesis of the bodily ego, I began with the claim that certain mental states are self-representing and I then went on to indicate the content that the theory ascribes to those self-representations and then to link this ascription with, in part at any rate, the efficacy of the mental state. This is obviously the correct expository order, but it is important to recognize that it reverses the evidential order. For the best reason that there could be for postulating self-representations of mental states – by which I mean both that certain states represent themselves and that they represent themselves in this or that way – relates to what such representations can do for the mental states they are of – or, ultimately, for the subject who has such states. In illustrating this point, which is a general point, I shall not confine myself to those mental states to which the thesis of the bodily ego applies, but I shall take states which are self-representing but where the self-representations are not distorted or are veridical.

I start with belief and a recent argument[2] designed to show that we cannot legitimately assign beliefs to creatures who lack the concept of belief. The argument – if I follow it – does not rest upon the presumably incontrovertible fact that anyone who can be said to hold a belief must be capable of reflecting upon the belief that he holds, or upon the fact that he holds the belief, and for these purposes therefore will certainly need to have the concept of belief. To argue in this way would be to make the necessity of having the concept of belief something that was consequen-

[2] Donald Davidson, 'Thought and Talk' in *Mind and Language*, ed. Samuel Guttenplan (Blackwell, Oxford, 1975).

tial upon holding beliefs, whereas what the argument under consideration wishes to establish is that having the concept of belief is part of, or
essential to, holding beliefs. For it the central consideration would seem
to be this: we form beliefs, we revise them; these are the vicissitudes of
belief, and we have to allow both if belief is going to enter appropriately
into the explanation of behaviour. Now if we consider the formation of
beliefs it is evident that the subject in order to form a belief must have the
concept of truth: for truth is what belief aims at, and so without the
concept he would have no reason to choose this rather than that as what
he believes. However, if we now turn to the revision of beliefs, we can see
that the concept of truth is not enough. To make intelligible to himself
the switch from one belief to another, the subject must also have some
such concept as that of holding true, where what is held true may or may
not actually be true. And further reflection shows first that this concept
has also a real part to play in the formation of belief too, and secondly
that this concept is just the concept of belief.

If this argument works, it does so by showing that beliefs could not
achieve what they do for the subject – that is, explain his behaviour and
his changes of behaviour – unless the subject had the concept of belief. In
this way the argument is of the pattern I suggested. It is, it is true, not
explicit in the argument that the concept of belief should actually be used
in the formation or revision of beliefs – that it should figure representationally rather than be kept in reserve, as, say, an idle part of the subject's
recognitional capacity – but the argument seems not to carry the reader
along without such an assumption. And so, if I am right about arguments
of this kind and what they show, the proper conclusion to the present
argument is that beliefs are necessarily self-representing.

Belief is a disposition, and it is natural to think that the case for the
self-representation of mental states gets stronger as we turn our attention
from dispositional to occurrent states. The occurrent mental states whose
specific efficacy seems most readily explicable by reference to the way in
which they are represented, hence represent themselves, are memory and
imagination (or at any rate one form of imagination, which I shall call
make-believe). Memory does what it does for the subject in part because
memory states are labelled as states whose content relates to the past.
Make-believe does what it does for the subject in part because states of
make-believe are labelled as states whose content is not to be assessed
against considerations of truth. I have argued[3] for both these proposi-

[3] Richard Wollheim, 'The Mind and the Mind's Image of Itself', *Int. Journal of
Psycho-Anal.* 50 (1969), 209–20, reprinted in his *On Art and the Mind* (Allen Lane,
London, 1973): and 'Identification and Imagination' in *Freud*, ed. Richard Wollheim
(Doubleday, New York, 1974), 172–95.

tions and hence for (on my view) the conclusions that derive from them – namely that memory states and states of make-believe are self-representing – and now I want simply to add one point which will turn out to be germane to the topic of this essay. In the case of memory, though not as far as I can see in the case of make-believe, there seems to be a connection, not lost on philosophers, between the self-representation of memory (whether this is how they saw it or not) and the phenomenology, or, more specifically, a crucial part of the phenomenology, of memory – I mean the sense of pastness or of familiarity that permeates at least one kind of memory. It is in part because memory feels as it does that it labels itself as such – just as it is in part because it labels itself as such that it is enabled to do what it does. It is a fine point whether phenomenology and self-representation are fundamentally distinct aspects of a mental state like memory or whether one isn't ultimately derivative from the other. But they certainly collude in a variety of ways, and this collusion will recur within the scope of the thesis of the bodily ego, to which I now turn.

4. In the essay 'Negation' (1925h, XIX) Freud considers the origins of intellectual life and in particular he concentrates upon a phenomenon which anticipates the formation of belief. Let us call this the formation of proto-belief. Belief and proto-belief differ in this respect: that whereas belief is, as we have seen, a truth-directed phenomenon, proto-belief is pleasure-directed. The formation of belief issues in holding something true or false: the formation of proto-belief issues in finding something good for us or bad for us. Holding something true or false conditions our expectations and contributes to the initiation of action. By contrast finding something good for us incites us to maintain it before the mind, finding something bad for us incites us to expunge it from the mind, and in neither case is the question of any match or mismatch between the thing found good or bad and the world paid heed to. With proto-belief there is, as Freud puts it, no 'reality testing'.

In the preceding summary 'something' is clearly to be glossed as 'a thought' or 'a judgment'. But then it might be asked how could a thought ever be retained or dismissed for reasons that were altogether independent of truth? Of course, we may – as in make-believe – suspend considerations of truth, but then equally we don't accept or reject what we make-believe. So how could we accept or reject a thought, as we are alleged to do in the case of proto-belief, and yet take no interest in its truth-value? It is of this that Freud offers an explanation, and he does so by reference to the way in which the thought represents itself. It represents itself as something corporeal: or, more specifically, either as something that can be brought into the body and made part of it, or as something that starts off as a part of the body and can then be pushed out of it. Freud characterizes the formation of proto-belief in the following way:

Expressed in the language of the oldest – the oral – instinctual impulses, the judgement is 'I should like to eat this', or 'I should like to spit out'; and, put more generally: 'I should like to take this into myself and to keep that out'. That is to say: 'It shall be inside me' or 'it shall be outside me'. As I have shown elsewhere, the original pleasure-ego wants to introject into itself everything that is good and to eject from itself everything that is bad (op. cit., 237).

A thought makes itself suitable for this kind of treatment by the way in which it represents itself: it represents itself as a piece of food, or as a piece of vomit, or (since proto-belief not merely persists into, but flourishes during, the anal phase) as a piece of shit.

A feature of the discussion in 'Negation' is that – at any rate for all that Freud says – the thoughts he has in mind are not singled out by reference to their content. They are, by and large, thoughts which arise from perception or from sensation: and the fact that they misrepresent themselves in this special way is just a reflection of the mode of mental functioning that currently prevails within the subject. It is the stage of development the subject is at, or that he is still in the grip of the primary process, that accounts for the occurrence of his mental states under these confused images, and what is of psychoanalytic interests here is the fragment of psychological development to which it introduces us.

However, the thesis of the bodily ego also ranges over certain mental states in virtue of their content rather than of the stage of development to which they attest, and in the case of such states, barely surprisingly, their content is of inherent psychoanalytic interest. Such states occur originally during the ascendency of the primary process and therefore their later occurrence is, strictly speaking, regressive, but they nevertheless play a crucial role not only in the evolved life of the individual but also in the evolution of his life. I am thinking particularly of the mental states that make up the two psychic mechanisms of introjection and projection. These mental states are phantasies, and to see just how these phantasies add up to a psychic mechanism the thesis of the bodily ego is of real importance. I shall here discuss only introjection, since the structural similarities between introjection and projection suffice for the case to carry over.

In the best account of introjection, which can partly be derived from the interpretation of Freud's writings[4] but which needs to be supplemented by later writers,[5] phantasy appears twice over.

In the first of its two appearances phantasy manifests itself in an occurrent form. A figure in the environment is perceived by the subject either as particularly loving and benign or as especially frightening and malign. This perception is itself most likely due to phantasy, but this phantasy would be a manifestation of projection. Whichever way round the figure is perceived, but in either case because it is perceived the way it is, the subject engages in a phantasy in which the figure before it or before its mind is depicted as being brought into the subject's body. Typically entry is effected through the mouth but sometimes through the anus. This first appearance of phantasy I call 'the incorporative phantasy'. In its second appearance phantasy manifests itself in a dispositional form. As a result of the incorporative phantasy the subject acquires a disposition to phantasize in a certain way. The figure who in the incorporative phantasy he took into his body is now phantasized as engaging in a variety of activities, all of which take place within the confines of the subject. Just how the location of these activities is represented in the phantasies will, as we shall see, vary. The second appearance of phantasy within introjection I call internalization – though this is an idiosyncratic use of the term – and the connection between the occurrent phantasy and the dispositional phantasy is at once causal and intentional: internalization is the effect of incorporation, and there is an identity of figure between the two.

However, to achieve cogency the account needs supplementation, and this is what the thesis of the bodily ego can provide. The thesis adds that the two phantasies essential to introjection represent themselves corporeally or that their self-representations assimilate them to bodily activities. There are two claims here. The first is that these phantasies are self-representing: which, as we have seen, means that a representation of them within the subject is essential to their efficacy. The second claim is that these self-representations are a specific kind of self-misrepresentation, and once again the justification of the claim depends – though this time

---

[4] 1915c, XIV, 136–8; 1917e [1915], XIV, 243–58; 1922b, XVIII, 105–16, 129–34; 1923b, XIX, 28–39; 1924c, XIX, 167–8.

[5] Karl Abraham 'A Short Study of the Development of the Libido' in his *Selected Papers*, trans. Douglas Bryan & Alix Strachey (Hogarth, London, 1949); Susan Isaacs 'The Nature and Function of Phantasy', *Int. J. Psycho-Anal.* 29 (1948), 73–97; and Melanie Klein 'A Contribution to the Psychogenesis of Manic-Depressive States' in *Love Guilt and Reparation and Other Works*, *The Writings of Melanie Klein*, ed. Roger Money Kyrle, vol. I (Hogarth, London, 1975), *The Psychoanalysis of Children*, *Writings* vol. II (Hogarth, London, 1975), and 'Some Theoretical Conclusions Regarding the Emotional Life of the Infant' in *Envy and Gratitude and Other Works*, *Writings* vol. III (Hogarth, London, 1975). Cf. W. W. Meissner 'Notes on Identification, I & II', *Psychoanalytic Quarterly* 39 (1970), 563–89, and 40 (1971), 277–302; and Roy Schafer *Aspects of Internalization* (Int. University Press, New York, 1973).

not wholly – upon an appeal to efficacy. (For the rest of the claim reflects the libidinal stage that exerts hegemony over the subject.) I shall concentrate upon the stronger claim and show how it fills a lacuna in the account of introjection given.

The account begins with a perception, in which a figure in the environment is perceived by a subject as either very benign or very malign, and this figure the subject then phantasizes taking into himself. If the perception is what motivates the phantasy, it is reasonable to suppose that what the subject wishes to achieve is, in the case of the malign perception, to protect himself from the harm that the figure might do him. But why should the subject think that either of these aims could be achieved by phantasizing that the figure enters his body? The subject may phantasize anything he wishes, but surely the figure, still out there in the environment, will remain either just as vulnerable or just as dangerous as he was initially perceived to be. Is there any source from which the subject can acquire confidence that, if he phantasizes in a certain way, a certain effect in the world will be assured? Or is there any belief that the subject could have which would justify him in his own eyes in resorting to incorporative phantasy as an appropriate response to a situation of danger?

An answer suggests itself. The subject's resort to incorporative phantasy would be explicable if it could be shown that the subject believes that in phantasizing the incorporation of the figure he thereby alters the situation of the figure: he is removing him from a position in which he can endure, alternatively in which he can inflict, harm to a position where he is safe, alternatively where the subject is safe from him. The simplest belief of this kind would be that in phantasizing the incorporation of the figure the subject thereby incorporates him, and this in turn could be accounted for if not merely did the subject's phantasies include a representation of themselves but these representations represented them as the very bodily activities that they are of. It is essential to the incorporative phantasy that it represents itself as an actual incorporative process, and this bridges the gap, which otherwise would open up, between resort to phantasy and the lowering of anxiety. This, it hardly needs to be pointed out, is an appeal to efficacy in that what the subject needs from introjection is relief from fear. (At this point the retort might be made that this isn't an appeal to efficacy in that the subject's aim is security for or from the external figure not just the belief that the figure is secure or that he is secure from the figure. But though this retort is generally sound, it is not so in this case since just what defines this case is that for its duration the distinction is lost on the subject.)

However, this is not the only respect in which the initial account of introjection needs to be supplemented and the thesis of the bodily ego invoked. Corporeal self-representation cannot stop short at the incorporative phantasy, it must extend to internalization, and this is something that we are required to accept for two distinct reasons. In the first place, unless this is so, the efficacy of the incorporative phantasy, which was the reason for introducing corporeal self-representation initially, would be in jeopardy. For once the external figure has been (as he experiences it) brought inside him, the subject needs to be reassured that such security as has already been achieved will not be at risk: in other words, he must believe that the incorporated figure will remain inside him. And a way of doing this that suggests itself is that the subject should experience the dispositional phantasy as a corporeal process of containing the figure in the very place where he is phantasized as being: that is, inside the subject's body. But, secondly, this result is independently assured, and that is because how mental states are represented or self-represented is not a piece-meal issue but is determined on the level of overall psychic organization. Corporeality of representation reflects a mode of psychic organization so that, given closely associated phantasies or phantasies linked by a common function, if one is represented corporeally, the other will be too: if the incorporative phantasy is represented corporeally so also must be the dispositional phantasy to which it gives rise.

The plausibility that attaches to this account of introjection is still not completely before us until we see how phenomenology enters the picture and makes its distinctive contribution to efficacy. It is a long-standing thought of Freud's that an experience that has a powerful visual or kinaesthetic content can readily be taken by the subject for the very thing that it is of – with, at any rate in the case of waking experiences, the immediate discharge of energy. Under the impact of the wish a 'false identity' is established between an image – or a memory, as Freud is inclined to call any image that owes its content to previous perception – and a phenomenologically similar percept, and in consequence the subject undergoes an hallucination. Such thinking is already much to the fore in those parts of the *Scientific Project* (1950a [1887–1902], I) where Freud discusses early mental functioning, so much so that two recent commentators on the *Project* have summarized his position by saying that 'hallucination is in a sense *the* mechanism of the primary process.'[6] Hallucination in this sense is of crucial importance in *The Interpretation of Dreams* and it appears as a premiss in an empirical argument that

[6] Karl Pribram and Morton Gill, *Freud's 'Project' Re-assessed* (Hutchinson, London, 1976), p. 141.

Freud adduces to substantiate a central tenet of his dream-theory. Freudian dream-theory maintains not just that dreams express wishes but that they provide wish-fulfilment, and in direct support of the theory he cites the 'infantile' or 'intelligible' dreams of children (1900a, IV, 127–31; 1916–7, XV, 126–35) in which manifest and latent content coincide and where, say, a child wanting strawberries dreams of having strawberries. But this would be no evidence unless we believed that in the subject's perspective the representation of a wish as fulfilled appears to fulfil that wish. Dreams can constitute wish-fulfilment only if, in being dreams of gratification – and the advantage of infantile dreams is that this is an evident fact about them – they are thereby believed to gratify (cf. 1917d [1915], XIV).

Freud cites the phenomenon of hallucination to show how a mental state of one kind can come to serve the same causal or functional role as a mental state of another kind and do so in virtue of a phenomenological link: so, for instance, memory, which resembles or seems like perception, comes to function as perception, i.e. it regulates discharge of energy. Now as far as Freud's explicit account is concerned, there is no suggestion that this false identity operates through the self-representation of mental states, so that, for instance, when a memory state acts for the subject like a percept, it includes a self-representation that represents it as a percept. Nevertheless this might be the right way of reconstructing Freud's account of hallucination. (Similarly an appeal to self-misrepresentation of mental states might be the right way to explain Freud's account of what he variously calls 'the omnipotence of thoughts' or 'the over-valuation of psychic phenomena' (1909d, X, 233–5, 298–301; 1912–13, XIII, 83–90; 1917a, XVII, 139). Indeed the right way to explain this latter phenomenon might even be by an appeal to a corporeal self-misrepresentation of mental states.[7] However, in this essay I do not intend to pursue these questions, closely related though they evidently are to its topic. For, if I am right, within the scope of the thesis of the bodily ego, there is already reason to suppose that certain mental states do misrepresent themselves and do so by representing themselves corporeally. This supposition in part derives, as we have seen, from considerations of efficacy and in part it gains credibility from its link with the theory of psycho-sexual development: for the precise corporeal form that mental self-misrepresentation takes depends upon the stage of development that the subject is at. Now my present suggestion is that, given there are such errors of self-representation amongst certain mental

---

[7] See my 'Wish-Fulfilment' in *Rational Action*, ed. Ross Harrison (Cambridge University Press, Cambridge, 1979), 47–60.

states, might we not be well advised to see if the phenomenology of those mental states contributes to that outcome – given further that phenomenology can give rise to a confusion or false identity between mental states of different kinds? Certainly, on the face of it, it is not implausible that, say, the phantasy of devouring an external figure should, on the basis of how it seems or feels, help to lure the subject into thinking that he was actually devouring the figure or that the experience in itself, or in virtue of its sensory character, should strengthen the illusion that Freud called 'psychic cannibalism'. But at this point I leave the suggestion.

5. I have said that in introjection the link between the two constituent phantasies – the incorporative phantasy and internalization – is twofold. It is causal and it is intentional. It is causal in that the earlier phantasy is productive of the later phantasy, and it is intentional in that the earlier and later phantasy are about the same thing or there is an identity of figure between the two. The second point is not quite right. The incorporative phantasy is a phantasy about an external figure and taking it into oneself: the phantasies of internalization are about a figure taken into oneself and they concern his doings inside the body. Strict identity, i.e. identity, does not hold between the external figure and the internal figure that results from its incorporation. The best way of mirroring the relationship between the two seems to be as that between a real-life person and a fictional character modelled upon that person.

In those passages in which Freud talked of introjection, he would seem, with varying degrees of explicitness to think of the product, or output, of the incorporative phantasy as an internal figure. The boldest claim of this kind evidently concerns the super-ego which is the internal version of the father in the Oedipal drama. But as he came to recognize the frequency of introjection in an individual life – which in turn must mean that introjection transcends a purely defensive role[8] – Freud was led to believe in a wide variety of internal figures, and in the late *Outline of Psychoanalysis* he posits an 'internal world' (1940a [1938], XXIII) which is populated by such figures. Freud's insight was, of course, intensively exploited by Melanie Klein and her followers. In reaction against what are held to be the excesses of Kleinian theory and in defence of a greater parsimony ascribed to Freudian theory defenders of psychoanalytic orthodoxy have come to obscure Freud's point.[9] By proposing the terms

[8] See my *Freud* (Collins, London, 1971) pp. 200–2.
[9] Cf. J. Sandler and B. Rosenblatt, 'The Concept of the Representational World' in *The Psychoanalytic Study of the Child* 17 (Int. Univ. Press, New York, 1963) pp. 128–45.

'mental representation' and 'representational world' for 'internal object' and 'internal world' they have misrepresented the point as though it were, in the first place, a point about what phantasies are rather than about what phantasies are of, and secondly, a point about all phantasies rather than about certain phantasies. It did not require the genius of Freud to discern that phantasies as such are internal events. What Freud did discern was that there are certain phantasies such that the only adequate way of describing their content is to say that they are of an object that is located inside and persists within the subject's body. There are, in other words, phantasies of external objects and phantasies of internal objects, and phantasies of internal objects derive by an appropriate causal route from incorporative phantasies. It is significant that in Kleinian theory where internal objects are made so much of, the distinction between the two kinds of phantasy and the specific causal origins of one kind are insisted on.[10]

That introjection should in this way bring into being an internal object at once clarifies, and may be clarified by reference to, what may now be identified as two discrete applications of the thesis of the bodily ego to mental phenomena. In the essay 'Negation' Freud was talking about how a thought or judgment, where this may be equated with the content of a mental act, may come to represent itself as a bodily phenomenon – in this case, a bodily part. By contrast, in the discussion of introjection (and projection) Freud was talking about how a mental act might come to represent itself as a bodily phenomenon – in this case, a bodily process. Continuous with this second line of thinking is the corporealization of what the mental act is directed upon: and that is not a thought or judgment but that which the thought or judgment is of. Bodily representation extends from phantasy to the figure in the environment who occurs in the phantasy: and given that the phantasy is represented as a bodily process, the figure is represented as the kind of thing that the bodily process would be directed upon. Psychic cannibalism, in other words, consumes a person.

However, it is one thing to see why psychoanalytic theory when it is conceptualized in such a way as to preserve the subject's perspective needs to introduce internal objects, but it is another thing to resolve the difficulties that attach to such a notion. I shall consider two obvious difficulties.

In the first place, in what sense are internal objects *internal?* I have

[10] Cf. 'I do not interpret in terms of internal objects and relationships until I have explicit material showing phantasies of internalizing the object in concrete and physical terms.' Melanie Klein, *Narrative of a Child Analysis, The Writings of Melanie Klein*, ed. Roger Money-Kyrle vol. IV (Hogarth, London, 1975) p. 31.

already said that the marks of internality are varied and it might be useful to bring them under two broad headings. On the one hand there are what I call the substantive marks of internality, by which I mean a subset of those properties which the object is phantasized as having. Amongst such properties would be ambivalence, the pursuit of archaic sexual aims, implacability or an exaggerated radiance of character, and an immediacy of access to the subject's mental processes. On the other hand there are what may be thought of as the formal marks of internality where these derive not from the content of the phantasy but from the structural properties of phantasy as such. Such marks would include radical incompleteness of character, deathlessness, a mutability of goodness or badness in accordance with the psychic ups and downs of the subject, and an imperviousness to reality-testing or to any matching against the external prototype.

The second and more serious difficulty is, in what sense are internal objects *objects*? The seriousness of the difficulty comes from the combination of three factors. Internal objects are non-actual: the explanatory role for which they are cast requires them to be the subjects of *de re* truths: and they give the appearance of not having well defined identity conditions. I have already given a hint of where to my mind the likeliest analogy for internal objects is to be found: in fictional characters – though the third factor is present only in some fiction. I do not know of an altogether satisfactory theory of fictional characters, but the most adequate accounts,[11] by rooting fictional characters in the imaginative experiences or the make-believe activity of their authors, prepare us for the way in which internal objects derive their existence from the incorporative phantasies of the subjects they inhabit.

6. Thus far in talking of the thesis of the bodily ego I have talked of the bodily ego itself solely in so far as it makes a benign contribution to individual development. This, however, is not the whole story, and that it isn't enhances the value of the thesis. For it enlarges its explanatory scope. Corporeal representation is, we have seen, obedient to the phase-specific intimations of psycho-sexual development, and in consequence if and when this development meets with setbacks, there will be corresponding disturbances and inhibitions amongst those mental phenomena which are represented in a way that makes reference to it. Even within normal development, Freud, following Abraham, pointed out that any internal object that owes its existences to a phantasy of oral incorpora-

[11] G. E. Moore, 'Imaginary Objects' reprinted in his *Philosophical Papers* (Allen & Unwin, London, 1959); and Robert Howell, 'Fictional Objects' in *Body, Mind and Method: Essays in Honor of Virgil C. Aldrich* (Reidel, Dordrecht, 1979).

tion is susceptible to a defect characteristic of the oral phase: ambivalence (1905d, VII, 198; 1921c, XVIII, 105). But in 'The Psycho-analytic
View of Psychogenic Disturbance of Vision' (1910i, XI), an essay which
for some reason he seems to have held in low esteem, Freud went well
beyond this and produced a general account of how a bodily organ that
'enters into close relations' with the sexual instinct exposes itself to just
those risks of functional disturbance to which sexual development itself
is prone, and an account of this sort is presupposed in much of the work
of Melanie Klein and W. R. Bion.[12]

The philosophical interest of the thesis of the bodily ego is that it ties
not just the mind to body but the development of the mind to the
development of the body. This tie turns out to be a mixed blessing.
Within a different psychology mental states might have been different –
different in their essence – and they might have represented themselves as
states of the outside world or states of another's body. If Freud is right
and his thesis true, it leads us to an important though well-kept secret of
human psychology.[13]

[12] Melanie Klein, 'The School of Libidinal Development' in *Writings*, vol. I (Hogarth,
London, 1975), and 'A Contribution to the Theory of Intellectual Inhibition', in *Writings*,
vol. III (Hogarth, London, 1975); and W. R. Bion, *Second Thoughts* (Tavistock, London,
1967), secs. 8, 9. Cf. Richard Wollheim, *The Sheep and the Ceremony* (Cambridge
University Press, Cambridge, 1979).

[13] I am grateful to W. D. Hart for comments on an earlier draft and to Jonathan
Sinclair-Wilson for helpful suggestions about the present version.

9

Norms and the normal[*]

RONALD DE SOUSA

A System must have its utopia. For psychoanalysis, the utopia is 'genitality'.

E. ERIKSON

Freud denied that psychoanalysis has 'moral' implications beyond those of the scientific attitude in general (1933a, XXII, 158ff.). Yet any comprehensive vision of human nature such as he provides must have implications for the nature of happiness, and for the relation of man's natural capacities to his normal or ideal state. Classical theories of man might be forced into a dichotomy between what we might tag the 'biological' and the 'theological'. The former derive normative conclusions from the innate and specific endowments of man, the latter start from an ideal model somehow revealed. (In this sense Aristotle's vision is biological, Plato's theological.) Freud's view contrasts with both: the normal man in maturity is not 'natural', he is the outcome of a complex development the course of which is not determined by innate capacities alone. Yet no source exists, outside that development itself, for an ideal of maturity. This third way blurs the venerable distinction between Fact and Value: in the developmental vision of the normal human, we should find both a source of therapeutic values – whether or not these coincide with conventional morals – and a relative measure of the worth, in relation to happiness, of different levels of experience and activity. My central object in these pages is to give a qualified defence of this approach, and to show how Freud's version of it fares in the face of criticism. A particular charge I shall consider is that of 'reductionism', often levelled against psychoanalysis: that the effect of Freud's theory is to degrade the higher manifestations of human life by reducing them to lower ones.[1]

[*] This is a reprint of an essay which appeared under the same title in *Freud: A Collection of Critical Essays*, ed. Richard Wollheim (Doubleday, New York, 1974), from which it is reprinted with permission of the author and the publisher.

[1] This view finds both support and disavowal in Freud's own writings: 'Man's judgments of value . . . are an attempt to support his illusions with arguments.' (1930a, XXI, 145); but ' "to blacken the radiant and drag the sublime into the dust" is no part of [the] purpose' of psychoanalysis (1910c, XI, 63).

I The pleasure principle, wants and happiness

In the opening sentence of *Civilization and Its Discontents*, Freud remarks: 'It is impossible to escape the impression that people commonly use false standards of measurement . . . and that they underestimate what is of true value in life' (1930a, XXI, 64). How is the implied distinction to be made? 'The idea of life having a purpose stands and falls with the religious system' (ibid., 76): if value is determined by life's 'purpose', the idea of 'true value' must then fall. Instead of questions about transcendent purpose or value, Freud asks 'what men themselves show by their behaviour to be the purpose and intention of their lives' (ibid.). His conception of value is a naturalistic one, grounded in experienced wants. But if people's actual wants are the measures of value, what criteria can be used to show that they are using 'false standards of measurement'?

We might interpret Freud's view thus: wants are conceived as a mode of perception having as its proper object pleasure-at-a-future-time (or rather: on-a-possible-occasion) (cf. 1900a, V, 565–6); then wanting is *veridical* if the experience it envisages is, when it occurs, actually pleasurable, otherwise *mistaken*. But could one not be mistaken about the value of *occurrent* pleasure? The present assumptions leave room for a mis-estimation of this only where there is a mistake in the perception of the pleasure itself; and perhaps such a mistake could not occur unless pleasure were somehow experienced without adequate awareness. And Freud does not seem to allow for such a possibility. For pleasure is an affect, and 'strictly speaking,' he says (though in a somewhat different context), 'there are no unconscious affects' (1915e, XIV, 178). So far then, this essentially utilitarian account of value seems to work. Still, there are fatal difficulties for the view that what is of value for man is determined by what his choices and behaviour *show* him to want. Both his choices and behaviour may belie his *real* wants. First, because a man may be mistaken at the moment of choice about the pleasurable qualities of the object chosen: wants are sometimes not 'veridical'. Secondly, in so far as the reality principle takes the place of the pleasure principle in determining rational choice (1933a, XXII, 76), we cannot infer from any given choice that its object is of 'genuine value' (or genuinely wanted): it might be chosen as a compromise or for the sake of something else.

These difficulties appear to stand in the way of distinguishing, on Freud's assumptions, between real and illusory wants. Yet Freud offers a way. Through the theory of instinct and development, the variegation of human tastes becomes encompassed in a system; different balances of elements give us different normal types (1931a, XXI, 215), from which deviations are more or less pathological. This results in a subtle shift: it is not individual men who 'show by their behaviour' what the purpose of their life is. A *theory*, based on facts about individuals, to be sure, but which need not reflect the subjective preferences of any particular one, determines the normal wants and pleasures of men in general. This is how the developmental perspective provides a 'third way' contrasting both with the 'biological' and with the 'theological'. The account is rooted in natural fact: Freud calls instinctual stimulus 'need' (1915c, XIV, 119). But for a capital reason we cannot simply identify even instinctual wants with biological needs. Some needs are without corresponding felt wants (say, the need for vitamins), and we are interested just in those needs that have a 'psychical representative' (1905d, VII, 168). For only those can ground an account of the vicissitudes of mental phenomena. Moreover it follows from the long helplessness of human infants that the development of their instincts must be shaped by social influences. Normal development, therefore, cannot be *reduced* to natural fact: 'We may characterize [the development of civilization] with reference to the changes which it brings about in the familiar instinctual dispositions of human beings' (1930a, XXI, 96). And in so far as happiness 'is a problem of the economics of the individual's libido' (ibid., 83), we have an answer to the question: How is *normal development* to be defined? Namely, by reference to the best economic solution both within the individual and between the claims of the individual and those of the group (ibid., 96).[2]

This line of thought ties in with the determination of value by 'pleasure and unpleasure'. But it suggests that the relation between developmental theory and human values is not a simple one. For while a moment ago developmental psychology promised to justify a distinction between real and illusory wants, we are now led to the curious conception of a psychology itself partly grounded in a Utilitarian theory of value. Yet, as we shall see, the psychological theory obscures rather than clarifies the basic notion on which Utilitarianism must rest: that of pleasure or satisfaction. To see why this is, let us turn first to a cursory sketch of instinct theory.

II The theory of instinct

Instinct, Freud repeatedly emphasized, is 'the most important and the most obscure element of psychological research' (1920g, XVIII, 34. Cf. 1915c, XIV, 118; 1930a, XXI, 117). The most basic part of psychologi-

---

[2] Note that there is something misleading about this opposition between the individual and the group. Though the claims of the group impinge on the freedom of the individual, they are derivative of the claims of the group's member individuals. Only individual consciousness can experience 'pleasure and unpleasure'.

cal theory must exhibit the relation between our mental life and its roots in our organic constitution. More particularly it should relate the physiological mechanisms operative in our bodies to the intentionality of mental life and behaviour. This is the fundamental task of instinct theory: 'although instincts are wholly determined by their origin in a somatic source, in mental life we know them only by their aims' (1915c, XIV, 123). It is 'a concept on the frontier between the mental and the somatic' (ibid., 122; cf. 1905d, VII, 168).[3]

This frontier role of instinct may help us to understand the point of asserting that 'the course of mental events is automatically regulated by the pleasure principle' (1920g, XVIII, 7). The pleasure principle is often attacked as either false or vacuous. As a psychological principle perhaps it is indefensible. Yet Freud is only one of many thinkers who have felt its attraction. Its true role may be not its ostensible one of explanation, but rather to remind us that in explaining behaviour we need to use mentalistic terms even where our explanation refers to natural needs or chemical facts. Freud postulates that the task of the nervous system is to reduce stimuli (1915c, XIV, 120) and adds: 'We can hardly reject the further hypothesis that [feelings belonging to the pleasure–unpleasure series] reflect the manner in which the process of mastering stimuli takes place'. The regions amenable to explanation in terms of instinct are those in which this parallelism may be expected to hold: the area of what we do, as opposed to what our organism achieves in response to needs that lack a 'psychical representative' (e.g. digestion). (One may well feel, however, that in so far as the theory of instincts aims to *explain* this passage from the organic to the mental as well as draw attention to it, the task it sets itself is an impossible one. This point will be pursued below, pp. 152ff.

Outside psychoanalysis, 'instinct' usually means something like 'fixed and innate determinant of behaviour', where what is innate is what is not changed by learning.[4] Freud, on the contrary, is interested in the transformation of instinct into modes of experience and behaviour that are not innate. He defines instinct as a stimulus that differs from others in being *internal* and *continuous*. This carries the idea of innateness, since if the stimulus is strictly continuous it does not have an onset, and if it is

[3] Actually Freud's terminology is not consistent: he says elsewhere that 'an instinct can never become an object of consciousness – only the idea that represents the instinct can' (1915e, XIV, 177). In those terms what interests us is the representative idea. What he there calls an instinct is what he usually terms its (somatic) *source* (see below, p. 143 an exact knowledge of which is 'not invariably necessary for psychological investigation' (1915c, XIV, 123). This matter is discussed by Strachey in his Note to 1915c.

[4] N. Tinbergen, *The Study of Instinct* (Oxford, London, 1951), p. 2.

internal its source must be genetic. But the emphasis is first on function not on origin, though, of course, from a developmental and evolutionary point of view the two converge.

For his definition Freud claims two benefits: explanations, first, of the distinction between 'outside' and 'inside', and, second, of the complicated development of higher animals. Both rest on the 'necessary' (ibid., 124) postulate cited above (p. 142) about the biological role of instinct in controlling stimuli. Outside stimuli are picked out as those that can be controlled by mere locomotion. (It might be more prudent, to avoid a Kantian objection, to speak of how objects of experience are classed as inner or outer, rather than of the origin of the distinction itself.) The second point is meant to be a corollary: the satisfaction of hunger or sex requires more complex manipulation of the outside world than the mere avoidance of its impingement (ibid., 120).

The postulate that the aim of instinct is to master stimuli applies to all instincts. They differ, however, from each other in their *force*, 'the measure of the demand for work which [they] represent' (ibid., 122). They differ also in their intermediate *aims*, which are means to the general aim of satisfaction, and are in turn determined by their organic *source*. (This simply means that, while both hunger and sex demand to be satisfied, we don't generally go about it in the same way.) However, this distinction between instincts is blurred by the fact that these intermediate aims 'are combined or interchanged with one another' (ibid.). This will prove to have important consequences.

The aim of instinct is different from its *object*, defined as 'the thing in regard to which or through which the instinct is able to achieve its aim'. The object is not intrinsically attached to an instinct, but 'becomes assigned to it in consequence of being peculiarly fitted to make satisfaction possible' (ibid.). The intermediate aims of instinct (the manner in which the object is used to provide satisfaction) are more narrowly limited by genetic disposition, but still admit of a wide range of conditioned variation. On this point note the contrast with the ethologist's conception, which posits specific aims ('responses') and predetermined objects (or 'innate releasing mechanisms'). To be sure, these are hardly real objects: the animals concerned are easily fooled by dummies. But their responses are highly specific and tied to innately determined sign stimuli.[5] For Freud, on the other hand,

---

[5] See ibid., pp. 37 ff. After prolonged absence of stimuli the threshold at which they become effective may become lowered so far as to reach zero. This results in what are sometimes called 'vacuum activities' (K. Lorenz, *On Aggression* [New York, 1967], p. 49). It has led Lorenz and Tinbergen to a view that on this point is rather close to Freud's: that 'automatic centres ... send out a continuous flow of impulses to central nervous mechanisms' (Tinbergen, *The Study of Instinct*, p. 75).

the factors determining the connection of instinct with its aims and objects are complex. Maturation, environmental repression, and 'organic' repression (1905d, VII, 177–8) all play a part, as does an associationist mechanism that would not disgrace Hume or Russell: you learn what you like by induction from experiences of satisfaction (1900a, V, 565–6). The question of the relative importance of these various factors receives no settled answer (cf. pp. 146–7 below). What is clear is that no set of innate predispositions wholly determines a 'natural' relation between instincts and their aims and objects. Nevertheless, the character of that relation is crucial to the psychoanalytic conception of 'normal' development.

Within the development of the sexual instinct, different choices of object and aim are regarded in very different lights. An adult choice that reproduces too closely and exclusively the choice of an earlier stage of development is a 'fixation' (1905d, VII, 155 ff.). But the convergence of the sexual 'component instincts' on a single heterosexual object choice and their subordination to the genital aim is True Love and the 'utopia' of genitality (1915c, XIV, 138). Thus the theory of development imposes criteria of normality on those choices, though they are not determined by the nature of the instincts. Freud says this clearly, in a long footnote about bisexuality:

... psychoanalysis considers that ... freedom to range equally over male and female objects ... is the original basis from which, as a result of restriction in one direction or the other, both the normal and the inverted types develop. Thus from the point of view of psychoanalysis the exclusive sexual interest felt by men for women is also a problem that needs elucidating and is not a self-evident fact based upon an attraction that is ultimately of a chemical nature (1905d, VII, 145–6).

This illustrates the theme sketched in the last section: the developmental story gives rise to judgments of value, but does not do so simply by laying down what is 'natural': for that is insufficiently determinate. How then is the range of the 'natural' narrowed down to yield the 'normal'?

A clue to the answer may be obtained if we consider the notion of *regression*. Freud distinguishes three sorts of regression: (a) *topographical*, in terms of the model of the mind in which the systems *Pcpt* (Perception), *Mnem* (Memory), *Ucs* (Unconscious), *Pcs* (Preconscious), and *M* (Motor) are arranged in sequential order; (b) *temporal:* 'harking back to older psychical structures', both in terms of the individual and in terms of the race; (c) *formal:* 'where primitive methods of expression and representation take the place of the usual ones'. 'All these three kinds of regression', Freud observes, 'are one at bottom and occur together as a rule,[6] for what is older in time is more primitive in form and in psychical topography lies nearer to the perceptual end' (1900a, V, 548). Here the language carries an almost inevitable evaluative force: the view that associates 'primitive' with earlier and primary processes seems naturally to go with a comparative judgment which exalts what is later in development, more complex, and closer to conscious thought than to perception.

In their context, which concerns dreams, the observations just quoted imply the superiority of waking life to dreaming. But what does this consist in? Clearly, in the capacity to *act rationally* in the *real world*. This suggests a rationale for the additional determinants of normality: behind the value judgments implied in the developmental view are the ideals of *objectivity* and *rationality*. Yet it is quite unclear how this rationale applies to judgments of normality relating to genitality and the component sexual instincts. This is a central theme to which I shall return below (sections V and VI).

III Perversion

I now turn to the concept that provides the most obvious foil for normality: the concept of perversion. It will throw light on Freud's approach to see how his treatment of perversion, in contrast to some others, carries legitimate implications of value.

Broadly speaking there are five possible approaches to perversion: (1) Denial: the notion is purely theological and once God is removed there is no more to be said. This view seems to me intellectually fainthearted: I ignore it. (2) The moral view: judgments of perversion are neither more nor less than moral judgments. (3) The biological (or Roman) view: anything is a perversion which interferes with the ascertainable biological ends of some act or process. (4) The phenomenological view: once the phenomenological essence of an experience is discovered by careful disciplined attention, anything is a perversion which leads away from that essential experience.[7] (5) The developmental view: perversions are 'seen to be on the one hand inhibitions, and on the other hand dissociations, of normal development' (1905d, VII, 231).

The second view must be wrong, as Thomas Nagel has pointed out, since it is assuredly not a sufficient condition of being a perversion that

---

[6] Though – according to a later paper – 'not necessarily always' (1917d, XIV, 227). This is a general statement which applies to the aims and objects of instinct, and also to the aspects of the ego that are not directly manifestations of instinct (1917d, XIV, 222).

[7] This is the view defended by Thomas Nagel in 'Sexual Perversion', *Journal of Philosophy* 66 (1969), 5–17.

an act be morally wrong. Nagel also argues that the third view is wrong, because it omits the essential element of mentality: otherwise the accidental death of a pregnant mother would be a perversion. Once more: we are on the frontier between the mental and the physical. However, this element could easily enough be built into the Roman view, and then – apart from the silly choice of reproduction as the end of sex – the Roman view comes rather close to Freud's. But there remains a crucial difference, as we shall see. As for the phenomenological view, it suffers from the fault for which Freud repeatedly criticized Jung (perhaps wrongly): it 'loosens the connection of the phenomena with instinctual life' (1914d, XIV, 60), and so hangs in an explanatory void. Moreover, it harbours its own refutation. For, if consciousness is the only guide to the essence of sex, one cannot exclude the possibility that some will experience sex in terms, for example, of the intention to procreate. Or simply that they will not recognize the characterization of that essence which Nagel discovers when he practises sex with *epoche*. To show that such people are missing something, we require the sort of shift from individual experience to human nature in general which we saw to be characteristic of the developmental view (cf. p. 141 above). But this mere phenomenology cannot provide.

I am less concerned, however, with the relative merits of these approaches than with a contrast that can be drawn between the developmental view on one side and the two extreme views – the biological and phenomenological – on the other. The Freudian view, in spite of its scientific stance, implies moral judgments: the extreme views do not. I take 'moral' here in the broad sense of 'evaluative in relation to the happiness of men as such'; and I shall argue that taken in this sense the approach involving moral judgment is the right one.

It may sound surprising to hear that the Roman view is morally neutral. For it generally comes firmly backed by a doctrine of Natural Law from which it follows that what is against nature is immoral. Even if that doctrine were coherent, however, the identification of perversion by the biological criterion could be independent of its moral evaluation. It is not hard to think of examples in Roman doctrine of matters where 'conforming to biological nature' and 'morally good' are not equivalent. The point applies even more obviously to the phenomenological view. Determining the essence of sex may ground a scale on which to measure how good something is *as sex*. But this bears no special relation to moral questions until it is determined what role is played by sex in the happiness of men.[8] By contrast, Freudian theory does attempt to

[8] Cf. ibid., p. 16.

determine that role. It turns out to be so central that we are justified in inferring that, *if* there is a sexual norm, a deviation from it will have moral import. The condition is secured by the developmental theory of the sexual instinct.

(This argument exhibits the shift of which I spoke, from the individual consciousness to the race or culture, in the determination of standards of happiness. If the developmental theory is correct, this shift involves no fallacy. It implies that, even if the individual experiences no awareness of frustration, he would experience more satisfaction if his desires were different in specifiable ways. This move, however, transfers the burden of defining normality to the notion of satisfaction. And as we shall see, the theory is not clear enough on this point to yield practical precepts of any great precision. [Cf. section IV below.])

If the argument just given for the moral significance of sexuality sounds too short and deductive, there are further considerations that are suitably complicating. The developmental history in terms of which normality is contrasted with perversion is not, as I have already pointed out, merely a process of maturation.[9] It is highly dependent on social interaction, and it involves the sacrifice of instinctual gratification of the purest sort. So even though the control of instinct allows some satisfactions, they are not comparable to those afforded by 'the wild instinctual impulse untamed by the ego. . . . This irresistibility of perverse instincts . . . finds an economic explanation here.' (1930a, XXI, 79). In this context, 'perverse' means 'natural': such is the distance that separates the natural from the normal:

A disposition to perversion is an original and universal disposition of the human sexual instinct and . . . normal sexual behaviour is developed out of it as a result of organic changes and psychical inhibitions occurring in the course of maturation . . . [including] the structures of morality and authority erected by society (1905d, VII, 231).

Alteration or removal of these structures cannot eliminate anxiety.[10] Nevertheless, we are led to expect that character traits predominant in a given culture, and institutions – such as property – have been fostered

---

[9] Like locomotion in birds, for example, which seems to have nothing to do with learning or imitation. Cf. Tinbergen, *The Study of Instinct* pp. 128 ff.

[10] Freud himself seems to have become less optimistic on this point in later years. In 1907c and 1908d, he seems to imply that the removal of repression would also do away with neurotic anxiety. But in 1926d this view is retracted and anxiety, traced primarily to the demands of the libido, is itself what 'sets the repression going' (1926d, XX, 109). More recent writers agree. Cf. Anna Freud, *Normality and Pathology in Childhood* (Hogarth, London, 1969), p. 8; D. W. Winnicott, *The Child, the Family, and the Outside World* (Penguin, London, 1964), ch. 15.

by particular infant-rearing techniques. And it appears that cross-cultural studies confirm this.[11]

Although socialization takes different forms in different cultural contexts, the bare fact of socialization is necessarily a part of human 'nature'. There is no reason to suppose that babies can survive its absence any better than monkeys,[12] and what may be their most important innate skill can only mature in a social environment. I mean language. To learn to speak requires a passage from the primary processes to the secondary ones. This passage, according to Freudian theory, involves limitations on the pleasure principle and transformations of instinct (1911b, XII, esp. 221–2). The way seems open to make a distinction between the amount of repression (or suppression) necessary to perpetuate *some* sort of social organization and civilization, and the 'surplus repression' which serves only to maintain the dominance of a particular segment of society.[13] Occasionally Freud is inclined to take such a view: 'neurosis could be avoided if . . . the child's sexual life were allowed free play' (1940a [1938], XXIII, 200; cf. 1912d, XI, 187; and 1908d). But mostly he adopts a standoffish attitude:

Psychoanalysis has no aim but that of disclosing connections. It can but be satisfied if what it has brought to light is of use in effecting reforms. . . . It cannot, however, predict whether other, perhaps even greater sacrifices may not result from other institutions (1912d, XI, 187).

And again: 'For a wide variety of reasons, it is very far from my intention to express an opinion upon the value of human civilization' (1930a, XXI, 144). This attitude is in part grounded on the conviction that interpersonal comparisons cannot rationally be made. For in attempting to compare ourselves with people in alien situations,

---

[11] Cf. E. Erikson, *Childhood and Society* (Norton, New York, 1950, 1963). Erikson is careful not to attribute simple causation to such factors: 'We are not saying . . . that their treatment in babyhood *causes* a group of adults to have certain traits – as if you turned a few knobs in your child-rearing system and you fabricated this or that kind of tribal or national character. . . . We are speaking of goals and values and of the energy put at their disposal by child training systems. Such values persist because the cultural ethos continues to consider them "natural" ' (pp. 137–8). Doubtless what raises the problem of normality so acutely for us is that we have no 'culture' in the relevant sense. Insofar as our psychological make-up is conditioned by the ethics of the containing culture, we are therefore without guidance as to *who* we are. Conversely, of course, one's identity conditions one's values: so we are uncertain about those. Hence the familiar talk of an Age of Anxiety, of Alienation, and so forth. The problem is real, for there is no philosophical mistake in the underlying tendency for ethics and psychology to pass the buck back and forth. Such is the burden of much of this chapter.

[12] See H. H. Harlow and M. K. Harlow, 'Social Deprivation in Monkeys', *Scientific American* 207 (1955), 136–46.

[13] Cf. H. Marcuse, *Eros and Civilization, a Philosophical Inquiry into Freud* (Beacon Press, New York, 1955), esp. p. 40.

It is . . . impossible . . . to divine the changes which original obtuseness of mind, a gradual stupefying process, the cessation of expectations . . . have produced upon their receptivity to sensations of pleasure and unpleasure (1930a, XXI, 89).

Yet isn't psychoanalytic theory precisely designed to provide rational grounds for such 'divination'? Inferences of this sort would not seem impossible if we had a complete account of instincts, their modes of satisfaction, and the transformations to which their objects and aims are susceptible. So I now return to the theory of instincts, and its bearing on the normative implications of developmental theory. The transformations of instinct raise the following issue: Does Freud propose a reduction of man's higher activities to his 'lower' instincts, in such a way as to impugn the difference of value between the two?

IV   Reductionism and the aims of instinct

On the exact nature and number of instincts that should be postulated Freud is not firm; but in the strict sense 'only primal instincts – those which cannot be further dissected – can lay claim to importance' (1915c, XIV, 124). His conception of these primal instincts evolved over time. He first distinguished a self-preservative instinct, or group of instincts, from a sexual one. This distinction was supposedly grounded in biology, with the observation that 'all our provisional ideas in psychology will presumably some day be based on an organic substructure' (1914c, XIV, 78). But Freud admits that we have no access at present to the underlying biochemical facts. We can only speculate. The speculation is that the two groups of instincts are chemically different by reason of their different evolutionary function (ibid.). But this has little plausibility. For the fact that individual and phyletic survival are different ends does not show that the two must be secured by different means. An additional minimal criterion of distinction seems implied, namely, that two instincts are different if they can conflict. We shall shortly see how much weight can be placed on this test.

Later the concept of narcissism threatened the dualism of ego and sexual instincts. But the dualism survived, and in 1920 a new theoretical postulate led to its reformulation in terms of Eros or Libido and Thanatos or the Death Instinct. Here again there were (somewhat abstruse) biological considerations (1920g, XVIII, 45 ff.), and the more straightforward arguments appealed to the 'ubiquity of non-erotic aggressivity' (1930a, XXI, 120). This fact might simply have suggested an instinct of aggression, but for rather abstract theoretical reasons Freud chose to interpret it differently.

This is not the place for a critique of the death instinct; nor is one necessary. But it will serve as a particularly good illustration for some points of more general relevance.

In its absurdity the death instinct once more shows Freud to be negligent about the bearing of evolution. If there had been organisms endowed with the capacity for self-destruction, their ability to propagate this trait would, by necessity of evolutionary mechanisms, have been inversely proportional to its efficiency. Thus if any trace of such an instinct by chance survived it would be guaranteed to be quite ineffectual. No wonder it 'was not easy ... to demonstrate the activities of this supposed death instinct' (1930a, XXI, 119).

Still, it might be retorted that the aim of this instinct has undergone transformations, so that it is mostly manifest in aggressiveness. This brings me to the central point. Freud's characterization of the aims of *all* instincts – including the libidinal – is unacceptably vague. He is not unaware of this: we have seen that he frequently laments that instinct theory is insufficiently developed, and in 1933a he says: 'Instincts are mythical entities, magnificent in their indefiniteness' (1933a, XXII, 95). But this indefiniteness has more important consequences than he allows.

It is generally assumed to be the chief strength of Freud's theory of sexuality that it displays the sexual instincts in their bewildering variety of forms. The explanatory power of psychoanalysis owes much to their interchangeability and the pervasiveness of their influence on our mental life.[14] Yet this strength is, as many critics have pointed out, too great for the theory's own good. There are no criteria for distinguishing one instinct from another. Conflict does not provide a sufficient criterion of difference, for two component instincts of the libidinal group can have opposite effects. This is particularly obvious once the libido comes to include both of the originally contrasting groups, the sexual and the ego instincts (1923a, XVIII, 257). Nor does Freud himself invariably assume that conflict proves distinctness. For though he seems to have assumed that the conflict leading to the transference neuroses 'compelled' him to posit two independent groups (1914c, XIV, 77), he was also willing to consider, at about the same time, the possibility that in repression 'it is precisely the cathexis which is withdrawn from the idea that is used for anticathexis' (1915e, XIV, 181). In other words, the force repressed and the repressing force might have the very same source.

It might be suggested here that only a certain kind of conflict is strong enough to provide the needed criterion of distinctness: essential conflict, conflict between the pure or primal forms of instinct. But this would be a

---

[14] Cf. Richard Wollheim, *Freud* (Collins, London, 1971), ch. 4, esp. p. 118.

mistake. For, strictly speaking, instincts cannot conflict at all as mental entities in their primal forms. For they belong to the *Ucs* (later, the id), which is indifferent to contradiction (ibid., 187). Therefore the only conflicts to which instincts are subject are practical conflicts, conflicts of effects.

If Freud gives us no adequate criterion of distinctness for his two main groups of instincts, we may still hope for a criterion of identity (or kinship) between instincts of the *same* group. We might then get a criterion of difference as a corollary. Let us see what links the 'components' of the sexual instinct to each other.

Each component instinct is tied to an erotogenic zone, and none, even that connected with the genital zone, is intrinsically related to reproduction. All acquire this link as a result of a development which brings them under the dominance of the genital zone, and of its mature aim and object (1905d, VII, 197). In these respects they are comparable to the 'tool activities' which, according to Lorenz, serve the 'big drives'.[15] Tool activities are decomposable into a number of specific mechanisms which develop and can operate independently of each other. They have evolved into hierarchical systems serving some biological purpose. All of this is indeed reminiscent of the role of the component instincts: but the differences are crucial.

First, Freud's component instincts are not innate mechanisms of specific response, but only internal stimuli. The responses provoked by these stimuli (the aim and object of the instinct) are determined at least in part by association. Apart from the location of the zone with which their intermediate aims are associated, there is therefore nothing to differentiate one component instinct from another:

In itself an instinct is without quality. . . . What distinguishes the instincts from one another and endows them with specific qualities is their relation to their somatic source and to their aims (1905d, VII, 168).

The second difference is this. We can presume that 'tool activities' became organized under a 'big drive' by the same process of selection and mutation that ensures the complex organization of an organ. The appearance of teleology is reducible to the mechanism of evolution. But Freud's instincts become parts of a hierarchy which is not only a biological one, and which is organized partly as a result of social conditioning. The teleology involved here is, therefore, of the very different sort, which must be traced to intentions, conscious purposes –

[15] See Lorenz, *On Aggression* (New York, 1967), p. 85, and cf. Tinbergen, *The Study of Instinct* pp. 102 ff. Tinbergen gives a more refined account of the hierarchical organization of the mechanisms that contribute to biological functions.

in short, the mental rather than the organic life (cf. 1913j, XIII, 188). The unity of aim achieved in the genital organization can therefore not be viewed, as can the role of 'tool activities', as a simple functional convergence of biological traits. Both Freud and the ethologists are interested in explaining complex behaviour in terms of hierarchies of simpler elements. Freud's task, however, is more ambitious in that his explicanda are essentially mental (cf. p. 141 above). He must therefore meet two more stringent adequacy conditions. First, the nature and scope of the elementary instinct – including its mental aspect – must be made precise. Secondly, it must be clear just how the instinct *explains* manifestations that go beyond its organic base: in sublimated forms of instinct, do we simply have another *effect* of the *same* instinct, or is there something more abstract which all forms have in common but which is not identical with any one form?

Unfortunately Freud's theory does not satisfy either requirement. The first is most obviously violated by the death instinct, which lacks a somatic source and has an excessively abstract aim. But, as we have seen, it is true also of the libido that the identity of its parts is assured only by the fact that they are all involved in a process which, under certain conditions, leads to their subordination to the monogamic reproductive aim. Given the vaunted versatility of the libido, it is also unclear what exactly happens in the case of sublimation. This is defined as a 'diversion of sexual instinctual forces from sexual aims and their direction to new ones' (1905d, VII, 178). If the second adequacy condition is to be met, we must know the nature of the 'forces' involved precisely enough to recognize them in a different guise. In fact, all we are told is that there is a source of 'neutral energy' which is 'desexualized Eros' (1923b, XIX, 44), but we are not told what marks it still as *Eros* when desexualized. It is clearly not enough to observe causal-like ('economic') correlations between forms of the libido: for the existence of causal relations argues no underlying substantial identity of 'energy'.

This presents us with a dilemma: if we are reasonably precise about the nature of this energy, and so satisfy the first of the two requirements just mentioned, then we are all the less likely to satisfy the second. On the other hand, if we manage a sufficiently abstract characterization of the instinct to cover all its forms ('uniting and binding'), for example (ibid., 45), then we fail of the first adequacy condition. Actually we fail in the second too: for such vague characterization cannot be said to *explain* the relation between direct and sublimated expressions of instinct. The attempt to explain too much results in a blurring of the concept of instinct which finally explains nothing at all. Much would be gained by narrowing the concept of instinct in such a way as to bring the psychoanalytic theory close to that of the ethologist. If we tie instinct firmly to somatic sources, there can be no death instinct, and we place limits on the plasticity of sublimation. We would then be free to contrast instincts with other innate characteristics, such as, for example, the disposition to play.[16]

Perhaps the second of our adequacy conditions cannot be met by any theory. We have seen that the sort of explanation we require is a psychological one: yet instinct is 'determined by its somatic source' (cf. p. 142 above). The hardest problem is therefore prior to any questions about sublimation. It concerns the relation between the somatic source and its 'representative idea' even in its simplest from. A striking and notorious example of this is provided by Freud's treatment of femininity. He assumes, plausibly, that there are 'psychical consequences of the anatomical distinction between the sexes' (1925j), but there is no satisfactory account of the relation between anatomy and its consequences. I am not asking here for a justification of the claim that a girl's penis envy has 'permanent effects on the development of her character' (1940a, XXIII, 155), but for an explanation of the claim that the lack of a penis must lead to penis envy in the first place. There is no *a priori* reason for the penis to be judged more enviable than the compact smoothness of a girl's external genitals. (There is no *a priori* reason for white to be more beautiful than black.) Of course, it may be replied that Freud does not know the subjective meaning of this lack *a priori*, but by analytic experience. But this misses the point, which is that the existence of penis envy is not explained simply by the lack of a penis. It may be – implausibly – that there is an innate expectation in every male and female to find a penis appended to every human being: so everyone is *naturally* disappointed. The mental factor for which we are looking would then be innately determined as is its source, but could not strictly be claimed to be determined *by* its source: for the organic fact *might* have had a different *sense*. On the other hand, it is more likely that the sense of the anatomical difference is given to the child by his environment. In that case, once again, it is not true that the lack of a penis determined penis envy. Still less does the sublimation of penis envy explain 'a capacity, for instance, to carry on an intellectual profession' (1933a, XXII, 125). On the contrary, the penis may act merely as a symbol of male freedom, and something else would have taken its place if anatomy had been different.

All this has important consequences for the issue of 'reduction'. 'Re-

[16] See D. W. Winnicott, *Playing and Reality* (Tavistock, London, 1971), esp. ch. 3. For Winnicott, the urge to play is innate, but not instinctual. Instinct and play compete for a child's attention and are thus far incompatible (p. 39). But play is not a transform or sublimation of instinct; nor is the former essentially linked to the repression of the latter.

duction' sometimes means simply 'explanation' ('Is chemistry reducible to physics?'): reduction in this sense establishes a causal dependence. But in a stronger sense reduction can establish an ontological dependence ('Are physical objects reducible to – nothing but – constructions out of sense data?'). It is safe to say that the Freudian account of mental life in general aims at reduction in the first sense. Even such weak reduction can, in practice, affect our attitude; but it is probably only in the strong sense that a reduction can legitimately show up a mistake in our conception of the nature and value of the reduced phenomenon. To sustain a charge of strong reductionism against psychoanalysis, one would have to show not merely that the 'higher' mental functions are explicable in terms of their origin in 'lower' instincts, but that the former are 'nothing more' than inhibited avatars of the latter.

We have seen that it is not clear enough what THE (natural) aim of an instinct is for this charge to be clearly assessed. And the considerations of the last page suggest that even the weaker form of reduction has not been shown to be involved. For it is not clear whether organic factors actually cause psychological ones; the possibility remains open that the role of the mental is to give a sense to the relevant organic facts without being caused by them.[17] Moreover, the process of sublimation, whether it leads to real transformations of instinct or merely to novel manifestations of the same instincts, may entail a modification of the value of satisfaction. We need a criterion of assessment over and above the determination of instinctual origins for human experience and activity.

In pursuit of such criteria, let us look at some Freudian explanations of particular states which are explicitly and pejoratively reductive. We shall see that they impugn the value of the states concerned not merely by tracing their origin in instinct, but for more specific reasons. By this route we shall be led to a partial answer to our earlier question about the character of Freud's 'normal' or ideal man.

V   The epistemic criterion

In Freud's view religious belief, 'so patently infantile, so foreign to reality' (1930a, XXI, 74), is thoroughly discredited by his explanation of it in terms of wish. Art is not, though it too is an indulgence in illusion: 'the mild narcosis induced in us by art can do no more than bring about a transient withdrawal from the pressure of vital needs' (ibid., 81). The

---

[17] This would not, of course, contradict the hypothesis of some sort of general psycho-physical parallelism. It would only cast doubt on the causal primacy of organic features (such as the presence, etc., of a penis) which affect the mental through one's *perception* of them.

crucial difference is that the illusions of art are recognized as such (ibid., 80; cf. 1908e, IX, 144), whereas religion is a mass delusion: 'No one, needless to say, who shares a delusion ever recognizes it as such' (1930a, XXI, 81).

The rationale is clear: wherever such a criterion can find application, the worth of a mental state is assessed in terms of *truth*, in terms of the extent of correspondence between the subjective and *reality*.[18]

One might seek to justify the value of truth itself in terms of its contribution to happiness, in so far as any enterprise will have greater chances of success if it is undertaken in the light of realistic appraisal rather than wish-fulfilling phantasy (cf. 1937c, XXIII, 237). But in that case truth will never be preferred to satisfaction in case of conflict, except by dint of the rule-utilitarian fallacy which infers a universal from a general truth. (Realism is usually advantageous, so it should be preferred even when it isn't.) In spite of what I have called Freud's Utilitarianism, however, it is clear that in his mind truth is an independent value which might even dominate the value of happiness. The fact that Freud did not assume that everyone shared this value explains in part his scorn for 'the great majority of mortals [who] will never be able to rise above [the religious] view of life' (1930a, XXI, 74). Whatever its justification, this concern for truth yields a criterion of value for those states or activities that are epistemically committed – such as psychoanalysis itself: 'psychoanalytic treatment is founded on truthfulness. In this fact lies a great part of its educative effect and its ethical value' (1915a, XII, 164). This epistemic criterion does not dismiss a belief merely because it is susceptible of a genetic explanation. On the contrary, the right kind of genetic explanation establishes a belief as legitimate. A belief constitutes knowledge if its coming into being can be explained in terms of the truth of its object. Its genesis can then be adduced as justification. But 'we call a belief an illusion when a wish-fulfilment is a prominent factor in its motivation, and in so doing we disregard its relations to reality, just as the illusion itself sets no store by verification' (1927c, XXI, 31).

The application of this epistemic criterion is straightforward in the case of epistemic states. But how does it extend beyond the realm of belief? Consider the contrast between *character* and *neurosis*. In a number of papers Freud traced the development of certain character types from the predominance of certain stages in the development of the

---

[18] This finds an illustration in Freud's praise of work: 'No other technique for the conduct of life attaches the individual so firmly to reality' (1930a, XXI, 80). The fact that realism does not always coincide with utility is attested by the fact that 'as a path to happiness, work is not highly prized by men' (ibid.).

libido – particularly anal-erotism (e.g. 1908b, 1917c). In theory every particular character is determined by some particular combination of dispositional and accidental factors. But neurotic symptoms are also explained in terms of such an interaction of factors. Whatever derogatory connotation attaches to neurosis, then, tends to spread over to character through the similarity of form in their explanations. Thus it may appear that psychoanalytic explanation *per se* is derogatory. But we have seen that this is a mistake: such evaluative implications are legitimate, if at all, only where the explanation shows a character trait, like a neurotic symptom, to be *irrational*.[19]

The epistemic criterion clarifies the difference between character and neurosis in so far as pejorative reductions are based on imputations of irrationality. Neurotic symptoms are obviously irrational, considered as actions in the light of the agent's beliefs and desires. For example, in those neuroses that are traceable to the repression of sexual impulses, the repressed impulses

find expression in other ways, which are quite as injurious to the subject and make him quite as useless for society as satisfaction of the suppressed instincts in an unmodified form would have done (1908d, IX, 191).

By contrast, character traits cannot be assessed so simply for rationality: they do not merely select means to independently established ends, but find their expression in the choice of ends themselves as well as styles of action. The epistemic criterion seems inadequate to assess such choices. Its applicability can therefore be taken to differentiate neurotic from character traits. Intuitively, however, character can also be evaluated in terms of rationality. It is now time to press the search for a broader notion of rationality which will make sense of this. We shall find that psychoanalysis is in the same ambiguous dialectical position in relation to rationality as in relation to pleasure and instinctual satisfaction. That is to say, while the notion is fundamental to the theory, the theory in a sense obscures it.

VI The rational and the real

What are the criteria that govern rationality of *emotion?* Freud speaks of the lover's 'overvaluation of the sexual object' (1905d, VII, 150), and

[19] One reason why the explanation of character in analytic terms is felt as degrading is that the development of instinct is frequently described in terms implying identity between its primal and its 'aim-inhibited' forms (cf. 1917c, XVII, esp. 128). But we have already seen that the sense of such identity is too unclear to bear much weight. Besides, the feeling that such explanations are degrading is itself subject to psychoanalytic explanation. Since the moral sentiments have their roots in the superego, it is to be expected that they should feel degraded by their origin in the Oedipal phase. For the superego itself has precisely come into being by repression of the Oedipus complex (1923b, XIX, 34).

presumably an overvaluation is an irrational valuation. In Simone de Beauvoir's *Les Mandarins* there is a character who is 'cured' of a life-long passion by its analytical interpretation as 'transference'; and presumably transference too is irrational. But what is *adequate* valuation? And when is love not transference? On the one hand, Freud says, 'it is the essential character of every state of being in love [to] . . . reproduce infantile prototypes' (1915a, XII, 168); but elsewhere, 'not every good relation . . . [is] to be regarded as a transference; there [are] also friendly relations which [are] based on reality. . .' (1937c, XXIII, 222). To be *based on reality* is at least to satisfy the epistemic criterion. In some cases, therefore, the rationality of emotion seems reducible to the rationality of the beliefs with which it is associated. Thus the lover's overvaluation consists in 'credulity'; 'his powers of judgment are weakened' (1905d, VII, 150). Similarly with the distinction between (normal) mourning and (pathological) melancholia: 'although mourning involves grave departures from the normal attitude to life, it never occurs to us to regard it as a pathological condition' (1917e, XIV, 243). In melancholia, by contrast, the characteristic 'self-reproaches are reproaches against a love object which have been shifted away from it onto the patient's own ego' (ibid., 248); this shift of object gives the attitude an automaticity and ineffectiveness which precludes the achievement of any relevant goals.

The systematic failure to secure an end is by definition irrational. Neurotic behaviour is in this sense irrational, as we saw. Nevertheless, this characterization is inadequate to define the ideal man of psychoanalysis. Under certain circumstances, frustration provides the energy for greater achievement:

What appears . . . as an untiring impulsion towards further perfection can easily be understood as a result of the instinctual repression upon which is based all that is precious in human civilization. The repressed instinct never ceases to strive for complete satisfaction, which would consist in the repetition of a primary experience of satisfaction (1920g, XVIII, 42).

To measure the relative worth of the frustration and the resulting achievements, we need to evaluate *ends*. The 'economic' point of view affords definite standards only if it is grounded on meaningful calculations of utility. But such calculations make clear sense only if the pleasure principle makes clear sense. The difference between satisfactions of different *kinds* has always caused trouble for systems akin to Utilitarianism. The usual solution offered, from Plato to Mill, is the appeal to the experienced judge: he who has experienced both can make the distinction between real and illusory wants, and higher and lower pleasures. This device has its Freudian counterpart in the *analysed man*.

But the various factors I have discussed confuse the issues. One factor is Freud's tendency to treat satisfactions other than primary as mere 'surrogates', from which one might infer that if any want is 'unreal' it is the sublimated want, not the primal instinct from which it derives its energy. Working against this is the lack of any clear criterion of identity through change for instincts. This means that no clear 'economic' relations between different modes of satisfaction can be defined. I have already mentioned the political scepticism that Freud derives from the difficulties of interpersonal comparisons. Indeed the modern practice of psychoanalysis, and Freud himself, have often been accused of taking an excessively conservative attitude to politics, morals, and society.[20] In Freud, the conservative stance stems not from approval of the social order as it is, but from scepticism about the effects of institutional reforms (see p. 148 above). Yet such scepticism is quite unexpected from someone inclined to Utilitarianism and equipped with a theory of satisfaction.

Another important factor is the difficulty attaching to the word 'Reality': what the 'reality principle' has to contend with is shaped by the containing society's expectations and sanctions. But these are partly determined by the characters of the society's members. The neurotic's behaviour may cause him suffering not because it is based on false beliefs about physical reality, but 'by raising difficulties in his relations with his environment and the society he belongs to' (1930a, XXI, 108).[21]

All these factors limit the applicability of the reality principle. But in his late works Freud brings to it a qualification from a different perspective. The ideal of rationality is often formulated in terms of the control of the whole person by the ego: 'Psychoanalysis is an instrument to enable the ego to achieve a progressive conquest of the id' (1923b, XIX, 56; cf. 1933a, XXII, 80). But the conquest can never be completed:

[20] See, for example, Marcuse, *Eros and Civilization*. It should in fairness be observed that Marcuse's charge applies chiefly to the 'Neo-Freudian revisionists' (Fromm, Horney, Sullivan) rather than to Freud himself, and that apart from the orthodox Marxist line the most serious attacks of this sort have been aimed at psychiatrists outside the analytic tradition. Cf., for example, T. Szasz, *The Manufacture of Madness* (Harper & Row, New York, 1970).

[21] In this way, of superficially identical patterns of behaviour that admit of analogous psychological explanations, such as obsessive or religious ceremonials (1907b), the one may be normal and the other pathological. Erikson (*Childhood and Society*) differentiates neurosis from primitive mentality as follows:

Neurosis is an individual state in which irrational trends are irreconcilably split off from a relatively advanced rationality; while primitivity is a state of human organization in which pre-rational thinking is integrated with whatever rationality is made possible by the technology [p. 184].

not merely in practice, but as a matter of logic. For the ego, like the rider of a horse, 'has borrowed its energies from the id' (ibid., 77). To conquer it altogether would be for the rider to kill off his horse the better to control him. Nor is the ideal type the one whose superego is dominant, the 'obsessional type', 'though from the social standpoint [men of this type] are the true, pre-eminently conservative vehicles of civilization' (1931a, XXI, 218). The ideal is the 'erotic-obsessional-narcissistic' who balances the claims of all three agencies:

such a type would no longer be a type at all: it would be the absolute norm, the ideal harmony. We thus realize that the phenomenon of types arises precisely from the fact that, of the three main ways of employing the libido in the economy of the mind, one or two have been favoured at the expense of the others (ibid., 219).

This represents an acknowledgment that the 'reality' faced by the ego includes both inner and outer reality. Freud occasionally seems to imply the contrary, as when he contrasts 'real' and 'instinctual' danger, and correspondingly 'realistic' and 'neurotic' anxiety (1926d, XX, 166). But this is misleading: the true basis of the distinction turns out to be whether the danger is *known* or *unknown*, and Freud recognizes that 'in so far as the instinctual demand is something real, his neurotic anxiety, too, can be admitted to have a realistic basis' (ibid., 167).[22] It is here, no doubt, that we might seek the unexplained link between rationality and the developmental view of normal mature sexuality (cf. p. 144 above). In man's total situation – faced with id, society, and external world – genitality is taken to be the most satisfactory compromise. This may or may not fit in with fact and theory; but at least it displays the unified perspective behind the 'norms' based on the developmental view.

The need for the ego to deal both with inner and with outer reality brings a new complication to the problem of 'real wants' or 'true values' with which I began. If we attempt to apply what I have called the 'epistemic criterion' of rationality to desires, we shall find the result particularly ambiguous. From the point of view of external reality, it is natural (though admittedly not necessary) to consider 'realistic' desires to be those that are likely to be fulfilled. From the point of view of internal reality, on the other hand, a realistic desire is one – as I suggested above,

[22] Freud speculates in two short papers (1924b, 1924e) that the difference between neurosis and psychosis lies in the fact that the former begins with a denial of the claims of the id, whereas the latter begins with a denial of (external) reality. Though he uses the word 'reality' to mean external reality, it is clear that the other demands on the ego are equally real.

p. 140 which strives for something that is actually satisfying: a correct perception of possible pleasure. Unfortunately the two sorts of 'realism' often conflict: what is of true value may be very unlikely to be attained, whilst what is 'realistically' desired in the light of external reality may bring but puny pleasure. There is no obviously acceptable principle of rationality that can reconcile these two sorts of 'realism'. So we have here another essential limitation on the ideal of rationality.

An adequate conception of rationality should recognize not only the multiplicity of human ends, but the existence of incomparable ends. It is on this point that there is a tension within Freudian theory. On the one hand, there is an insistence on an 'economic' point of view which presupposes the comparability of all ends, and perhaps hints at a measure of desire in instinctual 'force' (p. 143 above). On the other hand, Freud's account of the vicissitudes of instinct fails to provide instructions on how to apply any single measure to different sorts of satisfaction. Moreover, the separate demands of inner and outer reality cannot be brought together under a unified principle of rationality. Both these points hint at an implicit recognition that principles of rationality may conflict in the pursuit of incomparable goals. Thus they undermine the narrowly 'economic' point of view.

VII Summary

I have argued that Freud's comprehensive developmental view of human nature carries legitimate implications of value, but that these are severely limited by the detail and the defects of the theory itself.

The first reason was this: The theory aims to trace our mental life to its simplest elements, where these are intimately bound up with biological functions. Broadly speaking, this programme is obviously sound, though in carrying it out Freud is rather free with his assumptions about the mechanism of evolution. But he tends to conflate the kind of teleology involved in evolutionary explanations and that are inherent in intentional explanations. Since the main point of the 'frontier concept' of instinct is the explanation of intentionality in terms of its relation to biological finalities, this weakens the argument at the most crucial point. Primal instincts cannot adequately be characterized merely by reference to their somatic source. Their *psychological* nature demands to be identified in terms of *aims*. And the specifications of these aims are either too narrow to provide the far-reaching explanations demanded of them, or too vague and abstract to show their organic origins.

This may point to a limitation of principle on the whole enterprise.

Perhaps some of our mental endowments are simply tied to maturational properties of our nervous and endocrine systems, without any more specific links with any particular bodily zone or independently identified biological function. The best hope for the notion of instinct may lie in not forcing it to explain too much.

The second reason was a corollary of the first. Freud's theory lacks criteria of reidentification for instinctual forces, and partly as a consequence it lacks principles for the relative evaluation of the satisfactions correlated with different forms of instinct. It cannot, therefore, fulfil its promise to extract from a developmental account of the human mind an objective distinction between basic and derived wants, nor derive from such a distinction criteria for telling real from illusory values. By drawing attention to the complexity and obscurity of the fundamental notion of *satisfaction*, the theory undermines its own implicit Utilitarianism.

Nevertheless, there is a value clearly bound up with psychoanalysis, though the attempt to deduce it strictly from a conception of satisfaction or happiness must fail. This is the value of truth and rationality. In so far as rationality in behaviour can only be defined with reference to specific ends, or to a method for selecting ends, this notion is infected with the unclarities of instinct theory. It further suffers from the relativity of the 'reality' with which it is the business of the ego to contend. Finally, it is limited by the need to balance against each other the claims of the individual and of society, as well as the three agencies of the individual mind. Freud's theory provides no procedure for regulating these balances, and no hint as to how one might construct a fully unified and integrated notion of rationality.

The accusation of reductionism, however, should now be seen to be without foundation. Instinct theory is not a firm enough base for any degrading reduction, and in any case the charge is based on a confusion between eliminative (ontological) reduction and mere explanation.

On the other hand, it is also wrong to credit – or discredit – Freudian theory with a rigid model of ideal man. The normative implications of Freud's vision first present themselves as epistemological norms: they consist in the erection of standards of normality in a sense common in biology, and without which classification cannot proceed. Since what is being classified concerns the nature of man, however, these norms automatically acquire moral import, in a broad sense of the term. But it would be a misinterpretation of these norms to assume that they are bound to work in a rigid or conservative way. The complex relativities to which 'reality' is subject account sufficiently for Freud's inclination – and that of many of his followers – to a conservative stance: some variables have to be fixed in practice. Yet the only true utopia of psychoanalysis is rationality; at the same time, it teaches us how difficult an ideal this is to interpret.[23]

[23] I am grateful to the Canada Council, who provided a research grant in the summer of 1970, during which preliminary research for this paper was done.

I also wish to thank Richard Wollheim for many valuable criticisms of an earlier draft.

10

On the generation and classification of defence mechanisms*

PATRICK SUPPES and HERMINE WARREN

The work to be presented here is an attempt to work out the rudimentary principles of a theory of the defence mechanisms. More specifically, we will attempt to lay out a framework within which the defence mechanisms may be systematically defined, generated and classified. The recent literature, both psychological and psychoanalytic, is full of comments concerning the need for systematic treatment of psychoanalytic theory. A good summary of the situation may be found in Rapaport's monograph (1960).

The approach we have used in this paper falls generally within the framework of the use of mathematical models in psychology, although the developments are elementary and, we believe, totally self-contained within the framework of our discussion of the defence mechanisms. The problems in developing specific mathematical models for given parts of psychoanalytic theory are formidable, and we do not pretend to be clear as to how all these problems are to be solved. Nevertheless, the kinds of success that have been achieved by using mathematics in other areas of science, including other areas of psychology, suggest that a piecemeal approach may be useful at the present stage. We think that the elementary mathematical models we have used in the present paper to provide a definite scheme for generating and classifying the defence mechanisms provide an example of such a piecemeal approach.

By using elementary formal methods we have been able to bring a viewpoint to the classification of the defence mechanisms that seems not to have been previously presented in the literature. The advantage of these methods is that explicit elementary computations for deriving the number of mechanisms as well as for classifying them are introduced, so that we are able to augment intuition in deciding exactly what mechanisms are to be counted as separate and distinct.

* First published in the *International Journal of Psycho-Analysis* (1975) 56, 405–14. The authors wish to thank Dr Leonard Horowitz, Dr Ronald Spinka and Dr William Winter for their helpful suggestions.

We do want to emphasize the entirely modest beginning of the use of formal methods made in this paper. We are hopeful that in subsequent research we will be able to deepen and expand the effort.

Contents of the unconscious

One first question that concerned us was how to characterize the contents of the unconscious. Freud stated on more than one occasion that the unconscious may be thought of as consisting primarily of ideas that represent impulses. However, the concept of idea is a difficult one to define explicitly – as McIntyre (1958) has pointed out, the use of the concept of idea by Freud is part of a long philosophical tradition going back through Herbart and Kant all the way to Locke in the 17th century – and it is even harder to give a precise meaning to the concept of an idea that represents an impulse. For this and other reasons, it seemed to us desirable for our present purposes to draw upon a broad philosophical tradition and make use of the general notion of proposition. Thus we shall talk about propositions, rather than ideas, impulses and the like. In particular, we assume that propositions represent thoughts or impulses in the unconscious. Similarly, we shall speak of propositions as representing thoughts or feelings in consciousness.

Looked at in this way, it becomes natural to define the defence mechanisms as transformations of propositions. By a transformation we mean a function that maps unconscious propositions (thoughts or impulses) into conscious propositions; a transformation may also be thought of as a process that takes unconscious propositions and changes them in specific ways into conscious propositions. For example, denial would be defined as the mechanism that maps a proposition p in the unconscious into either its denial (its negation) or the null proposition in consciousness, meaning that the proposition is not mapped into any explicit proposition in consciousness but rather is blocked. Correspondingly, displacement would be defined as the mechanism that maps a proposition p in the unconscious into the proposition p' in consciousness, with the object x of the proposition p transformed into some object y of the proposition p', with y related to x in some respect. We will not at this point attempt to define all the mechanisms cited in the literature, although we assume it is possible to do so, but will instead return to a fuller treatment of the mechanisms in the next section.

There will be, of course, objections to the use of propositions in this way, for, in the same philosophical literature that extends back to the beginnings of modern philosophy, the concept of proposition, like that of idea, has had a chequered history. Nevertheless, the concept of proposition has, since the latter half of the 19th century in the hands of Frege and other writers, achieved a certain definiteness and precision which can be used to good effect in the present analysis. In the primary sense of Frege and subsequent writers, a proposition is the sense or meaning of a sentence, and although Frege (1892) actually used *Gedanke*, that is, thought, rather than proposition as the word to stand for the sense of a sentence, the subsequent philosophical practice has been primarily to talk about propositions rather than thoughts.

Psychologists too may well voice objections to the use of propositions in this context. It is not clear that the rigorous adherence to the use of propositions can catch the spirit of psychological discussions. Certainly in most cases psychologists speak of defence mechanisms as being expressed in complex behaviours rather than in propositions in consciousness. Still, we think it is possible to use the notion of proposition as a way of abstracting the general sense of what is in both the unconscious and consciousness, and that there are advantages to be gained from adhering to such a uniform way of formulating the matter. We will thus be able to keep distinct the explicit and immediate result of the mechanism's operation from the behavioural consequences of its operation.

We were interested to see, in this connexion, that Freud on at least one occasion represented unconscious contents by propositions, specifically of the form subject–verb–object. Thus, in his notes on paranoia (1911c, XII) Freud remarks that the most often seen forms of paranoia may all be represented as transformations of the proposition *I (a man) love him (a man)*. In this way he sheds light on the ways in which complex behaviours (in which the operation of one or more defence mechanisms is presumably embedded) result from the transformations of a proposition. Freud further comments that the possible number of ways in which the proposition *I love him* could be transformed is four: delusions of jealousy change the subject, delusions of persecution change the verb, erotomania changes the object, and megalomania rejects the proposition as a whole. We shall comment later about the attempt to work out the theoretical number of possible transformations involved in these changes.

Before concluding this section, we wish to make some general remarks about the above examples of mechanisms. Clearly the energy concept is not worked out. Although we are not negative about the concept of energy in the way some writers have been (Holt, 1967a, 1967b), we feel it premature at this time to try to incorporate the concept into our framework. However, we can make the suggestions that follow.

One possible way of thinking about the matter would be to speak of energy as being 'attached' to propositions in the unconscious. The weakness of this formulation is that at the very least one needs to keep track of the energy attached to propositions and to what happens to the energy as the mechanisms operate. The reader will notice that we do not say *cathected* because we are not sure whether it is appropriate to think of a proposition in the unconscious as being cathected. In neutral language it certainly seems reasonable to speak of propositions in the unconscious as having energy attached to them.

This means that formally we are thinking about the defence mechanisms as operating on ordered pairs (p, e). The first member of each pair would be a proposition p in the unconscious and the second member would be the energy e attached to the proposition. The result of the transformation would be a new proposition p' in consciousness and a new quantity e' of energy. Using the examples of denial and displacement once again, we would thus define denial as the defence mechanism that maps a proposition p in the unconscious into the null proposition in consciousness; the energy attached to the proposition p would remain as energy blocked in the unconscious. Similarly, in the case of displacement, the energy attached to x would become attached to y, the object into which x is transformed.

Two last points need to be mentioned about this concept. Although there is an intuitive meaning to speaking about energy as either being blocked in the unconscious or as being freed, a more exact characterization of this point seems necessary. Secondly, although we believe that the concept of energy can be usefully developed and that an amount of energy can be attached to each proposition in the unconscious, the question of whether conservation of energy is an appropriate concept is a more difficult matter. Indeed whether it is useful at the present time to seek a quantitative concept of energy is not clear.

Generation of mechanisms

Although the definitions we have suggested in the previous section are somewhat more explicit and systematic than those usually found in the literature, there is still a certain arbitrariness about a list of a limited number of mechanisms, such as that given by Anna Freud (1936); as is well known, this list of mechanisms included regression, repression, reaction formation, isolation, undoing, projection, introjection, turning against the self, reversal and sublimation. The definitions found in the literature do not provide a method for relating one to the other. Thus it is natural to ask whether there is a more systematic way of generating the possible mechanisms, and whether such a method of generation can give us any insight into whether the number of mechanisms is indefinitely large, or whether a relatively small number can be expected. Others have spoken of such a need for systematic study. Waelder (1960), for example, expresses a similar interest when he states 'there seems to be a need for an alphabet of defence mechanisms, i.e. a description of simple forms out of which the more complex mechanisms are composed'.

The central idea of the method we propose for generating the possible mechanisms can be explained in a few words. We have assumed that the content of the unconscious consists primarily of propositions, and we further assume that these propositions themselves may be thought of as being of the form actor–action–object.[1] In using this form, we assume that the 'action' is the carrier of the impulse or feeling expressed by the proposition. As already remarked, we do not consider here the energy that theoretically could be attached to each proposition. It is interesting to note that our decision to restrict ourselves to relatively simple forms of propositions actually coincides with a number of linguistic speculations about the deep structure of the generative grammars of spoken languages. Our actual view is that matters are undoubtedly more complicated than is indicated by our simple restrictions or than is indicated by the current speculations of linguists; nevertheless, it is a useful simplification to restrict the elementary forms for the present investigation.

Also, for our present purposes, we do not feel a need to commit ourselves to a linguistic expression of propositions. There is no reason not to accept the idea that a proposition is extracted from, or represented by, a memory of a visual scene, or a memory of a sequence of events, with the events being held in memory in terms of visual or auditory but not linguistic expression.

We now turn to the elementary transformations of propositions, out of which the defence mechanisms may be thought of as being built up. It is our hope, on the basis of a reading of the standard definitions of the major mechanisms, to be able to find the minimum number of transformations necessary to generate the basic mechanisms. Once having done so, we shall try to define a large number of mechanisms in terms of this relatively small number of transformations.

The elementary transformations we feel it necessary to consider are the following:

(i) The first is the transformation of the actor of a proposition from *self* to *other*.

[1] We use 'actor–action–object' rather than Freud's 'subject–verb–object' referred to above in order to emphasize the non-linguistic character of propositions. We use the word 'action' in a wide sense, as exemplified in the *Oxford English Dictionary* (definition 1d): 'The action expressed by a verb; properly of verbs which assert *acting*, but conveniently extended to *the thing asserted by a verb*, whether action, state, or mere existence, as *I strike, I stand, I live, I am.*'

(ii) Correspondingly, we have the transformation from *other* to *self*. It should be understood in each of these cases that the elementary transformation defined operates just on the part of the proposition indicated; the remainder of the proposition remains untouched.

(iii) The first transformation on the action of a proposition consists of the transformation from the action to its opposite, for example, from hating to loving, as in the mechanism of reaction formation.

(iv) The second transformation on the action of a proposition transforms the action so that it is nullified or denied. This transformation defines the defence mechanism of denial in its simplest form.

(v) The third transformation on the action of a proposition transforms the action by intellectualizing it. This is the intellectualizing or neutralizing transformation.

(vi) The fourth transformation on the action of a proposition transforms the action so that it is intensified. We think of this transformation as the transformation of affectualization.

(vii) We also transform the object of a proposition in various ways. The first transformation we consider transforms an object x that is not the self into an object y that is the self. This transformation characterizes the simple form of turning against the self.

(viii) We also transform an object x into another object y, neither object being the self. This is the elementary form of displacement. It is assumed in both these cases that in the unconscious, the object is not the self.

Thus, to summarize, we have introduced three types of transformations, i.e. transformations on the actor of a proposition, transformations on the action, and transformations on the object of a proposition.

The transformations may be shown in schematic form as follows:

1. *Actor transformation*
   Self as actor $\rightarrow$ Other as actor
   Other as actor $\rightarrow$ Self as actor.
2. *Action transformations*
   Action $\rightarrow$ Opposite of action
   Action $\rightarrow$ Denial of action
   Action $\rightarrow$ Intellectualization of action
   Action $\rightarrow$ Intensification of action.
3. *Object transformations*
   Object $x \rightarrow$ Self as object
   Object $x \rightarrow y$ as object, $x \neq y$, $y \neq$ self.

We can now examine how various defence mechanisms may be generated in terms of these elementary transformations. What we have in mind is, in general, that a transformation that is applied to a proposition in the unconscious will yield a new proposition that is part of consciousness. The proposition in consciousness may on occasion lead to action, but in the present abstract version of the theory we shall not distinguish between propositions in consciousness that lead to action from those that do not. We shall simply treat all transformations as producing from propositions in the unconscious new propositions in consciousness. We recognize that we have not said anything about the occasions on which these propositions are likely to be generated, and that there need to be both internal and external conditions of stimulation that lead to the operation of the mechanisms. In general, it is fair to say that what we have in mind is something that corresponds more to the production of conscious dispositions that endure across time, and not to the production of momentary propositions arising on a given occasion. From a technical standpoint it is also fair to say that the propositions leading to conscious dispositions are perhaps not always correctly characterized as being in consciousness but rather as being in the preconscious and thus accessible to consciousness.

Given the transformations listed above, and assuming that at most one transformation is applied to each part of the proposition, it is easy to compute the possible number of defence mechanisms that can be generated, namely, $2 \times 5 \times 3 - 1 = 29$, when the subject in the unconscious proposition is the *self*, and another 29 when the subject of the unconscious proposition is some *other*. Note that in computing the number of mechanisms the number for each component is one greater than the number of transformations, because any one component – actor, action or object – may remain unchanged by the action of the mechanism. Also, it is possible that all three components may remain unchanged because no mechanism is operating, and so we have subtracted one to eliminate this case. (More general results that take into account reiteration of transformations are discussed in the appendix.)

In Table 1 we show the 29 forms of propositions that result from the possible transformations, and that thereby reflect the operation of defence mechanisms. The propositional forms shown in Table 1 do not of course represent the mechanisms themselves but rather the result of the mechanisms' having been applied to unconscious propositions. For example, by applying the transformation for the opposite of actions to a proposition we generate the defence mechanism of reaction formation. Thus, from *I hate my mother* we obtain *I love my mother*, and this we may take as a prototypical instance of reaction formation. This is shown in Table 1 as line 3. Or, by applying the transformation for objects of a proposition, in the case in which neither object is the self, we generate the

Table 1. The 29 defence mechanisms generated by elementary transformations from unconscious propositions of the form Self + Action + Object.

	Mechanism	Number of transformations	Propositional form in consciousness
1	Displacement	1	Self + A + y
2	Turning against the self	1	Self + A + Self
3	Reaction formation	1	Self + Opp A + x
4	Reaction formation & displacement	2	Self + Opp A + y
5	Reaction formation & turning against the self	2	Self + Opp A + Self
6	Intellectualization	1	Self + Neut A + x
7	Intellectualization & displacement	2	Self + Neut A + y
8	Intellectualization & turning against the self	2	Self + Neut A + Self
9	Denial	1	Self + Denial A + x
10	Denial & displacement	2	Self + Denial A + y
11	Denial & turning against the self	2	Self + Denial A + Self
12	Affectualization	1	Self + Intensif A + x
13	Affectualization & displacement	2	Self + Intensif A + y
14	Affectualization & turning against the self	2	Self + Intensif A + Self
15	Projection	1	Other + A + x
16	Projection & displacement	2	Other + A + y
17	Projection & turning against the self	2	Other + A + Self
18	Projection & reaction formation	2	Other + Opp A + x
19	Projection & reaction formation & displacement	3	Other + Opp A + y
20	Projection & reaction formation & turning against the self	3	Other + Opp A + Self
21	Projection & intellectualization	2	Other + Neutral A + x
22	Projection & intellectualization & displacement	3	Other + Neutral A + y
23	Projection & intellectualization & turning against the self	3	Other + Neutral A + Self
24	Projection & denial	2	Other + Denial A + x
25	Projection & denial & displacement	3	Other + Denial A + y
26	Projection & denial & turning against the self	3	Other + Denial A + Self
27	Projection & affectualization	2	Other + Intensif A + x
28	Projection & affectualization & displacement	3	Other + Intensif A + y
29	Projection & affectualization & turning against the self	3	Other + Intensif A + Self

defence mechanism of displacement. Thus, from *I am mad at my boss* we obtain *I am mad at my wife*.

Fundamentally, we favour a process view of mechanisms and from this standpoint it is natural to think that some particular mechanism may result from more than one transformation. We have shown in the case of each line of Table 1 the type and number of transformations used, and we have shown in the left-hand column the best description of the mechanism that results from the transformations shown. In the most elementary cases, for example, displacement in line 1 of Table 1, or reaction formation in line 3, the mechanism arises just from one elementary transformation. In contrast, the mechanism in line 20 arises from three elementary transformations, one on the actor, one on the action and one on the object. Thus, when the initial proposition in the unconscious is *I love him*, the result of this mechanism is *He hates me*, as in the example already quoted from Freud. We have included only the 29 propositional forms that arise from beginning with an unconscious proposition that has the self as subject, and have not considered the propositional forms that would arise from beginning with some *other* as the subject. We shall comment on this in more detail later in considering the mechanism of identification.

Although Table 1 exhibits 29 distinct mechanisms, if we now return to Anna Freud's work we find that 6 of the 9 mechanisms she mentions have not been covered by our table (we do not here consider sublimation as a defence mechanism). In addition, if we look at the much longer list of Bibring *et al.* (1961) we again find that most of this list is not included in Table 1, although we have taken the term *affectualization* to stand for the intensification of feeling from their list.

There are two reasons for this relatively small overlap between Anna Freud's work, Bibring's work, and the work presented here. The first reason is the lack of clearly agreed upon intuitive but systematic definitions of the various mechanisms to be found in the literature. For example, in Anna Freud's work it is difficult to find any systematic statement which clearly differentiates reversal from reaction formation. It is also difficult on the basis of her discussion to state the characteristics that differentiate isolation from intellectualization. In this light, and working within the present framework, we are prepared not to treat isolation and reversal as separate identifiable mechanisms, and we are prepared to treat repression as simply the basic operation of placing propositions in the unconscious rather than treating it as a separate mechanism.

The second reason for the relatively small overlap is the severe restriction of our framework. Thus we believe that identification and introjection as a special case of identification can be introduced in a straightforward way by extending the framework of Table 1, that still a different framework will lead us to the mechanism of undoing, and that still a more powerful extension will lead us to regression. We discuss each of these extensions in turn.

For the mechanism of undoing, we extend our framework to include a transformation at time t followed by another transformation at some later time, say t', such that the propositional action at t' is the opposite of the propositional action at t. For example, the proposition *I want to hit my baby brother* transforms to *I want to console my baby brother*. Similarly, *I want a divorce* transforms to *I could never leave her*. Also, as far as we can see, it might be possible to pair each of the 29 mechanisms in conjunction with undoing, although this would introduce a refinement that has certainly not been empirically investigated by anyone.

In the cases of identification and regression (two of the mechanisms that have been extensively discussed in the literature) we feel it unwise to introduce additional elementary transformations in order to add these mechanisms to our table but rather prefer to think of identification and regression in terms of a hierarchy of mechanisms. All of the mechanisms defined in Table 1 in terms of elementary transformations are at about the same level of complexity and specificity. As in other matters, it seems natural to introduce a hierarchy for more general or complex mechanisms and this, we feel, is the proper approach to identification and regression.[2] In both these cases the hierarchy is introduced by defining identification and regression each as classes of elementary mechanisms, in the sense of those exhibited in Table 1. We will first consider identification because our approach to this mechanism is probably closer to that already explicit in the literature than is our approach to regression.

We have already indicated that corresponding to mechanisms 15 to 29 of Table 1, i.e. those involving transformations from the self as actor to some other as actor, we have inverse transformations from the other as actor to the self as actor. It is these additional 15 mechanisms that we believe constitute the class of identification mechanisms. All 15 of these mechanisms of identification are shown in Table 2. The first is the simple case of identification, i.e. where the only change is identification of the self with the other as actor. Thus, *He does it* transforms to *I do it*. We have called this the case of elementary identification and in the description of the remaining 14 mechanisms the transformation of the actor

---

[2] From a formal standpoint many other classes of elementary mechanisms can easily be defined, e.g. all those involving the elementary transformation of projection. However, we have only singled out the two classes that seem to have some special conceptual interest.

Table 2. *The 15 elementary defence mechanisms of identification*

Mechanism	Number of transformations	Propositional form in consciousness
30 Elementary identification	2	Self + A + x
31 Elementary identification & displacement	2	Self + A + y
32 Elementary identification & turning against the self	2	Self + A + Self
33 Elementary identification & reaction formation	2	Self + Opp A + x
34 Elementary identification & reaction formation & displacement	3	Self + Opp A + y
35 Elementary identification & reaction formation & turning against the self	3	Self + Opp A + Self
36 Elementary identification & intellectualization	2	Self + Neutral A + x
37 Elementary identification & intellectualization & displacement	3	Self + Neutral A + y
38 Elementary identification & intellectualization & turning against the self	3	Self + Neutral A + Self
39 Elementary identification & denial	2	Self + Denial A + x
40 Elementary identification & denial & displacement	3	Self + Denial A + y
41 Elementary identification & denial & turning against the self	3	Self + Denial A + Self
42 Elementary identification & affectualization	2	Self + Intensif A + x
43 Elementary identification & affectualization & displacement	3	Self + Intensif A + y
44 Elementary identification & affectualization & turning against the self	3	Self + Intensif A + Self

173

from other to self is characterized as elementary identification plus displacement, elementary identification plus turning against the self, and so forth. For example, *My mother hates my father* transforms by identification and displacement to *I hate my brother*, or by identification and turning against the self to *I hate myself*. We are thus using two concepts of identification, that of elementary identification as exhibited in the elementary mechanism and also that of complex identification as exhibited by the entire class of 15 mechanisms.

In Table 1 and Table 2 we have introduced altogether 44 elementary mechanisms and we now want to ask how these are to be related to regression. The approach we have adopted to regression does not seem to have been explicitly formulated before in the literature, and there may be proper objections to our conceptualization. We define regression as a broad higher-order mechanism that can be exhibited by any of the 44 elementary mechanisms if the elementary transformations are transformations that go backward in time in terms of the individual's experience. An example of this, in the case of displacement, is when the new object is an object from the past, or, in the case of denial, when the memory denied is a memory from the past, rather than a current perception.

This approach to regression introduces the mechanism without introducing explicit formal machinery for temporal reference. In a completely worked out process theory it would be necessary to show how regression operates in detail in terms of the life history of the individual and to introduce an explicit time variable to characterize the action of the mechanism. Within the present context, we are able to avoid this necessity by introducing the above informal characterization of regression. What we do feel is appropriate at this time is the characterization of regression as a higher-order mechanism and in fact a ubiquitous higher-order mechanism that can be exhibited in any one of the elementary mechanisms we have defined. What is important to note, however, is that although regression is a higher-order mechanism that can be exhibited in each of the 44 cases, it does not follow that it is more general, for example, than projection or identification. In other words, according to our schema there are many cases of projection or of identification that do not involve regression.

Comparison to other approaches in the literature

The kind of systematic formal approach to classifying the defence mechanisms that we have undertaken in this paper is, we believe, somewhat different from any of the approaches now in the literature, and we will try in this section to examine some of the similarities and differences.

To begin with, we have not mentioned the topic of computer simulation of defence processes, a subject that has been of some interest. The most detailed example of such an approach is perhaps the model presented by Moser, Zeppelin & Schneider (1969). To a large extent their developments are orthogonal to ours, as they are concerned more with a process formulation of cathexis and drives. The detailed structure and content of the defence mechanisms themselves is not a focus of their work, though their model makes more explicit than practically any other the possible role of cathexis in the operation of defence processes. We have deliberately avoided the concept of cathexis or the concept of energy in the present paper. Many current researchers are sceptical of the place of the concept of energy in psychoanalytic theory, and we have wanted to present our ideas avoiding involvement with this concept.

It is apparent that even if one does reject the concept of energy, other concepts of a related kind must be introduced in a complete theory in order to provide an account of what drives the organism. It is likely, of course, that for some time to come a detailed quantitative theory of energy will not be feasible, and in this respect we are sceptical of some aspects of the Moser model.

An information-processing approach to psychoanalysis is to be found in the recent monograph by Peterfreund (1971), but unfortunately his exposition of the defence processes is too general and too brief to permit detailed comparisons with our own approach. Peterfreund does not attempt any detailed analysis of any of the particular defence mechanisms, but his use of flow charts as developed in computer science (also used by Moser, Zeppelin & Schneider) may prove to be a useful innovation in psychoanalytic theory.

Two articles that are much closer in spirit to our own are the article by Bibring *et al.* (1961), in which 39 defences are listed and partially classified, and the more recent article by Holland (1973), in which an algebraic approach similar to our own is developed. The study by Bibring *et al.* is not intended to provide systematic methods for generating the mechanisms and we shall not examine the approach of this article in more detail. Holland, on the other hand, does attempt to introduce informally four kinds of displacement from which he would like to generate the bulk of defence mechanisms, at least the bulk of those considered classical in the literature. His four kinds of displacement are: displacement of direction, displacement in time, displacement in number, and displacement based on similarity. While Holland's theoretical development is suggestive (and the interested reader will probably want to compare it to our own) it is probably fair to say that our attempt, though less ambitious, is nevertheless worked out in greater detail. From a systematic standpoint we have not been able to fully understand the algebra that Holland proposes and we do not believe that in an ordinary mathematical sense he has actually introduced a well-defined algebra of explicitly characterized operations. It is not, for example, possible to derive from his paper specific combinatorial results about the number of mechanisms of a given kind, and so forth. On the other hand, we emphasize that by making our own analysis completely formal and explicit we had to sacrifice suggestive but informal developments relating our ideas to those of primary process or a variety of ego transactions. Holland has a number of useful things to say about these matters.

One of the most careful efforts made in the classification of the defence mechanisms is that of Gleser & Ihilevich (1969). They are the originators of the Defence Mechanism Inventory, which they have standardized as a clinical test instrument. In developing their inventory they divided the defence mechanisms into five clusters, which we feel have a fairly direct relation to the classifications we have given in Tables 1 and 2. Their five clusters are the following. (1) *Turning against object*. This cluster includes displacement and identification with the aggressor. (2) *Projection*. This cluster includes, as they put it, those 'defences which justify the expression of aggression toward an external object'. This cluster is close to the class of mechanisms that is generated by using our elementary transformation of projection. (3) *Principalization*. This cluster includes intellectualization, isolation and rationalization, and is thus very close to what we have termed intellectualization. (4) *Turning against self*. This cluster is close to our elementary transformation of turning against the self. (5) *Reversal*. This cluster includes negation, denial, reaction formation and (somewhat surprisingly) repression, which we have treated as a characteristic feature of all defence mechanisms. Thus their cluster of reversal is close to our two elementary transformations of denial and reaction formation.

What is distinctive about the Gleser and Ihilevich work is the careful effort made on both the standardization and validation of their inventory of defences. We wish to note, however, that the five clusters of mechanisms were derived intuitively and without appeal to more general elementary principles.

Summary

Following suggestions in the literature concerning the need for systematic treatment of psychoanalytic theory, we have attempted to introduce new means for generating and classifying the defence mechanisms. The classification results from a consideration of the elementary transformations that may be applied to unconscious propositions of the form actor–action–object. Elementary transformations on the actor, the action or the object of the unconscious proposition are introduced, and the defence mechanisms are then systematically generated by applying one or more of the transformations to unconscious propositions. The relation of the mechanisms thus generated to more classic work is examined, as are several different recent proposals for the study of the defence mechanisms.

Appendix

The computation of the number of defence mechanisms generated by the elementary transformations, as shown in Tables 1 and 2 and as discussed in earlier sections of this paper, does not explore in depth the more general structure of the transformations we have introduced. This is not done in the main content of the paper for the reason that we do not see any way in which the additional mathematical analysis that can be given of the transformations has any hope of being applied either theoretically or empirically in the near future. Since, however, the examination of algebraic structures of transformations has turned out to be important in a wide range of scientific disciplines, it seemed desirable to make our conception of the structure explicit in this appendix.

The two natural questions to ask are, first, whether the reiterated composition of the eight elementary transformations yields an algebraic group, with the operation of the group being that of composition of the transformations, and, secondly, whether the algebraic structure is finite or infinite in character. The answers to these two questions are intertwined.

Still a different question is whether each of the transformations is defined for any propositional form either before or after other transformations have been applied. For example, if we apply the transformation that maps the self as actor into the other as actor, how are we to define the effects of this transformation on a proposition that has other as actor rather than the self? This kind of question must obviously be settled for each of the transformations before the two algebraic questions raised above can be answered.

Clearly, the theory is simpler if the transformations are total functions defined for every proposition rather than partial functions, and it will be worth seeing how far we can go in this direction in a reasonably natural way. First of all, in the transformation of the actor we can collapse the two elementary transformations into one, a single transformation that maps self into other and other into self. The composition of this transformation with itself is then just the identity transformation. It is worth noting that this gives us at once a two-element subgroup with the identity transformation playing, of course, the role of the identity in the group.

The same applies to the transformation of the action to its opposite, with the composition of opposition with itself yielding the identity transformation, and so once again we have a two-element subgroup. In the case of the intensifier transformation leading to the elementary mechanism of affectualization, it is natural to introduce reiteration of the intensifier in such a way that the reiteration of the intensifier transformation leads to ever more intense affectualization. Thus we do not have a finite number of transformations but rather an infinite one under composition. Also, we do not have a natural inverse transformation, and although we could perhaps define one in terms of the neutralization transformation on which intellectualization is based, at the present stage of development of the theory this seems rather artificial. Consequently, the most we will want to say here is that we have a semi-group of transformations that are infinite rather than finite. In the case of composition of the neutralization transformation with itself, we may again want to be able to reiterate this transformation and in the same fashion obtain an infinite semigroup, although it is again not clear at the present stage of theory that the concept of potentially unbounded reiteration of the neutralization transformation can serve any useful purpose.

Concerning the transformation of the objects of propositions which lead to displacement and turning against the self, we do not seem to have at the present stage of investigation a natural algebraic structure to impose, and so we will not pursue these transformations in any more detail.

We can now answer the two questions we raised at the beginning of this appendix in tentative fashion. First, the algebraic structure looked at *in toto* of all the transformations is a structure with an infinite number of objects in its domain resulting from composition of one elementary transformation with another. Secondly, we do not, in general, seem to have a natural group structure but we do have some restricted and simple finite subgroups. Moreover, in the case of transformations of the objects of propositions it does not seem natural to impose much structure at all at the present time because of the openness of the way in which one object can be transfomed into another or into the self.

In summary, these remarks are meant to show how easy it is to go beyond the relatively small, finite number of defence mechanisms we have listed in Tables 1 and 2 to what is in fact an infinite number of distinct mechanisms, if we accept the unbounded iteration of certain transformations. It is for future investigation to decide whether concepts of the kind discussed in this appendix will turn out to be useful.

References

Bibring, G. L. *et al.* (1961). A study of the psychological processes in pregnancy and of the earliest mother–child relationship. *Psychoanal. Study Child* 16.

Frege, G. (1892). Über Sinn und Bedeutung. *Z. Phil. phil. Kritik* 100, 25–50.

Freud, A. (1936). *The Ego and the Mechanisms of Defence* (Int. Univ. Press, New York, 1966), rev. edn.

Gleser, G. C. & Ihilevich, D. (1969). An objective instrument for measuring defence mechanisms. *J. Consult. Clin. Psychol.* 33, 51–60.

Holland, N. (1973). Defence, displacement and the ego's algebra. *Int. J. Psycho-Anal.* 54, 247–56.

Holt, R. R. (1967a). The development of the primary process: a structural view.

In R. R. Holt (ed.), *Motives and Thought: Essays in Honor of David Rapaport* (Int. Univ. Press, New York).

Holt, R. R. (1967b). Beyond vitalism and mechanism: Freud's concept of psychic energy. In J. H. Masserman (ed.), *Science and Psychoanalysis*, vol. 11 (Grune & Stratton, New York).

MacIntyre, A. C. (1958). *The Unconscious: a Conceptual Analysis* (Routledge & Kegan Paul, London).

Moser, U., Zeppelin, I. von & Schneider, W. (1969). Computer simulation of a model of neurotic defence processes. *Int. J. Psycho-Anal.* 50, 53–64.

Peterfreund, E. (1971). *Information, Systems and Psychoanalysis* (Int. Univ. Press, New York).

Rapaport, D. (1960). *The Structure of Psychoanalytic Theory* (Int. Univ. Press, New York).

Waelder, R. (1960). *Basic Theory of Psychoanalysis* (Int. Univ. Press, New York).

11

Models of repression

W. D. HART

It is beyond any reasonable doubt that there are unconscious mental phenomena of decisive importance for understanding people's lives. But it is not quite so clear in what the unconsciousness of a mental phenomenon consists nor by what processes such a phenomenon is rendered unconscious. In this essay, I wish to direct my attention to these two problems. In particular, I shall focus on three models of unconscious states and repression, a process by which psychic conditions are rendered unconscious. It is important to treat the unconscious and repression simultaneously. For there is a crucial distinction between unconscious and pre-conscious mental states. The essential mark of an unconscious mental state is that one has powerful motives for excluding it from consciousness. After *Inhibitions, Symptoms and Anxiety* (1926d, XX), it is clear that Freud thought that in some cases of intrapsychic conflict, an unbearable anxiety arises which provides a motive for repression. Repression is thereby represented as an intentional, though nonetheless typically unconscious, mental action (which is not to deny that it might also be a causal process). In modelling repression, then, it is necessary to allow for a psychic phenomenon rendered unconscious, a motive arising from conflict for so rendering it, and means whereby a person can accomplish this aim. This requires characterizing both the state of a mental phenomenon rendered unconscious and means by which a person can render that phenomenon into precisely that state. These propositions impose adequacy conditions on any account of the unconscious and repression, and since they are like simultaneous equations in two unknowns, the unconscious and repression must be treated together.

I shall first focus on two solutions to these equations. One derives from Freud's essay 'Repression' (1915d, XIV). There Freud is primarily concerned to describe a means by which a psychic phenomenon is repressed, so we must supplement his account by asking whether the condition into which the phenomenon is thereby rendered is one of unconsciousness, and if so, in what this consists. The other derives from

Colin McGinn's essay 'Action and its Explanation'.[1] There McGinn is primarily concerned to 'demythologize the unconscious', that is, to describe the unconscious condition of a mental phenomenon in cogent, intelligible and down to earth terms. We must supplement his account by asking whether we can describe a means of repression whereby a person could render a psychic phenomenon unconscious in McGinn's sense. I shall focus especially on trying to articulate differences between the accounts of Freud and McGinn, but this focus does *not* mean that I think their views are incompatible or that even if they are distinct, their views could not correctly describe different aspects of the life of the mind. It is perfectly possible that more than one condition should be sufficient for unconsciousness and that there should be more than one way to render a psychic phenomenon unconscious. Nevertheless, it is of some interest to try to bring out differences between the two accounts (or alternatively to show them extensionally equivalent) so that we will be in a better position to compare their respective explanatory powers.

McGinn's model is lucid: not to be conscious that you believe or desire that p is not to know that you believe or desire that p. On McGinn's view, for example, a person has an unconscious belief that p if and only if he believes that p but he does not believe that he believes that p. Ordinarily, the belief that p gives rise, causally according to McGinn, to belief that one believes that p; and this is necessary and sufficient for the belief that p to be conscious or at least pre-conscious. But in repression a desire inhibits this causal process; as a result, one does not believe that one believes that p, and this is necessary and sufficient for the belief that p to be unconscious. Since it is an adequacy condition of any account of repression that it be an intentional action, I shall re-express McGinn's view as saying that the inhibiting desire is one's motive for performing an act of repression. But since, for all I know, motivated action may be an entirely causal process, this translation by no means represents an objection to McGinn's view.

There is an objection to the sufficiency of McGinn's analysis of the unconscious state. Consider Freud's thirst dreams, discussed in chapter 3 of *The Interpretation of Dreams* (1900a, IV–V). I shall assume that dreams are intentional, motivated actions performed by the dreamer and that the dreamer is conscious at most of the manifest content of his dream. The dreamer is asleep and wishes to continue to sleep. But he is also thirsty and so wishes to drink. Satisfying this second wish would require waking up to get a drink, thereby frustrating his first wish. Thus

---

[1] Colin McGinn, 'Action and its Explanation' in *Philosophical Problems in Psychology,* ed. Neil Bolton (Methuen, London, 1979), pp. 20–42, especially section V.

the dreamer has conflicting desires. His strategy for resolving this conflict has these elements. As a part of his primary process, the dreamer believes in what is called the omnipotence of thought; its application here is that the dreamer believes that fantasizing doing something is as good as really doing it or that he does not distinguish the two. Thus he believes that he can satisfy his desire to drink by fantasizing drinking, and do so without having to wake up and so frustrating his desire to sleep. For this reason, he represents to himself (hallucinates) as fulfilled in his desire to drink; this representation of himself as drinking is the manifest content of his dream. The point is that this explanation of the thirst dream requires attributing to the dreamer beliefs about his desire to drink, his desire to sleep and about the efficacy of his fantasies. Therefore, the second-order beliefs about first-order propositional attitudes which McGinn says are sufficient for the consciousness of those attitudes are present in the dreamer, even though the point of the dreamer's action is to exclude from his consciousness his desire to drink so that it will not awaken him. That the dream is temporarily successful in this aim is shown by the fact that the dreamer does not wake during his dream; that the desire to drink persists excluded from consciousness is shown by the fact that it sometimes wakes him after being unslaked by his dream. I conclude that the presence of McGinn's second-order beliefs about a propositional attitude is not sufficient to prevent that attitude from being unconscious. (A moment's reflection will show that adding beliefs of an order greater than the second will not remedy this insufficiency.) On the other hand, I think it is plain that the absence or attenuation of second-order beliefs about propositional attitudes is a necessary condition for those attitudes to be unconscious. (So little dreamwork contributes to the formation of the thirst dream that it may not be clear that the dreamer is unconscious of his desire to drink. But it is clear that where a long chain of associations separates the latent and manifest contents of a dream, part of the dreamer's aim is to render unconscious or preserve the unconscious state of the latent wish, the distorted representation of whose fulfilment is the manifest content of the dream. Here the dreamer must have many beliefs about that wish, and far from guaranteeing its consciousness, these (partly) explain his motive for rendering it unconscious. This point reinforces the insufficiency of McGinn's analysis.)

McGinn's model tells us nothing about how a desire might inhibit the formation of a second-order belief. Translated into the action mode, his model tells us nothing about how one might go about performing an action of repression. This is hardly surprising, since he aimed at neither. But in 'Repression', Freud sketches a mechanism whereby an emotion might be repressed. Let us suppose that an emotion is always a complex entity and, in particular, that an emotion always includes an idea or thought and a certain amount of feeling. Suppose, for example, that a man lusts after a certain woman. Then it is natural to expect him to think about making love to her and to expect that he has a strong desire that his thought should come true. Now suppose that he also has grounds for objecting to his lust for her; for example, since she is his best friend's wife, he thinks he ought not to lust after her and so he wants not to lust after her. He thus has a conflict, and repressing his lust is one strategy he may adopt for dealing with his conflict. Freud suggests that a technique for repressing his lust lies in splitting apart the thought stating the object of his desire and the feeling animating that desire. The thought then becomes unknown to the man while the affect, which may be altered by the split, might become displaced onto another idea.[2] Put so abstractly, it may seem implausible that there is such a technique. But I think the real question to ask is this: How must we conceive the unconscious state in order that the splitting of ideas from affects in an emotion could render the emotion, and its constituent thought, unconscious? Answering this question is a necessary condition for evaluating Freud's hypothesis on a technique of repression.

First, Freud's hypothesis can be brought much closer to everyday experience. It is a bit of folk medicine that one should try to forget a distressing experience. The folk prescription for this is to think about, get one's mind on, something else. For example, the lustful man mentioned above might throw himself into his work. By getting his mind on his work, he gets his mind off the idea of making love to his friend's wife; one can only attend to so much at any one time. And it is natural to suppose that he is in part working off his lust; that is, that part of the energy he expends in work is the energy which animated his desire for his friend's wife – after all, it is harder to be lusty when you are exhausted by or absorbed in work. Second, it seems to me that the best model for the repression effected on a thought or emotion by such an activity is Harry Stack Sullivan's concept of selective inattention.[3] Peripheral vision is a perceptual analogue of this psychic technique. One sees most clearly things at a reasonable distance in one's direct line of sight. One does not see at all clearly what lies on the edge of one's visual field. Now suppose that out of some motive, one just simply refused to turn so that something on the edge came to lie on one's line of sight. Here we have a motivated refusal to see and thus come to know things around one.

[2] For more on this, see Richard Wollheim, *Sigmund Freud* (Collins, London, 1971), p. 182.

[3] Harry Stack Sullivan, *Clinical Studies in Psychiatry* (Norton, New York, 1956), chapter 3.

Something like this may play a part in the devices a person uses to ignore an enemy when circumstances throw them together. Moreover, if we think of introspection as a kind of perception of the contents of the mind then the perceptual analogy may be an example of selective inattention rather than a mere analogy. Now let us put the pieces together. One represses an emotion, and its constituent ideas, by selectively refusing to attend to (introspect) it. This is accomplished by attending to something divorced from the subject matter of those ideas. The sequence of ideas in free association is a history of the ideas selectively attended to in order not to think of the repressed idea. The stratagem also has affinities with the technique of allusion with omission described by Freud in section 11 of chapter 2 of *Jokes and their Relation to the Unconscious* (1905c, VIII), and briefly in the third of the *Five Lectures on Psychoanalysis* (1910a, XI). One invests the energy of the emotion in thinking about that something else, and thereby ceases to attend to the ideas included in the emotion. The unconscious state achieved thereby for those ideas consists in the refusal to attend to them, and this satisfies McGinn's necessary condition for unconsciousness. (On the other hand, if the composition of an emotion from ideas and affects is essential to the emotion, and this mode of repression splits ideas from affects, then the emotion does not exist in a repressed state; instead, repression destroys the emotion, even if it can be reconstituted upon the occurrence of insight.)[4]

We have now gestured toward a technique of repression, whose description is due to Freud, which might perhaps suffice to render a mental phenomenon unconscious in McGinn's sense. But I think there are a number of points which it would be desirable to get clearer. Note first that Freud's splitting technique does not by itself account for the existence of unconscious mental states. When an affect and an idea constituting an emotion are split, the emotion is destroyed, not rendered unconscious; thus we cannot appeal to that emotion's presence in the unconscious to explain a man's subsequent actions and mental life. And splitting the idea from its affect will render the idea unconscious only if affective cathexis is a necessary condition for the consciousness of an idea. But my perhaps naïve impression is that I can be conscious of ideas to which I am quite indifferent, for example, the thought that there are at this instant exactly 10^{10} grains of sand on the planet Mars. And more important, it has yet to be explained how decathecting an idea could render it unconscious. What would the unconscious state have to be in order that decathecting an idea is by itself enough to make the idea unconscious? That is at least obscure. Even if consciousness and uncon-

---

[4] For more on this see Wollheim, *Sigmund Freud*.

sciousness are states we have motives for wanting some of our ideas to have, that does not mean that they are themselves affective states; rather, they are cognitive conditions. Note second that splitting is enough for the unconsciousness of the idea only when we add to it Sullivan's technique of selective inattention, and then only when we assume as a so far brute fact that we cannot attend to a vast number of distinct ideas at once. Indeed, it might be said that being unable to attend to a thought just is not being conscious of it, though put in other words, so that while perhaps we have noted a fact that makes repression possible, we have not really accounted for the unconscious state in any enlightening way.

All this suggests to me that perhaps we should start again. The basic hypothesis is that repression is a motivated action the aim of which is to render a psychic phenomenon unconscious. The essence of explaining an action consists in giving the beliefs and desires which, while perhaps not themselves all rational, suffice to make that action a rational thing to do. So let us look for beliefs and desires which would make repression a rational thing to do, and perhaps in stating the content of those beliefs and desires we can arrive at a statement of the intention with which repression is done that will yield insight into the nature of the unconscious state. And let us also look for ordinary, familiar actions which, performed in suitable situations, could be acts of repression rendering mental entities unconscious and which could be accounted for rationally by the beliefs and desires we have articulated.

We shall consider the beliefs and desires of a single subject S. It may increase perspicuity for those formally inclined if I represent S's beliefs and desires schematically. Thus 'Bp' is short for 'S believes that p' and 'Dp' is short for 'S desires that p'; the rest of my shorthand is standard and I shall translate attributions of beliefs and desires to S into this notation as a running aside. A major contribution by psychoanalysis to the understanding of our mental life is its discovery of our belief in the omnipotence of thought (OT) and how this explains some of our most intriguing activities. We can approximate this here by attributing to S a belief that what he believes is true or that what he wants is real. In symbols, $B(Bp \rightarrow p)$ and $B(Dp \rightarrow p)$; call these OT_1 and OT_2. The distinction is somewhat artificial, being forced on us by our having taken only belief and desire and not fantasy as well. Both beliefs are to be thought of as unconscious; otherwise they could not survive rational criticism. It is natural to attribute to S a species of means–end thought; he wants what he believes is sufficient for what he wants. In symbols, if $B(p \rightarrow q)$ and Dq, then Dp; call this MET. It is obviously too strong since it makes no allowance for choice among means. But making such an allowance would probably involve quantitative considerations my present apparatus is too simple to encode. Think of *MET* as a first approximation.

One might think of attributing to S a sort of wishful thinking; he believes what he wants to believe. In symbols, $DBp \to Bp$; call this *WT*. OT_1, *MET* and *WT* imply $Dp \to Bp$; S believes of what he wants that it is so. This consequence might look as though it describes a pathology of belief and desire, but it is not yet repression. There is not yet anything repressed, and there is as yet no representation of any conflict in S. It seems to me that *WT* is at fault; it is too simple a principle.

To construct a slightly better model of conflict resolution by repression, suppose S believes that p but desires that $\sim p$, that is,

(a) $Bp \ \& \ D(\sim p)$.

By OT_1 we have

(b) $B(B(\sim p) \to \sim p)$

and by MET we have

(c) $(B(B(\sim p) \to \sim p) \ \& \ D(\sim p)) \to DB(\sim p)$,

so since by (a) $D(\sim p)$, it follows that

(d) $DB(\sim p)$.

This will be S's motive for repression. In order to represent a conflict in S, it would suffice to discern in S a desire somehow 'contrary' to that described in (d). To this end, it suffices to suppose that desire mediates conscious belief in the sense that two further principles hold. First, suppose that

(e) $Bp \to DBp$,

(a principle tending to damp down cognitive dissonance), and second that *ordinarily* consciousness is such that

(f) $DBp \to BBp$,

(a perhaps weaker version of *WT*). By (a) we have Bp, so by (e) we get DBp. Since we now have $DB(\sim p) \ \& \ DB(p)$, if we had

(g) $(DB(p) \ \& \ DB(q)) \to DB(p \ \& \ q)$

we would get $DB(p \ \& \ \sim p)$. If we also had a desire for consistency, viz,

(h) $D \sim B(p \ \& \ \sim p)$,

then S would have incompatible desires, that is, a conflict. How is S to resolve his conflict? Suppose his desire that $\sim p$ is much stronger than his desire to believe that p. Then he can get more satisfaction by acting on his desire to believe that $\sim p$ than by acting on his desire to believe that p; so he chooses to act on his desire to believe that $\sim p$. He cannot do this by bringing it about that $B(\sim p)$; for since Bp, he will then be threatened by believing that $p \ \& \ \sim p$, which would frustrate his desire for consistency. So perhaps his next best strategy (since logic alone rules it out that $\sim Bp$) is to bring it about that $\sim BBp$, violating (f), the ordinary rule of consciousness. Since then $Bp \ \& \ \sim BBp$, S's belief that p would be unconscious in McGinn's sense.

I certainly do *not* intend the above model to be taken seriously. A vast number of devastating objections can be brought against it; (for example, it at best gets us only unconsciousness in McGinn's sense which, as we have seen, will not do for Freud's purposes). But the point which interests me is this: even if the above model works, it does so only by importing *quantitative* considerations – considerations the present purely qualitative apparatus is incapable of representing. Quantitative considerations are also relevant to our perceptual analogue to Sullivan's concept of selective inattention: in order to *keep* an object on the periphery of one's visual field (so as to *make* oneself unable to see it clearly), one has to be able to see it clearly *enough* to be able to know when and how to turn so that it will remain always at the edge. (This quantitative way of putting it suggests that the paradox with which Sartre charges Freud may not really be a paradox.) So I wish now to consider quantitative issues and perceptual models of consciousness.

Sullivan represents repression as selective inattention. This suggests a model of consciousness in terms of introspection; a person is conscious of only those of his psychic states and so forth which he introspects. Introspection is not popular in psychology these days. I am not sure why this is so, but two arguments against introspection occur to me which may influence philosophers' ideas on the subject. First, it seems that introspection requires a self, the person, who does the introspecting; but, though it is hardly open to psychoanalysis, some are reluctant to admit the existence of a self capable of anything, let alone introspecting. Second, one might admit that there is a self but deny that it can do anything like what introspecting should be. The point here is that introspecting is what Kant used to call inner sense and can only be understood as a form of perception; but perhaps one might deny that one can, or that it makes sense to say that one can in any way perceive any of one's own mental states. For instance, H. P. Grice has argued very convincingly that perception is *essentially* a causal process, that to perceive something one must interact with it causally, thereby acquiring knowledge of (or belief about) it.[5] (Not just any causation of veridical visual experience by that in virtue of which it is veridical suffices for seeing. If a mad scientist injects me with chemical C and the psychological effect of chemical C on me is that it causes in me a visual experience as of the mad scientist injecting me with chemical C, then I have a veridical visual experience caused by that in virtue of which it is veridical, but I do not *see* him injecting me. This is a case of the notorious problem of *appropriate* causation.[6] I will not go into it here.) But at the least we do not have a plausible model whereby we can acquire knowledge or belief about our own mental states, etc., by interacting with them causally. For senses like sight and hearing, we know that there are causal mechanisms involving light and sound; interacting causally with objects by means of the media of light and sound is how we can get information about them through sight and hearing. But what could be the carrier, the analogue of light or sound, the medium by which our mental events interact causally with our selves so that we acquire beliefs about our mental states? If there is no such carrier, then – so the objection goes – introspection is impossible.

I do not take the first objection to introspection, the doctrine that there is no self, seriously. Still, it may be worthwhile to rehearse some reasons for believing in the self. Here goes:

There is an observation concerning our self-knowledge which goes back at least to David Hume. People think, feel, imagine and decide, and we are sometimes aware of some of our thoughts, feelings, images and decisions. But we seem never to be acquainted with a self which thinks, feels, imagines and chooses. Hume wrote, 'For my part, when I enter most intimately into what I call *myself*, I always stumble on some particular perception or other, of heat or cold, light or shade, love or hatred, pain or pleasure. I never catch *myself* at any time without a perception, and never can observe anything but the perception' (*Treatise*, I, 4, 6). Introspect as you will, you will find only the contents of your consciousness; you will not find the subject of your consciousness. Since the eighteenth century, many people have been struck by our inability to confront the bearer of our psychological conditions – Husserl, Wittgenstein in the *Tractatus* and Sartre, to name but three. Hume toyed with the idea that there is no self beyond the bundle or container of the contents of consciousness. But even ignoring its reductive taint, this idea has seldom produced comfortable conviction; Hume himself expressed discomfort

[5] H. P. Grice, 'The Causal Theory of Perception' in *Perceiving, Sensing and Knowing*, ed. Robert J. Swartz (Anchor, Garden City, 1965), pp. 438–72.

[6] For further discussion of, and additional references on, this problem see Christopher Peacocke, *Holistic Explanation* (Clarendon Press, Oxford, 1979), part II.

with it in his appendix to the *Treatise*. Searching for an alternative view has produced some of the thorniest patches in human thought, but still resistance to the bundle theory persists. Husserl urges that there is a self distinct from the bundle of mental events and from the collection of the contents of consciousness; if it forever eludes acquaintance, so much the worse for dogmas of empiricism which would seek to deny it. This view has acquired an unfortunately pretentious title – the transcendence of the ego – and a due respect for tradition urges me to retain it. Try then to bear it in mind that the title names a fairly simple-minded and naïve view: there is a self which is the subject of the contents of consciousness, and indeed all psychic phenomena, but which is not acquainted with itself. (Transcendence is thus a purely epistemic attribute.)

There is a moderately evident reflection which supports the transcendence of the ego against the bundle theory: agency. A mere bundle or container of the contents of consciousness seems hopelessly passive. But thinking, imagining and deciding are things we all do. They are not impersonal happenings in an impassive medium, but instead the mental actions of an agent, even if that agent is not acquainted with itself. An agent acts; a bundle cannot; so the agent, the self, cannot be a mere bundle. We need not suppose an active component or faculty, a will, properly contained in the self. Instead the claim is that the self acts in thinking, imagining and choosing. This elusive agent of one's mental acts is the transcendental ego. The point of this current reflection on agency is that whatever the nature of the transcendental ego, a passive container of the contents of consciousness could not be active and so could not be the self.

(I think that nothing in the two paragraphs above is incompatible with a materialist view on the mind–body problem – though neither do I wish to endorse any such view.)

I suspect that behind resistance to the transcendence of the ego there lurks a sort of idealism with respect to the mind: minds, and mental phenomena generally, depend for their existence on being experienced or somehow known by those who have them (and, perhaps, depend for their natures on how they are experienced or what their possessors believe about them). The view that there is no self over and above the contents of consciousness comes closest to satisfying some such idealism with respect to the mind; for the contents of consciousness is that of which a person is conscious. Such issues have, of course, played a dominant role in twentieth century philosophy of mind, so there is not much point in trying to settle them here. But it is perhaps worth pointing out that Freud's discovery of the unconscious makes it at least highly likely that he should have denied idealism with respect to the mind.

Consider, for example, Freud's discussion of depression in 'Mourning and Melancholia', (1917e, XIV). Suppose that a man loves his mother, but at the time she dies, he feels very hostile toward her. As a result of an unconscious belief in the omnipotence of thought, he fears that his hostility killed her, so he feels guilty about his hostility and her death. His guilt is so strong that he feels unable to face up to his hostility and his guilt, so he represses them. Thereafter, all he feels consciously is a relentless, objectless depression; it may even prompt him to self-destructive behaviour. In this case the man is not conscious of his hostility or his guilt; but since those states explain his conscious depression, he is hostile and guilty. So, on Freud's view, the man's hostility and guilt do not depend for their existence on being contents of his consciousness. One might even go so far as to suppose that it is part of how he represses his hostility and guilt that he experiences them as objectless depression; if so, the man's unconscious mental states do not depend for their natures on how he consciously experiences them or on his conscious beliefs about them. One could say that, especially on the introspective, perceptual model of consciousness, the man does seem to have to be acquainted with his hostility and guilt (at least to some extent) in order to be able to exclude them from his consciousness. While that is true, his acquaintance with his hostility and guilt will typically be no more conscious to him than they are. And more importantly, the model commits us only to the view that his hostility and guilt depend for their *repression* on his acquaintance with them, not that they so depend for their existence or their nature.

(It might be asked how selective inattention to his mental state can bring a man to experience it quite otherwise than it really is; one might know less about an object one keeps on the edge of one's visual field, but how can this lead one to radically false beliefs about it? The question depends upon a false presumption; it is easy to make mistakes about things glimpsed only sidelong. But it should also be pointed out that the model of selective inattention is *not* committed to the view that the *only* analogue to repression is keeping an object out of or on the edge of one's visual field. As psychoanalytic work done after Freud makes clear, there are many mechanisms of defence, each resulting on occasion in repression. To continue the perceptual analogy, an object might be squarely in the centre of one's visual field, and yet one so concentrates one's focus of attention on a trivial part or aspect of it that it seems quite other than it really is; such might be an analogue to the defence mechanism of distortion. Viewed from too close up, a molehill might look like a mountain. Concentrating too hard on how a sentence was inscribed can make it very hard to understand.)

The second objection to introspection is rather more serious. The model of selective inattention draws an analogy between introspection and perception. Unless it takes introspection to *be* a kind of perception, the model is in danger of losing its content, its explanatory force. Perception, as Grice argues, is always and necessarily a causal interaction with what is perceived. But what could be the means or mechanism whereby we interact causally with our mental states when we introspect them?

Any positive response to this question will have to be speculative. The difficulty here has as much to do with the nature of causation as with the nature of the mind. For example, if we took a Humean, constant-conjunction view of causation, then in order to exhibit a causal model of introspection it would suffice to postulate a constant conjunction between mental states and acquaintance with them. The thinness of this model serves only to illustrate, I think, the well-known insufficiency of constant conjunction alone for causation. There are (at least) two sorts of counter-examples to the sufficiency of constant conjunction for causation. Those of one sort are known as accidental regularities. If, for example, all the coins in my pocket are made of silver, then there is a constant conjunction between being a coin in my pocket and being made of silver; but putting a penny in my pocket will not cause it to be made of silver. It has been noted that accidental regularities do not entail subjunctive conditionals (for example, 'If this penny were in my pocket, it would be made of silver'), while lawlike statements typically do. Thus, much recent work on causation has been directed at adding subjunctive conditionals of some sort to constant conjunctions in order to get conditions necessary and sufficient for causation. But there are counter-examples of a second sort to the sufficiency of constant conjunction for causation. For example, the falling of a (perfect) barometer is constantly conjoined with rain, but the falling barometer does not cause the rain. And yet, neither is their regular association accidental; it does entail the subjunctive conditional that if the (perfect) barometer were to fall, it would rain. Intuitively, the difficulty is that both the falling of the barometer and the rain are joint effects of a common cause; that is why the barometer is a good *sign* of rain but not a cause of it. (Equally clearly, it would be circular to add any such condition to an analysis of causation.)

But there is another view. Writing about the notion of causation, Quine says

It may have had its prehistoric beginnings in man's sense of effort, as in pushing. The imparting of energy still seems to be the central idea. The transfer of momentum from one billiard ball to another is persistently cited as a paradigm case of causality. Thus we might seek a simpleminded or root notion of causality in terms of the flow of energy. Cause and effect are events such that all the energy in the effect flowed from the cause. This thermodynamical image requires us to picture energy, like matter, as traceable from point to point through time. Thus let us picture an event simply as any fragment of space–time, or the material and energetic content thereof. Given an event e, then, imagine all its energy traced backward through time. Any earlier event that intercepts all of these energetic world lines qualifies as a cause of e.[7]

I put Quine's idea Kripke-style by saying that we now know (if we do) *a posteriori* that energy flow is the essence of causality. Much too briefly, the line of thought is that we know *a priori* that the conservation of some quantity or other which is traceable along intuitively identified causal chains is necessary for thoroughgoing causal explanation. (Consider a world in which nothing is conserved. Since time out of mind, there has been nothing at all. Then a rabbit pops into being *ex nihilo*, hops around for a bit, and vanishes without a trace. (You can imagine such a world, so one is possible; thus conservation principles are not necessarily true.) Since *ex hypothesi* there is nothing from which the rabbit came, the rabbit episode of that world's history has no cause; that world's gross violation of conservation deprives us of all material from which to construct a causal explanation of its rabbit episode. So there is no causal explanation without some sort of conservation.) The (local and global) conservation of a quantity through space–time is its flow. Then nature co-operates, and we learn from experience with her that there is in her a satisfactory basic conserved quantity traceable along causal chains. This is energy (or mass–energy). It seems to me reasonable to add these considerations up into Quine's view: causation is energy flow.

It is an advantage of Quine's view that it handles the second sort of counter-example to the sufficiency of constant conjunction for causation in a thoroughly *natural* way. Falling barometers are constantly conjoined with rain but do not cause it. In fact none of the energy expended in condensing rain drops out of water vapour flows from the falling barometer to the atmosphere (and if much of it did, falling barometers would cause rain). Instead, as moist air cools, the attractive forces between water vapour molecules and rain drop nuclei overcome dissociative heat energy. As there is a greater concentration of water, it interacts with, for example, the oldest barometer, human hair, causing it to contract, a contraction we now register as falling; electrochemical energy is transformed into the kinetic energy of motion. The energy flow view

---

[7] W. V. Quine, *The Roots of Reference* (Open Court, La Salle, Illinois, 1973), p. 5.

gets exactly right a prime counter-example to the regularity theory of causation.

Quine's view has other virtues. For example, suitably supplemented, it enables us to explain why lawlike statements entail subjunctive conditionals and to explain non-trivially why the causal relation is irreflexive (at least, that is, to the extent that it is). Moreover, since causation is energy flow, since flow is a matter of conservation, and since conservation is an intrinsically quantitative phenomenon, Quine's view explains why mathematics (thought of in the old way as the science of quantity) should have a substantial part to play in natural science, a circumstance which on most philosophies of science seems purely fortuitous. There are also objections to Quine's view. For example, in a refrigerator the action of the compressor causes ice to form in the freezer, but the (heat) energy flows from the freezer to the compressor; here the direction of the energy flow would seem to be the reverse of that of the causation. It may be possible to answer this objection by being quite careful to observe Quine's four dimensional view of events, by looking more closely into the thermodynamical structure of refrigerators, and by refining the requirements on energy flow for causation (by, for example, invoking further quantities like entropy), or by being willing to deny some intuitions about causation for the sake of good theory. But I will not expend further space–time on these interesting matters here.

It is well known that Freud took economic models in psychology very seriously. Such models are essential if we are to discern causal structures in the mind. For the essence of causation includes conservation, and conservation is of the essence of an economic model. Without a causal structure, the mind should probably be denied to have a nature; and if the mind had no nature, there would be precious little for a scientific psychology to discover. (The science of behaviour, whatever else it might be, is certainly not psychology.) It was perfectly natural and correct that in constructing economic models for psychology, Freud used a notion of psychic energy; an economic, causal model of mental functioning cannot but require the flow of a (relatively) conserved psychological quantity, and 'psychic energy' is just the right term for such a quantity. Many natural scientists with later nineteenth century educations were quite clear on the correctness of the view of causation which Quine rediscovered. (That a form of energy is psychic is not incompatible logically with its also being physical – say, electrochemical energy in the central nervous system. Freud was himself, at least earlier on, committed to materialism. But economic models in psychology and the flow of psychic energy are consistent with both materialist and dualist solutions to the mind–body problem. Of all the major theses in the philosophy of mind

193

on which Freud held views (for example, determinism, materialism, idealism with respect to the mind), he made the least use of his materialism; detaching that doctrine from his theory would do it considerably less violence than detaching any of the others. We probably should not hold that *psychic* energy is strictly conserved any more than kinetic energy is. If, on a materialist view, psychic energy is just electrochemical energy of the central nervous system, then what is strictly conserved is only energy (or mass–energy), although within neural transactions, electrochemical energy is relatively stable and conserved. Even a thoroughgoing dualism should probably deny that purely psychic energy is strictly conserved. Rather, it comes into being from, say, conversion of chemical energy in food or electromagnetic energy in light into alertness and the experiences and beliefs associated with vision, and is expended through, say, conversion into kinetic energy in locomotion. This dualist conception deserves a development I cannot give it here. Nonetheless, if psychic energy is to be worthy of its name, it should be relatively conserved within wholly intrapsychic transactions like introspection.)

Prevailing opinion seems not to have much sympathy with psychic energy these days. There seem to be at least two qualms responsible for this attitude. First, one sometimes hears rather impressionistic denials that the mind satisfies (relative) conservation principles. For example, it is said that it is just not true that the more one loves others, the less one can love oneself, as 'conservation of love' would require. Perhaps; but why assume that the energy expended in loving others can be drawn only off that which might be expended in loving oneself? The fact, if it is a fact, that love is not conserved does not show that no psychic quantity is conserved.

Second, it seems to be doubted that there are any intrinsically psychological quantities at all, let alone ones which might be conserved. (The two objections may not be consistent; for the first seems to concede what the second denies, namely, that there is more and less among mental phenomena.) The reply to this second objection is that it is probably false. The well-known von Neumann–Morgenstern axiomatization of utility is the beginning of a quantitative theory of strength of desire, and Leonard Savage's work (in an important tradition) on subjective probability is the beginning of a quantitative theory of degrees of conviction. Roughly, von Neumann showed that if a person's preference ranking among possible alternatives is rational in a broad structural sense (for instance, if it is transitive), and if he also ranks all gambles between alternatives he ranks (and, most importantly, when he prefers x to y and y to z, then there is a probability p such that he is indifferent between y and the gamble on which he has a p chance of x and a $1 - p$ chance of z), then he has an ordinal utility function (from alternatives into the reals) which is unique up to a positive linear transformation. This means that facts about his desires fix his utility scale except for its zero point and its unit length; if selected arbitrarily, these last two do not encode facts about the person's preferences. This in turn means that no significance can be attached to *sums* of values of his utilities; in particular, the concept of the total strength of a person's desire at a time has yet to be given a sense. Since the (global) conservation of a quantity consists in its total amount at any one time being identical with that total at any other time, the absence of a natural zero and unit from utility functions therefore means that we cannot even raise the question as to whether desire is conserved. But all is not lost; we may yet be able to fix zeros and units naturally. For zeros, suppose we had a notion of 'combining' alternatives; this might, for example, consist in getting both, or, to allow for combining an alternative with itself, in repeating it. Suppose then that there were an alternative p such that for any alternative q, the person is indifferent between q and the combination of q and p. It then seems thoroughly natural to say that alternative p has zero utility for the person. (Albin Goldman is responsible for this construction.) (Because indifference is transitive, a person is indifferent between any two of his alternatives of zero utility.) Units are harder to make out; we should consider which properties of them we need in alternatives. Taking a clue from vector spaces, recall that a unit length (of, say, a basis vector) is one such that the length of any vector (in a one-dimensional space) is a real number multiple of the length of that basis vector. So we might try to construct a concept of the 'product' of a real number a and an alternative p. If a is zero, its product with p should be an alternative with utility zero. Any positive real number a is the sum of a unique natural number n and a real r greater than or equal to zero but less than one. We can think of r as a probability. We might then construe the product of a and p as the alternative consisting of n repetitions of p combined with the gamble on which there is an r chance of another repetition of p and a $1 - r$ chance of an alternative of utility zero. (For a negative, suppose alternatives have clear-cut opposites; if for example p is getting a pound, its opposite might be losing or owing one. Granted such a notion of opposition, then when a is negative, the product of a and p should be the product of $-a$ and the opposite of p. We will be committed to holding that for any p, the utility of the combination of p with its opposite is zero, but that sounds rational enough.) Suppose then that there is an alternative p (preferred to some (and thus any) alternative of utility zero) such that for any alternative q, there is a real number a such that the person is indifferent between q and the product of a and p. Such an alternative as p might be a natural unit. (In general it is false that the person will be indifferent between any two units; which we choose is a choice of scale.) There would fail to be a unit if the person always preferred q to any multiple of p. So to say that there is a unit is to deny a strong form of the law of diminishing returns. (Roughly, our idea of products is a function π from reals and alternatives to alternatives such that for the utility function u, $u(\pi(a,p)) = a \times u(p)$. One other version of diminishing returns would seem to hold that for our π, when $a > 1$ and p is of positive utility, then $u(\pi(a,p)) < a \times u(p)$. It might be that there is an increasing function f from reals to reals such that $u(\pi'(a,p)) \times f(a) = a \times u(p)$; if there were then a function π' from reals and alternatives to alternatives such that $u(\pi'(a,p)) = u(\pi(a,p)) \times f(a)$, we might get round this problem of diminishing returns by replacing π with π'.) (In effect, we have been imposing on the set of alternatives, ordered by preference and indifference, the structure of a *one dimensional* vector space. There might be purposes to be served by allowing for larger dimensions, but I will not speculate here on more complex constructions toward that end.) Whether these constructions of a zero and units work in detail, they do justify, I think, concluding that despairing of intrinsically psychological quantities is premature; what is needed is thought, not despair.

The von Neumann–Morgenstern and Savage axiomatizations are theories about the quantities of desire and belief, not their measurement. One must be careful to distinguish quantity from measurement. Views on quantity are metaphysical views; a quantity is an object, namely, a function from other objects to (typically) real numbers. (The von Neumann axiomatization of utility can be abstracted into an analysis of conditions sufficient for any such function to be a quantity.) Views on measurement, in contrast, are epistemological views; techniques of measurement are techniques for *detecting* the values of a quantity at various of its arguments. To suppose that a quantity depends for its existence on being measurable is a form of verificationism, which is in turn a form of subjective idealism and thus anathema. It is no objection to the view that each desire has a determinate strength that we might be incapable of detecting it. Of course the *interest* of a quantity does depend on our being able to detect its values, even if only indirectly. For comparative strengths of desire (of a single person), we already do this in rough and ready ways.

The von Neumann–Morgenstern and Savage axiomatizations are theories of *rational* desire and belief. This does not mean that they require that all our desires and beliefs should be rational. They are not;

and such a requirement would make their models highly unsuitable for Freud. (On the other hand, economic models in psychology are distinctly Freudian and distinctly causal. For Freud, it is thus particularly important that we be able to quantify belief and desire. For belief and desire are the principal elements in any explanation of action, and part of what is distinctively Freudian is the theory that dreams, parapraxes and neurotic symptoms are *actions* explained by unconscious beliefs and desires. If such explanations are ultimately to be causal, then we must be able to quantify belief and desire.) The rationality required by the axiomatizations is not point by point but rather overall and structural. Yet even this may in fact fail; counter-examples to the transitivity of indifference are easy to construct.[8] Nor do I think it is particularly enlightening to be told that such rationality constraints are *normative* conditions. Instead, there is an analogy between *rational* belief and desire on the one hand and Newton's *rigid* bodies on the other. There are no (perfectly) rigid bodies, but the motions of real bodies can be understood in terms of their deviations from those of rigid ones. Similarly, rational belief and desire are idealizations, and their real counterparts may partly be understood in terms of their deviations from the ideal.

I am not for a moment suggesting that belief or desire is conserved or that utility or subjective probability is psychic energy. (Psychic energy, if there is any, is probably as unobvious a combination of basic variables as kinetic energy, $\frac{1}{2}mv^2$, is of the variables mass, distance and time.) These were intended only to show that intrinsically (rather than materially or behaviourally defined) psychological quantities exist. But then how might one get the idea that a (relatively) conserved psychic energy is possible and worth seeking? (It is to be sought by its conservation. It is not as if someone thought kinetic energy, $\frac{1}{2}mv^2$, was somehow intrinsically interesting and then noticed that it happens to be conserved in mechanical interactions. Rather one sought some quantity conserved along the causal chains of mechanics and discovered that kinetic energy is so conserved.) Let us try to imagine how a quantitative law of wishful thinking might go. Presumably, in all cases of wishful thinking, a belief that p is to be explained by a desire that p. It might turn out that when there is no input to the strength of the desire, any increase in the conviction that p follows a decrease in the strength of the desire that p. We might then account for such a law by supposing that there is an underlying quantity conserved in wishful thinking, perhaps Freud's

[8] But see Alfred F. MacKay, *Arrow's Theorem: The Paradox of Social Choice* (Yale University Press, New Haven, 1980), chapter 3, 'Preference, thresholds and transitivity', for an insightful discussion of the significance of such counter-examples.

psychic energy, which can manifest itself first in utility and second in subjective probability, and that in wishful thinking it is transformed from its first manifestation into its second. Its conservative feature is important to this account's being part of a causal model of wishful thinking. (But only part; we would also want to know the mechanism by which desire converts into belief.) Or, perhaps more plausibly, it might turn out that in wishful thinking *ceteris paribus*, the degree of conviction that p is directly proportional to the strength of the desire that p; when it is wished that p twice as hard, then it is believed that p twice as much. We might then account for such a law by supposing that both utility and subjective probability are forms of some underlying quantity, perhaps Freud's psychic energy again, and that when you pump twice as much of it into desire, then eventually twice as much of it must turn up in wishful thinking *because it is conserved* in wishful thinking. (Analogously, in the kinetic theory of gases, the pressure and temperature of a fixed volume of gas are directly proportional, and both are explained by the kinetic energy of the molecules constituting the gas.) The constant of proportionality between desire and belief in wishful thinking would be a factor for converting amounts of desire into amounts of belief; and especially if the reverse were also possible at the same rate (as, for example, in acceptance of what was distasteful or in the resolution of cognitive dissonance), then it might be reasonable to conclude that there is something more basic, Freud's psychic energy perhaps, of which both are more accessible manifestations. Again, the conservative feature of this account too is important to its being part of a causal, economic model of wishful thinking. We have not yet got the right to deprecate Freud's energic models in the way it is now fashionable to do.

Some such line of thought might also be able to shed light on some of the mysteries of sleep. One tends to think of food as a sort of fuel; one's bodily strength is roughly proportional to the regularity, quality and quantity of one's diet. Similarly, one's alertness is roughly proportional to the regularity, quantity and quality of sleep one gets. But what is to fatigue as food is to hunger? It does not seem as though during sleep there is a stuff, analogous to food, which one consumes. It is almost as if one could refuel one's automobile by leaving it parked overnight with the motor running; some sort of magic, some sort of violation of conservation, can seem to be involved in sleep. Most physiological thinking about sleep seems to run along the following sort of lines: presumably, during sleep, some anabolic process produces some substance more rapidly than it would be consumed by catabolic processing during wakefulness. Of course, such chemical manufacture expends overall energy, but the substance it produces is then available for expenditure in alertness and attention during wakefulness. So viewed economically, sleep consists in trading overall energy for usefully accessible energy. But – and this is the point – such lines of thought must remain impressionistic until we can independently identify two conceptually distinct quantities, one presumably the physical amount of some bodily substance and the other some intrinsically psychological quantity of awareness, attentiveness, wakefulness or even consciousness, and demonstrate that these two quantities vary together. I suggest it is not mad to suppose that this second, psychological quantity might have something to do with Freud's psychic energy.

Let us now try to put the pieces together. We wanted a model of introspection. Introspection was to be literally a species of perception (Kant's inner sense), perception is essentially a causal process, and causation is energy flow. In a typical visual case of perception, an object is illuminated and the reflected light ultimately causes in us an experience which in turn ultimately results in our forming beliefs about the object seen. As a very rough, crude first approximation to the quantitative aspects of the causation essential to visual perception, we might hypothesize a correlation between, say, the intensity with which the object is illuminated and the number and intensity of conviction of the beliefs we form about it. These are among the elements which a model of introspection ought to mimic. One sometimes knows introspectively what one thinks or wants; one can introspect some of one's beliefs and desires. These will be our analogues to objects seen; they come with intrinsic intensities (analogous to those of glowing objects). *Generally speaking*, the more intense a psychological state, the more one is aware of it and the harder it is to concentrate on anything else (unless one has, for example, a strong desire not to be in that state). One also has a sort of overall background psychic energy which, roughly, varies inversely with one's fatigue; this will be our analogue to the illumination of objects seen. (As that background energy decreases, as one gets tired, one's need or wish or tendency to sleep, to be somehow unconscious, increases; so, very roughly, consciousness varies inversely with fatigue, and so directly with psychic energy. It is especially one's ability to concentrate, a kind of deliberate selective attention or inattention, which varies inversely with fatigue; when tired, one's mind wanders. So again we have evidence that consciousness as selective attention *and inattention* varies directly with overall mental energy. This adds a dimension to Freud's discovery that unconscious mental states tend to surface especially during dreams, and thus sleep, when overall mental energy, in the process of being restored, is reduced, and so one's capacity to direct one's attention selectively is reduced.) If we follow McGinn, it is at least a constituent of one's consciousness of one of one's mental states that one believes oneself to be in that state; such 'second-order' beliefs will be our analogues to the beliefs about objects formed as a result of seeing them. Suppose then, to continue the analogy, there is a correlation between the strengths of one's first-order beliefs and desires together with the intensity of one's overall mental energy on the one hand and, on the other, the number and intensity of conviction of the second-order beliefs, about those first-order beliefs and desires, which one forms. Then, as blind creatures might sensibly infer the existence of a sense of sight by noting that the more brightly an object shines or is illuminated, the stronger and more extensive are the convictions people have about it, so too might we sensibly infer the existence in us of an inner sense whereby we introspect the contents of consciousness.

This causal model of consciousness does not require introspection to be a species of perception in the strictest possible sense. In sight, for example, the illumination of an object causes in us a visual experience which in turn causes us to form beliefs about that object; experience mediates between objects and beliefs in perception. Our model of introspection has some mental phenomena, i.e. those of which we are conscious, causing others, i.e. beliefs about those mental phenomena. The model does not commit us to the existence of anything like experiences intervening between the contents of consciousness and the consciousness of them. So if experience is essential to perception, then the model does not make introspection out to be perception. On the other hand, the model does not rule out experiences mediating between our mental states and our introspective consciousness of them. Extra argument would have to be brought to bear to decide whether we should add experiences to our account of introspection.

The above is a (very crude first approximation to a) perceptual, causal model of consciousness. Admittedly, it does not specify a mechanism whereby first-order mental states result in second-order consciousness of them (analogous to the way light reflected from objects causes beliefs about them). (There is another problem as well. If we are to have a *causal* model of consciousness, then psychic energy must *flow* from first-order beliefs to second-order beliefs. Flow is motion, continuous change of place. This in turn appears to require beliefs to be located in space. Some mental phenomena, like experiences and sensations, are relatively easy to locate; but others, including the propositional attitudes, do not seem to be located in space at all. I think this problem can be solved, but I will not go into the matter here.) But it does suggest ways we might try to flesh out Sullivan's model of repression and the unconscious in terms of selective inattention. What I mean is this: One of one's intense desires might be irradiated by psychic energy, so one can introspect it. Ordinarily, such introspecting will result in a certain degree of conscious conviction that one has that desire. But suppose one also has a powerful desire not to have that, or anything like that, first desire. In *some* such cases, depending presumably on a vast range of complex factors, introspection might channel psychic energy away into anything but a strong conviction that one had the first desire; for example, by focusing introspection on a neurotic, obsessive thought one might drain off the psychic energy that would ordinarily turn up in conscious awareness of one's first desire, and since it does not turn up, that desire is now repressed. A careful scrutiny of the modes of ordinary perceptual inattention might suggest a catalogue of defence mechanisms whereby introspective selective inattention can repress unwanted psychological states. We might also be able to use our model to defend Freud against Sartre's objection to the unconscious: what is repressed must be known in order to be repressed and so cannot be unconscious. Suppose a second-order belief that one has a first-order belief must reach a certain degree or level of conviction before that first-order belief can be conscious. We might allow that in repressing the first-order belief, one does have to have the second-order belief (in order to know where not to attend selectively). But this second-order belief need only be held with a degree of conviction less than that necessary for the first-order belief to be conscious. The strategy of repression consists in diverting into something else (what else will depend on the case) the energy that would ordinarily bring the degree of conviction of the second-order belief up high enough for the first-order belief to be conscious; this is being selectively inattentive to, or repressing, the first-order belief. Notice that if this reply to Sartre does work, it does so only by invoking those quantitative considerations we have insisted on taking so seriously. (None of this requires that repression proceeds via articulated calculation or practical reasoning from propositions. Neither does ordinary perception so proceed. It is enough that we should know how to do these things.) We might also be able to use our model to incorporate certain features of Freud's splitting model. Suppose one is in an intense emotional state *S*, that this intensity includes lots of psychic energy which would ordinarily show up in part in a strong (and so conscious) conviction that one is in state *S*, but that one has a very strong wish not to be in state *S*. This strong desire might motivate one to direct the energy of *S*'s intensity away from the belief that one is in state *S* and into some otherwise feeble state which then engages one's introspective attention. This is, in a way, to split the ideas of the emotion off from its affect. The ideas, perhaps, one now believes oneself to have only to a degree of conviction insufficient for these ideas to be conscious.

(Moreover, that psychic energy is (relatively) *conserved* perhaps explains why we cannot attend to indefinitely many ideas at once, thus rendering this last not quite so objectionably brute a fact as it seemed above.) And the energy of the intensity of state S has been split off and invested in another state (for purposes of selective inattention), so one might even say that second state presents a delusive awareness of state S; it is (part of) S experienced falsely.

The introspective model of consciousness may also help us make sense of an aspect of insight in analysis. A man comes to analysis, let us suppose, suicidally depressed. He associates eventually to his father's recent death. After a time the analyst explains that the patient has a powerful anger against his father, that he wished him dead and wants to kill himself because, he fears, his wish magically killed his father. Suppose, following 'Mourning and Melancholia' (1917e, XIV), that the analyst is correct; the patient is angry (even now) with his father. Moreover, let us suppose the patient believes his analyst and is thoroughly justified in doing so because his analyst is good at his job and is known to be so by the patient. The patient is then angry at his father and knows full well that he is angry with his father. But this is not yet insight, not yet the return of the repressed; the patient has not yet experienced his anger consciously (and so cannot yet deal with it). What is missing? *We* may say that his belief in his anger has yet to be caused *appropriately* by introspecting his rage; his defensive selective inattention has yet to be undone. Introspective experience is essential to insight.

12

Mauvaise foi and the unconscious*

JEAN-PAUL SARTRE

The human being is not only the being by whom *négatités* are disclosed in the world; he is also the one who can take negative attitudes with respect to himself. In our Introduction we defined consciousness as 'a being such that in its being, its being is in question in so far as this being implies a being other than itself'. But now that we have examined the meaning of 'the question', we can at present also write the formula thus: 'Consciousness is a being, the nature of which is to be conscious of the nothingness of its being.' In a prohibition or a veto, for example, the human being denies a future transcendence. But this negation is not explicative. My consciousness is not restricted to *envisioning* a *négatité*. It constitutes itself in its own flesh as the nihilation of a possibility which another human reality projects as *its* possibility. For that reason it must arise in the world as a *Not*; it is as a Not that the slave first apprehends the master, or that the prisoner who is trying to escape sees the guard who is watching him. There are even men (*e.g.* caretakers, overseers, gaolers) whose social reality is uniquely that of the Not, who will live and die, having forever been only a Not upon the earth. Others so as to make the Not a part of their very subjectivity, establish their human personality as a perpetual negation. This is the meaning and function of what Scheler calls 'the man of resentment' – in reality, the Not. But there exist more subtle behaviors, the description of which will lead us further into the inwardness of consciousness. Irony is one of these. In irony a man annihilates what he posits within one and the same act; he leads us to believe in order not to be believed; he affirms to deny and denies to affirm; he creates a positive object but it has no being other than its nothingness. Thus attitudes of negation toward the self permit us to raise a new question: What are we to say is the being of man who has the possibility of denying himself? But it is out of the question to discuss the attitude of 'self-negation' in its universality. The kinds of behavior which

* This essay is chapter 2, first section of Jean-Paul Sartre, *Being and Nothingness*, trans. Hazel E. Barnes (Philosophical Library, New York, 1956). Reprinted by kind permission of the publishers.

can be ranked under this heading are too diverse; we risk retaining only the abstract form of them. It is best to choose and to examine one determined attitude which is essential to human reality and which is such that consciousness instead of directing its negation outward turns it toward itself. This attitude, it seems to me, is *bad faith* (*mauvaise foi*).

Frequently this is identified with falsehood. We say indifferently of a person that he shows signs of bad faith or that he lies to himself. We shall willingly grant that bad faith is a lie to oneself, on condition that we distinguish the lie to oneself from lying in general. Lying is a negative attitude, we will agree to that. But this negation does not bear on consciousness itself; it aims only at the transcendent. The essence of the lie implies in fact that the liar actually is in complete possession of the truth which he is hiding. A man does not lie about what he is ignorant of; he does not lie when he spreads an error of which he himself is the dupe; he does not lie when he is mistaken. The ideal description of the liar would be a cynical consciousness, affirming truth within himself, denying it in his words, and denying that negation as such. Now this doubly negative attitude rests on the transcendent; the fact expressed is transcendent since it does not exist, and the original negation rests on a *truth*; that is, on a particular type of transcendence. As for the inner negation which I effect correlatively with the affirmation for myself of the truth, this rests on *words*; that is, on an event in the world. Furthermore the inner disposition of the liar is positive; it could be the object of an affirmative judgment. The liar intends to deceive and he does not seek to hide this intention from himself nor to disguise the translucency of consciousness; on the contrary, he has recourse to it when there is a question of deciding secondary behavior. It explicitly exercises a regulatory control over all attitudes. As for his flaunted intention of telling the truth ('I'd never want to deceive you! This is true! I swear it!') – all this, of course, is the object of an inner negation, but also it is not recognized by the liar as *his* intention. It is played, imitated, it is the intention of the character which he plays in the eyes of his questioner, but this character, precisely because he *does not exist*, is a transcendent. Thus the lie does not put into the play the inner structure of present consciousness; all the negations which constitute it bear on objects which by this fact are removed from consciousness. The lie then does not require special ontological foundation, and the explanations which the existence of negation in general requires are valid without change in the case of deceit. Of course we have described the ideal lie; doubtless it happens often enough that the liar is more or less the victim of his lie, that he half persuades himself of it. But these common, popular forms of the lie are also degenerate aspects of it;

they represent intermediaries between falsehood and bad faith. The lie is a behavior of transcendence.

The lie is also a normal phenomenon of what Heidegger calls the '*Mit-sein*'.[1] It presupposes my existence, the existence of the *Other*, my existence *for* the Other, and the existence of the Other *for* me. Thus there is no difficulty in holding that the liar must make the project of the lie in entire clarity and that he must possess a complete comprehension of the lie and of the truth which he is altering. It is sufficient that an over-all opacity hide his intentions from the *Other*; it is sufficient that the Other can take the lie for truth. By the lie consciousness affirms that it exists by nature as *hidden from the Other*; it utilizes for its own profit the ontological duality of myself and myself in the eyes of the Other.

The situation can not be the same for bad faith if this, as we have said, is indeed a lie to oneself. To be sure, the one who practices bad faith is hiding a displeasing truth or presenting as truth a pleasing untruth. Bad faith then has in appearance the structure of falsehood. Only what changes everything is the fact that in bad faith it is from myself that I am hiding the truth. Thus the duality of the deceiver and the deceived does not exist here. Bad faith on the contrary implies in essence the unity of a *single* consciousness. This does not mean that it can not be conditioned by the *Mit-sein* like all other phenomena of human reality, but the *Mit-sein* can call forth bad faith only by presenting itself as a *situation* which bad faith permits surpassing; bad faith does not come from outside to human reality. One does not undergo his bad faith; one is not infected with it; it is not a *state*. But consciousness affects itself with bad faith. There must be an original intention and a project of bad faith; this project implies a comprehension of bad faith as such and a pre-reflective apprehension (of) consciousness as affecting itself with bad faith. It follows first that the one to whom the lie is told and the one who lies are one and the same person, which means that I must know in my capacity as deceiver the truth which is hidden from me in my capacity as the one deceived. Better yet I must know the truth very exactly *in order* to conceal it more carefully – and this not at two different moments, which at a pinch would allow us to reestablish a semblance of duality – but in the unitary structure of a single project. How then can the lie subsist if the duality which conditions it is suppressed?

To this difficulty is added another which is derived from the total translucency of consciousness. That which affects itself with bad faith must be conscious (of) its bad faith since the being of consciousness is consciousness of being. It appears then that I must be in good faith, at

---

[1] A 'being-with' others in the world. [Trans.]

least to the extent that I am conscious of my bad faith. But then this whole psychic system is annihilated. We must agree in fact that if I deliberately and cynically attempt to lie to myself, I fail completely in this undertaking; the lie falls back and collapses beneath my look; it is ruined *from behind* by the very consciousness of lying to myself which pitilessly constitutes itself well within my project as its very condition. We have here an *evanescent* phenomenon which exists only in and through its own differentiation. To be sure, these phenomena are frequent and we shall see that there is in fact an 'evanescence' of bad faith, which, it is evident, vacillates continually between good faith and cynicism: Even though the existence of bad faith is very precarious, and though it belongs to the kind of psychic structures which we might call 'metastable',[2] it presents nonetheless an autonomous and durable form. It can even be the normal aspect of life for a very great number of people. A person can *live* in bad faith, which does not mean that he does not have abrupt awakenings to cynicism or to good faith, but which implies a constant and particular style of life. Our embarrassment then appears extreme since we can neither reject nor comprehend bad faith.

To escape from these difficulties people gladly have recourse to the unconscious. In the psychoanalytical interpretation, for example, they use the hypothesis of a censor, conceived as a line of demarcation with customs, passport division, currency control, *etc.*, to reestablish the duality of the deceiver and the deceived. Here instinct or, if you prefer, original drives and complexes of drives constituted by our individual history, make up *reality*. It is neither *true* nor *false* since it does not *exist for itself*. It simply *is*, exactly like this table, which is neither true nor false *in itself* but simply *real*. As for the conscious symbols of the instinct, this interpretation takes them not for appearances but for real psychic facts. Fear, forgetting, dreams exist really in the capacity of concrete facts of consciousness in the same way as the words and the attitudes of the liar are concrete, really existing patterns of behavior. The subject has the same relation to these phenomena as the deceived to the behavior of the deceiver. He establishes them in their reality and must interpret them. There is a *truth* in the activities of the deceiver; if the deceived could reattach them to the situation where the deceiver establishes himself and to his project of the lie, they would become integral parts of truth, by virtue of being lying conduct. Similarly there is a truth in the symbolic acts; it is what the psychoanalyst discovers when he reattaches them to the historical situation of the patient, to the unconscious complexes

---

[2] Sartre's own word, meaning subject to sudden changes or transitions. [Trans.]

which they express, to the blocking of the censor. Thus the subject deceives himself about the *meaning* of his conduct, he apprehends it in its concrete existence but not in its *truth*, simply because he cannot derive it from an original situation and from a psychic constitution which remain alien to him.

By the distinction between the 'id' and the 'ego', Freud has cut the psychic whole into two. I *am* the ego but I *am not* the id. I hold no privileged position in relation to my unconscious psyche. I *am* my own psychic phenomena in so far as I establish them in their conscious reality. For example, I am the impulse to steal this or that book from this bookstall. I am an integral part of the impulse; I bring it to light and I determine myself hand-in-hand with it to commit the theft. But I *am* not those psychic facts, in so far as I receive them passively and am obliged to resort to hypotheses about their origin and their true meaning, just as the scholar makes conjectures about the nature and essence of an external phenomenon. This theft, for example, which I interpret as an immediate impulse determined by the rarity, the interest, or the price of the volume which I am going to steal − it is in truth a process derived from self-punishment, which is attached more or less directly to an Oedipus complex. The impulse toward the theft contains a truth which can be reached only by more or less probable hypotheses. The criterion of this truth will be the number of conscious psychic facts which it explains; from a more pragmatic point of view it will be also the success of the psychiatric cure which it allows. Finally the discovery of this truth will necessitate the cooperation of the psychoanalyst, who appears as the *mediator* between my unconscious drives and my conscious life. The Other appears as being able to effect the synthesis between the unconscious thesis and the conscious antithesis. I can know myself only through the mediation of the other, which means that I stand in relation to *my* 'id', in the position of the *Other*. If I have a little knowledge of psychoanalysis, I can, under circumstances particularly favorable, try to psychoanalyze myself. But this attempt can succeed only if I distrust every kind of intuition, only if I apply to my case *from the outside*, abstract schemes and rules already learned. As for the results, whether they are obtained by my efforts alone or with the cooperation of a technician, they will never have the certainty which intuition confers; they will possess simply the always increasing probability of scientific hypotheses. The hypothesis of the Oedipus complex, like the atomic theory, is nothing but an 'experimental idea'; as Pierce said, it is not to be distinguished from the totality of experiences which it allows to be realized and the results which it enables us to foresee. Thus psychoanalysis substitutes for the notion of bad faith, the idea of a lie without a liar; it allows me to understand how it is possible for me to be lied to without lying to myself since it places me in the same relation to myself that the Other is in respect to me; it replaces the duality of the deceiver and the deceived, the essential condition of the lie, by that of the 'id' and the 'ego'. It introduces into my subjectivity the deepest intersubjective structure of the *Mit-sein*. Can this explanation satisfy us?

Considered more closely the psychoanalytic theory is not as simple as it first appears. It is not accurate to hold that the 'id' is presented as a thing in relation to the hypothesis of the psychoanalyst, for a thing is indifferent to the conjectures which we make concerning it, while the 'id' on the contrary is sensitive to them when we approach the truth. Freud in fact reports resistance when at the end of the first period the doctor is approaching the truth. This resistance is objective behavior apprehended from without: the patient shows defiance, refuses to speak, gives fantastic accounts of his dreams, sometimes even removes himself completely from the psychoanalytic treatment. It is a fair question to ask what part of himself can thus resist. It can not be the 'Ego', envisaged as a psychic totality of the facts of consciousness; this could not suspect that the psychiatrist is approaching the end since the ego's relation to the *meaning* of its own reactions is exactly like that of the psychiatrist himself. At the very most it is possible for the ego to appreciate objectively the degree of probability in the hypotheses set forth, as a witness of the psychoanalysis might be able to do, according to the number of subjective facts which they explain. Furthermore, this probability would appear to the ego to border on certainty, which he could not take offence at since most of the time it is he who by a *conscious* decision is in pursuit of the psychoanalytic therapy. Are we to say that the patient is disturbed by the daily revelations which the psychoanalyst makes to him and that he seeks to remove himself, at the same time pretending in his own eyes to wish to continue the treatment? In this case it is no longer possible to resort to the unconscious to explain bad faith; it is there in full consciousness, with all its contradictions. But this is not the way that the psychoanalyst means to explain this resistance; for him it is secret and deep, it comes from afar; it has its roots in the very thing which the psychoanalyst is trying to make clear.

Furthermore it is equally impossible to explain the resistance as emanating from the complex which the psychoanalyst wishes to bring to light. The complex as such is rather the collaborator of the psychoanalyst since it aims at expressing itself in clear consciousness, since it plays tricks on the censor and seeks to elude it. The only level on which we can locate the refusal of the subject is that of the censor. It alone can comprehend the questions or the revelations of the psychoanalyst as approaching more or less near to the real drives which it strives to repress – it alone because it alone *knows* what it is repressing.

If we reject the language and the materialistic mythology of psychoanalysis, we perceive that the censor in order to apply its activity with discernment must know what it is repressing. In fact if we abandon all the metaphors representing the repression as the impact of blind forces, we are compelled to admit that the censor must choose and in order to choose must be aware of so doing. How could it happen otherwise that the censor allows lawful sexual impulses to pass through, that it permits needs (hunger, thirst, sleep) to be expressed in clear consciousness? And how are we to explain that it can relax its surveillance, that it can even be deceived by the disguises of the instinct? But it is not sufficient that it discern the condemned drives; it must also apprehend them *as to be repressed*, which implies in it at the very least an awareness of its activity. In a word, how could the censor discern the impulses needing to be repressed without being conscious of discerning them? How can we conceive of a knowledge which is ignorant of itself? To know is to know that one knows, said Alain. Let us say rather: All knowing is consciousness of knowing. Thus the resistance of the patient implies on the level of the censor an awareness of the thing repressed as such, a comprehension of the end toward which the questions of the psychoanalyst are leading, and an act of synthetic connection by which it compares the *truth* of the repressed complex to the psychoanalytic hypothesis which aims at it. These various operations in their turn imply that the censor is conscious (of) itself. But what type of self-consciousness can the censor have? It must be the consciousness (of) being conscious of the drive to be repressed, but precisely *in order not to be conscious of it.* What does this mean if not that the censor is in bad faith?

Psychoanalysis has not gained anything for us since in order to overcome bad faith, it has established between the unconscious and consciousness an autonomous consciousness in bad faith. The effort to establish a veritable duality and even a trinity (*Es, Ich, Ueberich* expressing themselves through the censor) has resulted in a mere verbal terminology. The very essence of the reflexive idea of hiding something from oneself implies the unity of one and the same psychic mechanism and consequently a double activity in the heart of unity, tending on the one hand to maintain and locate the thing to be concealed and on the other hand to repress and disguise it. Each of the two aspects of this activity is complementary to the other; that is, it implies the other in its being. By separating consciousness from the unconscious by means of the censor, psychoanalysis has not succeeded in dissociating the two phases of the act, since the libido is a blind conatus toward conscious expression and since the conscious phenomenon is a passive, faked result. Psychoanalysis has merely localized this double activity of repulsion and attraction on the level of the censor.

Furthermore the problem still remains of accounting for the unity of the total phenomenon (repression of the drive which disguises itself and 'passes' in symbolic form), to establish comprehensible connections among its different phases. How can the repressed drive 'disguise itself' if it does not include (1) the consciousness of being repressed, (2) the consciousness of having been pushed back because it is what it is, (3) a project of disguise? No mechanistic theory of condensation or of transference can explain these modifications by which the drive itself is affected, for the description of the process of disguise implies a veiled appeal to finality. And similarly how are we to account for the pleasure or the anguish which accompanies the symbolic and conscious satisfaction of the drive if consciousness does not include – beyond the censor – an obscure comprehension of the end to be attained as simultaneously desired and forbidden. By rejecting the conscious unity of the psyche, Freud is obliged to imply everywhere a magic unity linking distant phenomena across obstacles, just as sympathetic magic unites the spellbound person and the wax image fashioned in his likeness. The unconscious drive (*Trieb*) through magic is endowed with the character 'repressed' or 'condemned', which completely pervades it, colors it, and magically provokes its symbolism. Similarly the conscious phenomenon is entirely colored by its symbolic meaning although it can not apprehend this meaning by itself in clear consciousness.

Aside from its inferiority in principle, the explanation by magic does not avoid the coexistence – on the level of the unconscious, on that of the censor, and on that of consciousness – of two contradictory, complementary structures which reciprocally imply and destroy each other. Proponents of the theory have hypostasized and 'reified' bad faith; they have not escaped it. This is what has inspired a Viennese psychiatrist, Steckel, to depart from the psychoanalytical tradition and to write in *La femme frigide:* 'Every time that I have been able to carry my investigations far enough, I have established that the crux of the psychosis was conscious.' In addition the cases which he reports in his work bear witness to a pathological bad faith which the Freudian doctrine can not account for. There is the question, for example, of women whom marital infidelity has made frigid; that is, they succeed in hiding from themselves not complexes deeply sunk in half physiological darkness, but acts of conduct which are objectively discoverable, which they can not fail to record at the moment when they perform them. Frequently in fact the husband reveals to Steckel that his wife has given objective signs of pleasure, but the woman when questioned will fiercely deny them. Here we find a pattern of *distraction*. Admissions which Steckel was able to draw out inform us that these pathologically frigid women apply themselves to becoming distracted in advance from the pleasure which they dread; many for example at the time of the sexual act, turn their thoughts away toward their daily occupations, make up their household accounts. Will anyone speak of an unconscious here? Yet if the frigid woman thus distracts her consciousness from the pleasure which she experiences, it is by no means cynically and in full agreement with herself; *it is in order to prove to herself* that she is frigid. We have in fact to deal with a phenomenon of bad faith since the efforts taken in order not to be present to the experienced pleasure imply the recognition that the pleasure is experienced; they imply it *in order to deny it*. But we are no longer on the ground of psychoanalysis. Thus on the one hand the explanation by means of the unconscious, due to the fact that it breaks the psychic unity, can not account for the facts which at first sight it appeared to explain. And on the other hand, there exists an infinity of types of behavior in bad faith which explicitly reject this kind of explanation because their essence implies that they can appear only in the translucency of consciousness. We find that the problem which we had attempted to resolve is still untouched.

13

Self-deception and the 'splitting of the ego'*

HERBERT FINGARETTE

I

Who can doubt that we do deceive ourselves? Yet who can explain coherently and explicitly how we do so?

Recent philosophical attempts at such explanation have centred around the assumption that, in essence, the self-deceiver is one who has got himself to believe what he (still) does not believe. So soon as the matter is put thus starkly we are faced with deep paradox, and a good deal of the recent philosophical discussion has been directed toward trying to save the concept while dissolving the paradox.

In the following, I propose a quite different approach to the analysis of self-deception, one which does not centre on the coexistence of inconsistent beliefs, and indeed does not centre on the understanding of self-deception in terms of belief at all. In consequence, the paradox inherent in the 'two-belief' approach does not arise, nor does any other paradox.

The analysis of self-deception which I present here is set beside certain of Freud's doctrines. Setting my own account alongside Freud's work is

* This essay consists almost entirely of passages from Herbert Fingarette, *Self-Deception* (Routledge, London, 1969), which appeared in the series entitled Studies in Philosophical Psychology, under the editorship of R. F. Holland. The passages were originally selected and reordered in the present form by Professor Fingarette for *Freud: A Collection of Critical Essays*, ed. Richard Wollheim (Doubleday, New York 1974), from which it is reprinted with permission of the author and publishers. For ease of reading, Professor Fingarette has authorized omission of the usual typographical signs indicating editorial excision or minor editorial alteration. The brief introductory section was specifically prepared for the present text. The locations of the passages in the original text are indicated by the bracketed numerical superscripts at the end of each passage, thus:

[1] pp. 66–71
[2] pp. 82–5
[3] pp. 86–9
[4] p. 91
[5] pp. 111–12
[6] pp. 115–16
[7] pp. 125–33
[8] p. 142

appropriate inasmuch as his doctrine on defence and the unconscious constitutes the most elaborately worked out, the most extensively applied contemporary doctrine touching self-deception. The juxtaposition of these ways of talking about self-deception results, as I see it, in helping to identify and resolve a central incompleteness in Freud's doctrine, an incompleteness whose centrality Freud himself had just come to appreciate at the very end of his life. In addition, the juxtaposition of Freud's doctrine with my own account in non-psychoanalytic language tends to confirm the validity of the latter, and also makes directly available to it, in the empirical dimension, the depth and illumination afforded by the literature of psychoanalysis.

II

The self-deceiver is one who is in some way engaged in the world but who disavows the engagement, who will not acknowledge it even to himself as his. That is, self-deception turns upon the personal identity one accepts rather than the beliefs one has. It is the hallucinator who speaks, but he will not *acknowledge* the words as his; disowned by him and undetected by others, the voice nevertheless still speaks, and so it is assigned by him to some supernatural being. The paranoid is filled with destructiveness, but he disavows it; since the presence of destructiveness is evident to him, he eventually assigns 'ownership' of that destructiveness to others. With this as his unquestionable axiom, and with 'conspiracy' as his all-purpose formula, he interprets all that happens accordingly. In general, the self-deceiver is engaged in the world in some way, and yet he refuses to avow the engagement as his. Having disavowed the engagement, the self-deceiver is then forced into protective, defensive tactics to account for the inconsistencies in his engagement in the world as acknowledged by him.

Having afforded ourselves this bird's eye view of the matter, we need now to retrace our steps on foot.

An individual may be born of a certain family, nation, or tradition. Yet it is something else again for that individual to identify himself with that family, nation, and tradition. He may never do so. He may grow up doing so, but then, due to changes in life-circumstances, he may grow out of one or another identity. Even more dramatically, he may as a culminating and decisive act seize a particular occasion to disavow his affiliation, his identity as an American, a Christian, or, merely, a Rotarian. As the individual grows from infancy to adulthood, he identifies himself as a person of certain traits of character, having certain virtues and views, a certain bodily shape, having allegiances, enemies, obligations, rights, a history.

The phrase 'identifies himself as', certainly has some reference to discoveries the individual makes; but it refers as well to options adopted. Even with regard to something as 'concrete' and 'objective' as the body, it is interesting to note that *my* body as I identify it for myself is what the psychiatrist calls a 'body image'. He calls it my body image just because he sees that it reflects, in effect, my engagement in the world, the way I see things and take them to be, rather than the object the disinterested observer would describe.

A father announces: 'You are not my son. From henceforth I disown you.' Taken as biological description, the first sentence is false. Taken as the disavowal of identification which the second sentence reveals it to be, the first sentence can be lived up to or not – but it is not false. Although the use of 'avow' has in such cases a primary social or legal focus, it is related to the use I propose and is the model for it. The same holds true of typical proclamations such as 'I am an American', 'I am a union man', 'I am no longer a Democrat'. Of the existence of such public avowals and disavowals, and of their differences from mere description, there can be no doubt. The further assumption necessary for my thesis is that something significantly analogous can be done – is commonly done – in the privacy of one's own soul. Indeed my assumption is that the analogies between what is done in self-deception (and in undeceiving oneself) and what is done in the examples just cited are so many, so interrelated, and so fundamental that we would do well to talk quite generally of self-deception in the language of avowal and disavowal and in closely related language such as 'identify oneself as', and 'acknowledge'.

The distinction between being a certain individual and avowing one's identity as a certain person is dramatically evident in the case of the amnesiac who admits that the evidence proves he is John Jones, but who does not identify himself to himself as John Jones. Jones does not avow certain memories and commitments. As an individual he has a certain history but he does not avow that history. It is not merely that he will not avow these to us; he does not avow them to himself either. We could express all this by saying that the history in question is no longer his personal history for him. There is an important element of *authenticity* here: I refer to that respect in which, for the person before us, Jones is indeed alien, someone other. (The person before us is not sure just *who* he is, but he is sure that he does not identify himself to himself as Jones.) It is true that from the standpoint of the observer, Jones is here and is suffering amnesia. But from the standpoint of the person before us, i.e.

the subject as reflected in his own consciousness, it is important to say that he is not Jones. It is this latter standpoint which I have in mind when I speak of avowal and disavowal, of identification of oneself to oneself as a certain person or as a certain person being engaged in the world in certain ways.

To avow, then, is to define one's personal identity for oneself, not after the fact, but in that sense where we mean by 'defining one's identity' the establishing of one's personal identity in some respect. Moreover, we must include the maintaining of one's personal identity for oneself in the face of occasion for disavowal. Any such establishing or reaffirmation of one's personal identity may come to fruition in a climactic, public act; or it may be so slow and so evenly paced in its development as to seem to be natural evolution, or inherent stability in the face of stress rather than a dramatic act. Nevertheless, avowal and disavowal are always inherently purposeful self-expression rather than mere happenings suffered by the person. Avowal and disavowal are accomplished by a person; they are responses by him rather than effects upon him.[1]

We must seek now to establish more precisely what are the 'materials' which a man uses, what is it for an individual to 'possess' these materials *as* material ready for incorporation into, or exclusion from, a unified self; and we must ask what is the significance of such acceptance or rejection. For it is not ignorance or temptation but the authenticity of such exclusion from a self, or inclusion within a self, which is at the core of that spiritual disorder we call self-deception.

The phenomena of self-deception (I include here the phenomena covered by such terms as Sartre's '*mauvaise foi*', and Freud's 'defence') can be consistently interpreted within the framework of the doctrine that the self is a synthesis, an achievement by the individual, something 'made'. Avowal is the 'missing link' which is implicit in the doctrine of the self as synthesis. In order to show how this is so, I do not propose to present a tightly woven theory in a technical language, but to offer a broad and rapid sketch of the familiar course of the emergence of the self, a sketch unified by the view that the self is a synthesis, a creation. Naturally I shall highlight those features I have claimed are essential to self-deception. (The reader who desires to supplement his own observations in reflecting upon the following sketch is referred to such standard descriptive works as Gesell and Ilg's *Infant and Child in the Culture of Today*.)

Before achieving a relatively coherent unity as a self, the child learns relatively specific forms of engagement in the world. First these are quite rudimentary: using a spoon, opening a door, buttoning a coat. Then he learns complexes of interrelated motive, reason, emotion, relevant objectives, appropriate means, and, where relevant, moralistic judgmental tone. We do not normally see the latter sorts of specific engagements, at least not clearly, even at the age of two or three years. For example, the two-year-old does not rise to an insult by adopting a vengeful policy, selecting and using appropriate means to carry out his policy; nor perforce does he feel guilt for this. By the age of three years one has learned, for example, to appreciate both time of day and his own hunger as jointly justifying seating himself at table and eating in certain generally prescribed ways, to the ends of satisfying hunger and pleasing his parents, all the while enjoying the moralistic reaction of feeling 'good' (rather than 'naughty'). He has also learned that under certain conditions an object is his property, permanent or temporary, and that seizing it without his permission by his peers is occasion for anger on his part, for retaliatory action accompanied by a moralistic reaction which includes quite typically his feeling 'naughty' or 'bad', as well as feeling 'righteously indignant'. (The rationality of these moralistic reactions is characteristically not questioned; the pattern as a whole is learned, and only later, when a unified self and its larger perspective can be brought to bear, do moral criticism and personal moral judgment emerge.)

Yet even the four- or five-year-old, capable as he may be of engaging at last in a particular complex activity for childish reasons, with childish aims and methods, and in childish moods, still does not manifest an enduring centre, a personal core whose unity colours and shapes his various particular engagements. He shifts, eccentrically, at the behest of others, or because something in the environment distracts him, or because he is fatigued, from one project to another, each being relatively unaffected by the others; any one of these engagements is not noticeably judged by him with reference to the others, nor is it markedly coloured by them. The overall unity of personal style and attitude, the inwardly governed and relatively smooth transition, are as yet absent. The psychoanalysts tell us that in ways too subtle to be readily apparent, a unified core of personality evolves, at least in nucleus, by age two and a half to four (the oedipal phase); and the careful observer can even then notice certain gross patterns of temperament or style. Yet for the layman the evolution of a noticeable autonomous governing centre does not usually begin to manifest itself until the early school years. Indeed this is a traditional sign of readiness for school beyond the nursery or kindergarten level. At this period the child is able, at least for periods of time and with rudimentary success, to carry on autonomously. One engagement leads into, blends into, another; the child is not *merely* 'negative' or else 'obedient', but shows a degree of independence in his response to external demands. There begins to emerge a large 'plot' determined from within. After a few years, even the immediate moralistic reactions ('nice', 'naughty', 'shame', 'good', 'bad') soften – though this is one of the last stages of the process – as one specific form of engagement is related to another, as a coherent self emerges, and as the generality and many-sidedness of judgment which this makes possible nourish more 'personal' moral response.[2]

The child learns many particular forms of engagement; he 'plays' various roles continually, zestfully, as well as being tutored in some by adults. Some forms of engagement remain merely projects realized and then forgotten, roles learned and then abandoned. However, certain forms of engagement – or even some particular ones – are taken up into the ever forming, ever growing personal self, and they are modified as they become more and more an integral part of this 'synthesis'. To take some engagement into the personal self is not an act of physical incorporation (though Freud showed how important this image is in this connection). To take something into the self is an 'act' which our notion of personal identity presupposes. It is to commit oneself to treat something *as* a part or aspect of oneself, or as something inherent in the engagements which the person avows.

If there were no such thing as a person's *acknowledging* some identity as his and certain engagements as his, and disavowing other identities and engagements, there would be neither persons nor personal identity. Without this, man would be at most a highly co-ordinated, even highly intelligent animal, engaged in a sequence of pursuits in entire and inevitable unselfconsciousness. Such creatures might be numbered or named, and even referred to as 'persons', but they would not have the capacity for the moral or spiritual life.

Generally speaking, with the emergence of the person in the individual, there is a tendency for increasing correlation between what is avowed by the person and the actual engagements of the individual. It is in terms of the tacit ideal of perfect harmony in this respect that we tend to assess the individual. We are less disturbed by the discrepancies we see in the child; children are only 'half-formed'; they will 'grow up' and 'grow out of it'; meanwhile, they go in a hundred directions, and we are patient of this. Yet even for children we do have certain age-level expectations.

It can come about, for child or adult, that our expectations are not met. And, in particular, it happens – witness the self-deceiver – that an individual will be provoked into a kind of engagement which, in part or in whole, the person cannot *avow* as *his* engagement, for to avow it would apparently lead to such intensely disruptive, distressing consequences as to be unmanageably destructive to the person. The crux of the matter here is the *unacceptability* of the engagement to the person.

The individual may be powerfully inclined towards a particular engagement, yet this particular engagement may be utterly incompatible with that currently achieved synthesis of engagements which is the person.

The capacity to pursue specific engagements independently, as autonomous projects, without integration into the complex unity of a personal self, is, as we have noted, an early and a fundamental capacity of the human being. We may now add that the phenomena we classify under such headings as 'self-deception', 'defence', and *mauvaise foi*, are 'regressions' to this form of engagement; they manifest our capacity for such isolated engagements even after the emergence of a personal self, and in spite of unacceptability to the person. We judge from the totality of the conduct that the individual is engaged in a certain way, and he may even show signs of shame or intense guilt; yet we note what are in fact the characteristic features of disavowal: the person does not speak of the engagement as his, he does not speak *for* it, and he seems sincere; the engagement seems to exist in a certain isolation from the tempering influence of the person's usual reasonableness, his tastes, sensitivities, values; the person accepts no responsibility for being engaged in this way. On occasion we also distinguish the reparative measures being taken in order to minimize the discrepancies.

Let us imagine, for example, an individual who is intensely angered by his employer's attitude towards him. The individual, we shall suppose, is unable to rid himself of this reaction. Yet such anger towards such a person is radically unacceptable to this person. An unprincipled and humiliating subservience in spite of the anger would also be unacceptable, and in any case it would continue to bear the stigma of being his own anger, even if acknowledged to no one but himself. As a least evil, the person disavows the unquenchable anger and aggression: It is not 'I' who am angry; from henceforth I disassociate myself from it; it is utterly repugnant to me. By rejecting identity with the anger, the person avoids responsibility, but he also surrenders all authority and direct control.

Nevertheless, the fact remains that the individual is thereafter left to pursue this aggressive relationship as an isolated project. It readily manifests itself in harmful action and hurtful words towards the employer. There may be moralistic guilt reactions associated with it. These, too, are of course disavowed, though the evident manifestations of mood may be rationalized as 'depression' or undirected sulkiness.

Because of the moralistic guilt reaction, and also for purposes of protective camouflage against interference, the individual may initiate ameliorating and cover-tactics; he may find or invent some role to play – perhaps the role of the completely respectful and friendly employee. This may, by its practical effect, require a modification of the manner of being aggressive, or it may at least soften the practical impact of the effects of being aggressive. There is no problem, in supposing that an individual can invent congenial explanations or play various roles; what we further assume here is that these activities, too, are disavowed. The individual can speak more or less skilfully the lines which he has learned would in general be appropriate for a friendly and respectful employee. Since this is a generalized role rather than a personal response, and since the self-deceiver may not be a very good actor, we notice a certain artificiality in his friendliness, a tendency to overdo and 'ham' it, a certain insensitivity to the subtleties peculiar to the situation, a stereotypy in manner.[3]

In summary, then, I have treated as central the capacity of a person to identify himself to himself as a particular person engaged in the world in specific ways, the capacity of a person to reject such identification and engagement, and the further supposition that an individual can continue to be engaged in the world in a certain way even though he does not avow it as his personal engagement and therefore displays none of the evidences of such avowal.[4]

III

I find myself for a moment in the interesting position of not knowing whether what I have to say should be regarded as something long familiar and obvious or as something entirely new and puzzling. But I am inclined to think the latter.

I have at last been struck by the fact that . . .[1]

These are the provocative opening words in Freud's last paper, unfinished and posthumously published under the title, 'Splitting of the ego in the process of defence'. Freud's opening remark is all the more provocative because he had just previously made two attempts, both left incomplete by him, to present a definitive restatement of psychoanalytic theory. With these uncompleted efforts in the immediate background, he turned to the 'Splitting of the ego' and one naturally suspects that the provocative opening words of this last short paper may announce some fundamental new insight which he had been struggling to assimilate.

On its face, this last paper is merely a brief restatement of material quite familiar from discussions in a number of Freud's writings. These discussions go as far back as the early writings; they are found from time to time in later papers; and they constitute an unusually large propor-

---

[1] 1940e [1938], XXIII, 275.

tionate part of the highly condensed *An Outline of Psychoanalysis*, on which he had been working only a few months prior.

That the material in 'Splitting of the ego' should look familiar to us is to be expected, since Freud himself introduces it as having a 'long familiar and obvious' look. What was there about it, then, that was 'entirely new and puzzling'? It must have been a way of seeing the familiar 'fact' by which he was now 'struck' anew.

I believe that what struck Freud was a central insight analogous to that which I have developed in Section II above. He saw a new way of generalizing the role of the ego in defence, a way which for the first time could bring into focus certain fundamental implications of his entire theory, a way which had the potential for resolving certain deep conceptual problems internal to his theory. Freud did not live to develop the potential of this new insight. Some aspects of it have in effect been central to very recent theoretical discussions of defence and the unconscious in the psychoanalytic literature. But these discussions have still failed to expose the central, unifying element in Freud's insight because they are basically cast in the old terms.[5]

Why should the ego aim to keep anything at all unconscious, whether it be defence or impulse? This, which I take to be the fundamental problem at the core of psychoanalytic theory, has so far as I know been raised neither by psychoanalysts nor by contemporary philosophical reinterpreters of Freud such as Sartre or, more recently, Ricoeur. The question bears elaboration.

Let us suppose that the defensive rejection of an impulse is designed not merely to inhibit its expression but characteristically to 'hide' its existence. But from whom or what is the impulse to be hidden? Other persons in the environment? If this were all, it would merely be a case of ordinary deception, whereas what is characteristic of defence is that one 'hides' something from *oneself*. But where shall we locate the inner 'victim' of this secretiveness? Is the impulse to be hidden from the id? This makes no sense, for it is the impulse *of* the id. Is it to be hidden from the superego? No, for it is typically the superego which perceives the emerging id derivatives, and which typically initiates the defence by inducing anxiety in the ego. Is the impulse to be hidden from the ego? Surely not, for the ego is by definition that 'agency' which takes into account *both* the impulse and the conflicting superego demands, and which then designs and executes the defensive manoeuvre. Furthermore, since the impulse remains active in the id, defence is a continuing process; the ego must therefore remain *continuously* cognizant of all relevant factors if defence is to succeed. However, if nothing relevant is 'hidden' from id, ego, or superego, what is the point of keeping anything from being conscious? We can no longer assume it to be – as is usually assumed – some kind of hiding of the impulse from oneself, some kind of ignorance due to successful 'disguise'. However, in the present case the imputation of knowledge to consciousness, and ignorance to unconsciousness, seems to have lost its justification.

Defence aims to reduce anxiety, of course, and so long as the main outcome of defence was thought to be a form of self-induced ignorance, it made a certain sense to suppose that 'what you don't know won't worry you'. But once we abandon the notion that defence brings a kind of blissful ignorance to some 'agency' of the mind, the question forces itself upon one: why should anxiety be reduced by defence any more than, better than, or differently than would be the case if we merely curbed our impulses and/or deceived others quite consciously?[6]

The question we now face is a surprising question because, after all, one of the earliest and most characteristic insights of psychoanalysis was that the origin of much psychopathology lies in the tactic of defending oneself from threats, inner or outer, by keeping oneself unconscious of them. This distinctive and illuminating insight has suddenly been transformed into a source of puzzlement and obscurity. Recent psychoanalytic theorists have argued, though not always for identical reasons, that the concepts of consciousness, preconsciousness, and unconsciousness play little or no essential role in contemporary theory. I believe they are wrong. However, even if they are right, the problem of the usefulness of defence would remain a central problem unresolved within psychoanalytic theory. The problem is not only unresolved, it is not even recognized by psychoanalytic theorists. Everyone has for long taken it for granted that defence serves a vital purpose; no one has appreciated that the purpose so long taken for granted, the *only* purpose postulated by theory, no longer is adequate to its theoretical burden.

Arlow and Brenner have been among the leading proponents of the thesis that psychoanalytic theory can get along without the use of the 'conscious–unconscious' cluster of concepts. They hold that in the work of the analyst, 'To characterize a mental element as accessible or inaccessible to consciousness does not tell us what we need to know.'[2]

There is much force in their detailed argument. Yet a healthy respect for the oldest and most characteristic of psychoanalytic insights in psychoanalysis might suggest caution. In fact the seeds of inner inconsistency are to be found in Arlow and Brenner's own exposition of their thesis.

[2] J. A. Arlow and C. Brenner, *Psychoanalytic Concepts and the Structural Theory* (Int. Univ. Press, New York, 1964), p. 112.

For example, Arlow and Brenner present material from two different cases in which, in each instance, it is important to their commentary that certain interpretations, believed to be correct by the analyst, were nevertheless not presented to the patient at a certain time.[3] To have presented these interpretations at that point, say Arlow and Brenner, would have been inappropriate, in one case perhaps dangerous. In thus acknowledging the critical therapeutic role of interpretation, Arlow and Brenner accept in practice what in theory they reject; for, what is interpretation if not the attempt to make explicitly conscious what was not conscious?

It will not help their case to argue that the newer aim of psychoanalysis is not so much 'to make the unconscious conscious' but rather to bring it about that 'where id was, there shall ego be'. We may readily grant the historical shift of emphasis expressed in these familiar slogans. The fact remains that therapeutic interpretation, aimed at dynamic insight, remains a principal analytic tool to achieve this newer aim. As such, interpretation – and thus the making conscious of what was unconscious – must remain of profound interest for both practice and theory. The Arlow and Brenner monograph, however, has little to say about the nature of dynamic insight. This is a predictable oversight in an argument designed to induce us to dispense with the conscious–unconscious distinction.

It seems that, at least in therapeutic practice, we cannot dismiss the question of the consciousness status of a mental content; but neither can we dismiss the more recent, theoretical lines of argument exemplified in the Arlow and Brenner monograph.

I propose, in summary, certain postulates which I believe must be accepted and which in fact are accepted in the solution which I shall present to this dilemma. These postulates derive, respectively, from the traditional psychoanalytic viewpoint, the newer Arlow-Brenner type of emphasis, and my own analysis of self-deception.

(1) *The traditional element:* Defence is not merely the inhibition of discharge, for this in itself would amount only to self-control; defence characteristically has a self-alienating nature as well. Furthermore, this self-alienation in defence is characteristically reflected in an alteration of consciousness.

(2) *The Arlow–Brenner thesis:* What primarily counts in defence is the 'dynamic' aspect, not the presence or absence of some 'mental quality', i.e. some para-perceptual or cognitive element.

(3) *My own thesis:* The alteration of consciousness in defence

---

[3] Ibid., pp. 106–9.

should not be understood primarily in terms of knowledge and ignorance but, instead, by reference to the 'dynamics' of defence – that is, by reference to those features of defence which we would in everyday language refer to in such terms as 'purpose', 'will', 'motive', and, finally, 'action'.

It is fundamental to the solution I propose that one recalls how, from the very beginning, defence has been conceived psychoanalytically as the establishment of a kind of split in the psyche. Prior to the development of Freud's ego psychology, the split was conceived to be between the Conscious and the Unconscious, each eventually conceived as a system. By the 1920s, when the newer theses concerning anxiety and the ego–id–superego trio were developed, the split was conceived to be essentially between the ego (prodded by the superego) and the id. The two versions, however, retain a remarkable parallelism, a persistent cluster of insights, which is of special interest to us here. In both versions, the conflicting entities are conceived as systems which are quasi-autonomous, indeed incompatible, alienated from one another. One system contains what has been rejected by the other. The former system operates according to the 'archaic', 'primary process'; logical, temporal, and causal relations are ignored, part stands for whole, isolated similarities establish equivalencies, and so on. The latter system operates according to the more rational 'secondary process'. The two systems interact by way of conflict rather than co-ordination.

By virtue of the parallelism in these respects of the older and newer versions of the theory, neither system escapes certain problems. For example, unconscious fantasies are assigned in both the earlier and later versions of Freud's theory to the system which contains the repressed, the system which operates according to the primary process. As a matter of clinical fact, however, unconscious fantasies are found to be organized to a good extent according to the (rational) secondary process. Such paradoxes as this arise because both earlier and later versions are parallel in insisting correctly on the fact that there is a split in the psyche, but in failing to define the nature of the split adequately. In both versions, Freud *over*stressed the fact that the element split off from the ego takes on a markedly 'primitive' character, and he fails adequately to stress the great extent to which the element split off still retains fundamental characteristics of the ego (and superego).

If we correct this one-sidedness, the situation can be stated as follows. The result of defence is to split off from the more rational system (i.e. the system which is defended) a nuclear, dynamic complex. This nuclear entity is a complex of motive, purpose, feeling, perception, and drive towards action. It is, for example, an angry and competitive impulse to damage one's father as object of envy; or it may be an erotic and competitive impulse to arrange matters so as to be the adored son. And in such cases there is typically a sense of guilt as an element in the complex, the guilt being of a kind which is appropriate to a relatively infantile appreciation of the impulse and its expression. Also integral to such impulses is a limited but genuine capacity to adapt the expression of the impulse to varying reality situations.

Of course what we have been describing is a kind of split-off from the highly elaborated *ego*-structure. True, it is only a nucleus of an ego, split off from the highly elaborated ego. In relation to the ego it is rudimentary in organization, especially with regard to the way it now fails to reflect the richness of the ego's learning and many identifications. Isolated as it is from the learning and experimentation constantly engaged in by a healthy ego, the split-off nucleus remains relatively static (and therefore relatively rudimentary) as compared to the continually maturing ego. The longer it remains split off, the greater the disparity between split-off nucleus and the ego – and therefore the greater the tendency for it to remain split off.

Why is such an ego-nucleus split off from the ego? It is because the incompatibility between the ego-nucleus and the current ego is so great, relative to the integrative capacities of the ego, that the latter gives up any attempt to integrate the ego-nucleus itself. The ego then adopts some more or less sophisticated versions of the *Ur*-defence postulated by Freud: so to speak, the ego says, This is *not-me*. The ego treats this unassimilable but still ego-like system as 'outside' rather than 'inside'.

This earliest defence of the infant against stress, as postulated by Freud, is in fact, I maintain, the model of all defence. This proposal is squarely in the spirit of Freud's theory building, in which we find that it is a characteristic conceptual strategy to postulate the earliest form of any category of response as the model upon which later refinements and elaborations of that category of response are built.

The defensive outcome, then, is to establish what we may call a *counter-ego nucleus*, this nucleus being the structural aspect of counter-cathexis. The notion of the counter-ego nucleus is thus a generalization in 'structural' terms of the 'economic' concept of 'counter-cathexis'.

What I have said above constitutes, I believe, an account in essentially psychoanalytic language of facts known since Freud, though never before characterized in just this way. I have described these long familiar facts in such a way as to emphasize that the defensive process is a splitting of the ego which is not something that 'happens' to the ego but something the ego *does*, a motivated strategy. It is this which I believe at last 'struck' Freud and which furnished the central theme of his last paper, 'Splitting of the ego in the process of defence'. What Freud called the 'entirely new' yet 'long familiar and obvious' fact was that he was 'clearly at fault' to 'take for granted the synthetic (i.e. integrative) nature of the processes of the ego'.[4] For the ego has another major function which had always had a generic *name*, 'defence', but whose *character* as the exact complement of ego-synthesis had never been properly understood or appreciated. 'The defence mechanisms' had been the label on a basket into which a categorially mixed collection of items had been stored. It is true that the generic motive for defence – to reduce anxiety – was finally appreciated by Freud in the 1920s. However, the generic mode of operation – the ego's splitting off from itself a counter-ego nucleus – was never appreciated by him until the very last days of his life. At that time, if I am right, he saw this clearly in the course of final review and restatement of the fundamentals of his theory.

Freud on a number of occasions used language close to that which I have used. He spoke of defence as 'disavowal' or a 'rejection' in the case of what was 'outer' or 'inner' respectively.[5] He finally saw, I think, that the generic aim of defence is, in infantile oral terms, to 'spit out', or in the more everyday language which Freud used, to 'disavow' or 'reject'. This disavowal or rejection is the generic feature of defence, and it corresponds to what I have called disavowal.

When this process occurs for the first time there comes into being a nucleus and centre of crystallization for the formation of a psychical group divorced from the ego – a group around which everything which would imply an acceptance of the incompatible idea subsequently collects.[6]

The notion of a 'psychical group' was used with some frequency in the earlier writings of Freud,[7] but this notion became assimilated to the word 'complex', which in turn came to be associated with certain of Jung's early ideas. The words no longer appear in Freud's writing after his estrangement from Jung; and the Freudian notion they express seems likewise to have dropped below the surface – always implied, as I have argued, but no longer explicit or properly appreciated. (However, a doctrine of 'ego-nuclei' has been propounded for many years by the distinguished English psychoanalyst Edward Glover.)

The preceding remarks lead us to see in a new way something of the nature of that resistance which Freud called the resistance of the id. A counter-ego nucleus, however rudimentary, has its own dynamism; it has that thrust towards its own aims which establishes it as ego-like rather

---

[4] 1940e [1938], XXIII, 276.   [5] 1940a [1938], XXIII, 204.
[6] 1895d, II, 123.   [7] 1906c, IX, 100–2.

than id. Herein is a source of that persistence which Freud ascribed to the id as repository of the repressed. Herein is also a source of what has been called the cathexes from the id which 'attract' additional material into the unconscious.

Psychoanalytic therapeutic technique is basically designed to offer to the counter-ego the possibility of some substantial gratification in altered form and harmoniously with the ego, and to offer to the ego the possibility of a bearable avowal of the counter-ego. The therapist thus makes possible avowal (removal of counter-cathexis and integration of the counter-ego into the ego).

The most markedly noticeable expression of avowal is usually associated with the new ability to hypercathect, i.e. the readiness of the patient to explicitly avow (not merely to 'intellectualize' about) the impulse which had been disavowed. Thus the patient's *explicit* acceptance of a therapeutic interpretation is a distinctive, but not a necessary condition, of the giving up of the defence. Or in still other words, dynamic insight, the becoming conscious of what was unconscious, is not the essence of dissolving the defence, nor is it the absolute aim of therapy, but it is a distinctive and natural expression of one's having abandoned defence. The 'dynamic' essence of defence is what I have called disavowal. This way of putting the matter, which follows from the theoretical critique I have presented, also is consistent with the traditional emphasis by Arlow, Brenner, et al., on the dynamics of defence.

Though I have stressed the ego-like character of what is disavowed, this is by way of corrective compensation for the usual emphasis on its id-character. The rudimentary character of counter-ego nuclei, their isolation from the civilizing influence of the ego, and the consequent lessening of concern with strict logical, causal, temporal, and other highly rational relationships, make counter-ego nuclei much cruder, more 'primitive', in the form of their expression. They are indeed 'closer' to the id insofar as the latter constitutes the uncivilized, highly unspecific basic drives.[7]

IV

Freud eventually appreciated that his therapy had always been oriented primarily to self-acceptance (removal of counter-cathexes) rather than to 'knowledge' (consciousness) as curative. Avowal of one's engagements is the optimal goal of classical psychoanalysis. Such avowal is the necessary condition of moral action, but is not itself moral action. It establishes the person as such in a particular respect and thus makes engagement in the moral life possible. As Freud said, the aim of psychoanalysis is not to tell the person what is good or bad, right or wrong in a specific context, but to 'give the patient's ego freedom to decide one way or the other'.[8] The medical aim is thus in substance a spiritual aim. It is to help the individual become an agent and cease being a patient; it is to liberate, not indoctrinate.[8]

[8] 1923b, XIX, 50.

14

Freud's anthropomorphism*

THOMAS NAGEL

Freud was a materialist, and at an early stage of his psychological inquiries attempted to construct an explicitly physiological psychology based on the interaction of neurons. This attempt, by now well known under the title 'Project for a scientific psychology', was abandoned shortly after Freud sent the draft to Fliess in October 1895. And when he learned in 1937 that Marie Bonaparte had unearthed the manuscript, he sought to have it destroyed.

His subsequent theories were of an entirely different character, for they contained only psychological terminology and did not refer explicitly to neuron interaction. Nevertheless, there is a good deal of structural continuity between the earlier and later views, and Freud continued to be convinced that the psychic apparatus which he was investigating and describing in mentalistic terms was in its true nature a physical system — though too little was known about neurophysiology to permit anyone to think about psychology in physical terms. That is why Freud felt it necessary to abandon the line of investigation represented by the *Project*.

The question therefore arises in what sense it is possible to think about a physical system in mentalistic terms, taken from the vocabulary of experience, perception, desire, etc., without having any idea of the physical significance of those descriptions. This question bears not only on psychoanalytic theory, but also on current disputes about the status of mentalistic hypotheses in linguistics, and in other areas where it is maintained that a mentalistically or anthropomorphically described process or function can be assumed to have a physical realization. What is the meaning of such claims?

Freud was not silent on the subject, and his explanations of how it is possible to think anthropomorphically about a physical system when one lacks an explicitly physical understanding of that system are among the

* This is a reprint of an essay which appeared under the same title in *Freud: A Collection of Critical Essays,* ed. Richard Wollheim (Doubleday, New York, 1974), from which it is reprinted with permission of the author and the publisher.

most philosophical passages in his writings.[1] They also contain a contribution to discussion of the mind–body problem, which deserves examination.

The remarks which will occupy us form part of Freud's general defence of the existence of unconscious mental states. There are four main locations: *The Interpretation of Dreams*,[2] 'The unconscious',[3] *An Outline of Psychoanalysis*[4] and 'Some elementary lessons in psychoanalysis'.[5] It will be useful to quote one typical passage at length.

The hypothesis we have adopted of a psychical apparatus extended in space, expediently put together, developed by the exigencies of life, which gives rise to the phenomena of consciousness only at one particular point and under certain conditions – this hypothesis has put us in a position to establish psychology on foundations similar to those of any other science, such, for instance, as physics. In our science as in the others the problem is the same: behind the attributes (qualities) of the object under examination which are presented directly to our perception, we have to discover something else which is more independent of the particular receptive capacity of our sense organs and which approximates more closely to what may be supposed to be the real state of affairs. We have no hope of being able to reach the latter itself, since it is evident that everything new that we have inferred must nevertheless be translated back into the language of our perceptions, from which it is simply impossible for us to free ourselves. But herein lies the very nature and limitation of our science. It is as though we were to say in physics: 'If we could see clearly enough we should find that what appears to be a solid body is made up of particles of such and such a shape and size and occupying such and such relative positions.' In the meantime we try to increase the efficiency of our sense organs to the furthest possible extent by artificial aids; but it may be expected that all such efforts will fail to affect the ultimate outcome. Reality will always remain 'unknowable'. The yield brought to light by scientific work from our primary sense perceptions will consist in an insight into connections and dependent relations which are present in the external world, which can somehow be reliably reproduced or reflected in the internal world of our thought and a knowledge of which enables us to 'understand' something in the external world, to foresee it and possibly to alter it. Our procedure in psycho-analysis is quite similar. We have discovered technical methods of filling up the gaps in the phenomena of our consciousness, and we make use of those

---

[1] Freud often gives the impression of being hostile to philosophy, but in a letter to Fliess of January 1, 1896, he says, 'I see that you are using the circuitous route of medicine to attain your first ideal, the physiological understanding of man, while I secretly nurse the hope of arriving by the same route at my own original objective, philosophy. For that was my original ambition, before I knew what I was intended to do in the world' (Letter 39 in *The Origins of Psychoanalysis*, p. 141).

[2] 1900a, V, esp. 612–13, 615–16.

[3] 1915e, XIV, esp. 166–71.

[4] 1940a, XXIII, chapters 4 to 8, esp. 157–60 and 196–7.

[5] 1940b, XXIII, esp. 282–3 and 285–6.

methods just as a physicist makes use of experiment. In this manner we infer a number of processes which are in themselves 'unknowable' and interpolate them in those that are conscious to us. And if, for instance, we say: 'At this point an unconscious memory intervened,' what that means is: 'At this point something occurred of which we are totally unable to form a conception, but which, if it had entered our consciousness, could only have been described in such and such a way.'[6]

Freud appears to have arrived at this position by the following process of reasoning. If one tries to construct a science of psychology dealing only with conscious processes, the task seems hopeless, for there are too many evident causal gaps. The conscious material is fragmentary and unsystematic, and therefore unlikely to be theoretically understandable in terms that do not go beyond it. It is natural to suppose these gaps filled in by neurophysiological processes, which give rise from time to time to conscious states. And the purposes of theoretical unity are served by supposing that, instead of an alternation and interaction between unconscious physical processes and conscious mental ones, there is a causally complete physical system, some of whose processes, however, have the property of consciousness in addition, or have conscious concomitants. The mental then appears as the effect of a certain kind of physical process.[7]

Further reflection, however, suggests that it may be wrong to identify the mental with these conscious effects, and that it should be identified with the physical processes themselves. These can appear to consciousness but are in themselves unconscious, as all physiological processes are. And since the true nature of the mental processes that appear to consciousness is physical, with consciousness being just one added quality of them, there can be no objection to also describing as mental those intermediate processes, occurring in the same physical system, which do not appear to consciousness even though they may be in many respects physically and functionally similar to those that do. Moreover, as we do not have the requisite physical understanding of the nervous system to be able to think about these processes in physical terms (perhaps we will never be able to reduce them to *cellular* terms), our best hope of progress in understanding the physical system is to think about it

---

[6] 1940a, XXIII, 196–7.

[7] This is the view expressed in Freud's monograph *On Aphasia:* It is probable that the chain of physiological events in the nervous system does not stand in a causal connection with the psychical events. The physiological events do not cease as soon as the psychical ones begin; on the contrary, the physiological chain continues. What happens is simply that, after a certain point of time, each (or some) of its links has a psychical phenomenon corresponding to it. Accordingly, the psychical is a process parallel to the physiological – 'a dependent concomitant' (1891b, XIV, 207).

in terms of the conscious aspects under which some mental processes appear to us. This is analogous to our use of visualization in thinking about physics – even about physical phenomena that are not actually visible. By thinking about mental processes in terms of the appearances of consciousness, we do not imply that their intrinsic nature is conscious. In fact, the intrinsic nature of both conscious and unconscious mental processes is unknown to us, and both types are merely represented, and not exhausted, by conscious imagery. Thus all of the psychical, and not only the unconscious, is *in itself* unconscious.

Just as Kant warned us not to overlook the fact that our perceptions are subjectively conditioned and must not be regarded as identical with what is perceived though unknowable, so psycho-analysis warns us not to equate perceptions by means of consciousness with the unconscious mental processes which are their object. Like the physical, the psychical is not necessarily in reality what it appears to us to be.[8]

I want to consider three questions about this view. First, is the analogy with the use of visual imagery in physics accurate? Secondly, does the view imply a particular position on the mind–body problem (e.g. materialism), or is it compatible with several alternatives? Thirdly, does the view supply a rationale for the employment of mentalistic concepts, taken from the psychology of consciousness, in theorizing about processes of whose physiological or chemical nature we are unable to form a conception?

It is certainly true that we find visual imagery helpful in thinking about structures that are invisible, invisible either because they are too small or because they do not reflect light. Thus we can imagine the DNA molecule as a double helix. Does this mean that we believe that if our vision were acute enough, that is how it would look to us? Perhaps so; but for some objects, such as atomic nuclei, the supposition that our vision should become acute enough to enable us to *see* their structure makes doubtful sense. It is more plausible to suppose that *if* we believe the hypothetical proposition, it is because we believe something else: namely that there is a similarity in structure between the invisible thing we are talking about and other, visible things that look a certain way; and that this structural feature is responsible for their looking that way. If the structural feature is what we see in the case of the visible objects, then we can use this kind of visual image to represent the same structural feature in invisible objects. Hence our image of the DNA molecule.

An important aspect of such cases is that the structure being imagined can be independently characterized. A double helix can be described in

[8] 1915e, XIV, 171.

purely geometrical terms, without reference to its visual appearance, and it is the former, not the latter, that the DNA molecule and a visible model have in common.[9] But if the significance of the hypothetical, 'If we could see it, it would look like this', depends on the availability of an independent characterization in non-visual terms, then the usefulness of this example as an analogy for the relation between conscious and unconscious mental processes is problematic. For in the latter case we have no independent way to characterize the unconscious mental process 'which, if it had entered our consciousness, could only have been described in such and such a way'.

However, we can still make sense of the supposition in terms of the *possibility* of an independent characterization of the unconscious process. We may be supposing that, although we are at present totally unable to form a conception of it, nevertheless it shares features with a corresponding conscious mental process, and that these features are partly responsible for the latter process appearing to consciousness in the form it does. This supposition seems to legitimate the peculiar counterfactual conditional, even if we do not now possess the vocabulary or concepts for describing the common features. They need not, for example, be features describable in the terms of current neurophysiology. They may be describable only in the terms of a future psychology whose form will be in part determined by the development of psychoanalytic theory. And there may be no reduction of the general terms of that theory to the terms of current neurophysiology (though it is possible that Freud himself thought there would be). I believe that this interpretation makes Freud's mentalistic discourse about what he regards as a physical system comprehensible, and makes the analogy with visualization in physics acceptable, though not so close as might initially appear. Instead of inferring specific similar causes from similar effects, he infers *similarity* of causes in unknown respects from observed similarity of effects.

Our knowledge of the unconscious, he says, is very like our knowledge of another person's mind, for it rests on circumstantial and behavioral grounds.[10] Since we have standard reasons of this kind for believing that certain features of our own and others' behavior have a psychical explanation, and further reasons to deny that these psychic phenomena

[9] Similarly, it is possible to speak of sounds so faint or so high that they cannot be heard by any organism, because we have a physical theory of sound.

[10] In neither case does he believe these grounds have to operate as the premises of a conscious *inference*, however: 'It would no doubt be psychologically more correct to put it in this way: that without any special reflection we attribute to everyone else our own constitution and therefore our consciousness as well, and that this identification is a sine qua non of our understanding' (1915e, XIV, 169).

are conscious,[11] the natural conclusion is that they are unconscious but otherwise similar to the potentially or actually conscious mental processes to which our ordinary explanations refer. Since they do not appear similarly to consciousness, the resemblance must be found in other, presumably physical, characteristics.

Since consciousness does not exhaust the nature of, for example, conscious hostility, it is possible to employ the imagery of consciousness to think about that which is common to both the conscious and the unconscious forms, as we use visual imagery in thinking about the structure of both visible and invisible double helices.

The main difficulty with this view is that it may assume too much, even though what it assumes is less specific than in the case of visual images of submicroscopic or invisible entities. It assumes that there *is* some definite objective character or disjunctive set of characters common to the states that are ordinarily grouped together by their similarity of appearance to consciousness (and their contextual and behavioral connections and significance). Only if that is true can we pick out a type of state of the nervous system by a mentalistic concept without implying anything about its conscious manifestations. But it is by no means obviously true, at least for many of the examples important to Freud, like beliefs, wishes, identifications.

It is most implausible, of course, that there is a general *neurological* character or set of characters common to all instances of the desire to kill one's father; but that is not the problem. A defender of the Freudian view need not claim that the objective character of these states can be accounted for in terms of any existing physical concepts. Perhaps it is only a developed psychology, not reducible to current neurophysiology, that can accommodate them.[12] But even to assume this, i.e. to assume

[11] He may be overhasty in this assumption. His main reason for refusing to extend the analogy with other minds to the attribution of consciousness to the Unconscious is that 'a consciousness of which its own possessor knows nothing is something very different from a consciousness belonging to another person, and it is questionable whether such a consciousness, lacking, as it does, its most important characteristic, deserves any discussion at all' (1915e, XIV, 170). But of course if the Unconscious were conscious of *itself*, then it would have a 'possessor' distinct from the subject of ordinary consciousness in the same person, and it would be only the latter who was unconscious of these conscious states of the Unconscious. However, Freud also offers other reasons against their consciousness, namely problems of inconsistency, peculiarity and incoherence, as well as indeterminateness in the number of subjects required to accommodate all other states consciously in more or less unified fashion.

[12] See, however, *Beyond the Pleasure Principle*: 'We need not feel greatly disturbed in judging our speculation upon the life and death instincts by the fact that so many bewildering and obscure processes occur in it – such as one instinct being driven out by another or an instinct turning from the ego to an object, and so on. This is merely due to our being obliged to operate with the scientific terms, that is to say with the figurative

that an objective psychology, whose concepts refer to physical phenomena, will roughly preserve the distinctions and categories embodied
in common-sense mental concepts, is to assume a great deal. (It is
perhaps less implausible in the case of sensations than in the case of
thought-related mental states.) If this criticism should be correct, and the
assumptions of Freud's account too strong, there may be other accounts
of the significance of the attribution of unconscious mental states which
would involve weaker theoretical assumptions: dispositional accounts
referring only to the behavioral and circumstantial similarities, perhaps
with an added condition that the unconscious state can reach consciousness under certain conditions. Certainly such accounts have been offered
by philosophers. But they are different from Freud's, and in this case his
remarks about what he means are not so easily dismissed as the
philosophical *obiter dicta* of a scientist commenting on the nature of his
primary professional activity.

Let us now turn to the second of the three questions we have posed:
since Freud's view is that both conscious and unconscious mental
processes are *in themselves* physical – though we can think of them at
present only in mentalistic terms – it might appear that he is committed
to a materialistic position on the mind–body problem. However, I believe
that this is not the case. Freud apparently *accepted* a materialist position, but it is not *entailed* by the views we are now considering. Everything depends on what is said about consciousness itself. Only if it,
too, is a physical phenomenon or a physical feature of those brain processes which are conscious mental processes, would Freud's account be
materialistic.

In the *Project* this is in fact his position, for he posits a special class of
neurons, the ω-neurons, whose activation is in some sense identified with
conscious experience. His most careful statement of the view is as
follows:

A word on the relation of this theory of consciousness to others. According to an
advanced mechanistic theory, consciousness is a mere appendage to physiologico-
psychical processes and its omission would make no alteration in the psychical
passage (of events). According to another theory, consciousness is the subjective
side of all psychical events and is thus inseparable from the physiological mental
process. The theory developed here lies between these two. Here consciousness

language, peculiar to psychology (or, more precisely, to depth psychology). We could not
otherwise describe the processes in question at all, and indeed we could not have become
aware of them. The deficiencies in our description would probably vanish if we were
already in a position to replace the psychological terms by physiological or chemical ones. It
is true that they too are only part of a figurative language; but it is one with which we have
long been familiar and which is perhaps a simpler one as well' (1920g, XVIII, 60).

is the subjective side of one part of the physical processes in the nervous system, namely of the ω-processes; and the omission of consciousness does not leave psychical events unaltered but involves the omission of the contribution from ω.[13]

To say that consciousness is the *subjective side* of a certain kind of neurophysiological process is not compatible with dualism, although it may also be a mistake to call it materialism. The view appears to combine the following points. (1) Every conscious mental process is [14] a physical process, of which consciousness is an aspect. (2) The consciousness is not an *effect* of the physical process; its existence is not compatible with the non-occurrence of that physical process, nor is its absence compatible with the occurrence of the physical process. This view, though not developed, is subtle and interesting. His later views on the subject are probably contained in the lost metapsychological paper on Consciousness, written in the same year as 'The unconscious'.[15] Unfortunately it was never published, and appears to have been destroyed.

Freud might have retained the double-aspect view (if that is what it can be called), in which case the other doctrines we are considering could provide a justification for thinking about physical phenomena in mentalistic terms, without implying the existence of any non-physical processes. It would also be possible, however, to hold that consciousness makes us aware of psychic processes that are in themselves physical and can exist unconsciously, *without* allowing that the events of consciousness are themselves physical. In either case the rationale for thinking about the unconscious psychical in terms of conscious appearances is the same, and the analogy with physics can be appealed to.

But the position that consciousness too is a physical process, or the 'subjective side' of certain physical processes, while obscure, is more interesting philosophically. It is worth saying a few words about how such a view may be construed, since it may bear on current discussion of the mind–body problem. Ordinarily, when the phenomenal appearance of something is contrasted with its objective nature, the former is explained as an *effect* of the latter on human observers. Thus ice feels cold in virtue of its effect on our sense of touch, and the physical property which we identify with its coldness – viz. low average kinetic energy – is

---

[13] 1950a, I, 311.

[14] The identification is made explicitly in the following passage: 'Thus we summon up courage to assume that there is a third system of neurones – ω perhaps (we might call it) – which is excited along with perception, but not along with reproduction, and whose states of excitation give rise to the various qualities – are, that is to say, *conscious sensations*' (1950a, I, 309).

[15] See the editor's introduction to the papers on metapsychology, XIV, 105–7.

something distinct from this sensory effect. If a corresponding view were taken about the relation between consciousness and the brain processes of which it is an appearance, then the conscious state would have to be described as an *effect* of the brain process on the subject's awareness, the brain process being something distinct.[16]

The view suggested by Freud, however, is that the brain process corresponding to a conscious state is *not* something distinct from the consciousness which is the awareness of it. The conscious qualities do not supply a complete description of the process, since its objective nature is physical, and consciousness is only its 'subjective side'. But consciousness is not an *effect* of this physical process any more than the surface of an object is an effect of *it*. Nor is it a detachable part. Philosophers of mind do not at present have much to say about the hypothesis that a neural process could appear to its subject as a conscious process, without producing subjective *effects*, simply in virtue of its own subjective qualities. This seems to me a question worth pursuing.

Let me turn to the last of the three questions posed above. Does Freud's view provide a justification for *theorizing* about the central nervous system in mentalistic terms? This question is not, I think, settled in the affirmative by the discussion so far. We have argued that Freud's account explains how mentalistic terms, with or without the implication of consciousness, may in principle *refer* to physical processes of which no explicitly physical conception can be formed at present. This does not mean, however, that a useful theory of these matters can be constructed using the mentalistic concepts, as may be seen if we return to the analogy with the role of visual imagery in physics.

Visualization is useful in thinking about molecular or atomic structure, but most of the important quantitative concepts used in physical or chemical theory are not represented visually, but more formally. Even our understanding of the visible world depends on concepts such as weight, energy, and momentum, that can be represented in visual terms only crudely. Physical theory depends on the development of non-phenomenal concepts.

Why then should it be expected that our understanding of the brain can be advanced by theorizing with phenomenal concepts of a mentalistic type? Desires and aversions, pleasures and pains, intentions, beliefs, and thoughts certainly provide very useful explanations of what people do. But is there any reason to expect that further refinement and systematization of these explanations will yield a theory of how the central nervous system operates? Freud argues persuasively that a complete theory is not

---

[16] See Saul A. Kripke, *Naming and Necessity* (Blackwell, Oxford, 1980).

to be expected if we restrict ourselves to describing the connections among states that are actually conscious. But is it enough to expand our field of investigation to include unconscious psychical states, i.e. those that are analogous, in structure and causes and effects, to conscious psychical states? That would be like trying to do physics entirely in terms of visible substances and phenomena plus invisible substances and phenomena structurally and causally analogous to them. The result would be some kind of mechanism. Is not psychologism a correspondingly narrow view about the brain?

The idea that we may expect to discover something about the brain by developing mentalistic theories in psychology and linguistics has been revived recently in connection with the mentalism of Noam Chomsky.[17] It is not necessary to offer this as one of the justifications for mentalistic linguistics, which is after all the only promising method currently available for investigating how natural languages function. We can at least try to discover phonetic, syntactic and semantic rules that people talk as if they were following. Linguists have had considerable success with this mode of description of grammar. But it is important to recognize that if people do not *consciously* follow certain statable rules in some area of activity, there is no *guarantee* that rules can be discovered which they may be said to be *unconsciously* following – rules which they behave *as if* they were following, and to which their judgments of correct and incorrect usage conform.

This should be evident to anyone who reflects on the failures of conceptual analysis in philosophy, for conceptual analysis is a type of mentalistic theory that tries to formulate rules for the application of concepts, which users of those concepts speak *as if* they were following. Wittgenstein's *Philosophical Investigations* devotes much energy to combating the assumption that such statable rules must always be discoverable behind our intuitions of correctness and incorrectness in the use of language.

Moreover, even if a mentalistic theory of the *as if* type succeeds reasonably well in accounting for human abilities or competence in some domain, as has been true of grammar, there remains a further question: what significance is to be attached to the claim that people don't merely talk *as if* they were following certain rules, but that they actually *are* (unconsciously) following them? The grounds for this further assertion are unclear.

Chomsky suggests, without making it a central part of his view, that

[17] See Noam Chomsky, *Aspects of the Theory of Syntax* (MIT Press, Cambridge, Mass, 1965), p. 193.

when a mentalistic theory of some domain like grammar is successful, it may come to have physical significance. His cautious but interesting comment on this possibility, at the end of *Language and Mind*, is as follows:

I have been using mentalistic terminology quite freely, but entirely without prejudice as to the question of what may be the physical realization of the abstract mechanisms postulated to account for the phenomena of behavior or the acquisition of knowledge. We are not constrained, as was Descartes, to postulate a second substance when we deal with phenomena that are not expressible in terms of matter in motion, in his sense. Nor is there much point in pursuing the question of psycho-physical parallelism, in this connection. It is an interesting question whether the functioning and evolution of human mentality can be accommodated within the framework of physical explanation, as presently conceived, or whether there are new principles, now unknown, that must be invoked, perhaps principles that emerge only at higher levels of organization than can now be submitted to physical investigation. We can, however, be fairly sure that there will be a physical explanation for the phenomena in question, if they can be explained at all, for an uninteresting terminological reason, namely that the concept of 'physical explanation' will no doubt be extended to incorporate whatever is discovered in this domain, exactly as it was extended to accommodate gravitational and electromagnetic force, massless particles, and numerous other entities and processes that would have offended the common sense of earlier generations.[18]

This is consonant with the outlook we have found in Freud, but it raises the question how a mentalistic theory would have to develop before its subject matter was admitted to the physical world in its own right. A theory from which the mentalistic character can be removed without explanatory loss is not essentially mentalistic. One might, for example, construct a mentalistic version of Newtonian mechanics, describing the attractions of bodies to one another and their stubbornness in moving in a straight line unless acted upon by an external force (all these psychic states being unconscious, of course). But the explanatory content of such a theory could be given in clearer, more formal, quantitative and non-mentalistic terms.

If, on the other hand, a theory is essentially mentalistic in that its explanatory value cannot be recaptured by a non-anthropomorphic version, then it may be doubted whether the things it describes will be admitted to the domain of physics. This is because mentalistic descriptions, connections, and explanations have to be understood by taking up, so far as is possible, the point of view of the subject of the mental states

---

[18] Noam Chomsky, *Language and Mind* (Harcourt, New York, 1968), pp. 83–4.

and processes referred to. Even where the mental states are unconscious, the understanding such a theory gives us requires that we take up the subject's point of view, since the form of explanatory connection between unconscious mental states and their circumstantial and behavioral surroundings is understood only through the image of conscious mental processes, with all the appeals to meaning, intention, and perception of aspects that this involves.

Since it appears to be part of our idea of the physical world that what goes on in it can be apprehended not just from one point of view but from indefinitely many, because its objective nature is external to any point of view taken toward it, there is reason to believe that until these subjective features are left behind, the hypotheses of a mentalistic psychology will not be accepted as physical explanations. The prospects for such an objectification of psychology are obscure, as is the form it might conceivably take. But this is a difficult topic which cannot be pursued here.

It should be mentioned that some psychoanalysts have maintained that Freud's theories are already far advanced toward objectivity – that his psychodynamics are impersonal and scientific, that the anthropomorphic terminology is only metaphorical and plays no essential theoretical role.[19] But these claims have been very persuasively challenged in a paper by William I. Grossman and Bennett Simon,[20] which is also an excellent guide to the psychoanalytic literature on this subject. Subjective anthropomorphic thinking seems indispensable to the understanding of such statements as this:

The analytic physician and the patient's weakened ego, basing themselves on the real external world, have to band themselves together into a party against the enemies, the instinctual demand of the id and the conscientious demands of the super-ego.[21]

Psychoanalytic theory will have to change a great deal before it comes to

[19] For example, H. Hartmann, E. Kris and R. M. Loewenstein, 'Comments on the formation of psychic structure', in *The Psychoanalytic Study of the Child* 2 (1946), pp. 11–38. Also in *Psychological Issues* 14 (Inter. Univ. Press, New York, 1964), pp. 27–55. The claim that Freud's theories are essentially mechanistic is sometimes also offered as a criticism. See for example A. C. MacIntyre, *The Unconscious* (Routledge, London, 1958), p. 22: 'Although Freud abandoned finally and decisively the attempt at neurophysiological explanation . . . it is my contention and the most important contention in this part of my argument that Freud preserved the view of the mind as a piece of machinery and merely wrote up in psychological terms what had been originally intended as a neurological theory.'

[20] 'Anthropomorphism: motive, meaning, and causality in psychoanalytic theory', in *The Psychoanalytic Study of the Child* 24 (1969), pp. 78–111.

[21] 1940a, XXIII, 173.

be regarded as part of the physical description of reality. And perhaps it, and other mentalistic theories, will never achieve the kind of objectivity necessary for this end. Perhaps, finally, the physical explanations of the phenomena in question will not be reached by progressive refinement and exactness in our mentalistic understanding, but will come only in a form whose relation to mentalistic theories cannot be perceived by us.[22] Now, as in 1896, it is too early to tell.

[22] A similar view is found in Donald Davidson, 'Mental events', in *Experience and Theory*, ed. Lawrence Foster and J. W. Swanson (Univ. of Mass. Press, Amherst, Mass., 1970), pp. 79–101.

15

Freud's anatomies of the self*

IRVING THALBERG

1. *The philosophical knot*   If you study clinically the sorts of behaviour Freud dealt with, you may justifiably feel tempted to say that they manifest conflict of the individual with himself or herself. You might regard this self-conflict as a clash between forces within the person. And you might wonder, as Freud did: what items contend inside of us? What forms do their struggles take? With great originality and boldness, Freud put forth quite heterogenous theories of the mind's components, and of how their operations result in various types of normal as well as disturbed behaviour. I find many of his speculations altogether spellbinding. Yet despite my unqualified enthusiasm, I fear that none of these ingenious and suggestive partitioning explanations will turn out to be both illuminating and coherent. I plan to illustrate why it was nevertheless reasonable for him to propose such 'dynamic' accounts of human activity and affliction. I hope it will be instructive to see which features of behaviour threw Freud into conceptual confusion. These few deep muddles cannot possibly discredit Freud's innovative work. Our appreciation of the difficulties he seems to have encountered should advance our understanding, in philosophy of mind and action, of the person and his reflexive acts.

I realize that the doctrinal thickets I want to rummage in have been staked out by a legion of Freud experts. But I think most of the sceptical commentators have not argued their case in detail. Those who have done so devote insufficient attention to Freud's, and our own, profound theoretical need to subdivide the self. Few distil conceptual vaccines from his philosophically enlightening confusions.

To start with, Freud is remembered for his tripartite divisions of the self into unconscious, preconscious and conscious 'systems',[1] from

---

* This is a revised version of an essay which appeared under the same title in *Freud: A Collection of Critical Essays*, ed. Richard Wollheim (Doubleday, New York, 1974).

[1] When I discuss Freud, I shall reserve quotation marks for expressions which he himself used, as translated in the Standard Edition (SE). I quote him abundantly because I want readers to judge for themselves what his words mean. When I foresee exegetical controversy, I parenthetically record the SE dating of a work's publication, the SE volume and page numbers – and if the work was composed by Freud long before it was published, the date of its composition.

roughly 1900 until 1923, and id, ego and superego thereafter. But his accounts of our mental processes made use of countless other items within us. In conformity with tradition, he assumed that 'ideas' populate our minds and their compartments. By the slippery term 'idea' he seemed to mean images, concepts, propositions and thoughts. In addition, Freud always supposed that our mental machinery runs on some kind of 'energy' – which resembles but is not a species of electrical current. In the guise of emotive 'affect' and conative pushiness, this psychical energy adheres to some of our ideas. However, from the time he began theorizing, Freud conceded that 'we have no means of measuring' psychical current. And in a posthumous monograph he declares that 'in mental life some kind of energy is at work', though we will not 'come nearer to a knowledge of it by analogies with other forms of energy'.

Freud also consistently gave top billing to our drives, impulses or 'instincts' (*Triebe*), which he regarded as somehow derivative from psychical energy. This creates a minor puzzle. For while Freud recognizes just one kind of psychical energy, from relatively early in his theorizing he makes it a methodological principle that 'instincts occur in pairs of opposites' (1910a, XI, 44). To the end he believed that '[o]nly by the concurrent or mutually opposing action of the two primal instincts' and 'never by one or the other alone, can we explain the rich multiplicity of the phenomena of life' (1937c, XXIII, 243). In this sense, *not* in the Cartesian 'mind-*versus*-matter' sense, Freud's explanatory schemes are dualistic. One competing instinct he regularly calls 'libido', and says that it propels us toward erotic endeavours. At first its rival is the 'ego-instinct' of self-preservation (1910i, XI, 214). From 1920 on, the destructive instinct, directed at oneself and others, becomes the antagonist of libido.

Since I mentioned the ego instinct, I should post a warning. Freud's conception of the ego (*das Ich*) was unsettled prior to 1923. Frequently he seems to mean by 'ego' the whole person (1894a, III, 54; 1920g, XVIII, 11). Other passages, occasionally in the same works, suggest that the ego is only part of us, and that Freud is contrasting the ego with parts that we are not conscious of (1894a, III, 48; 1920g, XVIII, 19). At times Freud makes the ego a delegate within us of conventional morality, and has it keep shameful thoughts away from our 'consciousness' (1900a, V, 526). On this view, we would not be fully conscious of everything our ego does. Particularly when it censors thoughts, we are no better apprised of its activity than we are of whatever it manages to exclude from our consciousness (see section 6). Yet another characterization of ego appears in Freud's 1895 *Project*. There ego is nothing but a sub-system of 'neurones', whose job is to maximize 'discharge' of psychic energy from our whole homeostatic mental apparatus.

2. *A distinction between strictly physical and broadly anthropomorphic models* Since we are taking a census of the items Freud invokes to explain conflict behaviour, we should notice that he portrays their relationships in correspondingly varied terms. Because of his commitment to materialism, you would expect him to describe psychological phenomena in the language we reserve for inanimate objects and events. Thus Freud's topographical account of the person makes 'reference . . . to regions in the mental apparatus, wherever they may be situated in the body'. We also remember his mechanistic imagery of tensions and tugs. For instance, he says 'the repressed [idea or thought] exercises a continuous pressure in the direction of consciousness, so that this pressure must be balanced by an unceasing counter-pressure'. Equally familiar is Freud's hydraulic talk – of flow and 'blockages'. We hear of libidinal instincts pouring through 'channels'. If libido is dammed up, after leaving its 'reservoir', it 'may . . . move on a backward course . . . along infantile lines'. Freud occasionally draws upon crystallography, and imagines the fusion of repressed, hysterogenic memories around a 'nucleus'. When we dream, our childhood experience may operate as a 'nucleus of crystallization attracting the material of the dream thoughts to itself'. Sometimes resorting to botany, Freud compares a repressed idea with a fungus that 'proliferates in the dark'. A recurring zoological simile is that libido goes out to objects, and then returns, much like the pseudopods of an amoeba. From pathology Freud takes the notion of 'strangulated affects', along with the comparison between a repressed memory-idea and a wound that contains some irritating 'foreign body'. Toxicology also enriches Freud's theorizing. He supposes that libidinal currents, or 'sexual substances', become poisonous if they do not escape from our mental apparatus.

Freud's anthropomorphic models come from several domains of social life. When we perform an 'erroneous action', Freud says that 'control over the body' passes from one's ego, and its 'will', to an opposing 'counter-will'. Freud regularly speaks of 'two thought-constructing agencies' within us, 'of which the second enjoys the privilege of having free access to consciousness for its products'. Other political and social arrangements besides 'privilege' and 'free access' enliven the relationship between parts of the self. There are upheavals too. Freud explains that the

soul . . . is a hierarchy of superordinated and subordinated agents, a labyrinth of impulses striving independently of one another towards action . . .
Psychoanalysis . . . can say to the ego: 'a part of the activity of your own mind has been withdrawn from your knowledge and from the command of your will. . . . [S]exual instincts . . . have rebelled . . . to rid themselves of . . . oppression; they have extorted their rights in a manner that you cannot sanction.'

Freud describes the psychoanalyst's task in similar language: 'the physician . . . works hand in hand with one part of the pathologically divided personality, against the other partner in the conflict'; his or her goal is to 'give . . . back command over the id' to the neurotic's ego. Freud brings in more political terminology when he says that neurotic symptoms themselves, as well as dreams and slips of the tongue, are like negotiated 'compromises' between our unruly impulses and our moralistic inclinations.

Social life provides Freud with yet another model when he calls his theories 'economic'. He deploys financial imagery at least twice, likening an instinct to a 'capitalist', who loans us energy for our undertakings (1905e, VII, 87; 1916–17, XV, 226). Now and then he describes an individual, or his ego, as acting on 'economic' grounds when they maximize pleasure (1920g, XVIII, 7). But Freud's term 'economic' usually has to do with the relative 'strength' or 'pressure' exerted by psychical or neural forces (1950a [1895], I, 283; 1915e, XIV, 181; 1924b, XIX, 152).

More intimate relationships also have a place in Freud's doctrines. He says that a person becomes narcissistic when his or her ego 'offers itself . . . as a libidinal object to the id, and aims at attaching the id's libido to itself'. In melancholia, however, 'the ego . . . feels itself hated . . . by the superego, instead of loved'. Finally we should note a model that appears already in Plato's *Phaedrus* Freud's variant is that the ego 'in its relation to the id is like a man on horseback, who has to hold in check the superior strength of the horse'. Here again, as we noticed in most of Freud's analogies with person-to-person dealings – and with inanimate phenomena – the underlying pattern is discord, tension.

I trust that my hurried conspectus of Freud's schemes for explaining conflict behaviour has exhibited their great diversity, sophistication and attractiveness. Before we start evaluating them, you might wonder if it is fair – or philosophically rewarding – for us to subject his so-called 'metapsychological' doctrines to close scrutiny. Perhaps they are only metaphors, not meant to be taken literally, and thus they should be immune from philosophical prosecution. Indeed, Freud himself cautions: 'What is psychical is . . . so unique . . . that no one comparison can reflect its nature'. But far from being a prohibition, this is an encouragement to consider seriously as many images as possible. For Freud continues: 'The [therapeutic] work of psychoanalysis suggests analogies with chemical analysis, but just as much with the incursions of a surgeon or the manipulations of an orthopedist or the influence of an educator' (1919a, XVII, 161). In regard to one of his favourite topographical *cum* social models, Freud assures us that his 'crude hypotheses [about] the two chambers, the doorkeeper on the threshold between them, and consciousness as a spectator at the end of the second room, must indicate an extensive approximation to the actual reality' (1916–17, XVI, 296). In any event, I would insist that if a metaphor is to be at all enlightening, we should be able to locate some points of contact between it and what it is intended to explain. But I want to put off such methodological issues until we consider some of the reasons a theorist might have to divide up the soul, either on the model of contrary inanimate forces, or of interpersonal wrangling.

3. *Evidence of strife within the person*   Freud reports that when he began working in psychiatric hospitals and in his own practice, he was not 'pledged to any . . . psychological system'; rather, he 'proceeded to adjust [his] views until they seemed adapted for giving an account of . . . the facts which had been observed'. Some of the behaviour he witnessed especially demanded an explanation in terms of inner discord. A good example is Freud's quite early theoretical response to the syndrome then called hysteria. He speculates:

if I find someone in a state which bears all the signs of a painful affect – weeping, screaming and raging – the conclusion seems probable that a mental process is going on in him of which those physical phenomena are the appropriate expression. . . . The problem would at once arise of how it is that an hysterical patient is overcome by an affect about whose cause he asserts that he knows nothing. . . . He is behaving as though he *does* know about it.

At the time Freud was convinced that hysterical afflictions of this type result mainly from a 'summation of traumas' – as a rule, sexual experiences. When patients began treatment, they seemed to have forgotten these traumas. But when they were helped to recall the incidents, their hysterical disorders vanished. Freud is driven toward a partitioning theory. He believes

everything points to one solution: the patient is in a special state of mind in which all his impressions or his recollections . . . are no longer held together by an associative chain . . . [and thus] it is possible for a recollection to express its affect by means of somatic phenomena without the group of the other mental processes, the ego, knowing about it or being able to intervene to prevent it.

Further evidence comes from work on hysterically blind patients. Freud asserts:

Excitations of the [supposedly] blind eye may . . . produce affects . . . though they do not become conscious. Thus hysterically blind people are only blind as far as consciousness is concerned; in their unconscious they see. . . . [O]bservations such as this compel us to distinguish between conscious and unconscious mental processes.

In the same essay, and repeatedly elsewhere, Freud says that other experiments with hypnotism also prove that unconscious mental activity takes place in us. He declares that a post-hypnotic suggestion must be 'present in the mind', since a person to whom it was given will obey it while candidly disclaiming knowledge of its origin. We will say more of Freud's notion of 'presence' later (section 10).

For now we should remark that in Freud's view dreaming appeared to call for a 'divided soul' theory. He staunchly held that '[t]here must be a force here which is seeking to express something, and another which is striving to prevent the expression'. One of his last discussions turns upon the memory we display in dreams of incidents we cannot recall when awake. Surely these recollections have been 'present' all along, but inaccessible? (1940a, XXIII, 160f).

One typical phase of psychoanalytical treatment itself also struck Freud as requiring an 'inner strife' explanation. Sincere patients who are progressing steadily all at once come to a halt. Abruptly they find themselves unable to bring forth dreams and associations; or on the other hand they become too obliging, and produce whatever material their analyst seems to expect. According to Freud, such 'resistance' behaviour proves that some internal impediment is at work. He argues: 'The existence of this force could be assumed with certainty, since one became aware of an effort corresponding to it if, in opposition to it, one tried to introduce the unconscious memories into the patient's consciousness.' Later Freud amplifies: 'There can be no question but that . . . resistance emanates from the ego.' In fact, '[n]o stronger impression arises from the resistances during the work of analysis than of there being a force which is defending itself by every possible means against recovery and which is absolutely resolved to hold onto illness and suffering'.

A final source of conflict theories we might call 'respect for the ordinary language of psychotics'. Freud conjectures about paranoid individuals, who stubbornly insist that they are being observed and criticized, and constantly 'hear' voices commenting unfavourably upon their deeds and attitudes. Freud wonders: 'How would it be if these insane people were right, if in each of us there is present an agency [viz., the superego] which observes and threatens to punish', and which they have 'mistakenly displaced into external reality?' (1933a, XXII, 59; see 1914c, XIV, 95). In his very last résumé of psychoanalytical doctrine, Freud similarly finds it significant that victims of hallucinatory confusion, when they recover, will often say that throughout their most disturbed periods, 'in some corner of their mind . . . there was a normal person hidden, who . . . watched the hubbub of illness go past him'.

Two distinguished recent commentators on Freud believe that there is also a close match between Freud's tripartite conception and the way sane people think and speak of themselves. Jerome Bruner says that the id–ego–superego story exemplifies 'the dramatic technique of decomposition, the play whose actors are parts of a single life', and its 'imagery . . . has an immediate resonance with the dialectic of experience'.[2] Richard Wollheim is more explicit; he says Freud's theory 'provides a model of the mind and its working . . . [that] coincides with, or reproduces, the kind of picture or representation . . . we consciously or unconsciously make to ourselves of our mental processes'.[3] Another virtue of nearly all Freud's theorizing is that it encourages us to break the link so firmly established by Descartes between mentality and consciousness. Whether or not it is correct, this dogma ought to be challenged.

Yet I have misgivings. I am persuaded that Freud's consistently non-anthropomorphic theories make sense. They could be true, or false. We have at least a rough understanding what the world might be like in either case. Despite that solid advantage, I believe Freud's non-anthropomorphic schemes fail to elucidate those aspects of mental life which most baffle us. I shall not address the much-belaboured question whether Freud's physicalistic theories of mind qualify as 'scientific'. As for his animistic accounts, I concur with Bruner and Wollheim that these generate illumination – no doubt because we already have a practical and theoretical understanding of social transactions, and Freud miniaturizes such events inside us. But I think a careful assessment will show these doctrines to be instructively unintelligible, in ways I shall point out. If I am right about this, it is a moot question whether Freud's paradigms drawn from social life are scientific. In any case, I begin the critical phase of my discussion by examining a strictly neurological theory of Freud's which I have already referred to more than once.

4. *A mental apparatus and its sub-systems of 'neurones'* Freud's homeostatic model, as we would call it nowadays, seems to be a marvel of relative cogency together with explanatory emptiness. It seems to be taking shape in his earliest metapsychological essays. He elaborates it with a treasury of details in his *Project* of 1895 (1950a, I, 295–387), and its silhouette hovers behind many of his subsequent writings. Freud

---

[2] Jerome Bruner, 'The Freudian Conception of Man and the Continuity of Nature', in M. Brodbeck, ed, *Readings in the Philosophy of the Social Sciences* (Macmillan, New York, 1968), p. 710.

[3] Richard Wollheim, *Sigmund Freud* (Viking, New York, 1971), p. 234.

envisages a 'mental apparatus' composed of three kinds of 'neurones', classed according to how 'permeable' they are to currents of psychic energy, called 'Quantity' or 'Q'. The system of least permeable neurones Freud labels 'the ego'. As I noted at the end of section 1, this 'ego' system operates to maximize 'discharge' of Q from the whole apparatus – hence my comparison with present-day homeostatic devices. More philosophically intriguing is Freud's name for the most permeable system, which receives 'stimuli' from our 'external' surroundings. This neurone system he baptizes 'consciousness'. If you wonder what these neurones have to do with the phenomena ordinary folk associate with consciousness, my hunch would be this: whenever these neurones transmit Q, notably upon receipt of external stimuli, we will be conscious – that is, at least we will be awake, and probably we will be conscious *of* one thing or another.

This is a coherent empirical hypothesis. It makes sense. I can easily imagine that whenever some particular neurones buzz with Q, we are conscious. Or perhaps *no* brain activity of the right sort coincides with our moments of lucidity and contact with our environs. My complaint about Freud's neurological model is that it furnishes us no clues regarding those aspects of our consciousness which are most puzzling to curious laymen and to practising therapists. In Bruner's and Wollheim's terminology, the Freudian neural apparatus has no 'resonance with . . . experience'; it lacks kinship with our 'picture . . . of our mental processes'. You would not expect anyone to say, 'Ah, so consciousness is the passage of Q energy through this group of neurones!'

One shortcoming of Freud's neural theory is obvious: it leaves out, and thus fails to elucidate, three aspects of our conscious mental states which greatly impress philosophers. Our ultra-permeable neurones have a definite spatial habitat, and the same goes for any currents of Q that shoot through them. Not so with consciousness. We have ordinary knowledge of neural events within us – knowledge acquired through perceptual snooping and grounded in evidence as well as previously accepted theory. We have a mysteriously different kind of authority to say that we are conscious, and that our conscious state is one of doubt, belief, or what have you, on such-and-such a topic. This last-mentioned 'aboutness', or intentionality, is a central feature of most states of consciousness; however it is unclear whether we can meaningfully say that the Q-transmissions of a neurone system are on a topic, or about anything. Now it would be unfair of me to criticize Freud because he did not go into these and similar philosophical niceties – which were not widely discussed in his time, particularly by psychologists. My gripe is not against Freud. I doubt that anyone could produce an account of neurones and brain events which doubles as a theory of what we experience as consciousness.

I shall not pursue these questions further. But I might as well add that difficulties just like those we had with Freud's neurological account of consciousness are bound to emerge elsewhere. Here is one last example. Freud says of our homeostatic neurone system that it is governed by 'the principle of constancy or stability', which he later re-names 'the pleasure principle'. Obviously Freud does not mean that neurones follow principles, or that they are unprincipled either. He must be claiming only that the apparatus, or a part of it, usually operates in a stabilizing manner – and maximum amounts of Q leave the apparatus. But what does this outcome have to do with pleasure? Well, Freud equates pleasure (in German: *Lust*) with discharge of Q, and the build-up of Q he describes as 'unpleasure' (*Unlust*). Again it is clear he does *not* mean that we enjoy the release of Q from our mental apparatus, or that our 'ego' or 'consciousness' neurone systems do. Freud is simply conjecturing about what quasi-electrical events take place in our brains when we are pleased or distressed.

His conjecture is meaningful, and may in fact be true – or false. Yet it cannot be the whole story of our joys and sufferings. Freud's and anyone else's neurological account will have the serious deficiencies that we just saw in his companion theory of consciousness. Moreover, it does not enlighten us about the important relationships, causal or otherwise, between our states of pleasure or displeasure and our beliefs, our purposes – including the unconscious ones so astutely discerned by Freud – as well as social convention and conditioning. I believe that any theorist who intends to produce an adequate, illuminating account of our conscious mental states generally, and of pleasure specifically, must have something to say about these aspects of our mental life.

I can give no transcendental proof of this, and I certainly cannot set forth all the requirements I think should be met by a philosophical theory of mind. But I believe I ought to illustrate how you risk incoherence if you try to enrich a neurological story with notions from the sphere of interpersonal behaviour.

5. *A mixed account of hysterical symptoms* Perhaps because he sensed that theories of the kind we have been examining leave out something vital, Freud often added anthropomorphic embellishments. Slightly before he wrote the *Project*, Freud was busy attempting to understand hysteria. I have already referred to a pair of his doctrines: that a form of psychic energy, emotional 'affect', clings to some of our memory 'ideas', and that this is the result of a series of 'traumatic' incidents, usually

during our childhood and sexual in character. Freud also believed that if this load of affect is not discharged, or 'abreacted', through our overt actions – including our emotional outbursts and our conscious recall of the incidents – then we are in for trouble.

What sort? When affect builds up inside of us, what happens to it and to us? As Freud develops his central theme of repression, and tells how repression causes hysterical and other troubles, his account begins to sound animistic. He says the affect-laden memory is 'objectionable'; the person's 'ego . . . decides on the repudiation of the . . . idea'; in somewhat different terms, one patient herself 'repressed her erotic idea from consciousness and transformed the amount of its affect in physical sensations of pain' (1895d, II, 123 and 164). Yet plainly Freud wanted to stay as much as possible within the bounds of a neurological or at least mechanistic explanation. Here is a typical result, from a landmark case study written a decade after the *Project*. Freud imagines that the potential victim of hysteria has

[c]ontrary thoughts . . . paired off in such a way that *the one thought is excessively intensely* [sic] *conscious while its counterpart is repressed and unconscious*. This . . . is an effect . . . of repression. For repression is often achieved by means of an excessive reinforcement of the thought contrary to the one which is to be repressed. . . . [T]he thought which asserts itself . . . in conciousness . . . I call a *reactive thought*. The two thoughts . . . act towards each other much like the two needles of an astatic galvanometer. The reactive thought keeps the objectionable one under repression by means of a certain surplus of intensity; but for that reason it itself is 'damped' and proof against conscious efforts of thought (1905e, VII, 55; see 1893a, II, 12).

Any theorist would be tempted to weave notions of personal agency and interpersonal conflict into the electromagnetic tapestry. *If* you restrict yourself to the terminology of psychical mechanics, all you can report is one entity bouncing another away from part of the mental apparatus which is inexplicably named 'consciousness'. You will be unable to express the fact that the 'reactive' entity is protecting the *person's* own *moral* beliefs, while the entity that it pushes under is 'erotic', and for that reason subject to 'repudiation'. You cannot go onto describe the person's hysterical symptom as a 'mnemic symbol' of the ancient trauma (1895d, II, 90). And how would you articulate the hypothesis that it is less unpleasant for the victim to have hysterical symptoms than to clamp down altogether on his or her nasty idea? Besides, the patient as well as theory builders might derive some gain if we blend in anthropomorphic elements. After listening to some of Freud's mixed accounts of their predicament, hysterics might claim enhanced self-understanding, and feel they are beginning to put things together. A purely electromagnetic explanation is unlikely to produce this kind of 'resonance' for victims.

So much for incentives to humanize our story. Why are concepts from personal and social life at odds with an otherwise mechanistic theory? My reasoning would be roughly as follows. Suppose that you introduce terms like 'objectionable', 'repudiation', and 'transform' – this latter verb being understood as it would be when you report, 'Mary transformed the flour sack into a blouse'. In contexts where it is indisputably meaningful to deploy these terms, it also makes sense to say other things. For instance, you can say why various people find X-rated movies objectionable, what a candidate for office intended to achieve by repudiating his or her party's programme, and how Mary went about transforming the flour sack. However, it is blatant nonsense to speak about any kind of electronic device, or any part of such a device – for that matter, any brain or neurone system – in these terms. You might have complex reasons for objecting to X-rated films. Perhaps you have evidence that many rapists seem to have been inspired by such films. Maybe you have a gut reaction against the genre, but no particular reasons for your negative attitude. Or possibly you consider it unobjectionable. However, what could you possibly mean if you discussed an electrical apparatus or a brain in this manner? At least on the genesis of hysteria, Freud himself admits:

I cannot . . . give any hint of how a conversion [of affect into symptoms] . . . is brought about. It is obviously not carried out in the same way as an intentional and voluntary action. It is a process which occurs under the pressure of the motive of defense in someone whose organization . . . has a proclivity in that direction (1895d, II, 166).

I shall not try to figure out how an electrical or neural process could result from 'pressure of the motive of defense'. My suspicion at this stage is that our animistic terminology, rather than our blending of it with neurological or electromagnetic schemes of explanation, must be to blame for nonsense here. We can test this by working through a relatively minor yet exemplary 100% anthropomorphic theory – Freud's altogether fascinating account of what it is to dream. A question will focus some of my misgivings.

6. *Is our ego awake or asleep when we dream?* This should be a dilemma for any Freudian account of dreaming, whether one means by 'ego' the whole person who dreams, or only part of him or her. I see no way around it, as long as we explain his dreaming by reference to what various agencies do within him, or what he does to them. A casual reader of Freud's pellucid prose may not be jolted by some of his lapses of

cogency on this topic. So here are samples, numbered to facilitate discussion:

(i) [T]he wish to sleep (which the conscious ego is concentrated upon . . .) must . . . be . . . one of the motives for the formation of dreams (1900a, IV, 234).

(ii) [D]reams are given their shape by the operation of two psychical forces . . . [O]ne of these forces constructs the wish which is expressed by the dream, while the other exercises a censorship upon the dream-wish and . . . brings about a distortion of the expression of the wish (*Ibid.*, 144).

(iii) [C]riticism . . . involved . . . exclusion from consciousness. The critical agency [has] . . . a closer relation to consciousness than the agency criticized . . . [and also] directs our waking life and determines our voluntary, conscious actions (1900a, V, 540).

(iv) [T]he ego . . . goes to sleep at night, even though then it exercises the censorship on dreams (1923b, XIX, 17).

(v) The critically disapproving agency does not entirely cease to function during sleep (1923a, XVIII, 268).

(vi) A dream may be described as . . . fantasy working on behalf of the maintenance of sleep. . . . It is . . . a matter of indifference to the sleeping ego what may be dreamt . . . so long as the dream performs its task (1925i, XIX, 126).

(vii) [B]etween the two agencies . . . a censorship . . . only allows what is agreeable to it to pass through to consciousness . . . [R]epressed material must submit to . . . alterations which mitigate its offensive features . . .

[T]he formation of obscure dreams occurs *as though* one person who was dependent upon a second person had to make a remark which was bound to be disagreeable in the [latter's] ears. . . . [O]n the basis of this simile . . . we have arrived at the concepts of dream, distortion and censorship (1901a, V, 676).

(viii) [W]hile this second agency, in which we recognize our normal ego, is concentrated on the wish to sleep, it appears to be compelled by the psycho-physiological conditions of sleep to relax the energy with which . . . [it holds] down the repressed material during the day . . . The danger of sleep being disturbed by [the repressed material] . . . must . . . be guarded against by the ego. . . . [E]ven during sleep a certain amount of free attention is on duty to guard against sensory stimuli, and . . . this guard may sometimes consider waking more advisable than a continuation of sleep (ibid., 679; see 1933a, XXII, 16).

(ix) [O]ur ego . . . gives credence to the dream images, as though what it wanted to say was: 'Yes, yes! You're quite right, but let me go on sleeping!' The low estimate which we form of dreams when we are awake . . . is probably the judgment passed by our sleeping ego . . .

[A]nxiety dreams . . . can no longer [prevent] . . . an interruption of sleep but . . . [bring] sleep to an end. In doing so it [*sic*] is merely behaving like a conscientious night watchman . . . suppressing disturbances so that the townsmen may not be waked up. . . . [He] awakens them, if the causes seem to him serious and of a kind he cannot cope with alone (1901a, V, 680; see 1933a, XXII, 17).

These statements and the overall account of dreaming which they belong to are initially plausible. But I believe that if we press for additional information about the characters in this story, and their multifarious activities, we are sure to elicit plain nonsense – a sign that the story was covert nonsense to begin with. I shall not worry that at some junctures Freud's narrative seems to have the distinct flaw of implying a vicious regress. In quotation (ix), for example, our *ego* is pictured as not only sleeping, but apparently dreaming too – hardly an auspicious way to explain *our* dreaming.

(i)–(ix) represent a dramatic conflict. The main antagonists are the unnamed 'agency' working on behalf of our illicit wishes and 'repressed material', and our ego – which keeps the material away from our 'consciousness' and prevents its discharge through 'voluntary, conscious action . Like a symptom, a dream is a 'compromise' between the opposed 'psychical forces' (see 1933a, XXII, 15). And since this compromise leads to relative calm within us, sleep is made easier.

Obviously Freud means that *we* slumber, but how about our ego? Well, the agency that 'constructs the wish which is expressed by the dream' is on the alert, ready to send forbidden material to consciousness. If there is going to be any struggle, or negotiated compromise, our ego must be reasonably awake. On the other hand, would it not sound incongruous if Freud said that our ego is fully vigilant as we snooze? After all, we tend to consider our ego the real us; and if we sleep when we dream, our ego should too.

If my reconstruction is near the mark, we can see why Freud inconsistently portrays our ego as wishing to sleep, definitely 'sleeping', wanting to 'go on sleeping' (i, vi, ix), and yet exercising 'censorship', imposing 'alterations' on the repressed material, doing guard duty (ii, vii, viii) – even simultaneously going to sleep and censoring our dreams (iv). No wonder that he often tries to slip between the horns of this dilemma with a drowsy ego (i, viii). Evidently that is no solution. The nearer our ego comes to being asleep, the less it can act as inquisitor and sentinel.

So far we have only illustrated how Freud's 'interpersonal action' model for dreaming and similar mental states may be self-contradictory. Next I shall try to elicit particulars about the identity and consciousness of his *dramatis personae*. The upshot is likely to be unmistakable nonsense.

7. *'Who?' questions* At this point I shall occasionally branch out from the numbered anthropomorphic statements of Freud's about dreaming. Now it seems to me that when we hear stories of this type about people, rather than about denizens of a person's mind, we legitimately seek to learn more. Hence my inquiries regarding the personified ego. Consider its 'wish to sleep' (i, viii). For *whose* sleep does it yearn? Does it want me

to sleep, or only itself? What relationship is there anyway between its repose and mine? Can I doze off while it remains on the *qui vive?* In this case there are other identification problems. For instance, whose 'free attention is on duty' (viii)? Whose 'waking' may the 'guard' think 'more advisable than a continuation of sleep' (viii)? Mine? Surely not his own! As for the somnolent 'townsmen', we should raise further questions. Given Freud's general view of human motivation, can we suppose that any 'watchman' is 'conscientious' enough to care what happens to his fellow citizens? Why does he call them from their beds to help him quell 'disturbances'? Does he otherwise risk harm? *Any* reply we make to such questions will sound capricious – or deranged. Yet if we were discussing ordinary sentries and villagers, we could find answers.

The puzzle is not isolated. Recall Freud's treatment of our instincts or drives. Freud says 'these processes strive toward gaining pleasure; psychical activity draws back from any event which might arouse unpleasure' (1911b, XII, 219). But whose enjoyment do they 'strive' for? Why mine? Surely it is unintelligible to suppose *they* enjoy escaping from my homeostatic mental apparatus.

Our bewilderment should become fairly general when we remember Freud's functional characterization of the ego. He always assigns it 'the task of self-preservation', which it carries out 'by learning to bring about changes in the external world to its own advantage (through activity)' (1940a, XXIII, 145f.). Again we ought to inquire: Which 'self' does my ego have the duty of preserving? How is its continued existence related to mine? Granted that it is unconcerned to promote *my* interests, what exactly do we mean by 'its own advantage'? Freud's notion of this prominent actor within us, the ego, now seems quite elusive.

Nor do we find it easier to characterize other performers in his troupe. Our superego must 'impose' our 'ego ideal' upon our ego (1923b, XIX, 34–39). Speaking more broadly, our superego has the 'functions of self-observation, of conscience and of maintaining the ideal' (1933a, XXII, 66). By analogy with similar descriptions of people, we should find out what goals an 'ego ideal' or superego can set for a mini-person, why it bothers to do so, and how it goes about its work. For that matter, whom does my superego watch when it engages in 'self-observation' – me, my ego, itself? Once more, things you can say about interpersonal goings-on seem to make no sense when the protagonists are inside your mental apparatus.

8. *A counter-argument*   Kathleen Wilkes has recently tried to block this kind of 'nonsense' objection. As she formulates it, the sort of 'charge' I have been making is

that only a *person*, not any part of him, can *literally* 'repress', 'censor' . . . and the like. Just as a man, and not his hand, signs a cheque, so a human being, and not a part of his brain, is the one who can perform actions such as 'displacing' or 'suppressing' emotions. Crediting the ego or superego with such functions is a solecism, a use of anthropomorphic metaphor.[4]

Against this, she wants to 'defend the allegedly anthropomorphic characterizations' of 'hypothesized structures in the brain – such as the ego or id . . . or information retrieval mechanisms' – 'claiming that [these characterizations] are *not* metaphorical but literal'; for instance, 'describing a cerebroceptive mechanism as . . . "suppressing id-impulses" can be a literal and accurate description of what goes on, and is not illegitimate but irreducible anthropomorphization' (p. 132).

In support of her claim, Wilkes has a string of examples:

a washing machine . . . cleans dishes by soaking, soaping, rinsing, and drying them. So also does a human being not possessing such a machine. Thus, a machine does something which humans also do (washes dishes), and, at one general level of description, 'in the same way' as a human, namely by soaking, soaping, rinsing, and drying them. . . . ['Same way'] must be tied to a specified level of generality in the task description. The point remains, however, that humans and simple machines undeniably share some abilities. A more sophisticated kind of machine plays chess . . . [and] has the capacity to learn from its mistakes, to anticipate and guess the moves of its opponents, to select . . . strategies . . . it plans, adapts, and follows through strategies, tries to win and can lose. . . . [T]he human chess player does also; researchers . . . would . . . say that the computer carries out many of these sub-tasks (at some fairly detailed level of description) 'in the same way' as the human. . . . [I]t is literally true to say of a machine programmed to φ that it φs: there is no need and no justification for insulating the verb in raised eyebrow quotes, saying that it 'φs' (p. 134).

Finally she pictures a 'highly sophisticated computer' which

cleans shoes, plays chess, does the accounts, minds the children . . . and similar tasks. . . . [W]e would be justified in saying that it did something intelligently, or perhaps stupidly. . . . [I]t might be said to act over-hastily, without thinking hard enough. Such attributions – adverbial comments on the manner of performance – would not be anthropomorphic. We can make *literal* attributions of many psychological states to it. . . . [C]ertain predicates hitherto restricted to humans . . . may be true of sophisticated computers also.

[T]he ego . . . is no more 'human' than our advanced robot – indeed, far less . . . [since] it shares far fewer predicates with us than does the robot. The id and superego are even more restricted in scope. . . . Yet they are capable of some

---

[4] Kathleen Wilkes, 'Anthropomorphism and Analogy in Psychology', *Philosophical Quarterly*, **25**, 99 (1975), 133.

highly complex tasks. . . . The inference . . . is . . . that . . . such predications [are] completely *literal* (p. 135).

Wilkes repeatedly underscores literalness. Apparently, then, she believes that theorists like Freud are not merely using 'anthropomorphic metaphor'. At any rate, she does say it 'is not illegitimate but irreducible anthropomorphization' to describe something inside us (or our brain) as 'suppressing id-impulses'. This entails that such descriptions *are* anthropomorphic — literally and not metaphorically. Yet when she introduces her 'sophisticated' — but I hope not jaded — robot, she declares that her comments on its 'manner of performance' are 'not . . . anthropomorphic' after all. So we have a choice. We can interpret Wilkes's counter-argument as *either* an attempt to legitimate anthropomorphization, *or* an attempt to prove that we are not really anthropomorphizing — not even metaphorically — when we say of an ego, a neurone system or a machine that it represses, censors, retrieves information, washes the dishes, plans and follows a strategy, wins, loses — and thereby acts intelligently, stupidly or over-hastily.

For my purposes, it scarcely matters how you read Wilkes, or how you define anthropomorphization. I believe Wilkes might agree with me on the essential point. We do speak quite 'literally' of secret policemen repressing dissidents; of bureaucrats censoring the newspapers; of historians retrieving documents; of girl scouts washing their mess gear; of a chess master devising and sticking to his plan, triumphing, conceding defeat — and doing so astutely, unwisely or prematurely. If any descriptions are anthropomorphic, these are. Presumably if we go on and give 'literal' reports, using the same verbs and adverbs, of what an ego, a neurone system, or a machine is up to, these verbs and adverbs retain the same 'literal' meaning. Whether or not you choose to say that our descriptions of ego, neurone or machine behaviour are anthropomorphic, you have to admit that they put the antics of policemen, bureaucrats, historians, girl scouts, chess masters, egos, neurones and machines into the same respective categories. We are ascribing the same behaviour to a human agent and to his or her counterpart.

Apparently Wilkes is untroubled by the discrepancy that has interested me since section 5. We can say many *other* things of the human agent which we cannot intelligibly say of his or her counterpart. My reviews of the Freudian scenario for hysterical symptoms and dreams had enough examples. Why does our ego find certain ideas 'objectionable', and therefore repress them? A human censor might either take pride in his work, or simply do it because the job offers high pay and retirement benefits; but how could an ego or a mechanical device be thus motivated?

Do Wilkes's computers play chess for the prize money or renown they will get – or only because the game fascinates them? Are they squeamish about cheating in order to win? Are they sore losers? Do they slip into despondency when they are behind? Do they go out of their way to humiliate opponents? I gather that Wilkes has no more inclination than I do to answer these otherwise appropriate questions. I am strongly inclined to reason that since you can answer inquiries of this type when you relate the carryings-on of paradigmatic agents – human beings – your verbs and adverbs must not mean what they do in those cases. Wilkes's counter-argument is largely negative: such characterizations 'are *not* metaphorical'; 'there is no need and no justification for insulating the verb in raised eyebrow quotes'; 'the ego.. . . is no more "human" than our advanced robot'. We are never told what the verbs and adverbs do or could mean. Hence my conclusion that as things stand, these delightful animistic stories of our mental life are incoherent.

To corroborate and amplify my misgivings toward animism, I shall devote the final two sections of this study to puzzles about the Freudian notions of consciousness and the unconscious. My immediate question will be:

9. *Can there be multiple centres of consciousness within us?* We have accumulated riddles about consciousness. For example, we noticed (in section 4) that Freud called a system of permeable neurones 'consciousness', and we considered the honorific title unwarranted. We struggled to make sense of Freud's doctrine that in hysteria, your 'charged' memory of a traumatic event gets pushed away from your consciousness (section 5). When we examined Freud's anthropomorphic model of dreaming (section 6), we saw no way to avoid saying that our ego is, or is not, endowed with waking consciousness while we dream. From our attempts to learn more about the agencies within us whose struggles create or disguise our dreams, and produce neurotic symptoms (section 7), we can derive another untoward result: We must distinguish our own consciousness from that of our alert or drowsy ego. For doesn't our ego consciously repress ideas? And how can it do so without being conscious of those which are dangerously erotic? Since our consciousness fails to register the harmful ideas and our ego's repressive behaviour, it follows that there are two separate arenas of consciousness within us – our ego's and our own. This *may* not be an unintelligible doctrine. Let's test it.

Freud briefly took over a 'multiple centres' view from Charcot, and beginning in 1892 wrote of an hysteric's 'second consciousness' (1940d [1892], I, 153; 1893a, II, 15; 1893h, III, 39). Later Freud objected to this view on methodological grounds. He vigorously rejected the argument that 'instead of subscribing to the hypothesis of unconscious ideas of which we know nothing, we had better assume that consciousness can be split up, so that certain ideas or other psychical acts may constitute a consciousness apart' (1912g, XII, 263). He condemned this proposal as

a gratuitous assumption, based on abuse of the word 'conscious'. We have no right to extend the meaning of this word . . . to . . . include a [second] consciousness of which its owner himself is not aware. If philosophers find difficulty in accepting . . . unconscious ideas . . . an unconscious consciousness seems to me even more objectionable. The cases described as splitting of consciousness . . . might better be denoted as shifting of consciousness between two different psychical complexes which become conscious and unconscious in alternation (ibid.; see 1915e, XIV, 170; 1925d, XX, 3).

Perhaps; but Freud's theories hardly conform to this rule. Turn back to his statements about dreaming which I quoted in section 6. Statements (i)–(v) and (vii)–(ix) all record activities which demand conscious mini-agents – at least two opponents, really – of whose machinations the dreamer himself is ignorant. Here and elsewhere, animistic theories inevitably saddle us with one or more 'consciousness of which its owner himself is not aware'.

Are there good reasons why Freud should allow but one consciousness per individual? He remarks that 'the assumption of consciousness' in a person other than oneself 'rests upon an inference and cannot share the direct certainty we have of our own consciousness' (1915e, XIV, 169). For the sake of argument, I shall accept Freud's inferential account of our knowledge of the other minds. Then I would ask whether it is any more dubious to suppose that other centres of consciousness exist within me, than to suppose they exist within other people.

My non-Freudian reply is that the cases are radically different. It makes sense to describe various procedures for identifying other people, deciding whether they are awake, and determining what they feel, think, fear, want, or intend to be doing. I can perceptually discriminate the body of another person. I can watch his facial expression and his gestures, both of which often convey his moods, wishes and intentions. Above all, he can verbally disclose his mental state; he can tell us – candidly, or perhaps exaggerating, understating or distorting – whatever he believes, feels and wants. We can meaningfully explain how we draw an 'inference' of this type, how it may go wrong, how we could double-check and rectify our mistakes. If you feel comfortable with jargon, you could say that this is part of our language game of inferring another person's consciousness.

If there were other centres of consciousness within me besides my own consciousness, they could not possibly have a role in these proceedings, these 'inference' language games. My ego, id, superego, neurone systems, and so on have a kind of body, I suppose, but it is nonsense to speak of their faces and limbs, their facial expressions and their gestures – their grins, frowns, blushes, shrugs. They have no voices, and consequently it is unintelligible to describe them as telling me their state of mind – or keeping it secret from me. When my psychoanalyst learns about the agencies he thinks I shelter, he or she cannot dispense with my consciousness. He must listen to *me* report or misreport my dreams and free-associate about them. So we have an additional reason against postulating egos and similar agencies within us: they must have their own consciousness, and we are unable to make sense of that implication.

In fact I believe there are deeply interesting general difficulties of a similar kind about consciousness and the unconscious. I think a key question is:

10. *What is it for an idea to be 'in' our consciousness or unconscious?* The doctrines I want to examine here seem largely animistic. The simplest account Freud gives is perceptual. He likens the presence of an idea before our consciousness with our 'perception of the outside world through the sense organs' (1915e, XIV, 171). Now I would admit some parallel between our awareness of happenings inside our bodies – digestion or indigestion, for example – and our tactile, auditory and other methods of perceiving the extra-somatic world. We can speak meaningfully of unawareness, inaccuracy and downright error in both cases. Not so with our ideas. What would it be like for us to misperceive or to overlook an idea? Until such details are explained, I would shelve Freud's perceptual model of ideas being in consciousness – or the unconscious.

Freud also proposes what I would call an 'attention' theory. He writes:

Becoming conscious is connected with the application of ... attention ... which, as it seems, is only available in a specific quantity, and this may have been diverted from the train of thought in question on to some other purpose. ... If ... we come upon an idea which will not bear criticism, we break off: We drop the cathexis of attention. ... [But] the train of thought ... can continue to spin itself out without attention being turned to it again, unless ... it reaches a specially high degree of intensity which forces attention to it (1900a, V, 593f.).

This doctrine is vulnerable to 'Who?' questions and also the charge of multiplying centres of consciousness within each person. For instance: Who directs attention to the ideas and trains of thought which run through our mind? Do we focus and shift our attention, or does a mini-agency have this job? Is the aiming done consciously by us or the agency? Who continues thinking our unattended train of thought? Is it perhaps not entertained by any agency – including ourselves – when our attention leaves it? Yet how could it reach 'a specially high degree of intensity' while there is no one attending to it whom it bothers intensely? If we were talking literally of people and any of the countless things they attend to – expectant mothers and their labour pains, machinists and their lathes – questions of this form would be answerable. Here all replies sound bizarre.

I would derive a third and last theory of ideas-in-consciousness from an attempt of Freud's to characterize 'preconscious' ideas. According to Freud, their peculiarity is that they are

brought into connection with word presentations . . .

These word presentations are residues of memories; they were at one time perceptions. . . . [O]nly something which has been a *Cs.* [conscious] perception can become conscious, and . . . anything arising from within (apart from feelings) that seeks to become conscious must try to transform itself into external perceptions: this becomes possible by means of memory traces . . .

The part played by word presentations now becomes perfectly clear. By their interposition internal thought-processes are made into perceptions. . . . When a hyper-cathexis [intensification, excitation] of the process of thinking takes place, thoughts are *actually* perceived – as if they came from without – and are consequently held to be true (1923b, XIX, 20–3; see 1915e, XIV, 201).

Again we will elicit nonsense if we try to identify the actors, and decide whether their consciousness is distinct from that of the person in whom these high jinks take place. Even if it made sense to say 'thoughts are . . . perceived', I would doubt, as a matter of humble fact, that such thoughts 'are . . . held to be true'.

We have not attained much clarity about ideas and thoughts which are in our consciousness. So, although Freud's notion of unconscious mental events is daring and original, we should expect to have analogous difficulties with it. We should be particularly hesitant to say, without preliminary questioning, that certain ideas and instincts are 'before' or 'in' our unconscious.

We should start with Freud's explanations. Mostly he seems to rebut objections of principle against his notion of the unconscious. He seldom attempts to spell out what it means to assert that there are ideas and various other mental goings-on in our mind which we are not aware of. The nearest he comes to furnishing a positive argument for his assumption is when he discusses one of Bernheim's experiments with hypnosis. Freud reports that the hypnotized subject

was ordered to execute a certain action at a . . . fixed moment after his awakening. . . . He awakes . . . [with] no recollection of his hypnotic state, and yet at the pre-arranged moment there rushes into his mind the impulse to do such and such a thing, and he does it consciously, though not knowing why. It seems impossible to give any other description of the phenomenon than to say that the order had been present in the mind of the person in a condition of latency, or had been present unconsciously, until the given moment came . . . (1912g, XII, 261).

Freud also proposes a more 'dynamic view of the phenomenon':

this idea became *active*. . . . The real stimulus to the action being the order . . . it is hard not to concede that the idea of the physician's order became active too. Yet this idea did not reveal itself to consciousness . . . it remained unconscious, and so it was *active and unconscious* at the same time (ibid.; see 1940b, XXIII, 285).

What does Freud's preferred 'description', and especially his 'dynamic view', amount to here? Could Freud mean that the *subject* of this experiment was thinking of Bernheim's order in between times? No, because Freud says the man was unaware that he had received it until a corresponding 'impulse' flooded his consciousness. Is Freud claiming that part of the subject's mind – for instance, the receptacle for unconscious ideas – was pondering Bernheim's command? If so, Freud would have to deal with awkward 'Who?' questions, and also postulate another centre of awareness within the subject. We already noticed this kind of difficulty in Freud's 'attention' theory of conscious ideas, when he said that a 'train of thought . . . can continue to spin itself out without attention being turned to it'. Our puzzlement should not diminish because now we are talking about unconscious ideas. What could we mean if we supposed that they unfold or persist, although neither the person in whom they occur, nor any agency within him – his id, his unconscious, his repressive ego – takes note of them? Surely the unconscious idea resulting from the hypnotist's order did not contemplate itself!

Defenders of Freud may retort that neither the subject nor any part of him must dwell upon the hypnotically induced idea: it is simply laid up within his psyche, but outside the range of his consciousness 'until the given moment'. I would ask for clarification of the spatial metaphor 'outside', and probably I would be told that it means simply 'not apprehended by the conscious mind' (1915e, XIV, 161). Now Freudians might attempt to enrich this 'warehouse' theory by adding that the hypnotist's command has left a 'permanent trace' in our unconscious (see 1925a, XIX, 230). But I would remain perplexed, for three reasons:

(i) The 'storage room' theory of unconscious ideas has an irreducibly negative ring. This is especially troublesome because we just drew a blank when we tried to make sense of Freud's positive-sounding notion, 'apprehended [perceived] by the conscious mind'.

(ii) The 'permanent trace' proviso helps very little – and certainly will not distinguish between conscious and unconscious ideas, since both could mark our unconscious.

(iii) A negative characterization of unconscious ideas – as 'not apprehended by the conscious mind' – with or without a 'permanent trace' clause, furnishes no support to Freud's highly original 'dynamic' hypothesis that some of our ideas may be *active and unconscious at the same time*'. Why suppose that an idea which 'does not reveal itself to consciousness' will be active? Scars, bruises and similar traces often have no 'dynamic' effect on us, even though we are not consciously aware that they exist.

So much for the attempt to illustrate how hypnotically induced ideas are in our unconscious. I am equally unimpressed by Freud's appeal to our capacity for calling up ideas we have not been conscious of in quite a while. He argues: 'When all our latent memories are taken into consideration, it becomes totally incomprehensible how the existence of the unconscious can be denied' (1915e, XIV, 167). No doubt human powers of recollection are mystifying, and we need some explanation of them. But will we do anything more than compound our bafflement if we account for these powers by means of an unintelligible 'active' theory, or an intolerably vague 'storage' doctrine?

Freudians may protest: 'How else can we explain our abilities, and sometimes peculiar inabilities to remember, our post-hypnotic behaviour – as well as our dreams, free associations, parapraxes and neurotic symptoms – unless we assume the presence of more ideas in us than we are conscious of?' Yet this 'How else?' begs the very question we have just been debating – what it means to say that unconscious ideas are present in us. Besides, nonsense explains nothing.

Generally, we have noticed that both Freud's mechanistic and anthropomorphic stories of our mental life require the existence of things within us of which we are not aware: streams of energy, high-voltage ideas, pressing instincts, battling agencies. In order to explain people's conflict behaviour as a clash of inanimate forces, or of contentious actors within the mental arena, Freud must find room for more than what appears in our stream of consciousness. However, he fails to elucidate what it is for mental goings-on to be in our consciousness or elsewhere – presumably in our unconscious. Since all of his explanatory schemes depend on this distinction, they would be premature even if they were both relevant and coherent. But in spite of these problems, I remain convinced that Freud's models of the mind, its component forces and their interplay, are extraordinarily novel and suggestive. They help us take unorthodox and fruitful perspectives toward aberrant as well as 'normal' human conduct.

The difficulties we have spotlighted should encourage us to repair and refine Freud's theories, as well as to pursue alternatives which are as bold and wide-ranging. Finally, any post-Freudian account of what goes on in a person must come to terms with the provocative data which he brought to our attention, and his ingenious attempts to explain them.

16

Motivated irrationality, Freudian theory and cognitive dissonance

DAVID PEARS

I Freudian theory and the philosophical problem

The kind of motivated irrationality that has attracted most attention from philosophers has been irrationality exhibited in a restrictive context. For example, someone has reasons for judging a particular course of action best and yet he yields to the temptation to do something else. If he yields intentionally and freely, this counts as *akrasia* (not being in command of oneself).[1] There is also another type of example much discussed recently by philosophers. Someone has reasons for forming a particular belief and yet under the influence of a wish he forms a different belief. That is self-deception or, at least, wishful thinking. Both these types of irrationality, one affecting action and the other belief-formation, occur in restrictive contexts. At one moment the subject stands equipped with certain beliefs about fact or value which put a constraint on the move that he is about to make and at the next moment he goes against them. The interest of such cases is that they are dramatic, unmistakable defeats of reason. The demands of reason are clearly identified and yet they are definitely rejected.

Freud's study of errors[2] overlaps the philosophical investigation of *akrasia* and self-deception. However, he is more interested in the culprit than in the precise nature of its victim. The culprit is, of course, a wish or desire, but the victim is not always a rational requirement which is dramatically flouted. True, the fault will sometimes be saying the opposite of what one has good reason to say, or believing the opposite of what one has good reason to believe. But Freud includes many examples of merely saying or believing what one has no good reason to say or believe. Also, his catalogue of errors includes forgetting and misreading and even if these count as actions, they are neither done for reasons nor analysable in quite the same way as self-deception or wishful thinking. So

---

[1] Aristotle compares the *akratic* agent to a city which passes good laws but does not enforce them (*Nicomachean Ethics* VII, 10).

[2] Parapraxes. See 1916–17, XV 25–79 and 1901b passim.

the overlap between Freud's study of errors and the philosophical investigation of motivated irrationality is only partial.

Freud's interest in the rebellious wish also leads to another, much greater difference between his results and the theories of motivated irrationality put forward by philosophers. They are concerned to show that a certain type of event, the direct flouting of reason, can occur in spite of its paradoxical character, or, at least, can occur in specifiable, favourable circumstances, and they do not say much about its cause, which strikes them as being very close to the surface, if not obvious. He investigates the deeper causes of a wider class of events which includes not only errors but also dreams and neurotic symptoms.

Let us look more closely at this difference. Naturally, philosophers choose examples where the culprit is a rebellious wish, but it is usually one that is easily identified by the subject. Someone who takes too many drinks at a party against his own better judgment before driving home will know perfectly well that he does it for pleasure and that desire is hardly likely to be the proxy of some other deeply repressed desire. No doubt there are examples in which the rebellious desire is a proxy but philosophers avoid them because they prefer examples of *akrasia* in which the rebellious desire wears its true colours both when it is defeated in deliberation and immediately afterwards when it emerges victorious in action. The conflict with reason is more open in such cases and its outcome more dramatic. In the other type of motivated irrationality, self-deception, the rebellious wish may not be so easily identified by the subject, because he may be ashamed to admit its existence to himself and, even if he is aware of its existence, he will be unlikely to be aware of its operation, because a wish is not the right kind of cause for a belief.[3]

Freud's interest in the rebellious wish goes much deeper. In the examples chosen by philosophers he would say that when it is not actually conscious, it is seldom unconscious (repressed and inadmissible to consciousness) but usually only preconscious (temporarily excluded from consciousness).[4] In most of the cases with which he is concerned it is unconscious, because it was repressed in infancy and thereafter only its proxies are admissible to consciousness. So not only is there not much overlap between his field of study and the field chosen by philosophers, but also, more important, the angle of his approach is different from theirs. It is like the difference between inquiring why some well con-

[3] Freud makes use of this distinction between lack of awareness of a wish and lack of awareness of its operation both when he is explaining slips of the tongue (1916–17, XV 64–5) and when he is explaining obsessional symptoms (XVI 282–3).

[4] ibid. 295–6, cf 1900a V 614–15 and 1940a [1938] XXIII 159–60.

structed buildings succumb to earth tremors and investigating the causes of earthquakes.

Nevertheless, there are certain elements common to Freudian theory and philosophical explanations of motivated irrationality. One such element is what Freud called 'dynamism'. Motivated irrationality, as its name implies, is caused by a wish or desire and so too are the deeper structures postulated by Freud. It is, therefore, interesting to inquire how the causation works and how it is related to the ordinary causation of rational action and belief-formation.

II The paradoxes

The philosophical investigation of motivated irrationality has concentrated on its paradoxes. How can anyone act against his own better judgment or form a belief against the total weight of the evidence available to himself? These two achievements are paradoxical only when they are intentional and free. The paradox would be removed if the subject were hypnotized or if he failed to appreciate the impact of his reasons on his choice, but, if it is not removed, it is very strong. It seemed to Socrates and to a long line of subsequent philosophers that, when the grip of reason has closed on a subject's mind, he can no longer evade it freely and knowingly.

This paradox is deeply rooted in the nature of reasoning. There is also a second paradox which at first sight seems more superficial. How can anyone deceive himself that such and such is the case given that deception requires him to maintain the opposite belief? This paradox does not affect *akrasia* but only wishful belief-formation. It looks superficial because it seems to depend on the gratuitious choice of a name. If the name 'self-deception' has a self-contradictory connotation, it would be better not to apply it to wishful belief-formation. Then the first paradox would still remain, because the belief would be formed freely and knowingly against the weight of the evidence available to the subject, but the second, purely verbal paradox would have been dispelled.

However, it may be that the second paradox is not purely verbal. For when we are most strongly inclined to use the name 'self-deception' there is a reason for our inclination. The tempting cases are those in which the wish to believe seems to be using a strategy in order to achieve its object. For example, the subject goes out of his way to avoid situations in which he might get evidence against the belief and seeks out situations of the opposite kind, or perhaps he behaves as if he already had the belief. 'Acting as if' is well known to be a good way of acquiring a belief or, at least, fortifying it. For a belief is stimulated by an action that needs rationalization, especially when the agent continues to invest in its truth.[5] These three types of behaviour seem to indicate some appreciation of the existence and strength of the evidence against the belief and they might even be taken to indicate the presence of the opposite belief and possibly some awareness of its presence.

There is a real distinction here. It can be admitted that a wish sometimes causes a belief without more ado. Those would be cases of mere wishful thinking. But there is also a different class of cases in which the wish to believe seems to adopt a strategy which may even be quite complex. It is to this class of cases that we are most inclined to apply the name 'self-deception' and our inclination marks a real difference in the nature of things. However, this difference is connected with the first paradox. For the distinguishing mark of this class of cases is seldom so strong as a clear indication of the presence of the opposite belief and, if we take the indication in a wider sense, what is indicated will be an appreciation of the evidence against the desired belief, which is precisely what generated the first paradox. So the first paradox is the more radical one.

III   The divided mind

Familiarity with Freudian theory is scarcely needed to suggest the question whether the first paradox forces us to conclude that the mind is in some way divided. But in what way? Since we are starting from cases of *akrasia* and self-deception or wishful thinking, we may follow Freud and use as a base those contents of the subject's mind of which he is aware at the time of his action or belief-formation. It is obvious that his mind will also contain much of which he is not aware at that time. His earlier and later history and plausible assumptions of continuity leave us in no doubt on that point. Let us say that those other contents are in 'the reservoir' (either in the preconscious or the unconscious mind). But should we use the simple principles of division that these facts suggest when we are trying to explain motivated irrationality, or should we use some more complex principle?

If we used the simple principle, the reservoir would include among its contents things temporarily forgotten without any motive. However, what was explained by mere forgetfulness would not be motivated irrationality. Such a fault would be purely intellectual, like lack of

---

[5] Theories of cognitive dissonance deal with this phenomenon. See below, pt. VI of this paper.

intelligence, which might prevent a subject from appreciating his evidence (except that in that case nothing needs to be attributed to the reservoir). In general, motivated irrationality is the outcome of conflict and the fault must be caused by one of the conflicting desires. So in the special case in which the fault results from the temporary unavailability to consciousness of something in the reservoir, the unavailability must be caused by a desire.

This requirement makes the principle of division dynamic.[6] We start with a conflict between two desires in the subject, perhaps his general desire for truth and a malicious desire to believe that someone whom he dislikes has done something disgraceful. Then it is likely that the malicious desire would be forced into the reservoir (preconsciousness) by the subject's desire to think well of himself, or, if not, that it would at least force its own operation into the reservoir. For how could he admit to himself that his counter-evidential belief had merely been produced by a wish without immediately undermining it?

Perhaps this example does not compel us to invoke the theory of the divided mind, but it certainly makes it natural to do so. It is worth observing that, if it did compel us to invoke it, the compulsion would not come from the sheer impossibility of the subject's forming the counter-evidential belief. There would be sheer impossibility only if the evidence was taken by the subject to entail the unwanted belief, but we may suppose that in this case it allows him some latitude.[7] So if we were compelled to invoke the theory of the divided mind to explain what happens in this example, that would be for a different reason: wishful thinking has to conceal its own origin.[8]

The point of the example is that it illustrates the most economical form of the hypothesis of the divided mind. There must be two conflicting desires which set up rival centres of activity. However, this in itself is not an explanatory hypothesis, but only part of the phenomenon to be explained. For the question posed by the first paradox was 'How can the subject's desire to believe in the other man's disgraceful action succeed in the teeth of the evidence available to him?' and this question presupposes that he has a general, overriding desire for truth. We do not begin to answer this question until we suggest that the desire that would normally be overridden might emerge victorious if it operated from the reservoir. Therefore, the hypothesis is that, if it has not been put in the reservoir by

[6] See: 1916–17 XV 65–7 and 1940a [1938] XXIII 160–1.

[7] D. Davidson exploits this kind of latitude in his theory of *akrasia*. See 'How is weakness of the will possible?' in *Moral Concepts*, ed. J. Feinberg (Oxford, 1967).

[8] H. Fingarette says that self-deception is a self-covering policy. See *Self-Deception* (London, 1969), p. 49.

another desire, it will, at least, put its own operation in the reservoir with this end in view.

There is then one centre of activity in the subject's contemporary consciousness and another in the reservoir (in this example probably in preconsciousness). We have to suppose that each of these two centres includes any information needed to give its desire a line of action. The centre in the reservoir produces actions which have two peculiarities. First, at least one of the two normal features of motivation is banished from the subject's contemporary consciousness. It might be the existence of the operative desire that is banished, or it might only be its operation. Secondly, the banishing agency is always a desire, in the first case another desire and in the second case the operative desire itself.

This extremely economical hypothesis is based on Freud's fundamental concept of a boundary dividing the conscious from the preconscious and the unconscious, and it includes the dynamism that was always essential to his theory but became more prominent in his later work. However, in comparison with his fully developed theory, it is a minimal hypothesis.

Freud pictures the reservoir as a single pool of ideas and affects, or, more strictly, as two pools, the preconscious and the unconscious, standing behind the continuous stream of consciousness and feeding it in a carefully controlled way. The minimal hypothesis only uses one or two things in the reservoir to explain each piece of motivated irrationality. The idea is that on a particular occasion a wish forms a rival centre of activity when either it or its operation is confined to the reservoir, but that, even when that has happened, it can still interact with whatever information gives it its line of action. This does not mean that the information has to be confined to the reservoir. It may be common to both centres of activity and, since no topography is implied, there is no suggestion that it has to be registered twice.[9] An element belongs to a centre of activity if and only if it interacts with the wish that is its nucleus. The criterion of grouping is simply functional and the groups of elements may be pictured as overlapping circles. It follows that there is no need to take a particular subject's successive centres of activity in the reservoir and treat them as a unity. True, the elements of the successive centres may interact with one another, but the immediate explanation of the successive pieces of irrationality does not require us to assume that they do.

This contrast does not indicate any incompatibility, but only a

---

[9] R. Wollheim discusses Freud's ideas about double registration. See *Freud* (London, 1971), pp. 167–72. See 1915e XIV 174–5. Cf. Ricoeur, *Freud and Philosophy*, trans. Denis Savage. (New Haven and London, 1970), pp. 120–1.

different interest and a different approach. If we merely want immediate explanations of particular pieces of motivated irrationality, the most economical hypothesis will give fewer hostages to fortune, and so we concentrate on the moment of irrationality and use the concept of a momentary reservoir. However, Freud needed an aetiology of symptoms that would trace them back to their origin in infancy and so his conception of the reservoir is historical. Each stage in the development of the subject has laid down its sediment and later disturbances throw up material from these strata. Which stratum is chosen will depend on the nature of the disturbance and nearly always the material will be heavily disguised. This is a theory that evidently requires far more resources than the minimal hypothesis. The unconscious is a unity developing through time in ways that need to be discovered and codified.

IV   Explanations of motivated irrationality

The first of the two paradoxes affects both types of motivated irrationality. It is hard to see how the subject can either act or form a belief freely and consciously against his own better judgment. This difficulty may make it necessary to suppose that other elements are confined to the reservoir besides the rebellious wish and its operation. For if conscious irrationality really is impossible there may be some feature of what the subject does that will have to be kept out of consciousness.

This possibility needs to be considered not only in cases of self-deception or wishful thinking but also in cases of *akrasia*. For the problem is located in what is done. It is therefore distinct from (though it overlaps with) the problem of motivation, which would be solved by the suggestion that the wish, or at least its operation, is confined to the reservoir. The acute form of that problem is peculiar to self-deception and wishful thinking. A belief tends to be undermined by the knowledge that it is caused by a wish because a wish is the the wrong kind of cause for a belief. It is, therefore, likely that in such cases the wish will keep itself, or at least its own operation, out of consciousness. *Akrasia* does not present this problem in such an acute form. There is no general reason why the motivation of *akratic* actions should be kept out of consciousness, though, no doubt, it sometimes is kept out.

Anyone who sets out to give an account of motivated irrationality will find that he has to explore a labyrinth of different possibilities. The guiding thread that I shall use is the question, 'When are we forced to invoke the minimal hypothesis of the divided mind?' I do not think that we are really forced to invoke it in all cases of wishful thinking because it is always possible, however unlikely, that the subject should realize that the balance of his judgment has been tipped by a wish that he can identify and yet that it should remain tipped that way. The cases that seem to force us to invoke the hypothesis are those in which what is achieved could not be achieved consciously. Or, to put the point in another way, they are those which present the first paradox in its most extreme form.

It is easy to identify some cases of this kind. No sane person can consciously adopt a self-contradictory belief or one that yields a contradiction when it is conjoined with evidence that he has accepted. Of course, such achievements are possible when the stipulation of consciousness is dropped, but, when it is retained, they are not possible. Moreover, he can consciously adopt a self-contradictory belief without realizing that it is self-contradictory because it is, in general, beyond his competence to recognize that type of contradiction. But when we have excluded that possibility, we really do seem to be forced to conclude that the contradiction was kept out of consciousness, and if the thinking was wishful, it would be natural to assume that it was kept out by the wish.

These cases should be contrasted with cases which allow the subject some latitude. When his irrationality does not involve him in self-contradiction, he may embark on it consciously. For example, he may judge that it is all right for him to continue smoking in spite of the fact that all his evidence points the other way. Or, to take a purely theoretical example, he may not believe the bad news contained in a telegram, in spite of the fact that all his evidence points to the reliability of the source. These examples raise an interesting question of detail about the wishful thought. Will it ever be the positive value-judgment that it is good for him to continue smoking, or the definite belief that the message is false? But the main point, that where there is latitude we are not forced to invoke the divided mind, is perfectly clear.[10]

Things become more difficult when we ask if there are any other types of case that force us to adopt this explanation. It is a surprising fact that many philosophers have maintained that we are forced to adopt it in all cases of free and conscious *akrasia* in which the subject really accepts the values on which his deliberation is based. Their idea is that, if he accepts the proposition that on balance the considerations available to him support the judgment that it is best to do a certain action, for example, to refuse a cigarette when he is trying to give up smoking, then, if he freely and intentionally takes it, he cannot possibly have judged it best to refuse it. They maintain that in such a case the fault cannot possibly be located between the judgment that it is best to refuse the cigarette and the act of

---

[10] D. Davidson makes good use of this point in 'How is weakness of the will possible?'

taking it and must, therefore, be located between the preceding proposition and the judgment that it is best to take it, or, at least, all right to take it. On this view the fault will always be intellectual, a piece of self-deception, but not, of course, purely intellectual, because it will be caused not by stupidity, but by the rebellious desire for the pleasure of smoking the cigarette.[11]

Two distinct arguments have been used in support of this thesis. One is that it is impossible to judge it best not to do an action and yet to do it freely and intentionally.[12] The other is that it is impossible to do an action freely and intentionally without judging it best to do it.[13] Both arguments are of dubious validity. The second seems to give the wrong answer to the question of detail posed above. For even if this kind of *akrasia* has to be caused by self-deception, it is surely a mistake to suppose that the agent always has to go so far as to persuade himself that it is best to do the action.[14] More generally, it does not seem necessary to suppose that there is always some self-deceptive bias in the agent's final value-judgment. The action itself neither is nor implies a value-judgment and experience confirms that the desire that produces it simply does not have to be filtered through any value-judgment, favourable or permissive. The first argument is equally questionable. In real life, when the rebellious desire wins, we do not immediately conclude that the agent could not have really judged it best to abstain. There are other possibilities to be considered.[15]

This controversy turns on the nature of the mismatch that would occur between the final value-judgment and the action. Obviously, it would be irrational to take the cigarette while judging it best to refuse it. But would it be a case of conscious self-contradiction? Anyone who doubts the validity of the second argument will be inclined to give a negative answer to this question. Would it then be some other kind of logically impossible achievement? Anyone who doubts the validity of the first argument will be inclined to answer that question too in the negative. If both questions are given negative answers, mismatch between final value-judgment and action may well be a real possibility. Somehow or other the centre set up by the rebellious desire achieves independent access to action without the screen of any intellectual fault.[16] It may just

[11] D. Davidson takes this line, ibid.

[12] R. Hare uses this argument in *The Language of Morals* (Oxford, 1952) pp. 19–20 and pp. 168–70 and in *Freedom and Reason* (Oxford, 1963), ch. 5.

[13] D. Davidson relies mainly on this argument, 'How is weakness of the will possible?'

[14] As D. Davidson supposes, ibid.

[15] See P. Gardiner, 'On assenting to a moral principle', *Proceedings of the Aristotelian Society* 60, (1954–5).

[16] This seems to be the line taken by Aristotle in *Eudemian Ethics* II. 8.

be a philosophical prejudice that the will cannot be split in this way without any limitation of consciousness.

Whatever the solution of this problem, there is no doubt that we are forced to invoke the minimal theory of the divided mind in order to explain the formation of an irrational belief without latitude. We are then free to consider the extension of the theory to other cases and to apply it when the evidence supports its application. So the first paradox has a useful function to perform. It obliges us to accept a theory which is resisted by those who have an exaggerated belief in the unity of the mind, and yet, ironically, it may be that it is applied too extensively by those who have an exaggerated belief in the unity of the will.

V Sartre's criticism of Freud

In *l'Être et le Néant*[17] Sartre argues that the second paradox shows that self-deception is impossible, and that the obstacle is not removed by the suggestion that the deceiving agency is in the unconscious (or, to generalize his argument, in the reservoir). The paradox arises from the requirement that throughout the time that the subject is acquiring the desired belief he must maintain the opposite belief. This can be taken as a trivial consequence of the gratuitous choice of the name 'Self-deception', but it is more interesting to take it as an extension of the first paradox, which arises in all cases of motivated counter-evidental belief-formation, whether they are classified as self-deception or as mere wishful thinking. The point would be that we tend to reserve the name 'Self-deception' for cases in which the deceiving agency seems to adopt a complex strategy and that in such cases it is plausible to credit it with some appreciation of the existence and strength of the evidence against the desired belief, and perhaps even with the opposite belief. This construal of the second paradox connects it with the first one and makes Sartre's criticism more interesting, because it gives it a less arbitrary target.

Sartre's argument, that the difficulty is not removed by supposing that the deceiving agency is in the reservoir, is presented as a dilemma. Either the deceiving agency will be aware or unaware of the illegitimacy of the desired belief. If it lacks the awareness, the lack will have to be explained, presumably in the same way that it is explained in consciousness: we shall have to say that the deceiving agency conceals certain facts from itself. But that leads to an infinite regress of deceiving agencies. On the

[17] Trans. H. E. Barnes (New York, 1956), ch. 2, which is reprinted in this volume, pp. 203–11.

other hand, if we say that the deceiving agency is aware of the illegitimacy of the desired belief, the phenomenon of self-deception will remain unexplained. Let it be granted that the deceiving agency only keeps the embarrassing facts out of consciousness. That, however, is not an explanation of self-deception, but simply a redescription of the phenomenon that has to be explained. We still need to be told how two systems, partly independent of one another, manage to coexist in a single person.

It is evident that, if this criticism damages Freud's theory of the unconscious, it will damage the minimal theory of the divided mind to the same extent. We may, therefore, examine its impact on the minimal theory. This theory starts from cases of conflict. The subject has a general desire for truth and, on the other side, perhaps, a malicious desire to believe, against the weight of the evidence available to him, that someone whom he dislikes has done a disgraceful thing. Reason would frustrate the second desire, but in fact it wins and the theory has to explain its victory.

However, the theory does not have to explain the fact that people are often arenas of conflict. That is a datum for any theory. So when Sartre presents the second part of his dilemma, the challenge to the theory is not that it must explain the mere coexistence of the two centres of potential activity, but rather, that it must explain the victory of the one that would be frustrated by reason. The explanation offered is that the two centres are partly independent of one another. But this immediately leads to a second, implied challenge. Can the theory give a credible account of the causes and effects of this partial independence?

It is clear that this is the important question raised by Sartre's criticism of Freud. The first part of his dilemma is uninteresting, because nobody would suggest that the rebellious centre of activity deceives itself in the preconscious or unconscious mind. It is, therefore, best to concentrate on the theory's account of the partial independence of the two systems.

A system is identified by the desire that forms its nucleus and so each of the two systems takes as its nucleus one of the two conflicting desires. If the two systems were not in any way independent of one another, each could produce its effect, the formation of a belief, only after it had interacted fully with the other. So the rebellious system could produce its preferred belief only after it had interacted fully with the general desire for truth. However, that would probably lead to its defeat, because, unless there were latitude, full interaction would give the victory to reason. It follows that, if there is no latitude, the defeat of reason can be explained only by some degree of independence between the two systems. The rebellious wish must have some independent access to belief-formation, so that its force will be able to produce its effect without being transmitted through the other system.

This is the first step in the construction of the theory. The second step is to postulate the minimal degree of independence that is required between the two systems: one of the cognitive features of normal agency must be lacking. Perhaps the existence of the wish, or at least its operation, will be kept out of consciousness. In the example chosen the wish is shameful and may be kept out of consciousness for that reason. In other examples the wish might be let into consciousness but it is unlikely that its operation would be, because that would tend to be inhibiting, to undermine the belief. So, in general, at least the second of these two cognitive features of normal agency is likely to be lacking. The nature of the achievement also imposes a constraint. If there is no latitude, the subject must not know exactly what he is doing, and so a third cognitive feature of normal agency will be lacking.

It is important to note exactly how much this postulate of independence explains. It explains how the rebellious centre of activity might have access to belief-formation, because it removes an obstacle to such access. If the subject were conscious of the existence, operation and precise object of the rebellious wish, its force would have to be transmitted through the other system and then, if there were no latitude, it would be inhibited. The removal of this obstacle makes independent access to belief-formation possible, but it does not explain how wishes actually succeed in causing beliefs. That would be a further step, but it is not the main point of impact of Sartre's criticism.

The main point of the second part of Sartre's dilemma seems to be that the postulated independence itself stands in need of explanation. For it is not enough to be told that this independence exists; we also need to be told what causes it. However, this demand is met by the theory, because it does identify the cause of the independence. The wish to believe puts its own operation or some aspect of its own object out of consciousness and sometimes it is itself put out of consciousness by another wish. That is the dynamism of the theory.

However, it might still be objected that, if the first operation of the wish is to banish something from consciousness, that operation will be conscious. This seems to be an implication of Sartre's criticism. The only possible reply is that the suppression of the consciousness that normally accompanies a particular type of mental event may itself be unconscious without having succumbed to a previous act of suppression. To put the point in another way, suppression can be self-reflexive. So there is only an imperfect analogy with a man putting on a disguise.

The dynamism of Freud's theory exposes it to a dilemma. If the suppressing agency is always a wish, then either there is an infinite regress of suppressing agencies or suppression is self-reflexive. The second option is clearly preferable even if we have no picture of the way in which this self-reflexiveness works.

Sartre's criticism is not very precisely formulated and other interpretations of it are possible, but they are of less interest. For instance, he may have meant that the postulated minimal independence of the two systems does not really explain the defeat of reason. But that would be a mistake. The relation between the two systems is sufficiently like the relation between two minds without being too like it. For the rebellious system includes elements which do not produce any direct reflection of themselves in the main system, and which often cannot even be inferred by it, and that is a feature of the relation between two different minds. On the other hand, the relation between the two systems is not too like the relation between two different minds. For the main system does not feel constrained, accepts the belief-formation as its own and is not aware of any lack of the cognitive features of normal agency.

It may be that one more thread can be discerned in the rather complex texture of Sartre's argument, but it too is of minor interest. His claim, that Freudian theory merely redescribes the phenomenon of self-deception without explaining it, may imply that it is a mere *façon de parler*, unsupported by any evidence besides the phenomenon to be explained. However, there are several ways of rebutting this. In many cases the wish is conscious and its operation may be inferred from the fact that there is no purely intellectual explanation of the formation of the counter-evidential belief. In other cases the wish only disappears temporarily from consciousness and ordinary considerations of continuity suggest that it did not cease to exist in the interval between its disappearance and reappearance.[18] In both kinds of case confirmation is often available from the subject's own admission.[19] There is also another very important piece of evidence in complex cases of self-deception: if the wish were not operating, its stepwise, apparently contrived fulfilment would be an unbelievable coincidence.

VI Underlying structures

The structure of a typical piece of rational deliberation and its normal sequel is, in general, straightforward. A desire meshes with a belief in consciousness to produce a final value-judgment, or perhaps, as in the

[18] See 1916–17, XVI, 277–8.
[19] See 1916–17, XV, 64–5 and XVI, 437.

cases considered earlier, the final value-judgment issues from two beliefs about values. Either way, the final value-judgment is followed by a decision and then, in the normal course of events, by a free intentional action. If the action is not routine, no part of this structure will be banished from consciousness and in certain cases efficiency requires that no part of it should be banished.

One common strategy of self-deception, already mentioned, is to behave as if one already had the desired belief.[20] It is a familiar if surprising fact that such behaviour often stimulates or fortifies the belief on which, in a rational structure, it would be based, and such rationalizations are especially likely when the agent continues to invest in the truth of the belief. The normal flow of causation from belief and desire to action is reversed and the reversal is exploited by this particular strategy of self-deception. Everything proceeds as if the preconscious centre of activity used the information that the reversal often occurs and so, by the functional criterion of grouping, it does possess the information.

There is an interesting parallelism between this strategy and the strategy that Freud attributes to the unconscious in some of his case-histories. He suggests that in certain cases a symptomatic action expresses a belief that the patient wishes to hold in his unconscious. His idea is that it expresses the belief by going proxy for the action that would be based on it in a rational structure, but which could be used to strengthen it in the irrational structure that has just been described. Naturally, this interpretation relies on evidence that the goal of the symptom really is the strengthening of the unconscious belief. The same is true of the suggestion that an ordinary action is preconsciously designed to strengthen a conscious belief. We do not get an example of this strategy of self-deception unless the goal really is to strengthen the belief. If it were the action itself, or one of its ordinary external consequences, any distortion of the belief would have to be interpreted as self-deceptive *akrasia* of the kind described by Davidson.[21]

The parallelism between Freud's diagnosis and the diagnosis of the strategy of self-deception that exploits the irrational structure might be worth exploring. Henceforth I shall call this particular strategy of self-deception 'The recoil strategy'. It is not the same as self-deceptive *akrasia*. In fact it will be necessary to establish a firm distinction between self-deceptive *akrasia* and the two parallel strategies with which I am concerned, the recoil strategy of self-deception and the strategy that

---

[20] This strategy occupies the central place in H. Fingarette's account of self-deception, which is existentialist in its emphasis on commitment. See *Self-Deception*, ch. 4.
[21] D. Davidson, 'How is weakness of the will possible?'

Freud sometimes attributes to the unconscious. This distinction will require an excursion into the theory of cognitive dissonance.

There are really four different cases to be considered. First, there is the normal structure of desire, belief and action in rational deliberation. Then there is self-deceptive *akrasia*, in which a rebellious desire exploits the rational structure by distorting a belief. Finally, there are the two strategies whose parallelism I want to develop, the recoil strategy of self-deception and the strategy that Freud attributes to the unconscious in certain case-histories. Both these strategies exploit the irrational structure.

It might be best to begin with an example of the fourth kind. Freud reports the case history of a lady whose husband had been impotent on their wedding night. He suggests that she had an unconscious wish to stimulate the opposite belief in her unconscious mind. For though she did not simply act as if she believed that he had not been impotent (that would have been the recoil strategy of self-deception), she did obsessively report a routine that went proxy for acting as if she believed that he had not been impotent. The simple action based on the recoil strategy would have been to show her maid the red ink stain that her husband had put on the sheet on their wedding night, but she did not do that; (it was several years later and she was separated from her husband). Instead, she developed an obsessive routine which included ringing for her maid and waiting near a table in such a way that, when the maid entered, she could not fail to see a conspicuous mark on it. It might be thought that the patient's unconscious goal was to keep her husband's impotence secret, but Freud gives further details of the case which, he thinks, prove that it was to produce in her unconscious mind the belief that her husband had not been impotent.[22]

The development of the parallelism between this unconscious strategy and the preconscious recoil strategy of self-deception will require a more detailed examination of the latter, and that, in its turn, will necessitate an excursion into the theory of cognitive dissonance. The excursion into what looks like a different field will help us to establish a firm distinction between both the parallel strategies and ordinary self-deceptive *akrasia*.

It is convenient to begin with this distinction. The fundamental

---

[22] 1916–17, XVI, 261–4. Freud also gives other case-histories which may be understood in this way, but it is often difficult to be sure that the unconscious goal really is the production of the unconscious belief, or that Freud thought that it was. R. Wollheim argues that Dora's unconscious goal was, and was taken by Freud to be the production of an unconscious belief [Her case is given in 1905e, VII, 3–122], and in an interesting discussion of the Rat Man's case he diagnoses and implies that Freud diagnoses the same strategy and the same underlying structure [his case is given in 1909b, X, 155ff.]. See *Freud* (London, 1971), p. 92 and pp. 132–5.

difference between ordinary self-deceptive *akrasia* and the recoil strategy of self-deception has already been mentioned. It is a difference of goal. In the example of self-deceptive *akrasia* used earlier, the goal of the rebellious wish was the pleasure of smoking the cigarette and the point of the self-deception about the balance of values was that it removed an obstacle to the attainment of that goal. So there is a sharp contrast between this kind of case and a case in which the goal is a change of belief about the balance of values. In order to get an example of the latter kind of case, we might suppose that the subject uses the recoil strategy of taking the cigarette in order to change his valuation. However, that would not be a very plausible example and it would be better to take the case of a worker who forces himself to help and support a fellow-worker in order to increase his feeling of loyalty to him.

It is obvious that this strategy exploits a remarkable, but common irrational structure. One usually does something because one has a reason for doing it, but in this kind of case the agent does something in order to give himself what would have been a reason for doing it. The structure exploited by this strategy, though irrational, is a familiar feature of our lives. There is the 'sour grapes' reaction of those who miss something good and what some call the 'sweet lemons' reaction of those who get something bad. This is the territory of cognitive dissonance.

The first step towards a clear distinction between the recoil strategy of self-deception and ordinary self-deceptive *akrasia* has already been taken. The goal of the self-deceptive *akratic* is the action that his rebellious desire facilitates by distorting a belief, but in a case of recoil self-deception the goal is the distorted belief itself. The next step would be to analyse the irrational structure exploited by the recoil strategy and to relate it to the ordinary structure of rational deliberation. That would require a detailed examination of the experiments done in the late fifties and sixties by social psychologists trying to establish a theory of cognitive dissonance. For their experiments were designed to discover the laws governing the kind of irrational structure to which our inquiry has led us and they are difficult to evaluate because they involve some distinctions that lie just below the surface of our investigations.[23] However, it is

---

[23] The idea that these areas are connected and might be covered by a single theory, is not fanciful. See R. Brown, *Social Psychology* (Toronto, 1965), pp. 607–8. His discussion of theories of cognitive dissonance ends with an expression of the hope that some unification might be achieved. 'In Freudian theory, as in Lewin's and Miller's conflict theories, we have a clear antecedent of the present concern with inconsistency, but . . . the antecedent does not make the contemporary development superfluous. Inconsistency theory explores cognitive adjustments and especially attitude changes; conflict theory explores actions of approach and avoidance in both animals and man; Freudian theory explores a range of extreme and sometimes pathological adjustments in both mind and body which occur as

obviously impossible to review all their experimental work in a *coda* to an already lengthy paper. So I shall end with a brief discussion of some of the main issues.

First, we need a description of the type of experiment that has been taken to establish cognitive dissonance, which is, roughly, the jarring relation that holds between beliefs, or between beliefs and actions, when they belong to an irrational sequence. E. Aronson summarizes the results of several experiments designed to explore this relation: 'According to dissonance theory, if a person says something he feels is untrue, he experiences dissonance: the cognition "I said *x*" is dissonant with the cognition "I believe *not-x*".' In order to reduce dissonance, he might attempt to convince himself that what he said was not so very untrue. Thus dissonance theory suggests that advocating an opposite position [*sc.* what one believes] 'increases one's tendency to believe in that position. However, if one is provided with a great deal of justification for advocating an opposite position (for example, if one is paid a great deal of money for telling lies), one experiences less dissonance. That is, if I told a small lie for $53,000, I would have ample justification for having lied: the cognition that I have received $53,000 is consonant with having lied' [*pace* Kant]. 'Consequently, I would have less need to justify my action by convincing myself that I really believed what I had said than if I had been paid a mere 53 cents for lying. This type of prediction has been confirmed by several experiments . . .. These experiments have shown greater attitude change for less reward across a wide range of topics; moreover it has been confirmed across a wide range of rewards . . .. Thus it would appear that this is a sturdy finding.'[24]

This raises many questions, some of which have been taken up by social psychologists and have led to more discriminating experiments designed to provide them with answers. Their main problem was that certain experiments produced the opposite outcome: the attitude change

reactions to intense ambivalence. There is encouragement in this overlap of ideas. There is the promise that psychology will produce something more satisfying than a collection of models for particular problems, that it will find a truly general theory.'

[24] In R. Abelson *et al.* eds., *Theories of Cognitive Dissonance: A Sourcebook* (Chicago, 1968), ch. 1. This kind of result suggests that self-deception might be designed to decrease cognitive dissonance. A. Oksenberg Rorty says that, on the contrary, it increases it. See 'Belief and self-deception', *Inquiry* 15, 387–410. It is, of course, true that in the experiments described by Aronson self-deception increases dissonance between the subject's information about the circumstances of the lie and his minimization of its seriousness. However, the original dissonance between the act of lying and the belief that the lie is a serious one is certainly reduced. The strategy of self-deception in such a case is to reduce the really uncomfortable dissonance by creating a less uncomfortable dissonance, which is, in any case, concealed from the subject, because self-deception is usually a self-covering operation.

turned out not to be inversely proportional to the size of the bribe but directly proportional to it (the so-called 'incentive effect'). Obviously, we do not have a theory of cognitive dissonance until we can predict which type of experimental situation will produce which outcome. No result is sturdy until it is precisely formulated in a way that yields the right predictions. Now my concern is with questions whose answers might help us to understand how the recoil strategy of self-deception differs from ordinary self-deceptive *akrasia* and how it resembles the strategy that Freud imputed to the unconscious in certain case histories. However, a brief review of some of the experiments might settle my questions as well as theirs.

Suppose that everyone in the situation described by Aronson starts with the same scruple about lying and that it is strong enough to prevent them from lying for either of the two bribes without *akrasia*. They are then divided into two groups, one of which is offered the large bribe and the other the small bribe, and everybody tells the lie, but those who receive the small bribe reduce the gap between what they believe and what they said further than those who receive the large bribe. In both cases there is no change in their general scruple about lying, but only self-deceptive minimization of the particular lie. It is, therefore, very imprecise to say that there is a change of attitude.

The first question to ask about this experiment is 'when did the minimization occur?' The answer must be that much of it occurred before the lie was told. So, what we have here is, in large part, ordinary self-deceptive *akrasia*. Everyone lied for money against his own scruple and, even if this should never be done, it is evidently more *akratic* to do it for a small sum than for a large sum. Consequently, those who were going to lie for a small sum needed more self-deceptive minimization of their lies to offset the fact that they would be more *akratic*. The same result could be predicted, and the same explanation could be given in cases in which the *akratic* action went against a maxim of prudence rather than a moral scruple.

Most experimenters claim that this result is surprising until it is seen that dissonance between action and belief had to be reduced. However, that is not quite right. If much of the reducing occurred before the act of lying, what was reduced was the jarring relation between the scruple and a belief about the *prospective* act. True, the reason for the reduction is similar: the bigger the gap between a general policy and a prospective *akratic* action, the more self-deception has to be done by the rebellious desire in order to reduce it and so to facilitate the *akrasia*. However, the reason for the reduction is not the same. For the act has not yet been performed and so what is reduced and in complete self-deceptive *akrasia* eliminated, is the conflict. This point has considerable importance for anyone interested in the connection between cognitive dissonance theory and conflict theory.

The next question to ask about the experiment is 'Does it indicate the presence of the irrational structure in which the normal flow of causation is reversed?' This is a more difficult question to answer. If we do not go beyond the point now reached in the analysis of the experiment, it merely indicates the dynamics of ordinary self-deceptive *akrasia*. At least it does that, whatever else it may do. Now we have seen that ordinary self-deceptive *akrasia* does not involve the irrational structure. All that happens is that the rebellious desire exploits the normal structure by distorting a belief. Consequently, the answer to the question should be that, so far, the experiment does not indicate the presence of the irrational structure. The action has not yet been performed and so there is nothing actual to rationalize.

However, in most experiments of this type the subjects were questioned after they had lied. This opens up the possibility that their minimization of their lies, which had already proceeded a long way prospectively in their deliberations, may have been taken further after their actions. Certainly this is to be expected. The action itself provides a stimulus to rationalization which may well go further than the self-deception that actually produced it. If this is what happens, it brings the irrational structure into the analysis of the experiment for the first time.

There are two ways of discovering whether this additional biasing actually occurs. One way would be to question the subjects just before their actions as well as after them. The other way would be to take cases in which an unforeseen consequence of a subject's choice produces a biasing and to argue that it is quite likely that a similar, but smaller effect is added by an action that was foreseen with all its consequences.

The first of these two methods would be better, because it would provide a direct test of the amount of additional biasing after the action, but I do not know if it has ever been tried. There are obvious practical difficulties. The second method is indirect and it relies on a questionable inference, but it has been tried and the result is worth recording because it raises a crucial question about cognitive dissonance theory.

An experiment was designed to find out whether the subject's biasing is ever confined to the period after the action has been done and all its consequences have come in. It was already known that after a difficult decision a subject often reveals that he has reduced dissonance by maximizing his reason for his action and minimizing the reason against it. The question then was 'How can we be certain that the spreading apart of the alternatives ... occurred after the decision? Could it not have occurred at the conflict stage?'[25]

The answer appeared to be provided by Jecker's experiment,[26] in which 'subjects were offered their choice between two phonograph records. In three conditions there was *low conflict*; i.e. subjects were told that there was a very good chance that they would receive *both* records no matter which they chose. In three other conditions *high conflict* was produced by telling them that the probability was high that they would be given only the record that they chose. All of the subjects rated the records before the instructions; in each of the conflict conditions subjects re-rated the records either (a) after they discovered that they received both records, and (b) after they discovered that they received only the record that they chose, or (c) before they were certain whether they would get one or both. The results were quite clear: no spreading apart occurred when there was no dissonance; i.e. when the subject actually received both records, or when he was not certain whether he would receive one or both, he did not re-evaluate the alternatives systematically. When dissonance did occur, there was a systematic re-evaluation, i.e. subjects spread their evaluations of the alternatives when they received only one record – this occurred independently of the degree of conflict.'[27]

The first point to note about this experiment is that the dissonance is not the kind of dissonance that occurs in open *akrasia* without any self-deception. It is residual dissonance between the result of the rational choice and the positive desire for the record that was not preferred. These subjects wished that they had not needed to resolve a conflict and so they re-wrote the history of their recent past in a way that reduced it.

We may now pose the crucial question about this experiment: 'Did the subjects back-date their later valuations to the time of deliberation?' Several possibilities have to be considered. First, someone may rationalize a choice by putting forward a consideration that simply did not occur to him while he was deliberating, but which might have occurred to him, because at that time he did foresee the actual result of his choice and did subscribe to the relevant valuation. This would be self-deception about the actual course that his deliberation happened to take, but not about the beliefs with which he was equipped at that time. Secondly, someone might embellish the result of his choice by exaggerating a valuation in

---

[25] E. Aronson in R. Abelson *et al.* eds., *Theories of Cognitive Dissonance*. It should be noted that the biasing does not always take the form of 'spreading apart'. It takes this form when the action is not *akratic*, but when the action is *akratic* the agent may bring the alternatives closer together in order to reduce the apparent *akrasia*.

[26] J. Jecker, *Conflict and Dissonance: a Time for Decision*, ibid.

[27] E. Aronson's account of the experiment, *Theories of Cognitive Discourse*.

order to be able to exaggerate his satisfaction with the result. This would be a more radical kind of self-deception, because it would be self-deception about his equipment, but it need not involve any self-deception about the actual course of his deliberation and it can occur in cases in which he has not made any choice. Thirdly, someone may embellish the result of a choice by exaggerating one of its features and this would be another radical kind of self-deception designed to exaggerate satisfaction by falsifying his equipment, but it too need not involve any self-deception about the actual course of his deliberation, perhaps because he would not even claim that at that time he could foresee the exaggerated feature of the result, and it too can occur in cases in which he has not made any choice.

It is quite clear which of these three things the subjects of the experiment were doing. They were embellishing the results of their choices by exaggerating their valuations in order to be able to exaggerate their satisfaction with the results. So Aronson is right when he sums up his report by saying, 'This experiment provides clear evidence that dissonance and conflict are different processes; whatever else dissonance theory may be, it is not "nothing but conflict theory" '.[28]

This gets some confirmation from the way in which the subjects themselves might look at the matter. Although it is likely that, when they were questioned for the second time, they also deceived themselves about their earlier valuations, that was not necessarily so. They might simply have been exaggerating their present valuations without giving a thought to their earlier deliberation. If so, their self-deception would have been a pure example of the 'sweet lemons' reaction, which can also occur in situations in which no choice has been made. This kind of embellishment is not the same thing as rationalization. That really is a sturdy result.

On the other hand it is important not to forget the point already made, that, when subjects do rationalize their earlier choices, it is often the case that much of the biasing actually occurred during deliberation. Naturally, this can happen only when the relevant result is foreseen. Apparently, it did not happen to the subjects in Jecker's experiment who reduced dissonance, because they did not foresee that they would only receive their first choice record. But there is no *a priori* reason why those subjects in the high conflict condition who were questioned at a time when they still did not know whether they would receive one record or both should not have already spread their valuations during deliberation in order to facilitate a difficult, but rational decision, made against the background of an uncertain future. If they had spread their valuations

[28] E. Aronson, *Theories of Cognitive Dissonance.*

during deliberation, in this way there would have been an analogy between their procedure and self-deceptive *akrasia*. For they would have been making a difficult decision easier, by reducing a conflict which later, in relation to a certain future decision, would have emerged as residual dissonance, if they received only one record. However, in the other experiment, in which subjects were bribed to lie, there is no doubt that much of the biasing really did occur when they were deciding what to do. In such cases, the boundary between conflict theory and dissonance theory is not so clearly defined.

Whether dissonance is reduced by reducing during deliberation a conflict which later, given a certain result of a particular choice, would have emerged as dissonance, or whether it is reduced later by embellishment of the actual result, with or without rationalization of the choice, the theory must predict in what situations it will be reduced and in what situations it will not be reduced. The difficulty, already mentioned, is that in certain experiments the outcome was not the reduction of dissonance in inverse proportion to the size of the bribe, but the exact opposite: the larger the bribe, the greater the minimization of the lie. This is the so-called 'incentive effect'.

There are several points that need to be made about the experiments that produced this outcome and they may help to fix the boundary between ordinary self-deceptive *akrasia* and the recoil strategy of self-deception.

First, in cases of embellishment, it is rather misleading to call the effect of an unforeseen good consequence of a choice 'the incentive effect'. It is true that an actual increase in satisfaction through an unforeseen good consequence of an action might work associatively and cause the subject to fabricate an increase in satisfaction through another consequence. But the first of these two considerations cannot be back-dated by the subject if he remembers that he did not foresee that particular good consequence, and so it cannot be regarded as an incentive even by him, and, though he might back-date the second consideration, he would be wrong to do so, because in this case the increase was fabricated. The point made by calling the two considerations 'incentives' would be better made by saying that the two increases, one real and the other fabricated, are directly proportional to one another and both positive.

Secondly, if a good consequence is foreseen, as it is in the case of bribery, it really is an incentive and it really does play a part in the subject's deliberation. However, if this is what happens, we have to be very careful how we identify and analyse the effect of the incentive on an opposed consideration, such as 'It will be a lie'. So far, we have only examined cases in which it leads to a minimization of the lie in the subject's deliberation, because he has a strong scruple about lying. These are cases of self-deceptive *akrasia* in which the inverse proportion between the amount of the bribe and the amount of the minimization is perfectly intelligible. But how can we understand cases in which the proportion is direct?

The third point that needs to be made is that the explanation of the direct proportion need not be the same in all the experiments that produced that outcome. What seems to be common to them all is that the subjects had no strong scruple about what they did, because the circumstances themselves reduced the seriousness of the lie to a point at which they genuinely believed it to be justified by the bribe. Consequently, they could tell the lie without *akrasia* and they had no practical need to deceive themselves by minimizing it.[29] True, the decision might be a close-run event and they might feel the need to spread the alternatives in order to reduce residual dissonance. But that need is much less urgent than the need to facilitate *akrasia* in cases where there is a scruple.

Suppose then that there was no scruple and that the decision was not a close-run event. Then the acceptance of the bribe and the ensuing action would not leave the agent with any problem. He would not reflect that the small bribe had made his decision very *akratic* or had made it difficult for him to be sure that it was quite correct. There would be no dissonance and, therefore, no reason to expect the smaller bribe to lead to a greater minimization of the lie. Nor would he reflect that the large bribe had made his decision less *akratic* (it was not *akratic* at all) or had made it less difficult for him to be quite sure that it was correct (there was no difficulty). In short, the bribe would not lead to a situation in which there was any dissonance and so they would be free to work associatively in the way already described. The large bribe would then produce more maximization of the reason for the action and more minimization of the reason against it. Therefore, the amount of minimization might be expected to be directly proportional to the amount of the bribe and in fact that was the outcome of the experiment. This really is an incentive effect, but one that works by irrational association.

However, there is a sub-set of these experiments in which the

---

[29] See Festinger and Carlsmith in *J. Abnorm. Soc. Psychol.* **58** (1959), 203–10; Carlsmith, Collins and Helmreich in *J. Pers. Soc. Psychol.* **4** (1966) 1–13; and Linder, Cooper and Jones, ibid. 1967, 6, 245–54. Aronson says that in these experiments the subjects felt themselves justified in lying, but he does not draw the essential distinction between *akratic* and *non-akratic* action. In *non-akratic* action the defeated consideration may produce some residual dissonance, but it produces far more dissonance if after its defeat in deliberation it emerges victorious in *akratic* action.

explanation of the direct proportion is quite different and really irrelevant to the whole inquiry. In this sub-set, the lie that the subjects were bribed to tell was 'I enjoyed being used as a subject in the experiment' (a different one, which was in fact boring).[30] The way to minimize this lie would be to persuade oneself that one really had enjoyed the experiment. Consequently, in this particular case the greater the minimization of the lie, the greater the (claimed) enjoyment, and *vice versa*. Now when a subject is offered a large bribe, the associative mechanism may cause him to maximize his enjoyment, blurring the distinction between enjoying getting a lot of money for a dull task and enjoying a dull task. But to maximize the enjoyment is to minimize the lie. So by this linkage he would expect to find a direct proportion between the amount of the bribe and the amount of the minimization, and this might even happen in cases of *akratic* lying. But surely the special linkage between enjoyment and lying is a flaw in the construction of these experiments and their outcome is irrelevant to the inquiry.[31] The interesting cases of direct proportion are those in which the lie is free from any special attachment to enjoyment. In order to avoid this confusion, it would be better to take cases in which the action was not lying at all, but something different. In such cases the explanation of the direct proportion is the one suggested above: they create no need for self-deceptive *akrasia* or for the reduction of residual dissonance and so the field is left open for the operations of the irrational association.

The analysis of these experiments has, I hope, contributed to fixing the boundary between conflict and dissonance, and so to fixing the boundary between self-deceptive *akrasia* and the recoil strategy of self-deception. The structure exploited by the recoil strategy is difficult to disentangle from the ordinary structure of rational deliberation when the latter is distorted and exploited by self-deceptive *akrasia*. However, we have to disentangle it if we are going to understand the common features

[30] See Festinger and Carlsmith, *J. Abnorm. Soc. Psychol.* **58**, 203–10 and Carlsmith, Collins and Helmreich, *J. Pers. Soc. Psychol.* **4**, 1–13.

[31] R. Brown overlooks this point when he writes: 'Not the least interesting aspect of these results [*sc.* inverse proportion between amount of bribe and amount of minimization of the lie] is the fact that they contradict a reward or reinforcement principle. To rate tasks as enjoyable is linguistic behaviour similar to the spoken declaration that those tasks were "a lot of fun". One might have expected that the subjects who were most strongly rewarded for the declaration would pick up a linguistic habit and so be inclined to a favourable rating. It turned out otherwise, however.' *Social Psychology* (Toronto, 1965), p. 588. But it is the special linkage between enjoyment and minimization of the lie that brings it about that, when no strong scruple is in play, the large bribe produces more minimization of the lie. This special linkage must be eliminated if we want to discover the general explanation of the direct proportion between amount of bribe and amount of minimization.

of the recoil strategy and the strategy imputed to the unconscious by Freud in certain case histories, and the parallelism is important because it provides some confirmation for one of the more audacious parts of his theory of the unconscious. If something like that can be shown to happen outside the unconscious, why not something not so very different inside it?

17

Paradoxes of irrationality*

DONALD DAVIDSON

The idea of an irrational action, belief, intention, inference or emotion is paradoxical. For the irrational is not merely the nonrational, which lies outside the ambit of the rational; irrationality is a failure within the house of reason. When Hobbes says only man has 'the privilege of absurdity' he suggests that only a rational creature can be irrational. Irrationality is a mental process or state – a rational process or state – gone wrong. How can this be?

The paradox of irrationality is not as simple as the seeming paradox in the concept of an unsuccessful joke, or of a bad piece of art. The paradox of irrationality springs from what is involved in our most basic ways of describing, understanding, and explaining psychological states and events. Sophia is pleased that she can tie a bowline. Then her pleasure must be due to her belief that she can tie a bowline and her positive assessment of that accomplishment. Further, and doubtless more searching, explanations may be available, but they cannot displace this one, since this one flows from what it is to be pleased that something is the case. Or take Roger, who intends to pass an examination by memorizing the Koran. This intention must be explained by his desire to pass the examination and his belief that by memorizing the Koran he will enhance his chances of passing the examination. The existence of reason explanations of this sort is a built-in aspect of intentions, intentional actions, and many other attitudes and emotions. Such explanations explain by rationalizing: they enable us to see the events or attitudes as reasonable from a point of view of the agent. An aura of rationality, of fitting into a rational pattern, is thus inseparable from these phenomena, at least as long as they are described in psychological terms. How then can we explain, or even tolerate as possible, irrational thoughts, actions or emotions?

* A precursor of this paper was delivered as the Ernest Jones lecture before the British Psycho-analytical Association on 26 April 1978. Dr Edna O'Shaughnessy commented and I have profited from her informative remarks. I am also indebted for further useful suggestions to Dagfinn Føllesdal, Sue Larson and Richard Wollheim.

Psychoanalytic theory as developed by Freud claims to provide a conceptual framework within which to describe and understand irrationality. But many philosophers think there are fundamental errors or confusions in Freud's thought. So I consider here some elements in that thought that have often come under attack, elements that consist of a few very general doctrines central to all stages of Freud's mature writings. After analysing the underlying problem of explaining irrationality, I conclude that any satisfactory view must embrace some of Freud's most important theses, and when these theses are stated in a sufficiently broad way, they are free from conceptual confusion. It perhaps needs to be emphasized that my 'defence' of Freud is directed to some only of Freud's ideas, and these are ideas at the conceptual, in contrast to the empirical, end of that vague spectrum.

Much that is called irrational does not make for paradox. Many might hold that it is irrational, given the dangers, discomforts, and meagre rewards to be expected on success, for any person to attempt to climb Mt Everest without oxygen (or even with it). But there is no puzzle in explaining the attempt if it is undertaken by someone who has assembled all the facts he can, given full consideration to all his desires, ambitions and attitudes, and has acted in the light of his knowledge and values. Perhaps it is in some sense irrational to believe in astrology, flying saucers, or witches, but such beliefs may have standard explanations if they are based on what their holders take to be the evidence. It is sensible to try to square the circle if you don't know it can't be done. The sort of irrationality that makes conceptual trouble is not the failure of someone else to believe or feel or do what we deem reasonable, but rather the failure, within a single person, of coherence or consistency in the pattern of beliefs, attitudes, emotions, intentions and actions. Examples are wishful thinking, acting contrary to one's own best judgment, self-deception, believing something that one holds to be discredited by the weight of the evidence.

In attempting to explain such phenomena (along with much more, of course) Freudians have made the following claims:

First, the mind contains a number of semi-independent structures, these structures being characterized by mental attributes like thoughts, desires, and memories.

Second, parts of the mind are in important respects like people, not only in having (or consisting of) beliefs, wants and other psychological traits, but in that these factors can combine, as in intentional action, to cause further events in the mind or outside it.

Third, some of the dispositions, attitudes, and events that characterize the various substructures in the mind must be viewed on the model of physical dispositions and forces when they affect, or are affected by, other substructures in the mind.

A further doctrine about which I shall say only a little is that some mental phenomena that we normally assume to be conscious, or at least available to consciousness, are not conscious, and can become accessible only with difficulty, if at all. In most functional respects, these unconscious mental states and events are like conscious beliefs, memories, desires, wishes and fears.

I hope it will be agreed that these doctrines are all to be found in Freud, and that they are central to his theories. They are, as I have said, far less strong and detailed than Freud's views. Yet even in reduced form, they require more defence than is possible, in the view of many philosophers. The criticisms I shall be attempting to meet are related in various ways, but they are essentially of two sorts.

First, the idea that the mind can be partitioned at all has often been held to be unintelligible, since it seems to require that thoughts and desires and even actions be attributed to something less than, and therefore distinct from, the whole person. But can we make sense of acts and attitudes that are not those of an agent? Also, as Sartre suggests, the notion of responsibility would lose its essential point if acts and intentions were pried loose from people and attached instead to semi-autonomous parts of the mind. The parts would then stand proxy for the person: each part would become a little woman, man or child. What was once a single mind is turned into a battlefield where opposed forces contend, deceive one another, conceal information, devise strategies. As Irving Thalberg and others point out, sometimes it even happens that one segment protects itself from its own forces (thoughts).[1] The prime agent may appear as a sort of chairman of the board, arbiter or dictator. It is not surprising that doubts have arisen as to whether these metaphors can be traded for a consistent theory.

A second, though related, set of worries concerns the underlying explanatory methodology. On the one hand, psychoanalytic theory extends the reach of teleological or reason explanation by discovering motives, wishes and intentions that were not recognized before. In this respect, as has often been noted, Freud greatly increased the number and variety of phenomena that can be viewed as rational: it turns out that we have reasons for our forgettings, slips of the tongue, and exaggerated fears. But on the other side, Freud wants his explanations to yield what explanations in natural science often promise: causal accounts that permit control. In this vein, he applies to mental events and states terms

---

[1] See Irving Thalberg, this volume.

drawn from hydraulics, electromagnetism, neurology and mechanics. Toulmin, Flew, McIntyre and Peters among philosophers have at one time or another suggested that psychoanalytic theories attempt the impossible by trying to bring psychological phenomena (which require explanations in terms of reasons) under causal laws: they think this accounts for, but does not justify, Freud's constant use, when talking of the mind, of metaphors drawn from other sciences.[2]

It seems then, that there are two irreconcilable tendencies in Freud's methodology. On the one hand he wanted to extend the range of phenomena subject to reason explanations, and on the other to treat these same phenomena as forces and states are treated in the natural sciences. But in the natural sciences, reasons and propositional attitudes are out of place, and blind causality rules.

In order to evaluate these charges against psychoanalytic theory, I want first to rehearse part of what I think is a correct analysis of normal intentional action. Then we can consider irrationality.

A man walking in a park stumbles on a branch in the path.[3] Thinking the branch may endanger others, he picks it up and throws it in a hedge beside the path. On his way home it occurs to him that the branch may be projecting from the hedge and so still be a threat to unwary walkers. He gets off the tram he is on, returns to the park, and restores the branch to its original position. Here everything the agent does (except stumble on the branch) is done for a reason, a reason in the light of which the corresponding action was reasonable. Given that the man believed the stick was a danger if left on the path, and a desire to eliminate the danger, it was reasonable to remove the stick. Given that, on second thought, he believed the stick was a danger in the hedge, it was reasonable to extract the stick from the hedge and replace it on the path. Given that the man wanted to take the stick from the hedge, it was reasonable to dismount from the tram and return to the park. In each case the reasons for the action tell us what the agent saw in his action, they give the intention with which he acted, and they thereby give an explanation of the action. Such an explanation, as I have said, must exist if something a person does is to count as an action at all.

The pattern of reason explanations has been noted by many philo-

[2] See, for examples, Antony Flew, 'Motives and the unconscious' in *Minnesota Studies in the Philosophy of Science*, vol. 1, eds H. Feigl and M. Scriven (University of Minnesota Press, Minneapolis, 1956); Alasdair MacIntyre, *The Unconscious* (Routledge, London, 1958); R. S. Peters, *The Concept of Motivation* (Routledge, London, 1958); Charles Taylor, *The Explanation of Behaviour* (Routledge, London, 1965).

[3] The example, though not the use I make of it, comes from footnote 23 of 1909d.

sophers. Hume puts it pithily: 'Ask a man why he uses exercise: he will answer, because he desires to keep his health. If you then enquire why he desires health, he will readily reply, because sickness is painful.'[4] The pattern is so familiar that we may miss its subtlety. What is to be explained is the action, say taking exercise. At the minimum, the explanation calls on two factors: a value, goal, want or attitude of the agent, and a belief that by acting in the way to be explained he can promote the relevant value or goal, or will be acting in accord with his attitude. The action on the one hand, and the belief–desire pair which give the reason on the other, must be related in two very different ways to yield an explanation. First, there must be a logical relation. Beliefs and desires have a content, and these contents must be such as to imply that there is something valuable or desirable about the action. Thus a man who finds something desirable in health, and believes that exercise will make him healthy can conclude that there is something desirable in exercise, which may explain why he takes exercise. Second, the reasons an agent has for acting must, if they are to explain the action, be the reasons on which he acted; the reasons must have played a *causal* role in the occurrence of the action. These two conditions on reason explanations are both necessary, but they are not sufficient, since some causal relations between belief–desire pairs and actions do not give reason explanations. (This complication will not concern us here, though there are no doubt irrational actions that hinge on the complication.)

This much of the analysis of action makes clear why all intentional actions, whether or not they are in some further sense irrational, have a rational element at the core; it is this that makes for one of the paradoxes of irrationality. But we also see that Freud can be defended on one important point: there is no inherent conflict between reason explanations and causal explanations. Since beliefs and desires are causes of the actions for which they are reasons, reason explanations include an essential causal element.

What can be said of intentional action can be extended to many other psychological phenomena. If a person intends to steal some Brussels sprouts, then whether or not he executes his intention, the intention itself must be caused by a desire to possess some Brussels sprouts and a belief that by stealing them he will come into possession of them. (Once again, the logical, or rational, aspect of the intention is obvious.) Similarly, most of our wishes, hopes, desires, emotions, beliefs and fears depend upon a

---

[4] David Hume, *An Inquiry Concerning the Principles of Morals*, ed. L. A. Selby-Bigge (The Clarendon Press, Oxford, 1957), Appendix I, p. 293.

simple inference (usually, no doubt, unnoticed) from other beliefs and attitudes. We fear poverty because we believe it will bring what we hold to be evils; we hope it will rain because we believe rain will help the crops, and we want the crops to prosper; we believe rain will help the crops on the basis of induction or hearsay or reading; and so on. In each of these cases, there is the logical connection between the contents of various attitudes and beliefs, and what they cause.

The conclusion up to this point is that merely to label a psychological state or event as being or entailing what is loosely called a propositional attitude is to guarantee the relevance of a reason explanation, and hence an element of rationality. But of course if such states and events can be irrational, the element of rationality cannot prevent their being at the same time less than rational. Consider the case of an action where the agent acts counter to what he believes, everything considered, is better. (Aristotle called such behaviour a case of akrasia; other terms are 'incontinence' or 'weakness of the will'.) It is easy to imagine that the man who returned to the park to restore the branch to its original position in the path realizes that his action is not sensible. He has a motive for moving the stick, namely, that it may endanger a passer-by. But he also has a motive for not returning, which is the time and trouble it costs. In his own judgment, the latter consideration outweighs the former; yet he acts on the former. In short, he goes against his own best judgment.

The problem of explaining such behaviour has puzzled philosophers and moralists at least since Plato. According to Plato, Socrates argued that since no one willingly acts counter to what he knows to be best, only ignorance can explain foolish or evil acts. This is often called a paradox, but Socrates' view is paradoxical only because it denies what we all believe, that there are akratic acts. If Socrates is right – if such actions are ruled out by the logic of the concepts – then there is nothing puzzling about the facts to be explained. Nevertheless, Socrates (or Plato) has brought our problem to a head: there is a conflict between the standard way of explaining intentional action and the idea that such an action can be irrational. Since the view that no intentional action can be internally irrational stands at one extreme in the continuum of possible views, let me give it a name: the *Plato Principle*. It is the doctrine of pure rationality.

At an opposite extreme is the *Medea Principle*. According to this doctrine, a person can act against his better judgment, but only when an alien force overwhelms his or her will. This is what happens when Medea begs her own hand not to murder her children. Her hand, or the passion of revenge behind it, overcomes her will. Some such treatment of weakness of the will is popular.[5] And given the thesis, the term is suitable, for the will of the agent is weaker than the alien passion. Moralists particularly have been attracted to this view, since it suggests that no more is needed to overcome temptation than greater resolve to do the right. Just the same, it is a strange doctrine, since it implies that akratic acts are not intentional, and so not in themselves actions for which the agent can be held responsible. If the agent is to blame, it is not for what he did, but because he did not resist with enough vigour. What the agent found himself doing had a reason – the passion or impulse that overcame his better judgment – but the reason was not *his*. From the agent's point of view, what he did was the effect of a cause that came from outside, as if another person had moved him.

Aristotle suggested that weakness of the will is due to a kind of forgetting. The akrates has two desires; in our example, he wants to save his time and effort, and also wants to move the branch. He can't act on both desires, but Aristotle will not let him get so far as to appreciate his problem, for according to Aristotle the agent loses active touch with his knowledge that by not returning to the park he can save time and effort. It is not quite a case of a conscious and an unconscious desire in conflict; rather there is a conscious and an unconscious piece of knowledge, where action depends on which piece of knowledge is conscious.

There are situations in which Aristotle's analysis is appropriate, and other situations ruled by the Medea Principle. But such situations are not the only ones, and they are not the defining cases of akrasia, where the agent acts intentionally while aware that everything considered a better course of action is open to him. For when the Medea Principle is at work, intention is not present; and in Aristotle's analysis, the agent is not aware of an alternative.

On reflection it is obvious that neither the Medea Principle nor Aristotle's analysis allows for straightforward cases of conflict, cases in which an agent has good reasons both for doing, and for refraining from, a course of action; or, what comes to the same thing, good reasons for doing each of two mutually exclusive things. Such situations are too familiar to require special explanation: we are not normally paralysed when competing claims are laid on us, nor do we usually suppress part of the relevant information, or drive one of our desires underground. Usually we can face situations where a decision must be made, and we decide best when we manage to keep all the considerations, the pros and the cons, before us.

[5] For further discussion of these issues, and references, see my 'How is weakness of the will possible?' in Donald Davidson, *Essays on Actions and Events* (Oxford University Press, London, 1980).

What requires explaining is the action of an agent who, having weighed up the reasons on both sides, and having judged that the preponderance of reasons is on one side, then acts against this judgment. We should not say he has no reason for his action, since he has reasons both for and against. It is because he has a reason for what he does that we can give the intention with which he acted. And like all intentional actions, his action can be explained, by referring to the beliefs and desires that caused it and gave it point.

But although the agent has a reason for doing what he did, he had better reasons, by his own reckoning, for acting otherwise. What needs explaining is not why the agent acted as he did, but why he *didn't* act otherwise, given his judgment that all things considered it would be better.

A person who appreciates the fact that he has good reasons both for and against an action should not be thought to be entertaining a contradiction. It follows that moral principles, or the judgments that correspond to desires, cannot be expressed by sentences like 'It is wrong to lie' or 'It is good to give pleasure'. Not, that is, if these sentences are taken in the natural way to express universal statements like 'All lies are wrong' or 'All acts that give pleasure are good'. For one and the same act may be a lie and an act that gives pleasure, and so be both wrong and good. On many moral theories, this is a contradiction. Or to take an even simpler case, if it is right to keep promises and wrong to break them, then someone who through no fault of his own has made incompatible promises will do something wrong if he does something right.

The solution to this puzzle about the logic of practical reasoning is to recognize that evaluative principles are not correctly stated in the form 'It is wrong to lie'. For not all lies are wrong; there are cases when one ought to lie for the sake of some more important consideration. The fact that an action is a lie, or the breaking of a promise, or a consumer of time is a count against the action, to be weighed along with other reasons for the action. Every action we perform, or consider performing, has something to be said for it and something against; but we speak of conflict only when the pros and cons are weighty and close to being in balance. Simple deduction can tell me that if I wish to keep promise *A* I must be in Addis Ababa on a certain date, and if I wish to keep promise *B* I must be in Bora Bora at that same time; but logic cannot tell me which to do.

Since logic cannot tell me which to do, it is unclear in what respect either action would be irrational. Nor is the irrationality evident if we add that I judge that all things considered I ought to keep promise *A*, and yet I keep promise *B*. For the first judgment is merely conditional: in the light of all my evidence, I ought to do *A*; and this cannot contradict the unconditional judgment that I ought to do *B*. Pure internal inconsistency enters only if I also hold – as in fact I do – that I ought to act on my own best judgment, what I judge best or obligatory, everything considered.

A purely formal description of what is irrational in an akratic act is, then, that the agent goes against his own second-order principle that he ought to act on what he holds to be best, everything considered. It is only when we can describe his action in just this way that there is a puzzle about explaining it. If the agent does not have the principle that he ought to act on what he holds to be best, everything considered, then though his action may be irrational from *our* point of view, it need not be irrational from his point of view – at least not in a way that poses a problem for explanation. For to explain his behaviour we need only say that his desire to do what he held to be best, all things considered, was not as strong as his desire to do something else.

But someone who knowingly and intentionally acts contrary to his own principle; how can we explain that? The explanation must, it is evident, contain some feature that goes beyond the Plato Principle; otherwise the action is perfectly rational. On the other hand, the explanation must retain the core of the Plato Principle; otherwise the action is not intentional. An account like this seems to satisfy both requirements: there is, we have agreed, a normal reason explanation for an akratic action. Thus the man who returns to the park to replace the branch has a reason: to remove a danger. But in doing this he ignores his principle of acting on what he thinks is best, all things considered. And there is no denying that he has a motive for ignoring his principle, namely that he wants, perhaps very strongly, to return the branch to its original position. Let us say this motive does explain the fact that he fails to act on his principle. This is the point at which irrationality enters. For the desire to replace the branch has entered into the decision to do it twice over. First it was a consideration in favour of replacing the branch, a consideration that, in the agent's opinion, was less important than the reasons against returning to the park. The agent then held that everything considered he ought not to return to the park. Given his principle that one ought to act on such a conclusion, the rational thing for him to do was, of course, not to return to the park. Irrationality entered when his desire to return made him ignore or override his principle. For though his motive for ignoring his principle was a reason for ignoring the principle, it was not a reason against the principle itself, and so when it entered in this second way, it was irrelevant as a reason, to the principle and to the action. The irrationality depends on the distinction between a reason for having, or acting on, a principle, and a reason for the principle.

Another, and simpler, example will make the point clear. Suppose a young man very much wishes he had a well-turned calf and this leads him to believe he has a well-turned calf. He has a normal reason for wanting to have this belief – it gives him pleasure. But if the entire explanation of his holding the belief is that he wanted to believe it, then his holding the belief is irrational. For the wish to have a belief is not evidence for the truth of the belief, nor does it give it rational support in any other way. What his wish to have this belief makes rational is that this proposition should be true: He believes that he has a well-turned calf. This does not rationalize his believing: I have a well-turned calf. This is a case of wishful thinking, which is a model for the simplest kind of irrationality. Simple as it is, however, the model has a complexity which is obscured by the ambiguity of the phrase 'reason for believing'.

In some cases of irrationality it is unlikely, and perhaps impossible, for the agent to be fully aware of all that is going on in his mind. If someone 'forgets' that today is Thursday because he does not want to keep a disagreeable social commitment, it is perhaps ruled out that he should be aware of this. But in many cases there is no logical difficulty in supposing the agent knows what is going on. The young man may know he believes he has a well-turned calf only because he wants to believe it, just as the man who returns to the park to replace the branch may realize both the absurdity and the explanation of his action.

In standard reason explanations, as we have seen, not only do the propositional contents of various beliefs and desires bear appropriate logical relations to one another and to the contents of the belief, attitude or intention they help explain; the actual states of belief and desire cause the explained state or event. In the case of irrationality, the causal relation remains, while the logical relation is missing or distorted. In the cases of irrationality we have been discussing, there is a mental cause that is not a reason for what it causes. So in wishful thinking, a desire causes a belief. But the judgment that a state of affairs is, or would be, desirable, is not a reason to believe that it exists.

It is clear that the cause must be mental in this sense: it is a state or event with a propositional content. If a bird flying by causes a belief that a bird is flying by (or that an airplane is flying by) the issue of rationality does not arise; these are causes that are not reasons for what they cause, but the cause has no logical properties, and so cannot of itself explain or engender irrationality (of the kind I have described). Can there be other forms of irrationality? The issue is not clear, and I make no claims concerning it. So far my thesis is only that many common examples of irrationality may be characterized by the fact that there is a mental cause that is not a reason. This characterization points the way to one kind of explanation of irrationality.

Irrationality of this kind may turn up wherever rationality operates. Just as incontinent actions are irrational, there can be irrational intentions to act, whether or not they are acted out. Beliefs may be irrational, as may courses of reasoning. Many desires and emotions are shown to be irrational if they are explained by mental causes that are not reasons for them. The general concept applies also to unchanges. A person is irrational if he is not open to reason – if, on accepting a belief or attitude on the basis of which he ought to make accommodating changes in his other beliefs, desires or intentions, he fails to make those changes. He has a reason which does not cause what it is a sufficient reason for.

We now see how it is possible to reconcile an explanation that shows an action, belief, or emotion to be irrational with the element of rationality inherent in the description and explanation of all such phenomena. Thus we have dealt, at least in a preliminary way, with one paradox of irrationality. But now a second source of paradox emerges which cannot be so easily dissipated.

If events are related as cause and effect, they remain so no matter in what vocabulary we choose to describe them. Mental or psychological events are such only under a manner of description, for these very events surely are at the same time neurophysiological, and ultimately physical, events, though recognizable and identifiable within these realms only when given neurophysiological or physical descriptions. As we have seen, there is no difficulty in general in explaining mental events by appeal to neurophysiological or physical causes: this is central to the analysis of perception or memory, for example. But when the cause is described in non-mental terms, we necessarily lose touch with what is needed to explain the element of irrationality. For irrationality appears only when rationality is evidently appropriate: where both cause and effect have contents that have the sort of logical relations that make for reason or its failure. Events conceived solely in terms of their physical or physiological properties cannot be judged as reasons, or as in conflict, or as concerned with a subject matter. So we face the following dilemma: if we think of the cause in a neutral mode, disregarding its mental status as a belief or other attitude – if we think of it merely as a force that works on the mind without being identified as part of it – then we fail to explain, or even describe, irrationality. Blind forces are in the category of the non-rational, not the irrational. So, we introduce a mental description of the cause, which thus makes it a candidate for being a reason. But we still remain outside the only clear pattern of explanation that applies to the mental, for that pattern demands that the cause be more than a candidate for being a reason; it must *be* a reason, which in the present case it cannot be. For an explanation of a mental effect we need a mental cause that is also a reason for this effect, but, if we have it, the effect cannot be a case of irrationality. Or so it seems.

There is, however, a way one mental event can cause another mental event without being a reason for it, and where there is no puzzle and not necessarily any irrationality. This can happen when cause and effect occur in different minds. For example, wishing to have you enter my garden, I grow a beautiful flower there. You crave a look at my flower and enter my garden. My desire caused your craving and action, but my desire was not a reason for your craving, nor a reason on which you acted. (Perhaps you did not even know about my wish.) Mental phenomena may cause other mental phenomena without being reasons for them, then, and still keep their character as mental, provided cause and effect are adequately segregated. The obvious and clear cases are those of social interaction. But I suggest that the idea can be applied to a single mind and person. Indeed, if we are going to explain irrationality at all, it seems we must assume that the mind can be partitioned into quasi-independent structures that interact in ways the Plato Principle cannot accept or explain.

To constitute a structure of the required sort, a part of the mind must show a larger degree of consistency or rationality than is attributed to the whole.[6] Unless this is the case, the point of the analogy with social interaction is destroyed. The idea is that if parts of the mind are to some degree independent, we can understand how they are able to harbour inconsistencies, and to interact on a causal level. Recall the analysis of akrasia. There I mentioned no partitioning of the mind because the analysis was at that point more descriptive than explanatory. But the way could be cleared for explanation if we were to suppose two semi-autonomous departments of the mind, one that finds a certain course of action to be, all things considered, best, and another that prompts another course of action. On each side, the side of sober judgment and the side of incontinent intent and action, there is a supporting structure of reasons, of interlocking beliefs, expectations, assumptions, attitudes and desires. To set the scene in this way still leaves much unexplained, for we want to know why this double structure developed, how it accounts for the action taken, and also, no doubt, its psychic consequences and

---

[6] Here as elsewhere my highly abstract account of the partitioning of the mind deviates from Freud's. In particular, I have nothing to say about the number or nature of divisions of the mind, their permanence or aetiology. I am solely concerned to defend the idea of mental compartmentalization, and to argue that it is necessary if we are to explain a common form of irrationality. I should perhaps emphasize that phrases like 'partition of the mind', 'part of the mind', 'segment' etc. are misleading if they suggest that what belongs to one division of the mind cannot belong to another. The picture I want is of overlapping territories.

cure. What I stress here is that the partitioned mind leaves the field open to such further explanations, and helps resolve the conceptual tension between the Plato Principle and the problem of accounting for irrationality.

The partitioning I propose does not correspond in nature or function to the ancient metaphor of a battle between Virtue and Temptation or Reason and Passion. For the competing desires or values which akrasia demands do not, on my account, in themselves suggest irrationality. Indeed, a judgment that, all things considered, one ought to act in a certain way presupposes that the competing factors have been brought within the same division of the mind. Nor is it a matter of the bald intervention of a fey and alien emotion, as in the Medea Principle. What is called for is organized elements, within each of which there is a fair degree of consistency, and where one element can operate on another in the modality of non-rational causality.

Allowing a degree of autonomy to provinces of the mind dissipates to a degree the problems we have discussed, but it generates others. For to the extent that the Plato Principle fails to explain the workings of the mind, mere causal relations replace it, and these explain best, or make most progress toward science, as they can be summarized in laws. But there is a question how far the workings of the mind can be reduced to strict, deterministic laws as long as the phenomena are identified in mental terms. For one thing, the realm of the mental cannot form a closed system; much that happens in it is perforce caused by events with no mental description. And for another, once we contemplate causal relations between mental events in partial disregard of the logical relations between the descriptions of those events, we enter a realm without a unified and coherent set of constitutive principles: the concepts employed must be treated as mixed, owing allegiance partly to their connections with the world of non-mental forces, and partly to their character as mental and directed to a propositional content. These matters bear directly on the important question what kind of laws or generalizations will be found to hold in this area, and therefore on the question how scientific a science of the mental can be: that is, however, a subject I have put to one side.

There is one other problem that springs from recognizing semi-independent departments within the same mind. We attribute beliefs, purposes, motives and desires to people in an endeavour to organize, explain and predict their behaviour, verbal and otherwise. We describe their intentions, their actions and their feelings in the light of the most unified and intelligible scheme we can contrive. Speech yields no more direct access into this scheme than any other behaviour, since speech itself must be interpreted; indeed speech requires at least two levels of interpretation, there being both the question what the speaker's words mean, and the question what the speaker means in speaking them. Not that an agent knows directly what he believes, wants and intends in some way that reduces observers to mere detectives. For though he can often say what is on his mind, an agent's words have meaning in the public domain; what his words mean is up to the interpreter as well as to him. How he is to be understood is a problem for him as it is for others.

What makes interpretation difficult is the multiplicity of mental factors that produce behaviour and speech. To take an instance, if we know that in speaking certain words a man meant to assert that the price of plutonium is rising, then generally we must know a great deal more about his intentions, his beliefs, and the meaning of his words. If we imagine ourselves starting out from scratch to construct a theory that would unify and explain what we observe – a theory of the man's thoughts and emotions and language – we should be overwhelmed by the difficulty. There are too many unknowns for the number of equations. We necessarily cope with this problem by a strategy that is simple to state, though vastly complex in application: the strategy is to assume that the person to be understood is much like ourselves. That is perforce the opening strategy, from which we deviate as the evidence piles up. We start out assuming that others have, in the basic and largest matters, beliefs and values similar to ours. We are bound to suppose someone we want to understand inhabits our world of macroscopic, more or less enduring, physical objects with familiar causal dispositions; that his world, like ours, contains people with minds and motives; and that he shares with us the desire to find warmth, love, security, and success, and the desire to avoid pain and distress. As we get to matters of detail, or to matters in one way or another less central to our thinking, we can more and more easily allow for differences between ourselves and others. But unless we can interpret others as sharing a vast amount of what makes up our common sense we will not be able to identify any of their beliefs and desires and intentions, any of their propositional attitudes.

The reason is the holistic character of the mental. The meaning of a sentence, the content of a belief or desire, is not an item that can be attached to it in isolation from its fellows. We cannot intelligibly attribute the thought that a piece of ice is melting to someone who does not have many true beliefs about the nature of ice, its physical properties connected with water, cold, solidity, and so forth. The one attribution rests on the supposition of many more – endlessly more. And among the beliefs we suppose a man to have, many must be true (in our view) if any are to be understood by us. The clarity and cogency of our attributions of attitude, motive and belief are proportionate, then, to the extent to which we find others consistent and correct. We often, and justifiably, find others irrational and wrong; but such judgments are most firmly based when there is the most agreement. We understand someone best when we hold him to be rational and sage, and this understanding is what gives our disputes with him a keen edge.

There is no question but that the precept of unavoidable charity in interpretation is opposed to the partitioning of the mind. For the point of partitioning was to allow inconsistent or conflicting beliefs and desires and feelings to exist in the same mind, while the basic methodology of all interpretation tells us that inconsistency breeds unintelligibility.

It is a matter of degree. We have no trouble understanding small perturbations against a background with which we are largely in sympathy, but large deviations from reality or consistency begin to undermine our ability to describe and explain what is going on in mental terms. What sets a limit to the amount of irrationality we can make psychological sense of is a purely conceptual or theoretical matter – the fact that mental states and events are constituted the states and events they are by their location in a logical space. On the other hand, what constrains the amount and kind of consistency and correspondence with reality we find in our fellow men and women is the frailty of human nature: the failure of imagination or sympathy on the part of the interpreter, and the stubborn imperfection of the interpreted. The underlying paradox of irrationality, from which no theory can entirely escape, is this: if we explain it too well, we turn it into a concealed form of rationality; while if we assign incoherence too glibly, we merely compromise our ability to diagnose irrationality by withdrawing the background of rationality needed to justify any diagnosis at all.

What I have tried to show, then, is that the very general features of psychoanalytic theory that I listed as having puzzled philosophers and others are, if I am right, features that will be found in any theory that sets itself to explain irrationality.

The first feature was that the mind is to be regarded as having two or more semi-autonomous structures. This feature we found to be necessary to account for mental causes that are not reasons for the mental states they cause. Only by partitioning the mind does it seem possible to explain how a thought or impulse can cause another to which it bears no rational relation.

The second feature assigned a particular kind of structure to one or more subdivisions of the mind: a structure similar to that needed to explain ordinary actions. This calls for a constellation of beliefs, purposes and affects of the sort that, through the application of the Plato

Principle, allow us to characterize certain events as having a goal or intention. The analogy does not have to be carried so far as to demand that we speak of parts of the mind as independent agents. What is essential is that certain thoughts and feelings of the person be conceived as interacting to produce consequences on the principles of intentional actions, these consequences then serving as causes, but not reasons, for further mental events. The breakdown of reason-relations defines the boundary of a subdivision. Though I talk here, with Freud, of parts and agencies, there does not seem to be anything that demands a metaphor. The parts are defined in terms of function; ultimately, in terms of the concepts of reason and of cause. The idea of a quasi-autonomous division is not one that demands a little agent in the division; again, the operative concepts are those of cause and reason.

The third feature on which we remarked was that certain mental events take on the character of mere causes relative to some other mental events in the same mind. This feature also we found to be required by any account of irrationality. It is a feature that can be accommodated, I argued, but in order to accommodate it we must allow a degree of autonomy to parts of the mind.

The three elements of psychoanalytic theory on which I have concentrated, the partitioning of the mind, the existence of a considerable structure in each quasi-autonomous part, and non-logical causal relations between the parts; these elements combine to provide the basis for a coherent way of describing and explaining important kinds of irrationality. They also account for, and justify, Freud's mixture of standard reason explanations with causal interactions more like those of the natural sciences, interactions in which reason does not play its usual normative and rationalizing role.

Finally, I must mention the claim that many mental phenomena which normally are accessible to consciousness are sometimes neither conscious nor easily accessible to consciousness. The reason I have said nothing about this claim is that I think the relevant objections to unconscious mental states and events are answered by showing that the theory is acceptable without them. It is striking, for example, that nothing in the description of akrasia requires that any thought or motive be unconscious – indeed, I criticized Aristotle for introducing something like an unconscious piece of knowledge when this was not necessary. The standard case of akrasia is one in which the agent knows what he is doing, and why, and knows that it is not for the best, and knows why. He acknowledges his own irrationality. If all this is possible, then the description cannot be made untenable by supposing that sometimes some of the thoughts or desires involved are unconscious.

If to an otherwise unobjectionable theory we add the assumption of unconscious elements, the theory can only be made more acceptable, that is, capable of explaining more. For suppose we are led to realize by a genius like Freud that if we posit certain mental states and events we can explain much behaviour that otherwise goes unexplained; but we also discover that the associated verbal behaviour does not fit the normal pattern. The agent denies he has the attitudes and feelings we would attribute to him. We can reconcile observation and theory by stipulating the existence of unconscious events and states that, aside from aware-ness, are like conscious beliefs, desires and emotions. There are, to be sure, further puzzles lurking here. But these seem to be puzzles that result from other problems; unconscious mental events do not add to the other problems but are natural companions of them.

I have urged that a certain scheme of analysis applies to important cases of irrationality. Possibly some version of this scheme will be found in every case of 'internal' inconsistency or irrationality. But does the scheme give a sufficient condition for irrationality? It would seem not. For simple cases of association do not count as irrational. If I manage to remember a name by humming a certain tune, there is a mental cause of something for which it is not a reason; and similarly for a host of further cases. But far more interesting, and more important, is a form of self-criticism and reform that we tend to hold in high esteem, and that has even been thought to be the very essence of rationality and the source of freedom. Yet it is clearly a case of mental causality that transcends reason (in the somewhat technical sense in which I have been using the concept).

What I have in mind is a special kind of second-order desire or value, and the actions it can touch off. This happens when a person forms a positive or negative judgment of some of his own desires, and he acts to change these desires. From the point of view of the changed desire, there is no reason for the change – the reason comes from an independent source, and is based on further, and partly contrary, considerations. The agent has reasons for changing his own habits and character, but those reasons come from a domain of values necessarily extrinsic to the contents of the views or values to undergo change. The cause of the change, if it comes, can therefore not be a reason for what it causes. A theory that could not explain irrationality would be one that also could not explain our salutary efforts, and occasional successes, at self-criticism and self-improvement.

Works of Freud cited

1891b	*On Aphasia*
1892–93	'A Case of Successful Treatment by Hypnotism'
1893a	(with J. Breuer) 'On the Psychical Mechanism of Hysterical Phenomena: Preliminary Communication'
1893f	'Charcot'
1893h	'On the Psychical Mechanism of Hysterical Phenomena'
1894a	'The Neuro-Psychoses of Defence'
1895d	(with J. Breuer) *Studies on Hysteria*
1896b	'Further Remarks on the Neuro-Psychoses of Defence'
1896c	'The Aetiology of Hysteria'
1899a	'Screen Memories'
1900a	*The Interpretation of Dreams*
1901a	*On Dreams*
1901b	*The Psychopathology of Everyday Life*
1905c	*Jokes and Their Relation to the Unconscious*
1905d	*Three Essays on the Theory of Sexuality*
1905e [1901]	'Fragment of an Analysis of a Case of Hysteria'
1906a	'My Views on the Part Played by Sexuality in the Aetiology of the Neuroses'
1906c	'Psycho-analysis and the Establishment of the Facts in Legal Proceedings'
1907c	'The Sexual Enlightenment of Children'
1908b	'Character and Anal Erotism'
1908c	'On the Sexual Theories of Children'
1908d	' "Civilized" Sexual Morality and Modern Nervous Illness'
1908e	'Creative Writers and Day-Dreaming'
1909b	'Analysis of a Phobia in a Five-Year-Old Boy'
1909d	'Notes upon a Case of Obsessional Neurosis'
1910a [1909]	*Five Lectures on Psycho-Analysis*
1910c	*Leonardo da Vinci and a Memory of his Childhood*
1910i	'The Psycho-Analytic View of Psychogenic Disturbance of Vision'
1911b	'Formulations on the Two Principles of Mental Functioning'
1911c	'Psychoanalytic Notes on an Autobiographical Account of a Case of Paranoia (Dementia Paranoides)'

Works of Freud cited

1912c	'Types of Onset of Neurosis'
1912d	'On the Universal Tendency to Debasement in the Sphere of Love'
1912g	'A Note on the Unconscious in Psycho-Analysis'
1912–13	*Totem and Taboo*
1913j	'The Claims of Psycho-Analysis to Scientific Interest'
1914c	'On Narcissism: an Introduction'
1914d	'On the History of the Psycho-Analytic Movement'
1914e	'The Representation in a Dream of a "Great Achievement"'
1915a	'Observations on Transference-Love (Further Recommendation on the Technique of Psycho-Analysis)'
1915c	'Instincts and their Vicissitudes'
1915d	'Repression'
1915e	'The Unconscious'
1916–17	*Introductory Lectures on Psycho-Analysis*
1917a	'A Difficulty in the Path of Psycho-Analysis'
1917c	'On Transformations of Instinct as Exemplified in Anal Erotism'
1917d [1915]	'A Metapsychological Supplement to the Theory of Dreams'
1917e [1915]	'Mourning and Melancholia'
1918b [1914]	'From the History of an Infantile Neurosis'
1919a	'Lines of Advance in Psycho-Analytic Therapy'
1920a	'Psychogenesis of a Case of Female Homosexuality'
1920g	*Beyond the Pleasure Principle*
1921c	*Group Psychology and the Analysis of the Ego*
1922b	'Some Neurotic Mechanisms in Jealousy, Paranoia and Homosexuality'
1923a	Two Encyclopaedia Articles
1923b	*The Ego and the Id*
1924b	'Neurosis and Psychosis'
1924c	'The Economic Problem of Masochism'
1924e	'The Loss of Reality in Neurosis and Psychosis'
1925a [1924]	'A Note upon the "Mystic Writing Pad"'
1925d [1924]	*An Autobiographical Study*
1925h	'Negation'
1925i	'Some Additional Notes on Dream-Interpretation as a whole'
1925j	'Some Psychological Consequences of the Anatomical Distinction between the Sexes'
1926d [1925]	*Inhibitions, Symptoms and Anxiety*
1926e	*The Question of Lay Analysis*
1926f	'Psycho-Analysis': an article in the *Encyclopaedia Britannica*
1927c	*The Future of an Illusion*
1928b	'Dostoievsky and Parricide'
1930a	*Civilization and Its Discontents*
1931a	'Libidinal Types'
1933a	*New Introductory Lectures on Psychoanalysis*

1937c   'Analysis Terminable and Interminable'
1937d   'Constructions in Analysis'
1939a [1937–39] *Moses and Monotheism*
1940a [1938]   *An Outline of Psychoanalysis*
1940b [1938]   'Some Elementary Lessons in Psychoanalysis'
1940d [1892]   'On the Theory of Hysterical Attacks'
1940e [1938]   'Splitting of the Ego in the Process of Defence'
1950a [1887–   *The Origins of Psychoanalysis* (including 'A Project for a
     1902]   Scientific Psychology')

Select Bibliography

Alexander, Peter. 'Rational behaviour and psychoanalytic explanation', *Mind* 71 (1962), 326–41.

Alexander, Peter and MacIntyre, Alasdair. 'Cause and cure in psychotherapy', *Proc. Arist. Soc. Supp.* 29 (1955), 25–58.

Audi, Robert. 'Psychoanalytic explanation and the concept of rational action', *Monist* 56 (1972), 444–64.

Bergman, G. 'Psychoanalysis and experimental psychology', *Mind* 52 (1943), 352–70.

Blumenfield, David. 'Free action and unconscious motivation', *Monist* 56 (1972), 426–43.

Cioffi, Frank. 'Wittgenstein's Freud', in *Studies in the Philosophy of Wittgenstein*, ed. Peter Winch (Routledge, London, 1969).

'Freud and the idea of a pseudo-science', in *Explanation in the Behavioural Sciences*, ed. Robert Borger and Frank Cioffi (Cambridge Univ. Press. Cambridge, 1970).

Review discussion of Richard Wollheim, *Freud*, in *Inquiry* 15 (1972), 171–86.

and Alexander, Peter. 'Wishes, symptoms and actions', *Proc. Arist. Soc. Supp.* 48 (1974), 97–134.

Colby, K. M. *Energy and Structure in Psychoanalysis* (Ronald, New York, 1955).

Dilman, I. 'The unconscious', *Mind* 68 (1959), 446–73.

'Is the unconscious a theoretical construct?', *Monist* 58 (1972), 313–34.

Eagle, M. 'Psychoanalytic interpretations: veridicality and therapeutic effectiveness', *Noûs* xiv (1980), 405–26.

Edelson, Marshall. 'Language and dreams: the interpretation of dreams revisited', in *Psychoanalytic Study of the Child* 27 (1972), 203–82.

Language and Interpretation and Psychoanalysis (Yale Univ. Press, New Haven, 1975).

Ellis, Albert. 'An operational reformulation of some of the basic principles of psychoanalysis', in *Minnesota Studies in the Philosophy of Science*, vol. I, eds. Herbert Feigl and Michael Scriven (Univ. of Minn. Press, Minneapolis, 1956).

Erwin, Edward. 'Psychoanalysis: how firm is the evidence?', *Noûs* xiv (1980), 443–56.

Ezriel, H. 'Experimentation within the psycho-analytic session', *Br. J. Phil. Sci.* VII (1956–7), 29–48.

Farrell, B. A. 'Can psychoanalysis be refuted?', *Inquiry* 4 (1961), 16–36.

'Introduction', in S. Freud, *Leonardo,* trans. A. Tyson (Penguin, Harmondsworth, Middlesex, 1963), pp. 11–91.

'The status of psychoanalytic theory', *Inquiry* 7 (1964), 104–23.

Comment on Frank Cioffi's 'Freud and the idea of a pseudo-science', in *Explanation in the Behavioural Sciences,* ed. Robert Borger and Frank Cioffi (Cambridge Univ. Press, Cambridge, 1970).

'The validity of psychotherapy', *Inquiry* 15 (1972), 146–70.

The Standing of Psychoanalysis (Oxford University Press, 1981).

Farrell, B. A., Wisdom, J. O., Turquet, P. M. 'The criteria for a psychoanalytic interpretation', *Proc. Arist. Soc. Supp.* 36 (1962), 77–144.

Fingarette, Herbert. ' "Unconscious behaviour" and allied concepts: a new approach to their empirical interpretation', *J. Phil.* 47 (1950), 509–20.

'Psychoanalytic perspectives on moral guilt and responsibility', *Phil. Phenomenol. Res.* 16 (1955–6), 18–36.

Self-Deception (Routledge, London, 1969).

Fisher, S. and Greenberg, R. P. *The Scientific Credibility of Freud's Theory and Therapy* (Harvester, Hassocks, Sussex, 1977).

Flew, Antony. 'Psycho-analytic explanation', *Analysis* 10 (1949–50), pp. 8–15. Reprinted in *Philosophy and Analysis,* ed. Margaret Macdonald (Blackwell, Oxford, 1954).

'Motives and the unconscious', in *Minnesota Studies in the Philosophy of Science,* vol. I, ed. Herbert Feigl and Michael Scriven (Univ. of Minn. Press, Minneapolis, 1956).

Fenkel-Brunswik, E. 'Psychoanalysis and the unit of science', *Proc. Amer. Acad. Arts Scien.* 80 (1954), 271–350.

Gedo, J. E. and Goldberg, A. *Models of the Mind* (Univ. Chicago Press, Chicago, 1973).

Glover, Jonathan. 'Freud, morality and responsibility', in *Freud: the Man, his World, his Influence,* ed. Jonathan Miller (Weidenfeld, London, 1972).

Glymour, Clark. *Theory and Evidence* (Princeton Univ. Press, Princeton, 1980).

Grossman, William, I. and Simon, Bennett. 'Anthropomorphism: motive, meaning and causality in psychoanalytic theory', in *Psychoanalytic Study of the Child,* 34 (1969), 78–111.

Grünbaum, Adolf. 'Is Freudian Psychoanalytic theory pseudo-scientific by Karl Popper's criterion of demarcation?', *Amer. Phil. Quarterly* 16 no. 2 (1979), 131–41.

'Epistemological liabilities of the clinical appraisal of psychoanalytic theory', *Noûs* xiv no. 3 (1980), 307–85.

'Can psychoanalytic theory be cogently tested "on the couch"?', in *Pittsburgh Series in Philosophy and History of Science,* vol. 8., ed. A. Grünbaum and L. Laudan (University of California Press: Berkeley and Los Angeles). Forthcoming.

Hartmann, Heinz. *Essays on Ego-Psychology* (Hogarth, London, 1964).

Hartmann, Heinz, Kris, Ernst, and Loewenstein, Rudolph M. *Papers on Psychoanalytic Psychology* (Int. Univ. Press, New York, 1964).

Hilgard, Ernest R. 'The scientific status of psychoanalysis', in *Logic, Methodology and Philosophy of Science:* Proceedings of the 1960 International Congress, eds. E. Nagel, P. Suppes, and A. Tarski (Stanford Univ. Press, 1962), pp. 375–90.

Hook, Sidney, ed. *Psychoanalysis, Scientific Method and Philosophy* (N.Y. Univ. Press, New York, 1959).

Hutten, E. H. 'On explanation in psychology and in physics', *Br. J. Phil. Sci.* VII (1956–57), 73–85.

Jones, David H. 'Freud's theory of moral conscience', *Philosophy* 41 no. 155 (1966), 34–57.

Jones, G. Seaborn. *Treatment or Torture?* (Tavistock Publications, London, 1968).

Jupp, V. L. 'Freud and pseudo-science', *Philosophy* 52 (1977), 441–53.

Klein, G. S. *Psychoanalytic Theory* (Int. Univ. Press, New York, 1976).

Kline, P. *Fact and Fantasy in Freudian Theory* (Methuen, London, 1972).

Kris, Ernst. 'Psychoanalytic propositions', in *Psychological Theory*, ed. M. H. Marx (Macmillan, New York, 1951), pp. 322–51.

Laplanche, J. *Life and Death in Psychoanalysis*, trans. and ed. Jeffrey Mohlman (Johns Hopkins Univ. Press, Baltimore and London, 1976).

Laplanche, J. and Pontalis, J. B. *The Language of Psychoanalysis*, trans. Donald Nicholson-Smith (Hogarth Press, London, 1973).

McGinn, Colin. 'Action and its explanation' in *Philosophical Problems in Psychology*, ed. Neil Bolton (Methuen, London, 1979).

MacIntyre, Alasdair. *The Unconscious* (Routledge, London, 1958).

Madison, P. *Freud's Concept of Repression and Defense, its Theoretical and Observational Language* (Univ. of Minn. Press, Minneapolis, 1961).

Martin, Michael. 'Mr Farrell and the refutability of psychoanalysis', *Inquiry* 7 (1964), 80–98.

Martin, Michael, Margolin, Sydney G., Christiansen, Björn. 'The scientific status of psychoanalytic clinical evidence', *Inquiry* 7 (1964), 13–79.

Meehl, P. E. 'Some methodological reflections on the difficulties of psychoanalytic research', *Psychological Issues* 8 (1973), 104–28.

'Theoretical risks and tabular asterisks: Sir Karl, Sir Ronald, and the progress of soft psychology', *J. of Consulting and Clinical Psychology* 46 (1978), 806–34.

Merleau-Ponty, Maurice. *The Structure of Behaviour*, trans. Alden L. Fisher (Methuen, London, 1965).

Miles, T. R. *Eliminating the Unconscious* (Pergamon, London, 1966).

Mischel, Theodore. 'Psychology and explanations of human behaviour', *Phil. Phenomenol. Res.* 23 (1962–3), 578–94.

'Concerning rational behaviour and psychoanalytic explanation', *Mind* 74 (1965), pp. 71–8.

'Understanding neurotic behaviour: from "mechanism" to "intentionality"', in *Understanding Other Persons*, ed. T. Mischel (Blackwell, Oxford, 1973).

Morris, Herbert. *On Guilt and Innocence: Essays in Legal Philosophy and Moral Psychology* (Univ. of California Press, Berkeley, Los Angeles, London, 1976).

Select Bibliography

Neu, Jerome. *Emotion, Thought and Therapy* (Routledge, London, 1977).

Noy, Pinchas. 'A revision of the psychoanalytic theory of the primary process', *Int. J. Psycho-Anal.* **50** (1969), 155–78.

'Symbolism and mental representation', in *The Annual of Psychoanalysis* **1** (Int. Univ. Press, New York, 1973).

'The psychoanalytic theory of cognitive development', *Psychoanalytic Study of the Child* **34** (1979), 169–214.

Peterfreund, Emmanuel. 'Information, systems and psychoanalysis: an evolutionary biological approach to psychoanalytic theory', *Psychological Issues* **7**, monograph 25/26 (1971).

Peters, R. S. 'Cause, cure and motive', *Analysis* **10** (1949–50), 103–9. Reprinted in *Philosophy and Analysis*, ed. Margaret Macdonald (Blackwell, Oxford, 1954).

'Freud's theory', *Br. J. Phil. Sci.* **7** (1956–7), 4–12.

The Concept of Motivation (Routledge, London, 1958).

Pribram, Karl. 'The neuropsychology of Sigmund Freud', in *Experimental Foundations of Clinical Psychology*, ed. Arthur J. Bachrach (Basic Bks., New York, 1962).

'Freud's *Project:* an open biologically based model for psychoanalysis', *Psychoanalysis and Current Biological Thought*, eds. N. S. Greenfield and W. C. Lewis (Univ. of Wisconsin Press, Madison, 1965).

Pribram, Karl and Gill, Merton. *Freud's Project Re-Assessed* (Hutchinson, London, 1976).

Pumpian-Mindlin, E., ed. *Psycho-Analysis as Science* (Basic Books, New York, 1952).

Rachman, S., ed. *Critical Essays on Psychoanalysis* (Macmillan, New York, 1963), vol. 19.

Rapaport, David. *The Stucture of Psychoanalytic Theory: a Systematizing Attempt* (Int. Univ. Press, New York, 1960).

The Collected Papers, ed. M. M. Gill (Basic Books, New York, 1967).

Ricoeur, Paul. *Freud and Philosophy: an Essay in Interpretation*, trans. David Savage (Yale Univ. Press, New Haven, 1970).

Rieff, Philip. 'Freudian ethics and the idea of reason', *Ethics* **67** (1956–57), 169–83.

Freud: The Mind of the Moralist (Gollancz, London, 1959).

Roazen, Paul. *Freud: Political and Social Thought* (Hogarth Press, London, 1969).

Rubinstein, Benjamin B. 'On the possibility of a strictly clinical psychoanalytic theory: an essay in the philosophy of psychoanalysis'. *Psychological Issues* **9**, monograph 36 (1976), 229–64.

'On the psychoanalytic theory of unconscious motivation and the problem of its confirmation', *Noûs* **xiv** (1980), 427–42.

Russell, Bertrand. *The Analysis of Mind* (G. Allen, London, 1921).

Rycroft, Charles, ed. *Psychoanalysis Observed* (Constable, London, 1966).

Sartre, Jean-Paul. *Being and Nothingness*, trans. Hazel E. Barnes (Philosophical Library, N.Y. 1956).

Savodnik, Irwin. 'Is undergoing psychoanalysis essential to the appraisal of psychoanalytic theory', *Inquiry* **19** (1976), 299–323.

Schafer, Roy. *Aspects of Internalization* (International Univ. Press, New York, 1968).

A New Language for Psychoanalysis (Yale Univ. Press, New Haven, 1976).

Scriven, Michael. 'The frontiers of psychology: psychoanalysis and parapsychology', in *Frontiers of Science and Philosophy*, ed. Robert G. Colodny (G. Allen, London, 1964).

Sears, R. R. *Survey of Objective Studies of Psychoanalytic Concepts* (Social Science Research Council, New York, 1943).

Sherwood, Michael. *The Logic of Explanation in Psychoanalysis* (Academic Press, New York and London, 1969).

Shope, Robert K. 'The psychoanalytic theories of wish-fulfilment and meaning', *Inquiry* **10** (1967), 421–8.

'Freud on conscious and unconscious intentions', *Inquiry* **13** (1970), 149–59.

'Dispositional treatment of psychoanalytic motivational terms', *J.Phil.* **LXVII** (1970), 195–208.

'Physical and psychic energy', *Philosophy of Science* **38** (1971), 1–11.

Siegler, Frederick A. 'Unconscious intentions', *Inquiry* **10** (1967), 251–67.

Skinner, B. F. 'Critique of psychoanalytic concepts and theories', in *Minnesota Studies in the Philosophy of Science*, vol. I, ed. Herbert Feigl and Michael Scriven (Univ. of Minn. Press, Minneapolis, 1956).

Starke, J. G. *The Validity of Psycho-Analysis* (Angus, Sydney, 1973).

Toulmin, Stephen. 'The logical status of psycho-analysis', *Analysis* **9** (1948–9), 23–9. Reprinted in *Philosophy and Analysis*, ed. Margaret Macdonald (Blackwell, Oxford, 1954).

Walker, N. 'Freud and homeostasis', *Br. J. Phil. Sci.* **7** (1956–7), 61–72.

Wilden, Anthony. *System and Structure* (Tavistock Publications, London, 1972).

Wilkes, K. V. 'Anthropomorphism and analogy in psychology', *Philosophical Quarterly* **25** (1975), 126–37.

Winter, Judith B. 'The concept of energy in psychoanalytic theory', *Inquiry* **14** (1971), 138–51.

Wisdom, J. O. 'Psycho-analytic technology', *Br. J. Phil Sci.* **7** (1956–7), 13–28.

'A methodological approach to the problem of hysteria', *Int. J. Psycho-Anal.* **42** (1961), part III, 224–37.

'Comparison and development of the psycho-analytical theories of melancholia', *Int. J. Psycho-Anal.* **43** (1962), parts II-III, 113–32.

'A methodological approach to the problem of obsessional neurosis', *Br. J. of Med. Psychology* **34** (1964), 111–22.

'What is the explanatory theory of obsessional neurosis?', *Br. J. of Med. Psychology* **39** (1966), 335–48.

'Testing an interpretation within a session', *Int. J. Psycho-Anal.* **48** (1967), 42–52.

'Freud and Melanie Klein: psychology, ontology, and *Weltanschauung*', in *Psychoanalysis and Philosophy*, ed. Charley Hanley and Morris Lazerowitz (Int. Univ. Press, New York, 1970).

313

Select Bibliography

'A graduated map of psychoanalytic theories', *Monist* 56 (1972), 379–409.

Wittgenstein, Ludwig. *Lectures and Conversations,* ed. Cyril Barrett (Blackwell, Oxford, 1966).

Lectures in Philosophy, Cambridge 1932–35, ed. Alice Ambrose (Blackwell, Oxford, 1979).

Wollheim, Richard. 'The mind and the mind's image of itself', *Int. J. Psycho-Anal.* 50 (1969), 209–20. Reprinted in Richard Wollheim, *On Art and the Mind* (Allen Lane, London, 1973).

Sigmund Freud (Collins, London, and Viking, New York, 1971).

ed., *Freud: a Collection of Critical Essays* (Doubleday, New York, 1974).

'Wish-fulfilment', in *Rational Action,* ed. Ross Harrison (Cambridge Univ. Press, Cambridge, 1979), pp. 47–60.